Black Baseball and Chicago

Black Baseball and Chicago

*Essays on the Players, Teams
and Games of the
Negro Leagues' Most Important City*

Edited by LESLIE A. HEAPHY

McFarland & Company, Inc., Publishers
Jefferson, North Carolina, and London

LIBRARY OF CONGRESS CATALOGUING-IN-PUBLICATION DATA

Black baseball and Chicago : essays on the players, teams and games of
the Negro leagues' most important city / edited by Leslie A. Heaphy.
    p.   cm.
Includes bibliographical references and index.

ISBN-13: 978-0-7864-2674-4
ISBN-10: 0-7864-2674-8 (softcover : 50# alkaline paper)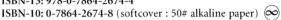

1. Baseball — Illinois — Chicago — History. 2. Negro leagues —
History. 3. African American baseball players — Illinois —
Chicago — History. 4. Baseball — United States — History.
GV863.I32C453 2006
796.35709773'11 — dc22   2006016327

British Library cataloguing data are available

On the cover: First baseman Thomas Turner of the Chicago
American Giants, 1947 *(Photograph from author's collection)*

Manufactured in the United States of America

*McFarland & Company, Inc., Publishers
Box 611, Jefferson, North Carolina 28640
www.mcfarlandpub.com*

Acknowledgments

Like any major project this one might never have been completed without the assistance and hard work of many people. This book would never have happened if it were not for the great careers of the many ball players and other baseball people who are talked about in the text. I must express my deep appreciation and gratitude for their stories.

I would like to thank all the contributors to the book who researched these men's stories and helped produce a sense of what the baseball scene in Chicago must have been like for so many years. I am grateful for their hard work in digging up the stories.

Much of the research for the different sections of the book was done with the assistance of the staff at the Kent State University, Stark Campus library. They filled endless interlibrary loan requests and helped track down other materials I needed. Melissa Salazar at the State Records Center and Archives in Santa Fe, New Mexico, went above and beyond in providing all the materials related to Bazz Owen Smaulding. The staff at the National Baseball Hall of Fame and Library in Cooperstown, New York, helped with every request I (and my students) made. They also provided some of the photographs in the text.

Two individuals deserve special thanks for their unfailing support and help in making this book a reality. The co-chairs of the Negro Leagues Committee of the Society for American Baseball Research (SABR), Dick Clark and Larry Lester, are ever gracious and the greatest sources of Negro League knowledge. I thank them for their willingness to share their expertise not only with me but with everyone who reads this book. Dick answered every request I sent him, checking on names, birth dates and other facts, while Larry provided photographs, articles he wrote and answers to my questions. Larry also answered every request for help from my students in their quest to put together their contributions to this book. Thanks to you both; I greatly appreciate all you've done.

The final thanks for this book has to go to a friend and fellow researcher who provided us all with the inspiration to develop this project and so many others. Jerry Malloy loved researching the Negro Leagues and he loved sharing what he discovered with anyone who wanted to know. That dedication, love and sense of mission gave rise to an annual Negro Leagues Conference named in Jerry's honor. This book grew out of the 2005 Jerry Malloy Negro League Conference held in Chicago. Thanks, Jerry.

Table of Contents

Acknowledgments   v

Preface   1

Introduction by Larry Lester   3

1. Early Black Teams in Chicago   7
2. The American Giants and Chicago's Negro League Era Clubs   18
3. Leading Black Ballplayers in Chicago   41
4. Management and Owners   142
5. The Ballparks, the East-West Classics, Integration and
    the Great Lakes Naval Team   173

Appendix A: Time Line of African American Achievements
    in Chicago Baseball   199
Appendix B: Rosters   202
Appendix C: Chicago Players in the Major Leagues   212
Appendix D: East-West Game Highlights, 1933–1953   214

Chapter Notes   217
Bibliography   225
About the Contributors   251
Index   255

Preface

A good argument can be made that the heart of black baseball always lay in Chicago. A number of the earliest teams were based in the city, most notably the Leland and the American Giants. It was the adopted home of Rube Foster, who founded the Negro National League while still a Chicago resident; he was later buried there. And while other cities sometimes hosted, Chicago was the traditional site of the Negro Leagues' wildly popular all-star game, the annual East-West Classic.

Yet while a good photographic history, *Black Baseball in Chicago*, has recently been published, along with a few biographies—detailed information about the teams, players, and scene is scarce. So when the opportunity opened up to publish a volume of papers from the 2005 Jerry Malloy Conference, with its focus on Chicago's independent and Negro Leagues past, the committee and its members seized it.

In 1997 the Negro Leagues Committee of the Society for American Baseball Research (SABR) decided to hold a conference focused solely on the history of black baseball. The conference has been held each year since, always in a city with connections to the leagues. The Chicago conference was the eighth annual meeting.

Along the way the name of the conference was changed. One of the longtime members of the Negro Leagues committee, Jerry Malloy, passed away, and a decision was made to rename the conference in his honor. Jerry was a tireless researcher who loved the history of the leagues and especially the story of the nineteenth century and events in Chicago. In recognition of his desire to share all his research with anyone who asked, it seemed natural to name the conference the Jerry Malloy Negro League Conference.

Since black baseball in the city was Jerry's main area of interest, it was decided we should try to do something a little different for 2005. McFarland was approached with the idea of developing a commemorative booklet for the conference with articles about Chicago's black baseball scene. They liked the idea and suggested turning the booklet into a full-length book when the conference was over. What follows is the culmination of that process. *Black Baseball and Chicago* includes papers delivered at the 2005 Jerry Malloy Conference. Most of these papers have been revised and expanded. In addition, a number of the profiles in the first three chapters were solicited, after the conference, to provide a more thorough accounting of Chicago's many players and teams. In every case, the author of the paper or the profile is identified in his biographical write-up, which appears at the back of the volume, in the section About the Contributors. The unattributed items in the book were written by the volume editor, in an attempt to further shore up coverage and to relate the many parts back to the general history of black baseball in Chicago.

The book has been divided into sections to help the reader follow the story. It begins with an introduction to the black baseball scene in Chicago. The book moves quickly into the nineteenth and early twentieth century, with the first chapter taking up the various independent teams based in the Windy City. The second chapter looks at the teams in and after 1920, when the Negro Leagues as we think of them took shape. Chapter three profiles players either from or having spent significant parts of their careers in Chicago. Not every player who donned a Chicago uniform is included in this section because there are many we know little about; but many of the big names and some of the lesser known players are included. Chapter four deals with the owners and managers involved with the Chicago clubs. The biggest annual event in black baseball history, the East-West All-Star game, is one of the subjects of chapter five. That chapter also focuses on three other specialized, important aspects of black baseball in the area. First the handful of ball parks used by the black teams are discussed. Then, it's the Great Lakes Naval Team, since a number of Chicago players made that team, which played in the Chicago area. The final part of chapter five looks at the question of integration of the two major league teams in the city, the Cubs and the White Sox.

The appendices include a timeline of major events in black baseball history in Chicago; a roster of players on the various Chicago area teams; a list of Chicago players who went on to the major leagues; and highlights of the East-West Game, 1933–1953. The book concludes with an extensive bibliography on Chicago black baseball.

Like the conference it grew out of, this book serves two ends. First the editor and contributors set out to deepen the reader's understanding — and their own — of an historically important baseball scene. Second we hope to add, with solid and narrowly focused research, to the record of black baseball in the United States. The history of this baseball community remains incomplete, but as interest spreads, the gaps grow smaller.

Leslie A. Heaphy

Introduction

Larry Lester

The saga of American Giants stomping through Chicago consists of two chapters. One chapter is pre–1932, "the early struggles," and the second is post–1932, "the Depression aftermath."

The early struggles began from seeds cultivated by Frank Leland, a native of Memphis, Tennessee. A Fisk University product, Leland began his baseball career with the Washington Capital Citys in the League of Colored Base Ball Clubs. When the league folded in mid-season, Leland moved to Chicago. Later, in 1901, he founded the Union Giants, a combination of the W. S. Peters' Chicago Unions and the Joe Miller Columbia Giants. In 1905, he christened a new team with his surname, the Leland Giants.

Around 1905, Andrew Foster, a brash, boastful son of a Methodist minister, was making a name for himself. As a pitcher for the Philadelphia Giants he defeated Rube Waddell and the Philadelphia A's in a post-season exhibition game. Not only did Foster take the glory of defeating this future Hall of Famer, he also took his name, Rube. Soon after, in 1907, Leland signed the young pitcher from Calvert, Texas.

By 1910, Foster was managing the Leland Giants. That year, the Giants finished with 123 victories against six losses. The talented tan contingent boasted such legendary stars as Bruce Petway, Pete Hill, Grant "Home Run" Johnson and future Hall of Famer John Henry "Pop" Lloyd.

The following year (1911) the Chicago American Giants were born. Foster stripped Leland's Giants of their best players; the entire starting rotation: Pat Dougherty, Frank Wickware and Bill Lindsay, along with their catcher Bruce Petway and two-thirds of the outfield, Pete Hill and Jap Payne, plus a couple of ringers. The new Giants had the nucleus of the strongest independent team in the Midwest. On any given Sunday afternoon, Rube's black brand of baseball often outdrew then cross-town rivals the White Sox and Cubs.

The American Giants were known for their flashy up-tempo brand of baseball, with hit-and-run plays, double steals, do-or-die sacrifice bunts. Foster's team was also renowned for their pitching and superb defense. Their innovative style of play became the benchmark for future black teams to be measured by. During the early teens, Foster's Giants often claimed the unofficial world colored championship.

As America entered World War I, Foster realized the drawbacks of independent baseball. He, like other black team owners, was at the mercy of white booking agents who scheduled games at the convenience of the resident white teams. The lack of permanency forced Foster to create a stable league as the best approach for establishing a continuity of scheduled games throughout black baseball.

In 1920, Foster met with independent team owners at the Paseo YMCA in Kansas City, Missouri. The meeting of these minds produced the Negro National League. Besides Foster's American Giants, charter members included Joe Green's Chicago Giants, John Matthews' Dayton (Ohio) Marcos, Tenny Blount's Detroit Stars, C. I. Taylor's Indianapolis ABC's, Lorenzo Cobb's St. Louis Giants and J. L. Wilkinson's Kansas City Monarchs. Wilkinson was the only white owner in the league's embryonic years.

Realizing the failure of previous attempts at an all-black league, Commissioner Foster initially moved players between teams in an effort for parity. A balanced schedule was created; meanwhile, he provided front money for financially meager teams. The end results were that the Negro National League (NNL) became the first black league to survive a full season. Providing a benchmark and model of consistency, the NNL structure was cloned in 1923 with the birth of the Eastern Colored League, with teams based mostly in the upper eastern United States.

The American Giants won the league championship the first three years, before the Monarchs stopped their reign. After a two-year hiatus, the American Giants returned to the summit with league championships in 1926 and 1927. Both years they faced the Bacharach Giants in the Colored World Series. Overcoming a no-hitter by Red Grier in the third game of the '26 series, they eventually won it behind Rube's young brother Willie's fine pitching performance. They repeated as world champions the following year.

Following the series victories, black baseball's kingpin, Rube Foster, was committed to a mental institution in Kankakee, Illinois. After the '27 series, the American Giants were sold to white businessman William E. Trimble, a florist. Trimble had visions of turning the Giants' home field, Schorling Park, into a dog-racing track. When politicians rejected the scheme, Trimble was stuck with a ball club he did not want.

Unable to withstand the devastation of the Great Depression, the American Giants folded with the NNL's collapse in 1931. Fittingly, they were reborn in 1932, under the new ownership of mortician Robert A. Cole, as they won the Negro Southern League championship. The next year, Cole's American Giants joined the reorganized Negro National League. In their first season, Cole's colored Giants won the championship, only to have it vetoed by league president Gus Greenlee, who owned the Pittsburgh Crawfords. Greenlee's Crawfords were declared titlist. In 1934, the American Giants lost four of seven games and the league title to the Philadelphia Stars.

In 1937, H. G. Hall became president of the American Giants, and led the creation of a Midwestern-based league called the Negro American League. The American Giants played here from 1937 through the 1952 season. While maintaining their historically top quality of play, they were unable to capture another league title.

Despite the lack of championships in the closing years, the American Giants were not the only attraction emanating from the great black metropolis on Chicago's South Side. The grand apex of any Negro league season, without question, was the East-West All-Star game. It was the shadow ball version of major league baseball's mid-season classic. Starting in 1933, the game was played annually at Comiskey Park. It brought thousands of fans from across the country to stay at the majestic Grand Hotel and other local lodgings.

Outside of a Joe Louis fight, the star-studded affair became the most important black sporting event in America, attracting roughly 20,000 fans in its inaugural game (despite inclement weather). Eventually, attendance grew to over 50,000, outdrawing the major league all-star contests in the early forties. Many historians, players and fans alike, argued that the success of the East-West Classics was the chief factor in the integration of major league baseball.

Foster's original American Giants, and subsequent forerunners, were truly gigantic in their accomplishments in presenting the national pastime with such a fine product of sports achievement.

1

Early Black Teams in Chicago

Black baseball in Chicago seems to have gotten an early start with local papers occasionally carrying reports of a variety of teams. Unfortunately, little is known about the teams or the individual players since reports tended to be rather sporadic. The team that got the most coverage was the Chicago Blue Stockings. Other early squads included the Uniques, the Oaklands and the Gordons.

In 1874 the Uniques roster appeared in a Peoria paper and the same club appeared again in 1879 in the *Chicago Times.* Players on both rosters included second baseman Brown, Hampton at shortstop, and Powell as catcher and at the hot corner. All the other players from 1874 were not listed in 1879. There were three Johnsons playing the infield, outfield and pitching. Shaw and Veney completed the outfield, while Watkins handled first base chores. In 1879 the additional players included Dyson at first, Jackson as catcher, Overland, Tilly and Davis in the outfield and Cleary as their pitcher.

The Oaklands appeared in the paper in 1878 and the Gordons in 1884. Neither article included more than the roster for each club, nor, unfortunately, as with the Uniques, were first names attached. Baylor, Ford and Waite patrolled the outfield and Bell handled the twirling duties for the Oaklands. The infield included Gordon, Grover, Kuehne and Reis, while Leslie handled the backstop duties. The Gordons relied on the twirling of W. Davis and the solid defense behind the plate of J. Harris. The outfield saw action by G. Campbell, T. Walker and A. Jones. Infield duties fell to the hands of J. Houke, R. Savoy, W. Turner and A. Curd.

Most of these early teams had to rely on word of mouth advertising and the like since newspapers came and went rather quickly. There were twenty-six African American newspapers established in Chicago between 1878 and 1920 but few lasted. Black baseball did not really begin to flourish until the 1890s when Julius Avendorph created the Chicago Society Baseball League. Included in the league membership were four black amateur baseball teams. Avendorph used his role with the Columbia Club to help arrange games and other events for the league.

In 1882 the creation of the Chicago Amateur Baseball Association (CABA) gave clubs a big boost. The association's primary function was to help book games for the local teams, which increased their opportunities to play the best opponents and secure good crowds. CABA worked hard to secure leases on local parks and then develop full schedules there.

Chicago Blue Stockings

Chicago's black baseball history extends back into the middle of the nineteenth century, with a variety of local ball clubs playing at the amateur and later the semipro level. Chicago had a strong history of sandlot ball and African Americans formed their own teams by the 1860s. One of the most well-known of these early squads, the Chicago Blue Stockings, received coverage in the local papers by 1870. One of the earliest reports claimed the team had been around for a number of years by 1870.

The Blue Stockings were resplendent in blue shirts with their monogram on the breast. They wore white woolen pants and blue stockings and topped it all off with caps with broad white and blue stripes. Their name came from the Blue Stockings they regularly wore. The club's secretary, W. P. Johnson, arranged for their uniforms as well as putting out a call for all challengers. Many of the players on the club worked in the local hotels and restaurants when not playing baseball.

According to the Chicago papers the Blue Stockings had some success in 1870, but that did not translate into full acceptance. They played a three game series against the champions from Rockford and beat them handily. In the first contest at Ogden Park the Blue Stockings took control of the game early and triumphed 48–14 behind the strong pitching of Charles Wing. Zack Daniels, the shortstop, led the club with seven runs scored, while Hampton crossed the plate six times. Their catcher and captain, George Brown, excelled in the field, showing off good judgment and an incredible arm. They won the second contest 28–18 at the fair grounds and called themselves the Colored Champions of the state after winning the third by a score of 30–18. According to the news accounts about 400–500 fans attended each of the contests.[1]

As a result of their victories over the Rockfords, the Blue Stockings were encouraged to put in an application for the Senior Amateur Championship Tournament. Captain George Brown submitted the application, but at the meeting held at the Goodrich law offices the decision was made to deny them admittance. The report said the Blue Stockings were "not deemed of sufficient strength to be entitled to consideration."[2] W. P. Johnson, the club secretary, issued a statement to the papers saying that the only reason they were denied entry was because the other clubs were scared to play them. Another article said that without the colored teams in the tournament attendance would suffer and the winners could not really call themselves champions because they had not defeated all the amateur clubs in Chicago. A challenge was then issued to any of the teams involved in the tournament to play the Blue Stockings but no one answered the call.

Though they beat the Rockfords, the Blue Stockings did not have as much success against the White Independents, the Red Stockings or the Uniques. They beat the Independents in one game 17–9 but lost to them 24–8, 17–15 and 25–24. The last game, the Blue Stockings claimed they actually won 23–22 because the game was called in the eighth inning and they were given the winner's purse. They lost another contest to the Red Stockings 22–5. In early 1871 they lost a game to the Uniques by the score of 39–5 to start the new season.[3]

The roster for the Blue Stockings in 1870 and 1871 included Charles Wing as their primary thrower. George Brown served as team captain and caught for the club. In one news report Brown was said to have such a strong arm that he shut down the opponents' running game entirely. He was a highly disciplined and energetic player. Zack Daniels turned the double play with ease, with either Johnson or Clery manning second base. The outfield consisted of Hampton, Smith, Adams, Shiner and J. Briddle. Thomas Hamilton and T. Brown covered the hot corner while Carter shared first base duties with T. Brown.

This amateur growth received a lot of support in 1887 with the creation of the Chicago Unions by Frank Leland, a new arrival from the South. The Unions and the semipro and professional teams that followed gave the local amateur clubs plenty of quality opponents to fill their schedules. Since the quality of their opponents was so high, clubs like the Blue Stockings and Key Stones attracted a good fan base.

Chicago Unions

The Chicago Unions dominated the amateur baseball scene in Chicago starting in 1886. The first roster included the main organizers of the club as they all played. William S. Peters played first base while Abe Jones caught and Frank Leland roamed the outfield, playing primarily in center field. In the early days the club played mainly on the weekends and passed a hat to meet their expenses. They often added side bets as incentives to get the best teams and encourage higher attendance.

In 1888 the Unions had the chance to play a series with the touring Pinchbacks of Louisiana. They won the first contest 4–1 and lost the second 6–5 in the ninth inning. Records for the third game have not been discovered, so it may not have been played because the Pinchbacks might have been concerned about losing to this relatively unknown Chicago club. They played again in 1889 but could not generate an agreement for an ongoing series.

In 1890 the Unions moved away from just the weekend approach and advertised as a full-time club. They wanted to be able to sign the best talent and be in the running for the colored championship of the world with the Cuban Giants.

In 1895 the Unions found some regular opponents in the Dalys and the Edgars. The Dalys challenged their supremacy so much that they scheduled a series of games in September to determine who was the best. The Unions won the first, lost the second and won the finale, in dramatic fashion, 9–8.

By 1896 their fortunes changed and they only played Sunday games in Chicago. During the rest of the week William S. Peters and Frank Leland arranged for them to tour the Midwest. They played all over because they had no home field. For a while they played at Sixty-seventh Street and Langley and then at Thirty-seventh and Butler. That year saw them playing another series with the Dalys. Harry Buckner lost the first game 1–0 but Chicago came back to win the second before succumbing again in the third. At the end of September the Unions found themselves in a series of games with the Edgars and the Cuban Giants to determine the colored champion. The Unions won a close contest with the Edgars, but they could not seem to contain the Cubans. They lost one contest 16–5 and a second 11–9.[4]

In 1897 the Unions tried to book a number of series with clubs from the south and east in order to be able to lay claim as champions. They defeated the Page Fence Giants in one contest behind the fine hitting of Harry Buckner. Their fielding deserted them in a series against the Cuban X-Giants and they came out on the losing side. They won late in the year over the Cuban Giants, 21–12, 11–9 and 14–12.[5]

Over the team's twelve year existence they were credited by Sol White with playing 731 games. Their record stood at 613–118 and 12 ties. The team developed a solid reputation as heavy hitters, excellent fielders and dependable pitchers. They also had good speed on the bases but tended to miss some of the fundamentals of the game. Since they won so regularly they did not spend a lot of time practicing. In 1899 the *Chicago Tribune* reported the club had a 100–10 record at the end of the previous season.[6]

The Columbia Giants joined the Chicago scene in 1899 and challenged the dominance of the Unions. In fact, in September the *Tribune* reported the Unions losing the colored championship to the Giants 1–0. Bert Jones took the loss while the Giants triumphed behind Wilson's shutout.[7] Examining the accounts of games included in the *Tribune* that season it seems the Unions had solid hitting and pitching but occasionally ran into trouble with their fielding. For example, the account of a game against the Joliet Standards in July stated that, while Chicago won 13–10, the game was "noted for many glaring errors by both teams."[8] The Unions committed five errors in a loss to the Spaldings in August, while earlier in June they made three miscues, though they defeated the Cuban Giants 16–6.[9]

In 1900 the Unions played a fourteen game series with the Cuban X-Giants. The Cubans won nine of the games due to their excellent hitting. The team was led by Captain Harry Hyde, outfielder David Wyatt and catcher Robert Jackson.

Among the many stars who played for the Unions was pitcher Harry Buckner, who later pitched for the Brooklyn Royal Giants. Third baseman William Monroe spent time with the Unions as well as the Philadelphia Giants. He played for the Giants in 1905 when they were considered one of the best teams around. Pitcher William Holland started with the Unions and then later followed Buckner to the Royal Giants. Robert Jackson caught the pitching for the Unions in later years; David Wyatt patrolled the outfield alongside William Smith and Albert Hackley. Wyatt became well-known in 1920 for helping to incorporate the new Negro National League.

In late 1901 players from the Unions joined with the Columbia Giants to form the Chicago Union Giants. This merger came about because the Columbia Giants had risen to challenge the Unions, which resulted in a player war. Frank Leland acted as the new club's manager, and Al H. Garrett from the Columbia team was his treasurer. This club played in the Chicago League through the 1904 season as the Chicago Union Giants and then the club split as Frank Leland formed his own club. The Unions kept playing as a barnstorming team well into the 1930s under the direction of William S. Peters and then Robert Gilkerson.

1899 Roster

William Holland, cf/p	Bert Jones, p/rf/cf
Willis Jones, lf	William Horn, p/rf
Harry Hyde, 3b/captain	Louis Reynolds, rf
Bill Monroe, ss	George Hopkins, 2b
Robert Jackson, c	Robert Footes, rf/c
Mike Moore, 1b	

Chicago Columbia Giants

In 1899 the famous Page Fence Giants had to move their home field and ended up playing the season in Chicago as the Columbia Giants. John W. Patterson managed the club and strengthened the team when he acquired pitcher Harry Buckner from the Unions to complement the rest of the staff. With Charlie Grant at second base and Grant Johnson at shortstop, the Giants hosted a solid nine each time they went out on the diamond. In addition to the strong athletes, the club also secured financial backing from the Columbia Social Club in Chicago. The men involved saw this as an opportunity to improve the prestige of their group by buying a winning ball club, the nineteenth century version of baseball in the twenty-first century. The players also received two uniforms, white for home games and gray for away contests, since they were expected to look the part of champions.

One of the key backers of the club was Major Robert R. Jackson. Jackson got involved with baseball in his hometown of Chicago through the Columbia team, later worked with Beauregard Moseley of the Leland club, and eventually took a position in the leadership of the Negro American League. In 1942 he also took on the position of president of the new Negro Major Baseball League, with Fritz Pollard as the vice president. Jackson was a local Chicago boy who went on to have a long and distinguished political career, never forgetting where he came from and using his position to help those in need, from the Home for the Aged to the Phyllis Wheatley Home for Working Girls. His baseball ventures were a part of his civic engagement and his social ties kept him in touch with the game.[10]

In 1900 the club claimed the local championship of Chicago. They played a five game series with the Union Giants and won all five contests, according to black baseball chronicler Sol White. The team played their home contests at the Wentworth and Thirty-ninth Street Park. They drew large crowds when they played at home on Sundays, as they had developed quite a local following. Unfortunately, their reputation was not as strong outside Chicago and their away games suffered. They ran into competition from the other black professional teams, such as the Cuban X-Giants, the Genuine Cuban Giants and the Norfolk Redstockings.

The Columbia club pooled its resources to form a new member of the Chicago baseball scene in 1901. The new player on the block was the Chicago Union Giants, who came to enjoy some success in the Windy City.

Chicago Union Giants

Frank C. Leland organized the Chicago Union Giants on July 17, 1901. He combined the talents of the Chicago Unions with the Columbia Giants to create this new entry in the Chicago League. They played in the league through the 1904 season with Leland, but in 1905 he left and formed his own club as the Leland Giants. William S. Peters, a former first baseman himself, kept the Union Giants playing.

The Chicago Union Giants played at Auburn Park at Seventy-ninth and Wentworth and had a number of talented stars on their roster. Their pitching staff included the Minnesota sensation Walter Ball, who made his Chicago debut in 1903. Future hall of famer Andrew "Rube" Foster appeared on the roster in 1902 for the first time. One of their regular starting players was third baseman and all around utility player Danger Talbert. He appears to have filled in at all the infield spots as the team needed him. Third baseman William Binga often appeared in the newspapers as the leading hitter for the Unions.[11]

Early in the 1902 season the Union club set the pattern for their season as they trounced the Eclipse by a score of 17–5. Clarence Lytle struck out five to go the distance for the Giants. They had reorganized their roster from the year before and hoped to make a strong showing not only in Chicago but throughout the Midwest. By the close of the year the Giants made good on their early strong showing by defeating the Columbia Giants for the title of best colored team in a three game series. The Union club won two out of three contests, including a thrilling 13–12 hitter's delight with William Binga leading the way with four hits.[12]

At the Chicago League's annual meeting in 1903 the Union Giants were accepted back into membership when the local Aurora club was dropped. The league had too many applicants and needed to trim its numbers. The Union Giants were welcomed because they provided a good match for whoever played them. For example, they beat the local Clinton nine 6–1 in August behind the four hit pitching of their new young star, Ross. In September they romped over the Joliet club 9–0 behind the solid pitching of Walter Ball.[13]

In 1904 the club had an excellent year and their play earned them the chance to play the Cuban Giants in a three game series for the Colored Championship of the world. The *Tribune* did not include accounts of all the games but did report that the Chicago club lost the title.[14] They won the final game of the series 3–2 at Auburn Park. They scored the winning run on an error in the ninth, but in the previous two games errors and bad weather had been costly for the Chicago club.[15]

Leland did run into some trouble in June 1904 over the club's name when William Peters, who had worked with him for years, decided to start a new club in Springfield with the same name. Leland decided to take him to court with the backing of the Chicago League. The league urged all its members to boycott games with the new Union Giants and play only Leland's club. While this caused some confusion it does appear that Leland's club triumphed.[16]

In 1905 Frank Leland decided to rename the club, but William Peters stayed involved with his club until 1917 when he sold his interests to former player Robert Gilkerson. Gilkerson's Union Giants barnstormed as an independent club into the mid–1930s before finally folding. The 1905 club challenged the new Leland Giants to the colored championship in Chicago as they won 112 and lost only 10 games that season.[17]

Rosters — 1902–1904

William Binga, c
Haywood Rose, c
Danger Talbert, 2b
Roberts, 2b
J. Patterson, 2b
Toney, ss
Barton, cf
Harry Moore, cf
Joe Miller, p
Harry Buckner, p
Green, lf
Willis Jones, lf

Rhodes, lf
Taylor, 1b
Harry Hyde, 3b
John Davis, rf
Newberry, rf
Means, rf
Mathews, p
Clarence Lyttle, p
Walter Ball, p
Ross, p
David Wyatt, rf

Leland Giants

In 1905 Frank C. Leland created the Leland Giants from the roster of the Chicago Union Giants. Leland had worked with William S. Peters since the Union Giants were formed in 1901. His inaugural team included on its roster outfielder Dell Matthews, first baseman George Taylor, David Wyatt, catcher Bruce Petway, outfielder Charles Joe Green, pitcher Walter Ball, second baseman Harris, Andrew Campbell, utility man Dangerfield Talbert, William Horn and shortstop James Smith. Wyatt later became known as one of the principal writers of the constitution for the Negro National League in 1920.

Leland's club got off to a fast start in 1905, winning 41 straight games by July. They won their forty-first game over the Auroras 7–0 at Auburn Park. In addition to their city league games they traveled to places like Fort Wayne, Indiana, and Decatur, Iowa, for more local competition. They easily defeated the local Decatur team 7–1 behind superb pitching and two rally-killing double plays. They continued to be a tough opponent the following seasons in the Chicago City League. The victories were enjoyed by an array of pitchers. For example, in 1907 Billy Norman had a number of stellar games, including a 2–0 shutout over the River Forests in September. Norman gave up only one hit and struck out five.[18]

Over the years, one of the regular Chicago opponents they played were the Gunthers. Team owner Charles Gunther, originally from Germany, moved with his family to America in 1842. After the Civil War Gunther opened a confectionery store in Chicago and later got involved in banking. He made a great deal of money and had a lot of political connections in the city. This allowed him to build his own ball park, which he opened to games with Frank Leland's club regularly because he wanted his team to claim the title of best in Chicago.[19]

When Foster returned to the Giants in 1907 he released most of the players from the previous season. He brought with him a number of players from the Philadelphia Giants, saying that if he was going to manage he wanted his own players. Leland objected to Foster's moves, but with his health failing and increasing responsibilities as a commissioner he gave in to Foster. The year 1907 also saw the Giants take a step forward in organization, with the incorporation of the club as part of the Leland Giants Baseball and Amusement Association. Beauregard Moseley and Robert R. Jackson became involved because of this larger association that oversaw not only the Giants but also a skating rink, a restaurant and other entertainment venues. This new venture garnered all kinds of publicity and political support for Foster and Leland. Though the amusement venture eventually failed it taught Foster a lot about organizations and how they run.

One of the highlights of the 1907 season for the Giants happened in a game against the South Chicago nine. Rube Foster pitched his second no-hitter, his first having come earlier against Newark. Foster struck out seven and walked only two batters to win 1–0.[20]

In 1908 the Leland club got involved in a bit of politicking when Charles P. Taft, brother to presidential candidate William Howard Taft, came to a game to watch the Lelands. He rooted for the Leland club as they beat the Gunthers 11–4. The players announced they would support Taft in his presidential run in return for the fine support they received.[21] During the 1908 season the Giants had the chance to test their skills against a number of eastern clubs. They first played the All-Havanas and beat them in a seven game series 5–2. They later won a five game series from the Cuban Giants that began with great pitching from Rube Foster in game one. They played a final series with the Philadelphia Giants that was advertised as a seven game tilt, but scores for only six games have been found and the series ended with three wins apiece. That may be why the seventh game never took place. Neither team wanted to concede to the other side.

The 1909 club enjoyed its best finish as they ended the season at 31–9 and found themselves in first place in the reformed Chicago City League. They won the pennant by beating the Gunthers 2–1 behind the solid pitching of Pat Dougherty. Pete Hill saved the game with a spectacular catch in center field.[22] They were led by a solid pitching staff that included Walter Ball, future Hall of Famer Rube Foster, Pat Dougherty and Big Bill Gatewood. Hitters hated facing Gatewood, who had a nasty spitter but also developed a well-earned reputation for throwing at batters who crowded his plate. The staff proved its mettle when they had to pick up the slack left in mid–July when Foster broke his leg sliding into home plate in the first inning of a game against the Cuban Stars at Gunther Park. Pete Hill led the team to victory in that game 13–6, with three hits and two runs scored.[23]

In addition to the fine pitching, the Leland club had some of the best talent in the game at the other positions. Andrew "Jap" Payne was considered by many to be the best right fielder in the game. He had a strong arm and loved to throw runners out at the plate. In addition, he wielded a solid bat and showed good speed on the bases. Heavy hitting outfielder Pete Hill gave them a long ball threat every time he came to the plate. Hill also covered a lot of ground in the outfield. In one game in 1909 Hill even showed his versatility as he came in to pitch four innings of no-hit ball against the Cuban Stars.[24] Danger Talbert played anywhere in the infield he was needed and had a solid glove. Another future hall of famer, John Henry "Pop" Lloyd, even joined the club for a short time.

At the end of the 1909 season the Giants found themselves in a three game series with the Chicago Cubs. They lost the first contest 4–1, the highlight being Joe Green's effort to score from first after he broke his leg. Bobby Marshall also made three errors, making things easier for the Cubs. They lost the second after a ninth inning rally pulled the Cubs ahead 6–5 and a questionable call from the umpire gave the Cubs an edge. The final game was called because of darkness in the seventh inning, the score knotted at one apiece. Pat Dougherty had pitched a superb game against the big leaguers.[25]

After the 1909 season, manager Rube Foster and general manager Frank Leland found themselves in court to settle financial disputes that stemmed all the way back to the 1907 season. Part of the claim involved 5,707 shares of stock that were not all sold at the time reported by Frank Leland. The challenge came from Beauregard Moseley, who said the team owed him nearly $10,000 for that stock. Moseley was a prominent politician and lawyer in the Chicago area.[26] The end result of their battles came with the splitting of the team into the Leland Giants and the Chicago Giants. Foster retained the Leland name while Leland kept many of the players. In 1911 Foster renamed his club the Chicago American Giants, who went on to be a mainstay in the Negro Leagues. Leland's club became the Chicago Giants, and he managed them until his death in 1914; then Joe Green took over the club.

A highlight of the 1910 season came in September when the Giants completed a triple play against the Oklahoma Giants. They beat the Oklahoma boys 5–0 and completed a rare play in the fourth inning. It started with a catch in center by Pete Hill who threw in to third base because the ball was ruled a trap. The ball was then relayed to second and first to catch the other runners.[27] One of the local reporters claimed that a victory by the Giants over the Gunthers at Gunther Park in August 1910 was one of the best games of the season. It was a pitcher's duel won by the Leland club behind the masterful twirling of Frank Wickware as he gave up only four hits and struck out nine.[28]

After the breakup of the Leland-Foster management team both men continued to be involved in black baseball. Leland's tenure lasted only a few more years, as he died in 1914, but Foster went on to have a long and successful career with the American Giants, which was an original entrant in the Negro National League in 1920. Foster became the "Father of Black Baseball" and stayed with the new American Giants until he became ill in 1926 and was forced to leave the team and the league. Unfortunately, he never returned to the game, but the Giants continued to play in Chicago into the 1950s.

Leland's team continued in 1911 and had some limited success. Smokey Joe Williams continued to pitch for him, and in one game shut out Foster's club 10–0 on five hits. In another game against the American Giants Williams did not fare as well, giving up a homerun to Pete Hill and a triple to Bill Monroe before giving way to Bill Gatewood. They lost that game 7–5. Walter Ball won the first game of that doubleheader 7–0, with Foster the losing pitcher.[29]

2

The American Giants and Chicago's Negro League Era Clubs

The American Giants were a mainstay of the Chicago baseball scene from the 1910s through the 1940s. In the early years they were led by the indomitable spirit and skill of Andrew "Rube" Foster, the father of the Negro Leagues. After he became ill in 1926 the Giants enjoyed a variety of leadership, though none of it quite as dominant as Foster's. One of their greatest seasons came in 1926 when they won the World Series, even though Foster did not get to finish out that season and enjoy the Series with his club.

Foster started the American Giants after he split with Frank C. Leland when they disagreed over how the Leland Giants should be run. In 1910 Foster made the split official and kept the Leland Giants name, initially, then changed the name to the American Giants.

Over the years, Foster guided many stars, rookies and just solid players on his roster. Many of them in later interviews would always talk about how much they learned from the big man who ran their club, Mr. Foster. In a recent interview Buck O'Neil acknowledged how much he owed to Foster, who inspired him with his drive, his ambition and his knowledge of the game. Dave Wyatt wrote that "Rube Foster is one of the most fair-minded sportsmen that I know of."[1]

Foster played and managed the Giants for a number of years before simply running the club. During the 1910s the Giants traveled all over the United States and beyond looking for the best opponents to play. For example, in 1917 they found themselves in a series of games with the All-Nations out of Kansas City, who were led by the incredible pitching of John Donaldson. In one contest against Donaldson and his club, the Giants sent their ace, Cannonball Redding, to the mound; he struck out twelve while only

The 1938 Eastern squad included a few players who spent some time on the roster of the American Giants. (Back row from left): Rev. Cannaday, Johnny Taylor, Thad Christoper, Sammy T. Hughes, Bill Wright, Biz Mackey, Barney Brown, Henry McHenry, Edsall Walker and Jim Brown. (Front Row from left): Jake Dunn, Buck Leonard, Dick Seay, Oscar Charleston, Vic Harris, Willie Wells and Sam Bankhead. (Photograph courtesy of NoirTech Research, Inc.)

allowing two hits, and still lost in twelve innings to the All-Nations.[2] They seemed to have had some trouble with a local club called Ragens Colts in 1917, while beating up on C. I. Taylor's Indianapolis club. Redding lost another 2–1 contest to the Colts in October, while Tom Williams and Redding helped the Giants win an earlier doubleheader from the ABCs 4–1 and 8–3.[3]

When Foster started the Negro National League (NNL) in 1920 he made Chicago one of the original entrants and anchors of the new league. He served as the league's first president and main booking agent. Some other owners objected to the influence Foster wielded for his American Giants but no one disagreed with his baseball smarts.

The Giants enjoyed a number of years of success beginning in 1920 when they won the first three pennants in the new Negro National League.

They lost the pennant in 1923 to the other powerhouse in the league, the Kansas City Monarchs. Then in 1926 they played the Kansas City Monarchs to get to the World Series, and in the World Series won five games to four. The following season the Giants triumphed in four straight games over the Birmingham Black Barons. Then in 1928 they returned again to the series but lost in a nine game series to the St. Louis Stars. In 1932, as an entrant in the Negro Southern League, the Giants beat out the Nashville Elite Giants to declare themselves world champions. When the Negro Leagues were revamped the Giants found themselves winning the second half of the league standings; Kansas City won the first but no series was played. They lost in the play-offs in 1943 to the Birmingham club in five games and enjoyed their final trip to the series in 1949, where they lost in four straight to the Baltimore Elite Giants.

Looking at the individual players who played over the years for the Giants, one finds some amazing names on their rosters. For example, there were nine future major leaguers who donned the American Giants uniform in the early stages of their careers. Thirteen Chicago American Giant players were later elected to a National Hall of Fame, in either the U.S. or Latin America. Seventy-four team members played in the East-West All-Star game from 1933–53. This is the caliber of player that Foster and others managed to entice to Chicago.

Rube Foster himself is in the Hall of Fame but so is his brother Willie, who also pitched for many years for his brother's club. When Willie Foster decided on a baseball career and wanted to come join the Giants, Rube did not encourage him because he thought he should finish college first. As a result, Willie did not begin his pitching with the Giants, but eventually Rube gave in and invited his brother to join him.

Another superstar on the Giants roster hailed from south of the border; Cristobal Torriente came to the Windy City in the 1920s. Torriente became a mainstay in the Giants outfield from 1919 to 1925. He joined Oscar Charleston and Jimmie Lyons to make up one of the best outfields in Negro League history. Torriente had speed and a strong arm and he could hit. In 1920 he won the batting crown with a .411 average.

Rube Currie came in to bolster the pitching staff in 1926 and helped lead the club to victory in the World Series. Currie also helped the Giants with his bat, ranking fifth in the league at .408. Currie joined a staff that consisted of Rube Foster and Webster McDonald, who hit .400 that same season.[4] Foster brought in star caliber players such as Bruce Petway to catch and John Henry "Pop" Lloyd to bolster the infield defense. He also relied on Pat Dougherty and Frank Wickware to strike fear in the hearts of opposing batters.

The Giants relied on their outstanding pitching to keep them competitive over the years. In addition to the Foster brothers, the Giants had twirlers such as Ed Rile, Tom Williams, Aubrey Owens, Gentry Jessup and Webster McDonald leading them to victory. With others like Lewis Wolfolk, Dan Bankhead, Chet Brewer, Rube Currie, Bill Gatewood and Juan Padrone, the Giants had a lot of depth they could count on as well.

In addition to Rube Foster acting as manager for so many years the Giants were blessed with a number of other excellent field generals. President J. B. Martin re-signed Candy Jim Taylor to the helm in 1945. Taylor joined the Giants after leading the Homestead Grays to the 1943 and 1944 championships. Taylor had previously managed the Giants from 1937 to 1942. He helped the Giants win the first half crown in 1937 and managed in the East-West Classic on five different occasions. Taylor came back to replace Lloyd Daven-port, who had had a rather

Rube Currie pitched for the Chicago Unions as well as the American Giants. One of the highlights of his career came in 1926 when he pitched a no-hitter. (Photograph courtesy of NoirTech Research, Inc.)

stormy one-year stint after replacing Double Duty Radcliffe.[5]

Over the years, the Giants played many memorable games. Some were memorable because of incredible pitching or fielding, others saw the Giants manhandle their opponents. Still others are remembered for a single play or because something happened involving the fans or umpires. Some of these events gives one a real feel for just how mighty these Giants were. For example, in 1926 Red Grier of the Bacharach Giants pitched the first no-hitter in Series history but the American Giants came back to win the Series. As Wayne Stivers makes plain below, one of the most exciting series that the Giants were involved in came in 1913 against a team called the Smart Sets:

THE RECORD BREAKING BACK-TO-BACK NO-HITTERS OF THE 1913 CHICAGO AMERICAN GIANTS
By Wayne Stivers

The first week of June in 1913 had Negro League baseball fans on Chicago's South Side talking about the upcoming four game series between the Smart Sets of Paterson, New Jersey, and their beloved Negro League team, Andrew "Rube" Foster's Chicago American Giants. The first game was scheduled to take place on Sunday afternoon, June eighth, at Schorling's Park, home of the American Giants.

The Chicago American Giants were fresh from successfully winning the Pacific Coast Winter League, and following that had barnstormed for over a month in the northwestern United States and into Canada, winning the vast majority of their games. They opened the regular season on April 25 in Schorling's Park, shutting out the Milwaukee White Sox 9–0. Since then, they had lost only two games in the regular season. This would be the season the American Giants would appear in over two hundred games, marking the first time a Negro League team would appear in that many games in one season.

On the other hand, the Smart Sets team was also having a great season on the East Coast, and had won twenty-one straight games before their appearance against the American Giants in Chicago. By all indications, it was expected to be a tough, competitive series between two talented Negro League teams.

The American Giants were a veteran team, with such outstanding players as Pete Hill playing center field and Frank "Pete" Duncan, Jess Barbour and Bill Lindsay sharing the other two outfield positions. Candy Jim Taylor was a solid third baseman, Bill Monroe was at second, Fred Hutchinson at shortstop and Bruce Petway and Bill Pierce traded off playing first base and catching. The pitching staff rested in the capable hands with Andrew "Rube" Foster, Charles "Pat" Dougherty, Louis "Dicta" Johnson, John "Steel Arm" Taylor, "Big Bill" Gatewood and Bill Lindsay.

The Smart Sets were well represented by pitchers Dan McClellan, Harry Buckner and another pitcher identified only by the name White. McClellan and Buckner would be in the lineup playing the outfield when they were not pitching. Ashby Dunbar played second base, with Clarence Williams, N. Williams, and Nathan Harris rounding out the infield.

The first game was held on a chilly Sunday afternoon on June eighth in front of a large crowd at Schorling's Park. Most would consider this game to be a pitchers battle with the spit-baller, Louis "Dicta" Johnson of the American Giants, facing one of the best pitchers of the early part of the century, Dan McClellan of the Smart Sets. Andrew "Rube" Foster may have had an inkling of what was to come, as he did not don his uniform, but watched his team from the *Indianapolis Freeman* press stand instead. It is not known if Rube managed his team from the press stand or if someone else was acting manager for this game. Dan McClellan never lived up to his billing, giving up thirteen hits while walking one batter. He received poor support from his teammates, who committed six errors behind him.

The American Giants took advantage of McClellan's poor pitching and the errors made by the Smart Sets, and put up six runs in the third inning and another three runs in the seventh inning to win the game 9–0. Candy Jim Taylor was the hitting star of the game, rapping out four hits, including three doubles for the only extra base hits of the game, the other nine hits all being singles. Jess Barbour and Bill Pierce had two singles each to help out with the victory.

The real hero of the game, however, was Louis "Dicta" Johnson, who had fine control of his spitter, striking out seven and giving up four walks, but allowing no hits for his first career no-hitter.

The next afternoon, Monday, June 9, the two teams would meet again at Schorling's Park, with the Smart Sets wanting revenge on the American Giants for being no hit by Louis "Dicta" Johnson. The veteran Charles "Pat" Dougherty of the American Giants would be going against a little-known pitcher for the Smart Sets by the name of White. Negro League baseball fans attending the game would not only see their home team American Giants dominate the Smart Sets again, but would see history in the making. The Giants got to White for only seven hits but scored in five of the eight innings they batted, and won the game easily, 8–0.

The real hero of the game, again, was the pitcher, Charles "Pat" Dougherty, who not only defeated the Smart Sets, but pitched a history making second consecutive no-hitter for the Chicago American Giants. The feat was never accomplished again in Negro League baseball. Less than four years later, and again in Chicago, the Major Leagues had their one and only back to back no-hitters by teammates. On May 5, 1917, Ernie Koob of St. Louis no-hit the Chicago White Sox 1–0. The next day, May 6, Bob Groom no-hit the White Sox again, this time winning 3–0.

The third game of the series would take place on Tuesday afternoon, June 10, at Schorling's Park. The Smart Sets must have thought that things could not get any worse, being no hit on two consecutive days. Bill Gatewood, the starting pitcher for the American Giants, must have felt the pressure to try to duplicate what his pitching teammates had accomplished in the two previous games. Fortunately for the Smart Sets, Bill Gatewood was not as dominant as his two previous pitching teammates had been against them, but he did manage to shut them out 5–0. The series, which had been billed to be tough and competitive, so far had been totally controlled by the home team American Giants. The two teams had played three games and the Smart Sets had yet to score a run, let alone come close to winning a game.

The final game of the series would take place on Wednesday afternoon, June 11, at Schorling's Park. The American Giants would send the veteran Bill Lindsay, "The Kansas Cyclone," to the mound to try and shut out the Smart Sets in four consecutive games. The Smart Sets would try to avoid another whitewashing, sending their ace, Dan McClellan, to the mound to try to salvage one game, at least. Even though he had been roughed up in the first game on Sunday afternoon, McClellan was one of the top pitchers of his day, and was capable of defeating any team on any given day.

The American Giants got off to a fast start, scoring one run in the first inning, scoring again in the fifth and seventh innings, and leading three to nothing going into the eighth. It looked like the Smart Sets were going to be shut out for the fourth consecutive game. They had gone thirty-four consecutive innings without scoring. As the eighth inning began, it looked like things might finally change as Ashby Dunbar and Dan McClellan hit back to back doubles and the long scoring drought was broken. The inning ended at three to one, and the Smart Sets must have thought they were finally getting back into a game. Bill Lindsay, however, toughened, and this would be the only threat in the game for the eastern team. The American Giants scored again in the bottom of the eighth, and went on to win four to one. Bill Lindsay would give the Smart Sets only four hits in the game, striking out twelve batters, while walking five, and getting a triple in the hitting department. The only player to get two hits in the game was Candy Jim Taylor, who got two singles. Bill Monroe and Bruce Petway got doubles for the Giants, and Dunbar and McClellan got their back to back doubles in the eighth inning for the Smart Sets. Dan McClellan, pitching a much better game in the fourth game than he did in the first, gave up nine hits, striking out only two, but walking none.

After their drubbing by the American Giants, the Smart Sets had to be glad to get out of Chicago. However, playing the St. Louis Giants in St. Louis later in the month during their western swing, they did not fare any better, and were swept in the three game series, eight to seven, seven to one and four to one.[6]

When the American Giants played the Tufts-Lyons in 1912 in California the result was not nearly as interesting as the paper's coverage of the game. The Giants lost 5–1 to Leverenz who struck out Rube Foster in the ninth inning when he represented the tying run. Foster entered the game as a pinch hitter for Fred Hutchinson. According to the news article, "Rube Fanned. He fanned furiously. He fanned with all the fervor of his ample being. Each time he swung the whole world swayed and 1000 of his compatriots gasped in astonishment."[7] The Giants also lost the opening game of the 1912 winter league season to the McCormicks 8–5. Dougherty took the loss after being knocked out in the sixth inning and replaced by Bill Gatewood.

In 1913 the Giants lost a game to the West Baden Sprudels 7–5. The local reporter called the game the most exciting of the year. It began with a parade followed by the unveiling of the flag from winning the California Winter League Championship. The team also sported brand new cream and blue uniforms. They won the Winter League behind the stellar pitching of Bill "Invincible" Lindsay and the batting of Frank Duncan. Their winning ways continued as they returned from the West Coast and reportedly collected a 62–10 record.[8]

At the close of the 1914 season Foster reported his club's record as

108–16. He included this accomplishment in a challenge issued through the *Tribune* to the winner of the Chicago Federal League, asking them to play the Giants in a seven game championship series. The purpose would be to determine the winner between the north and south sides of the city. Foster sent the challenge because he knew they would not be asked to play the winner.[9]

Dick Whitworth pitched a no-hitter against the Chicago Giants in September 1915. He gave up two walks and there was one error in the field as the American Giants won 4–0. John Henry Lloyd gave him all the runs he needed with the two he scored. The Giants and the Lincoln Giants planned a series of thirteen games together to decide the champion of black baseball in 1915. They played four games in New York, with the Lincoln's winning two and tying another. They played a five game series in Chicago with the home town team taking three of the contests to even the series at 4 wins each and one tie. The remaining four games were to be played in New York. During a 3–1 victory over the Cuban Stars a fight broke out at Schorling Park. Giant pitcher Crawford hit Torriente in the jaw with a pitch and when Torriente tried to steal third the umpire called him out. Torriente kicked the umpire and the players spilled out onto the field. Police had to be called in to quiet the ruckus down. The fight later resumed out on the street between Torriente and Crawford as they heaved paving stones at one another. Rube Foster finally broke it up.[10]

During the 1916 season local writers called the Giants the "bulldogs," which was considered slang for the best team around. (When they beat up on a local Indiana club called the Beavers with 17 hits and 14 runs this title was bestowed on them.) Whitworth and Wickware shared the pitching duties for this club while the big hitters included Pete Hill, Jess Barbour and Bruce Petway. Together they propelled the Giants to the City Championship; the flag was presented to the team and each player received a belt with a pearl buckle with their name and the championship engraved on it.[11]

David Brown showed off his stuff for the Giants in a 1921 victory (14–5) over the Staleys. He gave up only six hits while striking out 11 and walking only one. Bingo DeMoss led all hitters with four hits and three runs. Torriente followed with three base hits while every other Giant player had two hits in the game. Otis Starks showed off his stuff in a 1–0 defeat of the Indianapolis ABCs in mid-season. He gave up only four hits and struck out three while walking only one batter.[12]

One of the longest games of their history took place in 1922 in a twenty inning affair with the Bacharachs. Chicago won 1–0 with Torriente scoring the run. He came home on a single by Dave Malarcher after Foster had checked out the arm of the right fielder. The Bacharachs had put Ramirez in right for the last inning and as soon as the move was made Foster decided they would run on him if they got the chance. Torriente scored from second as a result.[13]

In 1923 Frank Young, reporting for the *Chicago Defender,* claimed 17,000 fans came out in early June to watch "one of the greatest baseball games staged in this city in many a day...." The Giants staged an amazing comeback victory against the mighty Kansas City Monarchs. They tied the game 2–2 in the seventh and then tied it again in the eighth 4–4. Tom Williams pitched through some tough jams to get his club to the tenth inning, when they scored the winning run on a double by Jim Brown, driving in Cristobal Torriente. Young claimed it was the largest crowd in the city to date to see two Negro League clubs play.[14]

The Giants also played in the City semipro league in 1923 and by the end of the season were fighting with the Pyotts for first place. The Logan Squares and the Normals filled out the rest of the schedule. All four clubs took this rivalry seriously, as they each wanted to win the coveted Silver Trophy. A 10–6 victory over the Logan Squares behind the solid pitching of Ed Rile and Dicta Johnson gave them a real shot at winning. Cristobal Torriente led the hitting attack with two hits, three runs knocked in and two runs scored.[15]

The Detroit Stars came to town in 1924 and defeated the Giants quite handily 13–1. They won the next contest 6–4 on a three run homer by Torriente. The highlight of the series was a triple play by the Detroit infield. It started on a hit by Dave Malarcher to Pryor, the first baseman. They shut out the Stars 8–0 in another game in the series; Juan Padrone picked up the win as the visitors could not figure him out.[16]

In mid–1936 the Giants went on a six-game winning streak. They defeated the Columbus Buckeyes and the House of David club. Hitters had a field day with the Buckeyes pitchers, winning 14–1, 15–1, 10–8 and 10–5. The House of David gave them better competition with 7–6 and 10–8 losses. One of the big hitters for the Giants was shortstop Wilbert Libeaux, who went 3–4 in one game with three runs scored. Ted Trent was the star pitcher, picking up three victories.[17]

In 1937 the Giants were on the wrong side of the score in a memorable game against the Monarchs. "Stringbean" Smith pitched a nearly perfect game in a 4–0 shut-out. The only runner to reach base against him was Mel Powell, who walked and then got erased in a double play. Willie Cornelius pitched a three-hitter himself but lost due to the poor fielding behind him.[18]

The Giants lost a heartbreaker in 1938 to the Birmingham Black Barons. They were ahead until the seventh inning and then the Barons scored ten runs in the inning to take the lead and the game 15–11, with Blackman picking up the loss. However, they did immediately follow that with a doubleheader victory over the Barons 11–3 and 4–1, with Tom Johnson picking up one of the victories.[19]

Satchel Paige came to Chicago late in 1940 to pitch for the Monarchs and he brought out so many fans there were not enough seats in the stands; nor were there enough ticket collectors, and some of the fans broke through the fence and got in for free before extra police came to restore order. Paige won the game 9–3 and struck out nine Giants along the way, so the fans got their money's worth.

The Giants swept the Cleveland Bears in four straight games when the Bears came to Chicago in 1939. They won the first 11–1 and then followed with a doubleheader sweep with scores of 3–2 and 4–3. The last game turned into a real seesaw contest with the Giants holding on for an 18–14 win. Byas seemed to be the hitting star in the series, as every big play had him in the middle with a couple of singles, a sacrifice fly and a double to center.

Receiving an invite to play the Great Lakes Naval team in 1943 was a first for the Giants. When they went to the training center to play, it was the first time a black team had been invited to play the naval squad, which was dominated by ex-major leaguers. The American Giants defeated the Bluejackets 7–3 behind the solid pitching of Gentry Jessup. Every Giant player except Jessup had at least one hit in a 19-hit attack. The big blow came as a triple by Lloyd Davenport, who went 3–4 and scored one run. Art Pennington and Ted Radcliffe had three hits each off losing pitcher Tom Ferrick.[20]

The Giants experienced another first in 1943 when they played Memphis on September 2. Their contest marked the first time two black teams would play under the lights at Comiskey Park. They lost the contest 2–0 with Verdel Mathis picking up the victory for Memphis. Gentry Jessup took the loss for the Giants; though he pitched well he was hurt by a Ralph Wyatt error. They split a doubleheader with the Cincinnati Clowns, winning the first game 5–2 but losing the second 3–2. Lefty Shields took the loss in the second, while Jessup won the first, helping his own cause with a double that knocked in two runs.[21]

The Giants actually won the second half of the Negro American League (NAL) race in 1943, forcing a playoff with Birmingham, which won the first half. The first game of the series got rained out and it became a best three out of five competition. Birmingham came away with the series, winning the final game 1–0 on a one-hitter by Johnny Huber. Huber gave up a single to Ralph Wyatt in the first and one walk and was masterful throughout the game. Jessup pitched nearly as well, giving up only four hits and one run in the losing effort.[22]

In a doubleheader with the Kansas City Monarchs in 1944 the Giants split the contest. They lost the first game 3–1 to Earl Bumpus. Gentry Jessup took the loss for the Giants. Chicago won the second game of the night 3–0 as Lefty McKinnis matched Paige pitch for pitch in the early going and came out on the high side of the score. The Giants scored their first run off Paige in the fourth inning when Alec Radcliffe stole home on Paige's long windup. Radcliffe had doubled and moved to third on a ground out by Art Pennington.[23]

During one stretch in 1945 the Giants won three straight from the Memphis nine. They won a doubleheader 5–1 and 4–1 with Gentry Jessup and Willie Cornelius taking the victories. McKinnis did come in to relieve Cornelius when he got in a little trouble in the second game. Cornelius helped his cause with a triple to center that drove in the first Giants run. Jessup struck out six and walked only two in the first game. The third loss

Group photograph of American Giants (from left) Pepper Bassett, Willie Ferrell, Jimmie Crutchfield and Willie Hudson. (Photograph courtesy of the National Baseball Hall of Fame Library, Cooperstown, New York.)

came after ten innings with a final score of 6–5. Jessup came in to relieve McKinnis in the eighth and left with the score tied. Jim Smith hit a tough high hopper to the infield to score the winning run in the tenth, giving Jessup two victories in the series. The Giants came out on the wrong side of a shutout to Birmingham in the first half of the season. They got only one extra base hit in the contest while the Barons had five extra base hits to win 2–0. Jessup took the loss for the hometown Giants, giving up ten hits while walking one batter.[24]

The 1946 season got off to a great start with Chicago playing the Monarchs in Comiskey Park. The doubleheader began with Governor Dwight Green throwing out the first pitch, as he did nearly every year. Dr. Martin arranged the festivities to get things off to a rousing start, which included bands and a parade on the field of local organizations. The best part of the day came when the hometown team triumphed in the first contest 9–2 behind the stellar performance of Gentry Jessup. Clyde Nelson gave Jessup all the support he needed, with a three run homer in the first inning. McCoy and Longest had solo homers in the second game. The Monarchs took the second game 4–3.[25]

Another memorable contest took place in 1946 when the Giants tangled with the Indianapolis Clowns at White Sox Park. Nearly 10,000 fans came out to watch the competition and got to see a beauty, as the game went twenty innings before being called due to darkness. Jim McCurrine hit a triple for Chicago in the ninth to tie the game and that was the last scoring of the night. The fans witnessed an incredible pitching duel as Gentry Jessup for the Giants and Peanut Davis for the Clowns both twirled the entire game. Jessup struck out eleven to keep the game close. In a twin bill with the Homestead Grays the Giants came up short both games. Gentry Jessup had his worst outing of the year, yielding 14 hits and losing 13–0. The Grays won the second 9–7 behind the long ball hitting of Josh Gibson as he treated the fans to a couple of heavy clouts.[26]

A four game series against Indianapolis in 1947 allowed all the Giants hitters to raise their batting averages. The Giants batters got 42 hits in four games. Manager Jim Taylor made some slight adjustments in the lineup and the club responded with four straight wins. In a twin bill with Memphis the Giants lost the first contest but came back strong in the second with 11 hits and 14 runs. Locke held the Red Sox to only one run on two hits while the Giants ran off three Memphis pitchers, who gave up 12 walks.[27]

After winning the Western division pennant in 1949 the Giants lost in four straight to the Baltimore Elite Giants, 9–1, 5–4, 8–4 and 4–2. Unfortunately for the American Giants they lost the final game at home in Comiskey Park to end the season. Gentry Jessup lost the first and last games of the series though he had pitched well all season for the Giants. For example, to clinch their pennant the Giants beat Indianapolis in a doubleheader, 1–0 and 2–0, with Jessup and Smith getting the victories.[28]

Toward the end of the Negro Leagues' existence the Giants tried to foster integration in their leagues with the signing of a number of white players. In July 1950 they signed Luis Clarizio, a twenty-year-old outfielder, and Lou Chirban, a nineteen-year-old pitcher, to contracts. (The two played their first game against the Indianapolis Clowns.) The Giants also signed Frank Dyll and Stanley Miarka.[29]

Midway through the 1950 season the Giants were in trouble when they lost back to back doubleheaders, one to the Indianapolis Clowns and the next to the Kansas City Monarchs. The Monarchs won 13–1 and 3–0, nearly shutting down the Chicago bats. The only hitter who seemed to be on the mark for the Giants was Clyde McNeal, who had three hits, including a long triple. Lou Chirban took the loss in the 13–1 Monarchs win.[30]

In both 1951 and 1952 the American Giants won the western division of the NAL. They won both halves of the division in 1952, led in hitting by third baseman Roy Williams with a .347 average and in pitching by Vincent Husband. Husband led the Chicago hurlers with a 7–1 record.

The Giants played their games in a number of parks over the years but mostly they called American Giants Park home. They moved to the park at Thirty-ninth Street and Wentworth in 1911 and leased it from John Schorling, a white saloon keeper. In the early 1930s the club lost the lease on the park and became a road team before returning in 1935, when Robert Cole bought the club. In 1941 a mysterious fire broke out in the grandstands and burned them down.[31]

The Giants were always an important part of the community as well. The players often worked in Chicago during the off-season and the club used a number of their games as benefits for a variety of community needs over the years. In 1923 the Giants played the Detroit Stars in late June and raised $618 for the local YWCA building project. The Giants defeated the Toledo Crawfords 9–8 in a 1939 contest staged to raise funds for the Chicago chapter of the NAACP. About 6,500 fans came out for the nail-biter, won by the Giants in the tenth inning. The Giants played the Cleveland Bears in Youngstown, Ohio, to raise money for the local Elks organization in May 1939. The club's 1940 home opener served as a fund-raiser for Herman Dunlap, who broke his leg at the end of the 1939 season and was still out when the new season began. In a 1941 contest they lost 8–3 in a benefit game for local Provident hospital. Joe Louis was there to throw out the first pitch and the ceremonies were planned by a committee headed by Mrs. Robert A. Cole. In 1945 the Giants hosted the Kansas City Monarchs in a fund-raiser for Meharry Medical College. The funds would be donated for the building of a new dormitory. Walter McCoy took the mound for the Giants. In 1949 they played the Louisville Buckeyes in a doubleheader in Syracuse. The game was arranged to benefit the local Syracuse Lodge of Negro Elks.[32]

Often local dignitaries and politicians could be found at Giants games. After they won the 1916 city championship, Edward Litzinger, a Republican candidate for the board of review, came and presented them with their flag. During the 1946 home opener against the Kansas City Monarchs, Governor Dwight H. Green threw out the first pitch after being escorted to the pitcher's mound by league president Dr. J. B. Martin. At a big game between the Monarchs and the Giants, local attorney James Herbert threw out the first pitch, while owners J. B. Martin and William Little sat and watched the festivities. The pregame activities also included a variety of bands, a local drum and bugle corps, plus the Elks and Boy Scouts parading around the field in support. Unfortunately for Chicago, the game did not live up to the hype beforehand, as they lost 13–3 to Kansas City.[33]

Over the years the Giants had a number of excellent owners and managers holding the reins. Some of the key men involved on the ownership side were H. G. Hall, Robert A. Cole, William "Bill" Little, William Trimble, and Dr. J. B. Martin. William Little first got involved with the club as a partial owner in 1936 when H. G. Hall invited him to invest at a time the Giants were struggling financially. In 1949 Little got controlling interest of the club, securing a five year lease from Dr. Martin, who had owned the team since 1941. Martin decided to bring in help to run the club since he had so many responsibilities to the league and he had no plans to give any of that up. Little was able to buy into the team because he owned his own tailoring company, Monarch Tailoring. He also owned the G. M. Porter Drugstore on the south side of Chicago. Little brought some financial resources to the club but also his business background and his education as a graduate of the Tuskegee Institute. He brought in Robert Simmons as his general manager.[34]

H. G. Hall worked for the Chicago Metropolitan Mutual Assurance Company as its first vice president and treasurer. Robert A. Cole, who owned the Giants and turned over his ownership to Hall, was also one of the co-owners of Chicago Mutual. Robert Cole amassed a large fortune working in Chicago, and supported the Negro Leagues in a variety of capacities. William Trimble took over the club in 1927. He was a white racetrack owner and florist from Princeton, Illinois.[35]

On the management side, the Giants were blessed with some excellent field managers. Starting with Rube Foster and going all the way to Winfield Welch in the 1950s, the leadership had great knowledge and inspired a number of players to go on and become managers in their own right. Winfield

Welch played and managed during his career for teams such as the New York Cubans, the Birmingham Black Barons, the Cincinnati Crescents and the Giants (in 1949). During the off-season he acted as secretary for the Harlem Globetrotters basketball team.[36] Candy Jim Taylor and Gentleman Dave Malarcher had the longest tenures with the Giants, as both enjoyed great success as managers.

Chicago Teams in the Negro Leagues Era

Chicago's baseball scene flourished from the earliest beginnings of the game, and it was no different in the local African American communities. There were lots of local sandlot teams, amateur clubs, company teams and semipro clubs and then the Negro League professionals, who toiled on the diamonds in the city from the mid-nineteenth century through the 1950s. The team that attracted the most attention was the world champion American Giants under the leadership of Andrew "Rube" Foster. Foster's Giants, Frank Leland's Giants and the Union Giants enjoyed some of their success because of the presence of so many good quality local teams throughout the city. These other teams provided many players their only opportunity to play when they had families or other obligations that kept them from traveling across the country.

THE CHICAGO BROWN BOMBERS

In the 1940s an effort was made to create a new Negro League that would help major league teams scout black players. The new league, called the United States League (USL), had six entries when it began in 1945. Chicago was represented by the Brown Bombers, a local team that had been around for a number of years as a semipro club. James Foster was president of the team and L. H. Gamble owned the ball club; over the years they brought in a number of Negro Leaguers to manage the club and play for the team.

In 1942 the Bombers signed Bingo DeMoss as their manager and they entered the Negro Major Baseball League. The other teams in the league were the Cincinnati Clowns, the Baltimore Black Orioles, the Boston Royal Giants, the Detroit Black Sox and the Minneapolis–St. Paul Gophers. DeMoss signed a number of excellent players to his roster, including pitcher Roosevelt Davis, "Stringbean" Williams, Johnny Reed and Sonny Parker.[37]

The Brown Bombers opponents represented the gamut of baseball, ranging from the local amateur teams to the major Negro League clubs. They started the 1942 season in Miami for spring training and then came north playing the Macon Red Wings, Winkler Motors and the Michigan City

Cubs. In early June 1942 they split a doubleheader with the touring House of David club while they were both in Minnesota. Chicago won the first contest 5–4 behind the solid pitching of Roosevelt Davis. He was helped by his fielders completing three double plays behind him. The House of David took the second contest 6–3. They lost a tough contest to the St. Paul-Minneapolis Gophers 3–0 in July 1942. Roosevelt Davis took the loss while former American Giants pitcher Gread McKinnis earned the victory. The East Chicago Giants made a trip to the Windy City from Indiana for a game on Bingo DeMoss Day and nearly spoiled the occasion for the home town team, but the game ended in a 3–3 tie, called due to darkness. They beat the Winkler Motors crew in two straight games in early August.[38]

The Ethiopian Clowns came to town and got shut out 1–0, with Roosevelt Davis again securing the win. The only run he needed came in the sixth inning after Williams had tripled and scored on Tyler's hit. They played a series with a local team in Muskegon, Michigan, and lost two, winning the final game to salvage a little pride. Mel Powell got the victory in that game. They also lost a doubleheader to the Birmingham Black Barons 8–0 and 10–5. They got shutout by Nat Shyer's All-Stars 7–0 in 1943. In 1944 they lost a doubleheader to the Detroit Cubs 16–4 and 6–4. Between games, Jesse Owens came out and ran a series of 100 yard exhibition races to entertain the fans. They beat the Cincinnati Clowns 5–1 and 3–1 with three home runs in the two contests. Nelson, Tyler and Stracham all hit the long ball to help the Bombers. They also defeated the Detroit Black Sox 7–5, with Tyler and Nelson again providing the fire power from the plate while Roosevelt Davis picked up the victory.[39]

Opening the 1943 season under Bingo DeMoss, the Brown Bombers had high hopes for their club because they had so many veterans. Their pitching staff continued to be anchored by Roosevelt Davis. Davis had previously pitched for the Miami-Ethiopian Clowns and in the Wichita and Denver tournaments. Stringbean Williams came to the club from the Black Barons and could pitch and play first base to keep his bat in the line up. Buddy Thompson from the Monarchs gave them a strong lefty while Johnny Reed and Sonny Parker rounded out the pitching core. Bernell and Jimmy Longest formed a solid right side of the infield while Wiggins and college player Eugene Tyler covered the rest of the infield. The outfield was patrolled by John Bissant of the American Giants along with "Putt" Powell, also of the Giants, and Bilbo Williams from St. Louis. Owner Gamble wanted to be sure his team gave the fans their money's worth when they came out to see the Bombers.[40]

When the USL opened in 1945 the Brown Bombers lost a doubleheader 8–7 and 3–2 to the Detroit Motor City Giants to kick things off. They had been ahead in the first game until Detroit took the lead in the ninth inning.

They lost a doubleheader to the Indianapolis Clowns in 1946, with Roosevelt Davis ending up with one of the losses. They defeated a Havana La Palomas nine 1–0 in July 1946. This was not the first time they had played the Cuban team. Their first encounter came in June in Council Bluffs, Iowa, and they played again in July and lost 11–8.[41]

The Palmer House All Stars

Working for the Palmer House Hotel in Chicago gave many young athletes an added bonus: they could play for the baseball team as well. The club owner L. M. Gamble, entered the All Stars in tournaments all over and they played exhibitions throughout the Midwest. The Palmer House All Stars competed in the Illinois State Semi-Pro Championship tournament regularly and often came away the winner. (For example, they won the tournament in 1939 and 1940.) They beat the Woodruff nine of Peoria in 1939 by a score of 15–5 as Norman Cross won his fourth game of the tournament. In 1940 they came in fifth in the Wichita National Semi Pro Tournament, relying on the solid pitching of Roosevelt Davis.[42]

When the All Stars began in 1934, Potter Palmer III wanted to create an intra-hotel league, with teams from all the departments at the hotel. That first season the championship was won by the club from accounting called the Tigers. This presented a challenge to the other divisions and the waiters set out to find good ball players who could also wait tables. They found a number of their future stars playing at Washington Park, where there were twelve ball diamonds always in use. In fact, Maurice Wiggins, their future shortstop, was found playing there. Along with Wiggins came Baby Doll Dial and Triple Duty Drake. The Caterers came away with the championship in 1935 and 1936 before the league folded because the other divisions could not compete. That was when the All Stars were created.[43]

Though the club was a semipro team the roster often sported the names of some of the biggest stars of the Negro Leagues. In 1940 Alec Radcliffe came on in relief to help the All Stars defeat the Puerto Rico nine 5–4. Radcliffe was also the manager of the club that season. Frank Duncan caught for them in 1940. Turkey Stearnes joined them after spending the 1939–1940 winter in Detroit. Jack Marshall, the American Giants infielder, joined them for the end-of-the-year tournaments. John Bissant, Bernell Longest, Norman Cross and Mel Powell played for the All Stars but also had previously been with the American Giants.[44]

During the 1941 season the club changed its name to the Chicago All Stars. Their first game after they made the switch resulted in a victory over the Sterman Elevators, a white ball club in Oklahoma. John Bissant led the club with three hits and scored three runs.[45]

The team often spent the early spring traveling in the South to get ready for the local season. In 1940 they traveled all through Texas and New Orleans before heading back to the Windy City, and in 1941 the club got its start in New Orleans. As the team traveled around the country their reputation grew and most Negro League clubs were interested in playing them because they were a worthy opponent. They also helped attract a crowd because they always seemed to have a few big names on the club.

Many of the Negro League clubs came to town to play the American Giants and would stay for another game or two with the Palmer House club. In 1940 the All Stars played the Kansas City Monarchs and nearly pulled off an upset victory against the legendary Satchel Paige. They lost the contest 2–1, as Paige struck out eight and did not walk a batter. Roosevelt Davis pitched for the Palmer House squad and constantly got harassed by the opposing manager, Andy Cooper, who accused him of roughing up the baseball. In fact, he ended up getting tossed from the game with Kansas City ahead 2–1, so he got charged with the loss. They lost a doubleheader to the Toledo Crawfords in 1939. The first game ended with the All Stars on the losing end of a 6–2 score and then they lost the second in a 7–0 shutout. Between the two games they had a ceremony honoring Frank U. Mesiah for his twenty-five years as head of personnel and training of waiters for the hotel. All the proceeds for the game were donated to Mesiah in honor of his commitment to the hotel.[46]

When they were not playing Negro League opponents the All Stars played a wide range of opponents such as the South Bend Studebakers in 1941. The Palmer House nine won that contest 7–1 with Johnson getting the victory. They defeated the Sheboygan Chairs 15–3 with Norman Cross picking up the victory and Andy Drake leading the hitting barrage with a homer, a triple and a single. They played a four game series with the Spencer Coals in 1940 and won the first two easily. Earlier that same season they lost a doubleheader to the Mills nine 10–5 and 7–5. Cross and Alexander took the losses.[47]

JOE GREEN'S CHICAGO GIANTS

Joe Green's Chicago Giants called the Windy City home for nearly 60 years. Green played third base himself before organizing the club. The Giants were a semipro team that often operated as part of the Chicago League but also barnstormed independently for many years.

Over the years the Giants played all challengers and had all kinds of stars on their roster. In 1935, though nearing the end of his career, John Donaldson pitched for Green's Giants and could still be counted on for a good game with lots of strikeouts.

The Giants dropped a doubleheader to the Duffy Florals in 1936, losing 10–4 and 8–4. The Giants had 22 hits in the two games but gave up 28 when their pitchers could not shut down the opposing hitters. They won a two game set from the Chicago Firemen, winning 5–3 and 4–2. Oliver Turner struck out nine for Green's club in the opener. Turner continued to shine for the Giants in 1938 as he recorded five straight shutouts at one stage, with the fifth being a 4–0 victory over the white Crystal Palace Blues.[48]

THE COLUMBIA GIANTS AND UNION GIANTS

Appearing on the local baseball scene in 1938 was a reorganization of the original Columbia Giants club. This semipro club had been organized by Frank Peters, Sr. and the new ball club was reinstituted by his son Frank Peters, Jr. Former standout pitcher Walter Ball was brought in to manage the new ball club in 1938. Walter Ball made his first move by signing Malvin Hayes as the new team captain. Hayes was a catcher, formerly with Detroit and Chicago. The other officers of the club were M. Ferguson as acting secretary and Benjamin Hickman as the club president.[49]

The Chicago Union Giants got their start in 1886 under the direction of W. S. Peters. This photograph is of the team in about 1913. Included in the photograph are Dick "Cannonball" Redding and Frank Wickware. (Photograph courtesy of NoirTech Research, Inc., and Golda Meir Library, University of Wisconsin.)

Ball's new roster included an array of players who came to the Giants with lots of experience. His players could previously have been found on the rosters of such clubs as the Evanston Giants, the Memphis Red Sox, the Homestead Grays, the Chicago American Giants, the Detroit Stars, the Hartford Giants, the Dayton Marcos and the Indianapolis ABCs. Ball expected to build his team around speed and fundamentals.

The Union Giants traveled all over the Midwest playing anyone who would meet their challenge. They often found themselves playing in local tournaments as well, those like the one in Joliet, Illinois, in 1940. They beat a local farm club 7–1 with Goff getting the win.[50]

MOUNDS BLUES

Allen Johnson of Mound, Illinois, started a local baseball team to compete in the Southern Illinois championship and the semipro state tournament. Under the leadership of George Mitchell the team posted a 53–7 record in 1936 and won the Southern championship in 1936 and 1937. They were runners-up in the state tournament in 1936. They also reported an undefeated record in 1935.

The Mounds Blues played all challengers, white and black, amateur to professional. In 1937 they played the Homestead Grays and the Kansas City Monarchs. They also challenged the American Giants and even went so far as Johnson wanting to enter his club in the Negro American League in 1938. Johnson attracted such strong competition because of the quality of his players and because he invested in his team. In 1937 he installed lights to allow night games at their park.[51]

CHICAGO MONARCHS

Armand Tyson, Sr., played, coached, managed and owned a number of semipro teams in and around the Chicago area from the 1930s through the 1950s. One of his strongest and best teams was the Chicago Monarchs. He began his first team in 1925, called the Tyson Athletics, and later changed the name to the Monarchs in the 1940s.

Over the years, the Monarchs played host to a variety of local and visiting clubs as well as attracting players of all caliber of play. For example, in 1946 one of their star pitchers was former American Giants star Gread McKinnis. McKinnis helped the Monarchs defeat the Manitowoc Braves 9–2 on a three hitter. Dick "Subby" Byas, also a former American Giant caught and managed the team. Alvin Spearman helped the club win its fifth straight victory over the Detroit Motor City Giants in 1944. John Humble pitched the team to a victory over the white Saulk City Red Sox 10–5 in 1946.[52]

GILKERSON UNION GIANTS

Under manager Bob Gilkerson the Union Giants traveled all over the Midwest as a barnstorming club. In one season the papers reported their final record as 122–26 with four ties. In 1922 the club claimed a record 89–29 and two ties. They even kept track of their overall run total for the season, which came to 916 against 402 for their opponents. They played in a number of tournaments, winning one in Canada. The roster for the club was often riddled with the names of stars from other Negro League teams such as Cristobal Torriente, John Donaldson, Double Duty Radcliffe and Hurley McNair.[53]

Robert Gilkerson played second base for a number of years before hanging up his cleats and taking on the role of owner/manager. Gilkerson bought the team in 1917 from former owner W. S. Peters. Peters had formed the Chicago Union Giants with Frank C. Leland and eventually the two men had separated and each formed their own Chicago Giants club. Leland changed his club's name to the Leland Giants in 1905, and Peters kept the name Chicago Giants until 1917.

Gilkerson worked hard at bringing together teams each year with a lot of veterans to make a good showing wherever they went to play. Ed Frick worked with Gilkerson as the team's booking agent. Though they did not win all the time they developed a reputation as a solid team who would give any opponent a run for their money. This guaranteed fans would turn out to see them play, thereby ensuring that the teams involved in any competition would make some money. The team barnstormed throughout the Midwest through the 1930s. Typical of many barnstorming teams, Gilkerson's club generally treated fans to some comedic action before the game and sometimes after.

In 1923 the local papers in Wisconsin carried a number of Gilkerson games. In one contest they lost to a team from Dodgeville by a score of 3–2 at Association Park. The report claimed the game was hotly contested. They won a fifteen inning game over Rice Lake by a score of 5–4. Another game ended in a tie with the local Portage Soldiers. The game got called after eleven innings because of darkness. The Portage squad had great fan support and they were proud of holding their own against a team with the reputation of the Gilkerson club.[54]

Showing off the speed in their lineup, the Union Giants defeated the Hurley nine 11–7, with runners having a field day on the bases. They did not just play local white semipro clubs but also other African American teams, as fans saw at Park Falls. Gilkerson's club triumphed over the Illinois Giants 13–4 due to the sloppy play of the Illinois contingent.[55] One of the local clubs called the Tomahawks defeated the Union Giants 2–0 on

1940 Chicago Black Sox, a local semipro club. (Photograph courtesy of the
National Baseball Hall of Fame Library, Cooperstown, New York.)

only one hit. The crowd loved the action and the result as their local boys
beat the out-of-towners.[56]

Bazz Owen Smaulding played for the Giants from 1931–35. He had previously played for the Kansas City Monarchs from 1928–30 and then the
Chicago American Giants in 1930 and 1931. Smaulding came from New
Mexico originally, where he had developed a reputation in high school as
one of the star athletes in the state. He played football and basketball and
ran track and field, where he set many state records.[57] While in high school
he played baseball for the Albuquerque Grays. In one game he pitched
against the local field artillery team, he lost 6–4, giving up eight hits to the
opposing side.

Smaulding pitched the Giants to a 1–0 shutout victory over the Stock
Yard Cowboys in one contest, and gave up only two hits in the game and
one walk. In 1921 the Giants won two contests from the Spencer, Iowa, nine.
They won the first contest 7–3 and the second 12–4, mainly on the strength

of seven home runs in the two games. Smaulding was the winning pitcher in the second contest.[58]

In 1924 the Gilkersons found themselves playing a contest against the Big League All-Stars led by pitcher Carl Mays. The final result of the game does not appear to have been published.

During a 1930 trek through North Dakota and Manitoba, the Union Giants beat up on all their opponents quite handily. Gilkerson had six pitchers with the team because they were playing so many games in a short period of time. One of the twirlers was Cristobal Torriente, who had played for a number of major Negro League squads. They played a Hope Nine and beat them 13–6 on ten hits and two errors, which kept the Hope club in the game.[59]

3

Leading Black Ballplayers in Chicago

Over the years many players found themselves donning the uniform of the American Giants or one of the other Chicago black teams. Some of the players went on to great fame and recognition, such as Oscar Charleston, Turkey Stearnes and Cool Papa Bell, who all played in Chicago and later earned entry into the Baseball Hall of Fame. Then there were the players such as Andy Anderson, Randolph Bowe and Leroy Morney, who no one recognizes today though they also graced the diamonds of Chicago. There are too many players to talk about because of Chicago's long history with black baseball, so what follows is a selective introduction to ballplayers from the different eras.

Curt "Andy" Anderson

Curt Anderson played left field in the 1951 East-West game for the American Giants. He went 1–4 in the contest.

Alfred "Buddy" Armour

Born April 27, 1915, Jackson, MS;
died April 1974, Carbondale, IL

Buddy Armour played in four East-West games in his career, two with the American Giants in 1947. He came to Chicago in 1947 in a trade with the Cleveland Buckeyes; the Buckeyes got Clyde Nelson in the deal. Armour came to Chicago at the request of Manager Candy Jim Taylor, along with Lyman Bostock, Sr., from Birmingham. Some years there were two All Star contests held and Armour played in both in 1947. In one game Armour had two doubles, knocking in one run and scoring two as the West won 12–3. Gentry Jessup really shut the East down, retiring all nine hitters he faced.[1]

41

George Walter Ball

Though he started his baseball career in Minnesota, Walter Ball quickly left the state and found himself in Chicago during the heyday of early black baseball. He arrived in Chicago in 1903 and became a star for the Chicago Union Giants. He pitched alongside the great Rube Foster, often being overlooked because he was not an overpowering pitcher.

Ball was born on September 13, 1877, in Detroit, Michigan. He lived there until his parents, John and Ella, moved to St. Paul in 1888. His father's work as a porter and barber took him to this new city, where Walter became a standout on the local sandlots.

He first appeared in the newspapers in 1896, pitching for a club known as the Nationals. It appears from local news accounts that Ball pitched for a number of teams as they needed him. All of these early teams he played on had rosters filled with primarily white ball players except for him.

In 1898 his father moved to Montreal, Canada, but Walter stayed in Minnesota and attempted to earn his way playing baseball. He played for anyone who would pay him and then found himself starting to travel more and more in 1899. The 1899–1900 seasons found him in Grand Forks, North Dakota, where he pitched brilliantly, but the team did not ask him back in 1901. They even won the championship his first season with the club, as he won 25 games. By 1902 he moved on to St. Cloud and played the season in a semiprofessional club that had never had a black man on their team before. The curiosity his presence aroused helped boost the club's annual attendance. St. Cloud also benefited from Ball's skills as he led them to the championship in eastern Minnesota.

He received a letter in 1903 from Frank Leland inviting him to Chicago to play for the Chicago Union Giants. This would be the first all-black team Ball had ever played for but he decided to make the switch because he knew he would not be released at the end of the season due to his skin color. Ball remained in Chicago for only one season before he made the decision to move on and join the Cuban X-Giants under E. B. Lamar. After a season and a half away from Chicago, Ball returned to the Union Giants for the second half of the 1905 season. Again he left at the end of the season to sign with the Quaker Giants, but they folded due to financial troubles so Ball returned to Chicago and pitched out the remainder of 1906 with the Leland Giants.

The following year found Ball back in Minnesota with the Colored Gophers, but in 1908 Frank Leland called him and asked him to return to Chicago. Ball came back to the Giants and finished the 1908 season for them. He remained in Chicago in 1909 and led the Chicago City League with a

12–1 pitching record. In one game in early August the Giants beat the Gunthers 5–3, with Ball getting the victory. The unusual part of the game was that Ball started, moved to right field at the start of the ninth inning and then returned to the mound to get the final out.[2] At the conclusion of the regular season the Giants played a three game set against the Major League Chicago Cubs. Ball pitched in the opening game and lost 4–1, then played in the final two contests in right field. In the final game he had one of only four hits managed by the Giants against Mordecai Brown.[3]

Ball stayed with the Giants through the 1911 season, though during the off-seasons he went to Cuba to continue pitching. In one contest against the American Giants in 1911, he lost 7–6 even though he gave up only seven hits and three walks.[4] Ball was on the move again in 1912 when he signed with St. Louis. He did not return to Chicago until 1915, when Rube Foster enticed him back to join the new Chicago American Giants. He remained in Chicago until his career officially ended in 1923. He also pitched in Cuba during the winters from 1908 to 1911, winning at least nine games and hitting in the .260s.

In addition to being a fine pitcher, Ball also played the outfield when he was not on the mound. He hit for power and he could field with the best. In one game in 1906, when the Leland club was playing a group of white All-Stars, Ball saved the day with an incredible catch in the field, made even more astounding when he came down with the ball and threw out the runner at home plate. In 1908 he made a great catch to save a game for the Leland Giants.[5]

After finishing as a player Ball continued to coach. In 1938 he was asked by a group of local businessmen to manage the newly reorganized Columbia Giants. Ball used his many contacts in the game to entice players to come and join him. The club joined the Chicago Midwest League and played at American Giants Park when they were out of town. He also coached in the Chicago Sports Association. He died on December 15, 1946, in Chicago, and was buried in Lincoln Cemetery, though no marker graced his gravesite. Ball was survived by his wife, Jeanette, and their four children.[6]

Jess Barbour

Jess Barbour played all over the infield for the American Giants in the early years. A reporter for the *Chicago Defender* called him "the best all-around ball player ever seen on a diamond." He also had a reputation for having a good eye at the plate, not chasing bad balls and helping his team with the bat.[7]

Herbert "Red Cap" Barnhill

Born July 12, 1913, Hazelhurst, GA

Herbert Barnhill earned his nickname playing most of his baseball career with the Jacksonville Red Caps, who were a member of the Negro American League (NAL). In the off-season he worked for the railroad as a redcap. After the Jacksonville team left the NAL, Barnhill caught on with the Kansas City Monarchs and the Chicago American Giants as their catcher.

Barnhill caught for the Red Caps for a number of years, traveling all over the South before joining the Monarchs, where he had a chance to catch Satchel Paige as a rookie. Unfortunately for Barnhill, Paige took a dislike to him as a catcher and his career quickly ended with the Monarchs; but he caught on with the American Giants under manager Candy Jim Taylor. During a game against Memphis, Barnhill was injured on a play at the plate that basically ended his career. Neil Robinson tried to score from third on a grounder to the second baseman and when he slid into the plate his spikes caught Barnhill's wrist and split his artery. Barnhill ended up returning to Jacksonville and going back to work for the railroad.[8]

He played part of the 1943 season and the next three years in Chicago. While catching for the Giants, Barnhill worked hard on improving his hitting. He got the best help from Candy Jim Taylor, who taught him how to hit a curve ball to right field. Charley Shields would pitch to him and Taylor showed his skills as a teacher of the game by forcing Barnhill to stay in the batter's box and hit the curve. Barnhill also spent a bit of time up North and played for Indian Head in 1951.

Sherman "Bucky" Barton

From 1899 to 1901 Barton pitched for the early Chicago black baseball teams. In 1902 he moved to join the Algona Brownies before returning to Chicago in 1904. He stayed in Chicago through the 1906 season and then returned again in 1911 for his last season.

Lloyd Pepper "Rocking Chair" Bassett

In 1934, the New Orleans Crescent Stars were not drawing many fans to their games. Being a time when baseball owners acted on many unusual ideas to put people into the seats, such as playing the game on donkeys or having a woman pitch against the men, it did not seem that absurd to ask Pepper Bassett, a young catcher in his first year with the Stars, to try a new gimmick. Bassett recalled in an interview with author Donn Rogosin: "I had to figure out a way to put some people in the park. So I went to the owner, and he said I should try catching in a rocking chair." The chair had the back out so Bassett could throw to the bases while sitting down. Thus began Bassett's rise in fame, earning him the nickname "Rocking Chair."

Bassett, however, was more than a gimmick player. At six feet three inches and 220 pounds Bassett was an excellent defensive catcher with a great arm, as well as a good handler of pitchers. He developed a "squeezer" type of catcher's mitt by taking out the excess padding. At a time when the bulky catcher's mitts forced catchers to use two hands in order to catch pitches, Bassett's innovation enabled him to catch with one hand, which allowed for a quicker release, making him hard to steal against.[9]

He was also a decent hitter throughout his 21-year career, despite not living up to the power that was expected of someone of his stature. According to Buck O'Neil, a fellow Negro Leaguer, "He [Bassett] didn't learn how to hit until his later years. Then he learned how to switch-hit, and he turned out pretty good." Spending the majority of his career batting from the lower part of the order, Bassett was not a consistent hitter. In 1937 and 1938, his first two years with the Pittsburgh Crawfords, he batted .395 and .308 respectively.[10] By 1941, his average had dropped to .176 before rising again to .400 during his time with the Cincinnati Ethiopian Clowns in 1943.[11]

Despite the inconsistency in his batting, Bassett was considered a good enough all-around catcher to be one of the three players involved in a trade between the Pittsburgh Crawfords and the Washington Homestead Grays, whom Bassett joined in 1936. Bassett was traded along with outfielder Clyde "Big Splo" Spearman and $2,500 to Pittsburgh for the great slugger Josh Gibson. Gus Greenlee, the owner of the Crawfords, called Bassett's arm the greatest in baseball, believing that, along with Satchel Paige, Bassett would be a bigger drawing card than Gibson.[12]

The transition to Pittsburgh in 1937 was the beginning of Bassett's baseball connection with the city of Chicago. He did spend three years of his career, from 1939 to 1941, catching for the Chicago American Giants, but the team never finished higher than fourth in the standings. Bassett, however, is remembered in Chicago more for his participation in the East-West All-Star Game. Bassett played in eight All-Star games, representing four different teams: Pittsburgh Crawfords in 1937 at age 18, Chicago American Giants in 1939 and 1941, Birmingham Black Barons in 1947, 1948, and 1950, Memphis Red Sox in 1953.[13]

Bassett did not have much personal success in his All-Star game appearances, batting .133 (two for 15 from the plate) with one double, one walk, and one error. In playing the first four innings of the 1939 contest, Bassett was part of a bases loaded double play where Mule Suttles, right fielder for

The 1937 Eastern All Stars played at Comiskey Park and defeated the West 7–2. The group included (back row from left): Barney Morris, Pepper Bassett, Andy Porter, Mule Suttles, Bill Wright, Biz Mackey, Barney Brown, Jake Dunn, Buck Leonard and Bill Holland; (front row from left): Ray Dandridge, Fats Jenkins, Willie Wells, Ches Williams, Jerry Benjamin and Leon Day. A number of these men played part of their career in Chicago. (Photograph courtesy of NoirTech Research, Inc.)

the Newark Eagles, hit to pitcher Theolic Smith, of the St. Louis Stars, who threw to Bassett at home, forcing Bill Wright, center fielder for the Baltimore Elite Giants, at the plate, and Suttles was out at first as Bassett threw to Jelly Taylor of the Memphis Red Sox. However, in his next All-Star appearance in 1941, Bassett let one of Hilton Smith's pitches get away from him, allowing a runner from third to score in the first inning. It was scored a passed ball. In the second inning, Bassett attempted a sacrifice bunt, but the catcher for the East, Roy Campanella of Baltimore, fielded the bunt and forced Tommy Sampson of Birmingham, who was hit by a pitch at second.[14]

Bassett finished first in All-Star catcher voting twice; the first time in 1937, when he finished fourth overall with 41,463 votes, and the second time in 1939, when he finished second overall with 502,394 votes. In 1941, he finished second in catcher voting, which secured him a spot on the West team. Bassett considered his most outstanding achievement in baseball to be playing in the East-West All-Star Game. He was a fan favorite who did whatever he could to entertain, even if it meant sitting down on the job.[15]

By Ryan Bucher

John Beckwith

Hailing from Louisville, Kentucky, John Beckwith started playing baseball at age 14 with the Montgomery Gray Sox. By age 19 he had joined the roster of the Chicago Giants. He remained with the Giants for seven years before a run-in with the law forced him to move on. He played for twenty-three years in the league by the time he quit the game.

Beckwith played a variety of positions in the field but really excelled at the plate. Lots of stories abound about home runs he hit out of different stadiums. Some of those who saw him play claimed he hit the ball farther than Ruth and Gibson. He often hit over .400 in the reported stats in the local black press and even led the league in home runs on more than one occasion. He kept up this ferocious pace against big leaguers as well, hitting an estimated .317 in those exhibition contests.[16]

James Thomas "Cool Papa" Bell

Born May 17, 1903, Starkville, MS;
died March 7, 1991, St. Louis, MO

James Bell grew up in rural Mississippi and eventually got his chance to travel and see the United States when he debuted in the Negro Leagues in 1922. He got his start as a pitcher and then moved into the outfield for the St. Louis Stars. One advantage he had was being a switch-hitter.[17] His manager, Bill Gatewood, was impressed with his speed and hitting and wanted him in the regular lineup. Gatewood is the one who gave him his nickname "Cool Papa." Bell played for a variety of teams until he quit the game after the 1950 season. Included on his resume would be teams such as the Homestead Grays, the Detroit Wolves, the Kansas City Monarchs, the Memphis Red Sox and the Chicago American Giants. He also played for four years in Mexico.

Bell developed his reputation as a speedster from the beginning and the legends grew as his career lengthened. Satchel Paige added the most to his mythical speed by telling the story of turning off the light switch in a hotel room and Bell being under the covers before the light went out. Being the storyteller he was, Paige neglected to mention the switch had a short in it. Others told tales of Bell scoring from first on an infield out or stealing his way from first to home. In a 1948 exhibition game against a team of major leaguers Bell scored from first on a sacrifice bunt off Bob Feller. Third base was left uncovered and when the catcher ran up the line to cover the base Bell scampered home. He was 45 years old at the time. Regardless of the truth of these tales, Bell created havoc whenever he got on base.

Bell played in eight East-West classics during his long career, mostly for the Homestead Grays, though he did represent the American Giants in 1942 in the two contests held that year. He went 2–6 in those two games. While playing for the Giants in 1942 Bell gave the club an experienced and first-rate outfielder who also filled in at first base when needed. Although he had been playing in the league for twenty years by that point, Bell could still run and hit. In a contest against the Baltimore Grays he helped the Giants win 8–2 with a 3–3 night at the plate and four runs driven in.[18]

In recognition of his accomplishments on the diamond Bell was elected to the National Baseball Hall of Fame in 1974. He became the fifth Negro Leaguer to receive that honor at the time.

William "Fireball" Beverly

Born May 5, 1930, Houston, TX;
died September 11, 1996, Houston, TX

William Beverly had a wicked fastball that earned him a start in the 1952 East-West game for the American Giants. He pitched three innings and gave up two hits while striking out a batter and walking one.

Junius "Rainey" Bibbs

Before starting his professional baseball career Bibbs played football and baseball at Indiana State University. He received Indiana Collegiate Honorable Mention in 1934 and 1935 for his play as a fullback. Bibbs joined the Negro Leagues in 1936 and played through the 1944 season. He played for the Cincinnati Tigers and the Kansas City Monarchs and did a short stint with the American Giants. Rainey Bibbs played in 29 games for the American Giants in 1944 and hit a solid .309 as the second leading hitter on the club. He got his nickname while playing baseball because reporters could not seem to spell his real name and he just decided to call himself "Rainey" instead.

John "Geechie" Bissant

John Bissant started his baseball career in 1934 with Cole's American Giants as their second baseman. He also played all the outfield positions.

In the second half of the 1930s and 1940s Bissant played for the Chicago American Giants.[19] He came to the Negro Leagues after having played for Wiley College. Bissant starred as a halfback on their football team. In 1938 he received a varsity letter for his accomplishments. He also was named to the all-conference team for the southwest and received All-American recognition as well. In 1939 Bissant stayed at Wiley and became an assistant coach under head coach Fred Long.[20]

Hailing from New Orleans originally, Bissant made quite a name for himself in college football before deciding on a professional baseball career. When he joined the Giants he made an immediate impact at the plate and helped strengthen the defense in the outfield. In one of his first games for the Giants in 1939 Bissant was sent in by Manager Jim Taylor to pinch hit for Simms in the tenth inning of a game against the St. Louis Stars. Bissant hit a hard liner to the infield that scored Wilson Redus with the game winning run. In 1947 he hit .354 as one of the league's leading hitters. During much of his time with the Giants he served as the captain of the team.[21]

John Bissant played in the 1930s in Chicago. He played in the outfield and at second base. Bissant came to the Negro Leagues as a college graduate, having gone to school and played football for Wiley College. (Photograph courtesy of NoirTech Research, Inc.)

James "Peter" Booker

Pete Booker caught for the Leland Giants from 1907 to 1910. He also played for the Chicago American Giants in 1914 and the Chicago Giants between 1915 and 1918. He had the opportunity to catch some of the greats of the game such as Rube Foster, Frank Wickware, Smokey Joe Williams, Walter Ball and Big Bill Gatewood.

Lyman Bostock, Sr.

Born May 11, 1918, Birmingham, AL

Lyman Bostock, Sr., became better known as a ball player after the short-lived career of his son Lyman, Jr., who played in the Major Leagues with the Angels and the Twins in the 1970s before dying at the age of 27 of a gunshot wound. Bostock, Sr.'s own career began with the Brooklyn Royal Giants in 1938 after a failed tryout with the New York Black Yankees. He played there only a year before having to go back to Birmingham because his father was ill. Bostock signed on with Birmingham after Jim Taylor saw him hitting for a local pipe works team. Right after making the All-Star squad in 1941 Bostock got drafted and served four years in World War II. After the service he returned to Birmingham for a year before they sold him to the Chicago American Giants. He played two years for the Giants in 1947 and 1949. In 1948 Bostock played for the New York Cubans. Then he decided to head to Canada to play since it seemed the Negro Leagues were starting to decline and there were fewer teams to play for. He played for the Winnipeg Buffaloes starting in 1950.

During the 1946 season with Birmingham Bostock hit .270 and then was sold to Chicago for the following year. Chicago picked him up to anchor their infield with a solid player at first base. Bostock brought some experience, a solid bat and the ability to catch everything that came his way.

After the 1954 season, Bostock went to work for the post office, where he remained for twenty-eight years. He considered himself something of a carpenter as he made all kinds of furniture over the years as well as bats.

Randolph Bowe

Born Mammoth Cave, KY

A left-handed pitcher for the Chicago American Giants, Bowe found himself in the news in 1940 as part of a contract dispute. He jumped his contract with the Giants before the end of the season to join the Ethiopian Clowns. He decided to jump because of some issues over his contract and the fact that other players seemed to be doing it and no one cared. The example Bowe had was on his own team, when Billy Horne jumped his contract and then was welcomed back by H. G. Hall without any penalty at all.[22]

Bowe pitched for the Giants in 1939 as well but got hurt and did not finish out the season. Before he got hurt he pitched a one-hitter against St. Louis. He gave up the lone hit in the second inning and the rest of the game was pretty much unhittable as he struck out 13 batters to mark his highest total in a single game. His previous high had been 11. He beat the Kansas City Monarchs in July in a 4–2 victory where he struck out nine batters and walked four. He came back strong in 1940 and pitched well for the Giants until he decided to jump. In a game against the Brooklyn Royal Giants he struck out six while giving up only six hits on the way to a 4–3 victory. Leroy Morney provided all the hitting Chicago needed with three hits and three runs knocked in.[23]

Chester Arthur "Chet" Brewer

Born January 14, 1907, Leavenworth, KS;
died March 26, 1990, Whittier, CA

Chet Brewer had a long and illustrious Negro League career. He traveled all over to pitch and is considered one of the top pitchers in the Negro Leagues by most researchers. He had an array of pitches that kept the hitters guessing, including an emery ball that he used in one game to strike out 19 Homestead batters, although he lost the game 1–0. He spent much of his early career with the Kansas City Monarchs, taking over the primary pitching duties as Bullet Rogan's career wound down.

Brewer grew up in Kansas and started his baseball career in 1924 with the Gilkerson Union Giants. He spent fifteen seasons with the Monarchs, five years with the Cleveland Buckeyes, and one year stints with the Washington Pilots, the New York Cubans and the Chicago American Giants.

Brewer pitched in the United States, all over Latin America, Canada and even in Asia. Wherever he went he won, which made him in high demand. He also had a lot of experience on integrated clubs in Jamestown and Bismarck, North Dakota. In 1946, while pitching for the American Giants, Brewer helped his club salvage one game of a doubleheader against the Cleveland Buckeyes. After losing the first game Brewer pitched the club to an 8–3 victory. John Bissant and Ralph Wyatt provided all the hitting he needed.

For all his years and all his apparent success Brewer only played in two East-West games at Comiskey Park, not because he did not have the skills but because he spent so much time playing outside the Negro Leagues. After he retired Brewer worked as a scout for the Pittsburgh Pirates from 1957 to 1974. Enos Cabell, Bob Watson and Ellis Valentine are just a few of the players he scouted. Brewer married Margaret Davis in 1924 and they had two children, Chester and Marian. The city of Los Angeles named one of their diamonds in his honor in 1978 as a way of recognizing his skills, his teaching and his commitment to young people.[24]

David "Dave" "Lefty" Brown
Born 1896, San Marcos, TX; died Denver, CO

A fine left-handed pitcher, Dave Brown twirled for the Chicago American Giants from 1918 to 1922. In addition to his excellent pitching Brown seemed to have a colorful life. He got involved in a robbery in 1918 and Rube Foster had to bail him out of that trouble. His later troubles got worse and eventually forced him to pick up an alias in the late twenties. Some suspect he may have been involved in a murder in 1925, but his role was never proven. At any rate, he dropped out of the game and reappeared later as Lefty Wilson.[25] It appears that Brown returned to the game with the Gilkerson Union Giants in the latter half of the 1920s.

Lefty Brown had a colorful career but none can deny his prowess on the mound. He had a wicked fastball, an even tougher curve ball and control that never seemed to desert him. It was not unusual to read in the box scores where he struck out 12–14 batters and did not walk a soul. He beat Cannonball Redding in 1924 with the Lincoln Giants to secure the New York City bragging rights among black teams. He also pitched a number of winters in Cuba, often for the Santa Clara club. During the winter of 1923–24 he posted a 7–3 record for Santa Clara.

Brown started his baseball career in 1917 with the Dallas Black Giants. He joined Rube Foster's Giants in 1918 and became a mainstay on the staff. He helped them win the first three NNL pennants from 1920–22. He left to try his luck with the Lincoln Giants in 1923 and 1924, and then went west to pitch in California.

After getting into some serious trouble Brown left behind the professional leagues and traveled throughout the Midwest playing for a variety of semipro clubs. According to some news accounts he even faced John Donaldson on more than one occasion, giving the fans a real thrill. He may have rejoined the Gilkerson Union Giants in 1926 and then pitched in places such as Bertha, Minnesota, and Sioux City, Iowa.

In 1945 a Dr. Claude Carmichael was asked to name his All-time Negro League Team. One of the three pitchers he included was Lefty Brown.

James "Jim" Brown

Died January 21, 1943, San Antonio, TX

James Brown started his baseball career catching for the San Marcos Giants. In 1919 he left Texas to join up with Foster's American Giants. He often caught their star lefty, David Brown. He later played and managed

Pitcher James Brown started with the Newark Eagles and then got drafted in World War II. He joined the Great Lakes Blue Jackets club in 1944. (Photograph courtesy of NoirTech Research, Inc., and Jerry Malloy.)

for the Palmer House All Stars. He also played in 1934 for the House of David club, hitting .356 for the season. He rejoined the Giants in 1935 as the backup catcher to Larry Brown. Larry Brown thought he would be a great addition because he was such a good judge of players. His last season was 1942, when he caught and managed for the St. Paul Gophers and then ended the year with the Lincoln Giants. He became ill immediately following the close of the 1942 season and died in January 1943.[26]

Larry "Ironman" Brown

Born September 16, 1901, Birmingham, AL; died April 7, 1972, Memphis, TN

Larry Brown played a long career for a variety of Negro League clubs. He earned his nickname for catching 234 games in 1930. Brown played in six East-West classics, starting with the inaugural game in 1933, and enjoyed a thirty year career in professional baseball. His career began in 1919 when he got the chance to join the roster of the Birmingham Black Barons as a seventeen-year-old kid.

Larry Brown caught for thirty years and played in seven East-West games. He never hit for power or even a high average, but that did not matter in the face of his defensive skills and his strong throwing arm. (Photograph courtesy of NoirTech Research, Inc.)

Brown grew up in Alabama, where he lived with his older sister and his mother. He played baseball for his high school team until 1918. In 1919 he got a job with the Tennessee Coal and Iron Company and played on their industrial team. He also occasionally caught an extra game or two for the Birmingham Black Sox just to make an extra buck.

Though he was not much of a hitter, that did not matter, because behind the plate Larry Brown had virtually no equal. He could throw out almost any runner, he never let anything get by him, and pitchers loved the way he called a game. In 1920 he joined the Knoxville Giants after working for a time for the railroads. The Memphis Red Sox gave him his

Larry "Ironman" Brown catching in Tampico in 1941. Brown caught for the American Giants in the 1930s. (Photograph courtesy of the National Baseball Hall of Fame Library, Cooperstown, New York.)

start in professional baseball and he played with them on and off throughout his career. He ended his Negro League career as a player/manager with
the Red Sox in 1948. In addition, Brown played for the Indianapolis ABCs
and the Detroit Stars and in the Havana Winter League from 1926 to 1931.[27]

Brown won his first championship playing for the Chicago American
Giants in 1927. During the World Series against the Bacharach Giants, Brown
showed off his arm by throwing out four of eight base stealers. This was
revenge for the 1926 series when there were 19 stolen bases.

During his long career Brown had the chance to work with some of
the greatest pitchers in the game. He called balls and strikes for the likes of
Satchel Paige, Willie Foster, and Double Duty Radcliffe. He threw out base
stealing phenoms such as Cool Papa Bell and got run over at home plate by
such legends as Oscar Charleston and Josh Gibson. His name is mentioned
with the best of the Negro League backstops, Josh Gibson, Biz Mackey and
Frank Duncan. In fact, for the first East-West Classic he led all catchers in
voting, including the phenomenal Frank Duncan. If Brown could have hit
to match his defensive skills more people would know his name today.

In 1935 Brown took on the job of managing Cole's American Giants.
His big task that year was trying to piece together a pitching staff that would
make it through the season. Robert Cole hired Brown because he knew
pitchers, and Willie Foster, the ace of the staff, had developed a sore arm;
therefore, the Giants needed some new blood.[28] Brown hit .308 in his six
All-Star appearances. He is also credited with a .259 lifetime batting average during his thirty-one-year career that saw him playing all over the Negro
Leagues. After retiring from baseball Brown worked as a waiter in Memphis for 23 years. He was married and had one son.[29]

Harry Buckner

Harry Buckner played his early years in Chicago for the Unions, the
Columbia Giants and the Union Giants. While he often pitched, Buckner
could also play shortstop and the outfield. He had decent speed and a pretty
good arm making him a versatile player. He could help himself at the plate
as well with good contact and a little bit of power.

Richard Thomas "Subby" Byas

Born March 19, 1910, Pineland, TX;
died October 2, 1985, Chicago, IL

Subby Byas earned his nickname as a backup catcher although he was a
strong hitter and played in two East-West classics in 1936–37. He represented

the American Giants in the contests. Byas later caught and managed for one of Chicago's strongest and fastest black semipro teams called the Chicago Monarchs.

Growing up, Byas played both basketball and baseball at Wendell Phillips High School and made the all-city team in both sports. He learned to play all infield positions on the baseball team but liked catching best. He also was a switch-hitter but preferred batting lefty.[30]

Byas began his career with Chicago and then was traded to the Newark Eagles. He returned to Chicago in 1933 to play for the Gilkerson Union Giants and then the American Giants in 1935. He played with the Giants through the 1941 season before ending his Negro League career playing with the Memphis Red Sox. He joined the military in 1943 and took on the task of managing an engineer aviation battalion team in New Guinea.[31]

Marlin Carter

Born December 27, 1912, Haslam, TX;
died December 20, 1993, Memphis, TN

Marlin Carter played the infield for Memphis, Cincinnati and Chicago. He got his start in Texas but later moved on to join the better known Negro League clubs. He played for a couple of years for the Mineola Black Spiders under manager Reuben Jones and then served in the Coast Guard during World War II. His career in baseball lasted through the 1950 season.

Clarence "Pops" Coleman

Born 1877, Louisville, KY

Pops Coleman played before the Negro Leagues ever got off the ground. After giving pitching a try, Coleman ended up behind the plate, where he caught for a variety of teams for nearly fifty years. One of the teams Coleman caught for was the Gilkerson Union Giants, where he had a chance to pass on his knowledge to a young catcher named Double Duty Radcliffe. Coleman also spent time with the All-Nations, catching John Donaldson, and with the ABCs catching Dick Redding.

Coleman spent over a decade with the Union Giants. For a time he also served as their manager. As a catcher he understood all the nuances of the game and he made an excellent field general.

William McKinley "Sug" "Willie" Cornelius

Born September 3, 1906, Atlanta, GA;
died October 30, 1989, Chicago, IL

Willie Cornelius had a long and distinguished pitching career with the Chicago American Giants during the 1930s and 1940s. As a young player, Cornelius gave a lot of teams trouble who had not seen him pitch before. In a 1935 series with the Pittsburgh Crawfords the Giants could not seem to have any luck winning except when Cornelius pitched a 7–4 victory to begin a long series. In a 1936 game against the Mills of Chicago Cornelius lost to Jim Vaughn, former Chicago Cub sensation, 2–1. Cornelius matched him pitch for pitch through the first eight innings and even hit a homer to tie the score at 1–1. He later tried to stretch a triple into an inside the park home run and got called out at home plate. Cornelius protested the call and got thrown out of the game. Ted Trent came in to work the last inning and actually picked up the loss rather than Cornelius.[32]

Cornelius enjoyed one of his best seasons when he won 22 games for the Giants in 1937, securing the twenty-second win over the Memphis Red Sox 4–2 in early September. He received the honor of representing the Giants in three East-West games in 1935, 1936 and 1938. He actually got the call to start the 1938 contest with Frank Duncan catching for him. He pitched in eleven innings and unfortunately got hit quite hard as he gave up five earned runs. Cornelius pitched a superb game in 1939 against the Sheboygan Chairmakers, defeating them 8–5. He struck out eleven, getting the crucial outs when he needed them. He got all the hitting he needed from Smith, Sparks and Young, who each had two hits in the contest. In 1940 Cornelius jumped to Mexico with teammate Pepper Bassett and did not return to the Giants lineup until 1941. In 1942 he started the season off with a bang when he helped the Giants take a doubleheader from the Red Sox. Cornelius won the first game 2–1 with John Bissant driving in the winning run.[33]

After returning from serving in the army during World War II he helped his own cause in winning an 8–4 contest over the Cincinnati Clowns. He hit a two-run homer in addition to allowing only eight hits. This made up for his first game back that season when he lost 8–0 to the Memphis Red Sox. They jumped all over him in the early innings and he had to give way to Ollie West and Gentry Jessup to finish the game for him. In September, Cornelius helped the Giants vault past the Monarchs into second place in the NAL. The Giants beat Kansas City in both halves of a doubleheader with McKinnis throwing a one-hitter in the first game. In the second, the score was tied 1–1 when Cornelius was used as a pinch hitter for Walter McCoy. He singled home Ralph Wyatt with the winning run.[34]

Cornelius pitched a number of games against nonleague opponents when the Giants barnstormed across the country. In one of these games he got knocked out of the contest by the Madison Blues in the seventh inning with the score 6–4. Ted Trent came on to finish the contest and pick up the victory 10–7 as Joe Sparks hit a grand slam home run in the ninth to seal the win.[35]

Samuel "Sam" "Cuban Tamer" Crawford

Sam Crawford had a long and successful career in the Negro Leagues, playing mainly for Chicago ball clubs. He pitched and played the outfield and second base, as well as managing and coaching. He relied on a fastball and knuckle ball to get batters out. In 1912 he actually pitched two no-hitters on the same day.[36] In addition to his days with Chicago, Crawford pitched for the Monarchs and Black Barons. He was with the Monarchs when they won in 1925.

Crawford is remembered by some for getting in a fight with Cristobal Torriente during and after one game. Crawford hit Torriente in the jaw with a pitch and when Torriente got called out stealing the players erupted onto the field. After the police quieted things down Crawford and Torriente continued their jawing out on the street. It quickly escalated into a more violent encounter as they began throwing paving stones left by city workers at one another. Rube Foster finally broke it up before either player got seriously hurt.

Crawford became a news vendor after his playing career ended. He earned some notoriety in 1955 when he shot and killed Pete William DeGraw. Crawford told the police that DeGraw came at him in a threatening fashion as he opened his newsstand one morning and he shot him. He also fired warning shots at DeGraw's companion, who had a knife at the time. An inquest was held into the incident but nothing further was reported in the papers about what happened to Crawford.[37]

Norman Cross

Norman Cross pitched for the American Giants and the Palmer House All Stars. In 1939 he helped the Palmer House nine win the Illinois State Semipro championship. In the 16 game tournament, Cross won four games, including the final game. He beat the E. N. Woodruff nine from Peoria 15–5. He gave up only six hits to the opposing hitters as Andy Drake called a great game for him.[38]

John W. "Jimmie" Crutchfield

Born 1910, Moberly, MO;
died March 31, 1993, Chicago, IL

In the August 17, 1935, issue of the *Pittsburgh Courier*, in an article talking about that year's East-West All Star game that had been played six days earlier in Chicago, readers came across the following: "Next in the parade of stars came young Crutchfield, fleet-footed outfielder of the Pittsburgh Crawfords, who made a sensational bare-handed running catch of Biz Mackey's mighty smash into center field. Sox park fans say it was a greater catch than any big league outfielder ever made in the Comiskey ball orchard."

Jimmie Crutchfield covered the outfield with his incredible speed; although many people said he'd never make it because of his size he proved them all wrong and played in the Negro Leagues for 16 years. (Photograph courtesy of NoirTech Research, Inc. and bucket number six.)

The "young" Crutchfield spoken of in the article was John W. "Jimmie" Crutchfield, a diminutive spark plug of a player who hailed from Moberly, Missouri. Only twenty-five years old at the time, Crutchfield, who was in his sixth season as a professional ball player, was the starting centerfielder for the 1935 Pittsburgh Crawfords, a team considered by many historians to be one of the greatest in black baseball history.

The road to fame had not been an easy one for Crutchfield, however. Due to his size, standing only five foot seven inches tall and weighing one hundred and fifty pounds, Crutchfield was ridiculed for his baseball aspirations.[39]

According to Crutchfield, "When I left my home in Moberly, Missouri, for the Birmingham Black Barons, everyone basically laughed at me and said I didn't have a chance in the world to make it. I weighed about 140 pounds, so they said things like, 'Hey Crutch, see you next week,' and 'Hey Crutch, you did buy your bus fare back, didn't you?'"

His critics were wrong, however, and Crutchfield proved as much on Opening Day 1930 when he garnered three hits, including a home run, and drove in three runs. Although he was not so successful in the rest of the games that season, such as the next day when he struck out five times, Crutchfield filled the role of starting centerfielder for the rest of the season, hitting a respectable .286.[40]

The first half of the 1931 baseball season found the Missouri native playing for the Indianapolis ABCs before jumping to the Crawfords. The Crawfords were at that time a semipro team that was beginning the transformation to a professional ball club. Crutchfield stayed there through 1936.

By 1932, the Crawfords under owner Gus Greenlee, the numbers king of black Pittsburgh, was attracting some of the finest talent the Negro Leagues had to offer. In addition to Crutchfield, the team included future Hall of Famers Josh Gibson, Oscar Charleston, Satchel Paige, Cool Papa Bell and Judy Johnson. The caliber of the team continued to grow until it peaked with the legendary 1935 club that hosted an outfield so fast "that raindrops could not fall between them." The outfield consisted of Bell, Sammy Bankhead and Crutchfield, who had appeared in the 1934 East-West game and would play in the next two for the Crawfords.

In 1937, Crutchfield would leave the Crawfords to play for Effa Manley's Newark Eagles. The Crawfords were losing players left and right to other clubs for bigger paychecks. Crutchfield stayed with the Eagles through the completion of the 1938 season. He hit .289 and .337 while in a Newark uniform. While with the Eagles, Crutchfield played with such luminaries as Hall of Famers Monte Irvin, Leon Day and Ray Dandridge.[41]

Crutchfield rejoined the Crawfords in 1939, although the club now called Toledo home, since the team's home park in Pittsburgh had been razed the year before. For reasons given only as "personal," he did not play in 1940, but returned in 1941, playing for the Chicago American Giants and making his fourth East-West appearance. The legendary American Giants team became Crutchfield's home through the start of the 1943 season. He entered the military and then came back in 1944 to play for both the Giants and the Cleveland Buckeyes. His final season was 1945 and he spent it with the American Giants in the Windy City. The Giants wanted him to come back for the 1946 season but according to Crutchfield, "I was tired of the traveling life. I knew that as much as I loved baseball, it was time to leave." After leaving baseball, Crutchfield remained in Chicago and went to work for the U. S. Postal Service, where he worked until he retired in 1971. In 1947, at the age of 36, Crutchfield married Julia R. Day, a Chicago school teacher.[42]

When interest in the Negro Leagues began to develop after Robert

Peterson wrote *Only the Ball was White*, Crutchfield found himself in the spotlight again. Named a Kentucky Colonel by the Governor of Kentucky, Crutchfield used the honorary title for the rest of his life. A favorite at reunions and card shows, Crutchfield became beloved around the country. In 1992, along with a number of other former players, Crutchfield was a guest of President Bush at the White House.

Crutchfield died in his south-side Chicago home on March 31, 1993, at the age of 83. According to media reports, they buried him with peanuts and popcorn and a baseball in his hands.

Perhaps the life of Jimmie Crutchfield can best be summed up by quoting from a list of his achievements that was passed out at his funeral. "His sacrifices on the field, in the army, and off-season as a bellhop and shoeshine boy paved the way for Jackie Robinson to integrate baseball and other Afro American athletes to realize their dreams" (Funeral Program). The most fitting tribute would have to be what he considered his greatest accomplishment. It was, according to the funeral program, that he never hated anyone.

By Sammy Miller

Reuben "Rube" Currie

Though hailing from Kansas City, Currie got his baseball start in 1919 with the Chicago Unions. He did return to Kansas City the following year before moving east and signing on with Hilldale. One of the highlights of Currie's career came in 1926, when he pitched a no-hitter for the World Champion Chicago American Giants. Later Currie joined with former teammates such as Bingo DeMoss to help form the Old Ball Players Association to help out former athletes in need, not just baseball players.

Lloyd "Ducky" Davenport

Born October 28, 1911, New Orleans, LA;
died 1988, New Orleans, LA

Lloyd Davenport had a long and varied Negro League career that began in 1935. He started playing with the Monroe Monarchs in the Southern League before moving up to join the Philadelphia Stars in 1935. He quickly established himself as one of the best outfielders of his time, making the first of five appearances in the East-West Classic in 1937. In 1943 he joined five of his Chicago teammates on the west squad.

Though only five feet five inches tall, Davenport could hit for power.

He had a great arm and a lot of speed in the outfield. He became a real favorite of longtime player and manager Double Duty Radcliffe. Radcliffe liked having him in his outfield and he often took Davenport along when he moved on to a new team. For example, Radcliffe managed Davenport during his time with the Chicago American Giants. Later, Davenport spent one season managing the Giants. He only lasted for the 1944 season because it was reported that he did not have a lot of patience with his players or the umpires.

Davenport loved to come through in the clutch and could be counted on to get on base when his team needed runners. Take, for example, a 1943 American Giants game before 10,000 fans at the Great Lakes Naval Training Center. Davenport went 3–4 and scored one run in his club's 7–3 victory. They were ahead by only one run when Davenport doubled and scored on an error on his hit.[43]

Davenport spent some of his winters south of the border. He played for Almendares in the Cuban League and helped them win the pennant under the direction of Adolph Luque. He jumped to Mexico in 1946 and got suspended for leaving during the season. Dr. Martin reinstated him for the 1949 season, as he rejoined the Giants after having been with the Louisville Buckeyes in 1944. He jumped again right before the World Series, to go to Venezuela to play.[44]

Johnny Davis

Johnny Davis pitched for a number of clubs during his long career, and spent a number of seasons with Chicago clubs. In 1903 he pitched for the Union Giants and in 1905 and 1906 for the new Leland Giants. After leaving Chicago he spent most of his career in St. Paul, pitching and managing a variety of local ball clubs.

Saul Davis

For much of the 1920s Saul Davis played for the Chicago American Giants. He played almost every infield position because he had speed and a strong arm. He was a part of the championship Giants club in 1926.

Davis played a solid shortstop but struggled at the plate for his entire career. He never hit for a high average and had no real power to speak of. Essentially, Davis was a slap hitter who liked to try to use his speed to disrupt the opposition.

His career began with the Birmingham Black Barons, but where he really wanted to play was Chicago. Davis wanted to play for the great Rube

Foster and he got that chance starting in 1925. He also spent time with the Gilkerson Union Giants, a traveling club that called Chicago home.

Davis's final stint in baseball involved his serving as the player/manager for the Zulu Cannibal Giants. The team traveled all over, entertaining fans with their attire as much as with their play. Jesse Owens often traveled with the ball club for an added attraction.

Walter C. "Steel Arm" Davis

Born 1902, Madison, WI; died 1935, Chicago, IL

Walter Davis earned his nickname not because of his size but because he often pitched both ends of a doubleheader early in his career. This did take its toll and later he had to move to the outfield and eventually to first base since he could not throw. Teams never took him out of the lineup however, because he could always hit and hit for power.

During the 1920s Davis played for both the Detroit Stars and the Chicago American Giants (1927–31). He often batted clean-up and would hit in the mid .300s. In 1933 Davis got elected to the first East-West All Star classic and had two hits. In 1934 he moved on to an integrated club in North Dakota. He joined Double Duty Radcliffe and Barney Brown on the Red Sox roster. The club dominated the semipro scene and also played the major Negro League clubs such as the Monarchs and the American Giants. That season Davis reported hitting .324 with 18 home runs.

In late 1934 Davis joined with some of the other semipro ball players to play a series with a group of Major Leaguers including Jimmie Foxx and Heinie Manush. They won the first two contests and Davis hit two homers and a double. Double Duty won game three for them with Davis adding one more hit to his total.

Davis moved on in 1935 to join the Brooklyn Eagles who had just signed pitcher Leon Day. In 1941 Davis could be found on the roster of the semipro Palmer House All Stars along with other famous Negro Leaguers such as Alec Radcliffe. Davis's career came to an abrupt and early end when he got into a bar fight and was shot and killed by Eugene "Red" Merrill.[45]

Elwood "Bingo" DeMoss

Elwood "Bingo" DeMoss was born in Topeka, Kansas, on September 5, 1889. Little is known about his childhood, though it is believed that DeMoss lived with his widowed mother, Eley, in 1910. He began his career in 1905 as a shortstop with the Topeka Giants, and was blessed with extraordinary speed to cover expansive portions of the infield. However, an arm injury suffered during a brief pitching outing forced his move to second base. Despite the injury and position change, DeMoss is viewed as the best second baseman in black baseball prior to the creation of the Negro League in 1920.

DeMoss made several appearances with strong independent teams, including the Indianapolis ABCs in 1915–16, owned by Tom Bowser and managed by the legendary C. I. Taylor. With the ABCs, fellow players gave DeMoss the name "Bingo," because it was said that wherever he wanted to hit the ball, bingo, it would go there. DeMoss was an excellent bunter, a master of the hit-and-run, and rarely a strikeout victim. In recognizing DeMoss's exceptional bunting skills, Kansas City Monarchs catcher Frank Duncan nodded, "I've never seen a man bunt a ball like DeMoss. Looked like when you play pool and draw a ball back. How he did it, I don't know, but he sure did it."[46] After losing to Rube Foster's American Giants in the 1915 playoffs, the ABCs exacted revenge by taking the 1916 series from the Giants five games to four. In 1917, DeMoss joined Foster's Giants, who exhibited a more up-tempo, aggressive, and audacious style of play that better suited his offensive skills. The entertainment value of this young player was also a great fit with the ostentatious Giants, with DeMoss always seen playing with a toothpick in his mouth. DeMoss replaced Pete Hill, an outstanding hitter and outfielder, as captain of the team for the six years following World War I.[47]

The Giants won the Negro National League pennant from 1920 to 1922 before surrendering the title to the Kansas City Monarchs in 1923. During the 1923–24 seasons, the newly formed Eastern Colored League raided the National League, immediately weakening some of the original teams. The 1925 season started unusually, as DeMoss would "save the season." DeMoss played a large hand in saving Negro League father and architect Rube Foster from asphyxiation due to a gas leak in his Indianapolis rooming house. The Chicago players grew concerned when they failed to see their manager that morning. DeMoss later led a group of players to check on Foster, only to find him unconscious against the bathtub gas heater. Foster was rushed by ambulance to Batiste Hospital, where he recovered.[48] Ironically, Foster, who also served as the league commissioner, sent DeMoss and George Dixon to the Indianapolis ABCs after the 1925 season, attempting to add a competitive balance in the league. Dave Malarcher, the Chicago American Giants manager, said that DeMoss "had the courage, confidence, and ability written all over his face and posture. He was the smartest, the coolest, the most errorless ball player I've ever seen."

DeMoss retired after the 1930 season, but returned to manage the Chicago American Giants in 1936. Seen by many as a smart baseball man

with a fanatical knowledge of inside baseball and young talent development, De Moss faced the terrific task of successfully assembling a young
Giants team that had been recently chosen by DeMoss's assistants, Jim
Brown and "Dizzy" Dizmukes.[49] DeMoss would resurface again in 1942 as
manager of the semipro Chicago Brown Bombers, capitalizing upon the
moniker of famed boxer Joe Louis. The short-lived team folded after one
year, forcing DeMoss back into retirement. In 1945 Branch Rickey started
the experimental United States Baseball League to develop black baseball
players for possible integration into the major leagues. One of the six teams
formed was the Chicago Brown Bombers, with DeMoss named as manager.
DeMoss won 57 percent of his games as manager, as his new team with the
old name played their home games at Wrigley Field when the Chicago Cubs
were on a road trip. After 1946, DeMoss left the baseball scene and lived a
quiet, ordinary life in Chicago until his death on January 26, 1965, survived
by his wife Maranda and two daughters, Mrs. Bessie Dearborn and Mrs.
Norma Jean Jackson. He did work with the Old Tymers Baseball group,
even serving for a while as their treasurer. Despite being a superb manager
and incomparable ball player, DeMoss's contribution to baseball history is
relatively unknown. Quite possibly, bias kept him out of major league baseball, where complete records are kept, and the fact that his career was at an
end long before many fans were born. Yet there will forever be unequaled
legends tagged to the memory of DeMoss that modern players may never
touch.[50]

                              By Michael Harkness-Roberto

Lou Dials

In the early 1920s, the Chicago American Giants, led by pitcher/man-
ager Rube Foster, were dominating the newly formed Negro National
League, winning the league pennant in each of its first three years, 1920 to
1922. From 1923 to 1925, however, the Kansas City Monarchs had become
the dominant team. Around this same time, Lou Dials began playing ball
for a semipro team, the Pasadena Monarchs, in the California Winter
League. Dials was an intelligent young man who was currently taking elec-
trical engineering classes at the University of California at Berkeley. He
would finish the program, receiving his bachelor's degree in 1927.[51]

It was while he was playing with the Monarchs that Dials' skills were

Opposite: Alonzo Odom "Lou" Dials played many years in the Negro Leagues,
including 1936 with the Chicago American Giants. (Photograph courtesy of the
National Baseball Hall of Fame Library, Cooperstown, New York.)

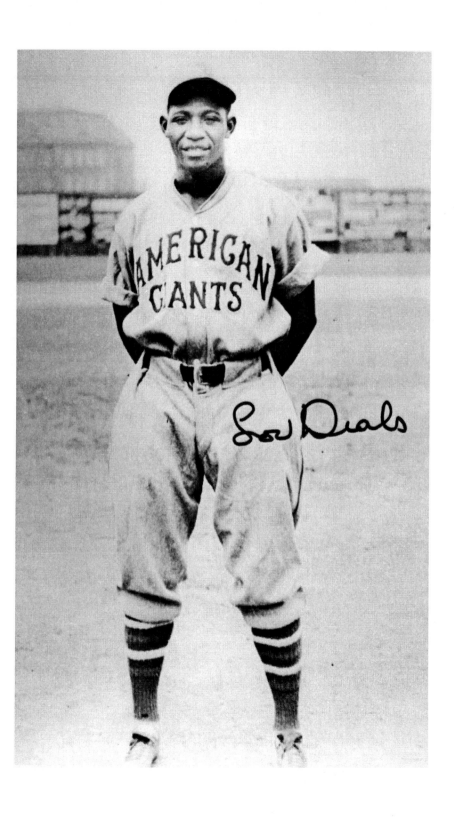

noticed by pro ball clubs. Because Dials was seen as a player who could help revamp his team and push the American Giants past the Monarchs, he received a letter from Chicago inviting him to join the team in 1925. At the time, rumors had been circulating about how pro ballplayers were being mistreated. Dials described one of these stories, which was about Rube Foster: "Rube once whipped Jim Brown (who had a reputation for scuffling during games). Rube told Jim to do something and Jim said he wouldn't do anything that old man told him to do. So, Rube took Jim into the clubhouse and everybody stayed out and Rube beat the devil out of Jim Brown. After that, Jim was a good boy." Most of these stories were not true, but they were enough to set his father against Dials going to play pro ball.

Despite his father's warnings, Dials left for Chicago, where, upon arrival, he first met Foster, whom Dials claimed "was a very big influence on my career." Dials, who played for the American Giants from 1925 to 1928 and 1936 to 1937, described this time as the most exciting period of his career. Because Foster wanted to fashion his team after the white teams, he spared no expense on traveling arrangements. Most of the time, the team traveled out west for games by train. Foster would rent a Pullman, and as Dials described it, "We'd travel in style." In addition to the traveling arrangements, each player was given a food allowance during trips. In his first year with Chicago, Dials received expense money of $2.50 in addition to his $250-a-month salary.[52]

Dials played for many teams throughout his twenty-six-year career (1925–1950), such as the Memphis Red Sox, Homestead Grays, and New York Black Yankees. In 1931 and 1933, he won the batting title, hitting .382 for the Detroit Stars and .370 for the Cleveland Giants. However, he will best be remembered for his days playing outfield and first base in Chicago.[53]

Dials was a member of the championship teams of 1926 and 1927. In 1926, Chicago pulled out two thrilling come-from-behind series wins. In the play-offs, the American Giants were down four games to one against the Kansas City Monarchs in a nine-game series. They won the next four games to win the series five games to four, placing them against the Atlantic City Bacharach Giants of the Eastern Colored League in the Negro League World Series.[54]

In a first to five wins series, Chicago came back from a 4–2 game deficit to win the World Series. In 1927, Chicago beat Bacharach five games to three; however, the team did have a lead of four games to none that almost got away from them. In that season, Dials batted .401 but did not win the batting title, finishing second behind teammate Walter Davis, who batted .409.[55]

In addition to helping Chicago win two championships, Dials was a part of the 1936 East-West All-Star Game at Comiskey Park. As the right fielder for the West squad representing the Chicago American Giants, Dials had no hits in two at bats and committed one error as the East won the game 10 to 2. In the game, Dials went up against Satchel Paige, who struck Dials out with his hesitation pitch. Dials said, "Satch pointed at me and told me, 'I told you I was going to get you.'"[56]

Foster, along with Bingo DeMoss, who was Dials' manager with Detroit, Cleveland, and Chicago, is one of the men who Dials credits for helping to shape his baseball career. This was a career that started with the Wentworth Club[57] in Chicago and almost led to Dials being the first black player to sign with a white professional team, the Los Angeles Angels of the Pacific Coast League, in 1943; but the Angels' owner, Phillip K. Wrigley, would not allow Dials to be on his team. Over fifty years after his career began Dials still remembered the first time he went up to bat at practice. Foster told him to bunt: "I did and he said, 'Good, I see you've been trained well.'"[58] Foster added greatly to Dials' training, giving him the control and fundamentals to have a long, successful career, not only as a player, but as a scout for several major league teams.

By Ryan Bucher

John Wesley "Iowa Wonder" Donaldson

Born February 20, 1890, Glasgow, MO; died April 14, 1970

While John Donaldson is probably best known for his twirling with the All-Nations club and the Kansas City Monarchs, he also spent some time with Foster's American Giants. Donaldson's exploits on the mound have become legendary, based on newspaper accounts like the one in the *Chicago Defender* in 1916. Donaldson was pitching for the All-Nations against Frank Wickware and the Chicago American Giants. The reporter expected a big crowd to see these two star twirlers battle it out. He said in one series of twelve games Donaldson had struck out 240 batters. In another stretch he struck out 110 in 110 innings. In an eighteen inning game Donaldson whiffed 35 batters and then set 27 men back to the bench in a twelve inning game. The stuff of legends.[59]

Donaldson started pitching in his hometown when he was only 13. In one contest against the local semipros he gave up three hits while striking out 18 men. It was from here that J. L. Wilkinson brought him to the All-Nations club to play first base and pitch. Donaldson's career lasted from 1911 to 1938 and he played for sixteen different ball clubs, including the Gilkerson Union Giants and the Chicago Giants.

Donaldson knew how to mix up his pitches and keep hitters guessing when he took the mound. Invariably, the newspaper accounts talk about his strikeouts as the highlight of the game. In a 4–0 shutout over a team from Brandeis, Donaldson struck out 19 batters in nine innings and gave up only five hits. In August 1912 he pitched a 13 inning game in Sioux Falls and struck out 23, winning 2–0. In 1913 he struck out 27 in a 12 inning game in Marshall, Minnesota. One of the other highlights of his career came in 1913 when he pitched three consecutive no-hitters.[60]

Later in his career, Donaldson pitched for a number of Minnesota ball clubs and often pitched against his former Negro League teammates. In 1926 he pitched for the Lismore Gophers against Lefty Brown and the Gilkerson Union Giants, losing the contest 6–1. In 1928 he pitched against the House of David and won 11–10 and then lost again to the Gilkerson nine 3–1.

Charles "Pat" Dougherty

Born 1879, Summer Shade, KY; died July 12, 1939, Chicago, IL

Pat Dougherty pitched for a number of Chicago clubs during his baseball career. From 1909–1911 Dougherty twirled for the Leland Giants and then from 1914 to 1917 he pitched for the American Giants as one of the mainstays of their staff. Often he was the only lefty on the roster which made him a rare and needed commodity on the staff.

In 1911, after a 6–1 victory over the Chicago Giants, Dougherty got called "the Black Marquard" in the papers, Marquard having pitched for the Cubs and set a record of 19 consecutive victories which Walter Ball broke with 23. In an earlier contest with the Cubs, Dougherty lost to Mordecai Brown 1–0, though he only gave up three hits. Brown actually gave up four but came away with the victory.[61] Dougherty became ill and died at his home in 1939. His wife and stepson, Melvin McNally, handled all the details for his funeral.

Jesse Warren Douglas

Born March 27, 1916, Longview, TX

In 1945 Jesse Douglas was named to the All-American team at second base. This was based on his .303 average at the plate and solid fielding for the American Giants. In 1950 Douglas still could be counted on to lead the Giants, as he hit .354 in the first seventeen games of the season. They named him the new captain of the ball club in recognition of his fine play and leadership. He played in the East-West game that year and had three hits to help the West to a 5–3 victory. He also knocked in two runs to help the cause. By the end of the year Douglas was declared the MVP of the NAL.[62]

Frank Duncan, Sr.

Frank Duncan was born February 20, 1901, in Kansas City, Missouri, into possibly the best city on earth for African American baseball. During the interwar years, Negro League baseball presented one of the only ways for blacks to earn a decent living (especially in southern states still dominated by Jim Crow laws). In addition, black baseball players were often afforded a level of respect not granted to those who worked as traditional laborers or domestic servants. As such, black ballplayers continually expressed their fond memories for their time in the game, even though their schedules and accommodations were worse than those of their white counterparts. Oftentimes, managers and owners of black teams would offer stars on opposing teams a chance to jump their contract and join them (even going so far as to approach a player on the field immediately following the final out to make the offer).

Like many Negro Leaguers, Duncan took advantage of the opportunities to be found in jumping teams when he got a better offer. Because of this he played for numerous teams over his career. He made his greatest mark with the Kansas City Monarchs and the Chicago American Giants but for very different reasons. While catching for the Monarchs during the 1920s, Duncan helped lead them to three straight Negro League World Series championships, including the first ever series against the Hilldale Club of Philadelphia. Duncan was never a serious threat at the plate. A career .252 hitter in his 517 games, teams played him because of his great work behind the plate. He caught a great game and was able to pick off runners with a cannon of an arm. After nearly 20 years as a player, Duncan was hired back to manage the Kansas City Monarchs during the 1940s. He guided the Monarchs to two more World Series appearances and coached Jackie Robinson in his only Negro League campaign in 1945. When word came that Robinson would be called to the majors, it was Duncan who warned Robinson against trying to play shortstop, telling him he didn't have the arm strength or range to be a major league shortstop.

Although he played with or managed a number of superstars and had a memorable career in his own right, Duncan is perhaps most famous for an on-field incident that occurred in Chicago against his future team, the Chicago American Giants. Duncan tried to score from second on a single. After fielding Jelly Gardner's throw to the plate, Chicago's catcher, John Hines, simply waited for Duncan to arrive. Duncan refused to concede the

Frank "Pete" Duncan played for the Leland Giants and the American Giants during his career. He was a speedy outfielder who also caused havoc on the base paths. (Photograph courtesy of NoirTech Research, Inc.)

out at home, though, and drove into Hines trying to dislodge the ball. The fury of the hit caused both benches to empty and led to one of the biggest brawls in the history of the Negro Leagues. The rumble continued until the Chicago police were called to the field in an attempt to restore order. By the time they arrived, even the majority of the spectators had rushed the field to support their chosen team and players. In the midst of the melee a policeman slugged Duncan with his nightstick and Gardner took the opportunity to kick the unconscious Monarchs catcher in the mouth. Understandably, the League tried to downplay such incidents in an effort to protect the credibility and integrity of the game and players.

Frank Duncan was never a superstar in the Negro Leagues, nor was he given the chance to play in the majors. When asked, he would likely say that his greatest thrill came in 1941 when he and his son Frank, Jr., became the first father-son combination on the same professional sports team. After retiring, Frank went on to coach baseball in Kansas City. A solid player who loved the game, Duncan never made a great name for himself in the annals of mainstream baseball history. He will always be remembered, however, for his professionalism and his role in bringing some of the game's greatest names into the public eye.

By Shawn Selby

Herman Dunlap

Herman Dunlap played in the East-West game in 1936 for the American Giants. He also missed significant playing time when he broke his leg and it did not recover as quickly as the doctors expected. In fact, his teammates played at least one benefit game for him to help with his expenses. When he was healthy, Dunlap had a reputation as a fine defensive player and a good bat to keep in the order.[63]

Joseph Vann "Winn" "Pop" Durham

Born July 31, 1931, Newport News, VA

Joe Durham came into the Negro Leagues in the later years but did get elected to the 1952 East-West game from the American Giants squad. He later became the second black player to play for the Baltimore Orioles (in 1954). Pitcher Jehosie Heard paved the way when he pitched two games. Durham played ten games at the end of the 1954 season and then did not reappear until 1957, with Baltimore again for 77 games and then in 1959 for six games with St. Louis.[64]

Willie Ferrell

Willie Ferrell pitched and played the outfield for the American Giants in the early 1940s. He played the outfield when he was not pitching because the club wanted to keep his bat in the lineup. In a 1942 doubleheader with the Kansas City Monarchs Ferrell got the nod for the second game after Lefty Shields pitched the first. The game benefited the South Side Boys Club.[65]

Robert Footes

Robert Footes played for the Chicago Unions and the Union Giants. He had the envious task of catching their star pitchers, such as Harry Buckner, Walter Ball and Pat Dougherty.

William Hendrick Foster

When the name Foster is mentioned in the context of Negro League baseball, especially in Chicago, Andrew "Rube" Foster immediately comes to mind. Rube was a towering figure in the history of Negro baseball in Chicago and central to the rise of Negro baseball throughout the Midwest. Another Foster, William "Bill" Hendrick Foster, half brother of Rube, also played a significant role in the history of Negro League baseball in Chicago.

Bill Foster was born on June 12, 1904, in Calvert Texas. "His mother died when he was only four ... and [he] was raised by his maternal grand-parents in Mississippi."[66] Fifteen years younger than Rube, Bill knew who Rube was but did not meet him until his teens. "I knew I had a brother, and I heard all about the great Rube Foster but I never met him till I went to Chicago to work in the stockyards. That was around 1918."[67]

Bill attended Alcorn Agricultural and Mechanical College in Mississippi. Alcorn College was part of the land-grant movement at the end of the nineteenth century. The school emphasized training more than education. As was common during the era, the school also provided training and education for a wide range of students. Alcorn College started out as a school exclusively for black males but began admitting women in 1895. After Bill's baseball and business career, he returned to Alcorn State University and coached the baseball team and served in other administrative capacities. Bill died in Lorman, Mississippi, on September 16, 1978. Widely regarded as one of the premier pitchers of his era by his peers and historians, Bill Foster was elected to the National Baseball Hall of Fame by the Veterans Committee in 1978.

Bill Foster's journey from Mississippi to Chicago in 1918 was part of the Great Migration of Blacks to the north from 1916 to 1919. Historians estimate that as many as half a million blacks moved north, providing a labor force to meet the demands of industrial expansion in Chicago, Detroit, Pittsburgh and Philadelphia. Not coincidentally, each of these cities played a pivotal role in the development of black baseball and other black economic enterprises. Chicago played a pivotal role in the success of Negro League baseball. Fan support and the entrepreneurial ability of Rube Foster helped other teams in the Negro National League enjoy financial success.

Bill returned to Mississippi after his initial foray to Chicago. "He [Rube] didn't want me to play ball ... he wanted me to do something else.... Well, I wanted to play."[68]

In 1925 Bill joined the Memphis Red Sox. His time there was cut short by the long reach of Rube. When Rube learned of Bill's playing with the Memphis team, he demanded that Memphis turn over Bill's contract rights to him. Memphis had no recourse but to comply with the wishes of the czar of Negro baseball, Rube Foster, league president and owner of the premier gate attraction, the Chicago American Giants.

Bill's transition from Memphis to Chicago was difficult: "...it was a sore spot between my brother and me.... I decided from then ... I was going to do everything like I wanted to do it."[69]

After little success and, one can only imagine, relentless counsel from Rube, Bill slowly began to use the techniques suggested by Rube. Rube's emotional collapse in 1926 provided an opportunity for Bill to put into practice Rube's mound preachings. "After he had a breakdown ... I went right through the same procedure that he had been teaching me. I went out there and won."[70]

Dave Malarcher, another giant of Chicago black baseball, who succeeded Rube as manager of the Chicago American Giants, said, "Bill Foster was my star pitcher, the greatest pitcher of our time, not even barring Satchel.... The art of pitching he learned from Rube."[71] "Cum Posey, an astute baseball man, called ... Foster the greatest lefthander Negro baseball ever saw."[72]

Foster's career record shows 137 victories in organized league contests and many more barnstorming victories during his long career. He was the ace of the Giants teams of the last half of the 1920s. He led the Giants to league championships in 1926 and 1927. His career also included a short stint as the Chicago manager in 1930.

In 1926 the Giants faced the Kansas City Monarchs, winners of the first half of the season, in a play-off series to determine who would face the Bacharach Giants, champions of the Eastern Colored League in the Negro World Series. The play-off had one of the legendary performances in all of

Negro League baseball. With Chicago a game down with two to play, a final doubleheader would determine which team would face the Bacharach Giants.

Game one of the doubleheader matched legendary Wilber "Bullet" Rogan against Bill Foster. The Giants pushed a run across in the ninth to beat the Monarchs and Rogan 1–0. Willie Powell was slated to start the second and deciding game. Bill Foster had other plans. Foster made it known he wanted to start the second game. "I'll go in and go as hard and as long as I can. You be ready to pick me up," said Foster. "Go ahead, I know you can take them," responded Powell."[73]

When Rogan saw Bill warming up for the second game, he convinced Kansas City manager Jose Mendez to let him face Foster again. Chicago quickly jumped on Rogan and took a 5–0 lead after two innings. Foster, meanwhile, was nearly unhittable, yielding just two hits in tossing his second shutout of the day, and Chicago was off to Atlantic City to face the Bacharach Giants. Bill Foster once again closed out the hard fought series with his second World Series victory 1–0 in the deciding eleventh game in Chicago.

In 1927 Bill posted a 21–3 season mark as Chicago faced a rematch with the Eastern Colored League champion, the Bacharach Giants. Chicago again bested the eastern league champion five games to four, with Bill Foster winning two and losing two.

Bill's league record in 1928 was 14–10 as he again led the Giants to the championship over the St. Louis Stars. The Stars lineup featured such greats as Cool Papa Bell, Mule Suttles and Willie Wells. In 1929 Bill Foster crafted a 15–10 record. "Instead of a World Series, the American Giants, plus Mule Suttles, Willie Wells and Cool Papa Bell, met the Homestead Grays, plus Clint Thomas and George Scales in five games."[74] The Chicago team won all five games.

As the Chicago Giants manager in 1930, and with the Negro National League battered and failing like many depression era businesses, Bill still posted a 16–10 record for the Giants. His club only won fifty-four games against fifty-two losses and finished out of the play-offs. In 1931, Bill Foster jumped to the Homestead Grays, joining one of the greatest Negro League teams ever assembled. The 1931 Grays featured some of the biggest stars of black baseball: Oscar Charleston, Josh Gibson, Willie Wells and Smokey Joe Williams. Late in 1931, Foster was permitted to switch to the Kansas City Monarchs, where he finished the season. Bill returned to Chicago in 1932 and 1933, fashioning a combined 20–15 record and leading the Giants to a Southern League play-off series victory in 1932 against Nashville.

In 1933 Chicago was the center of the Negro baseball universe with the advent of the East-West All-Star Game. From the start, the game was one of the most significant sporting events in the black community. Two of the country's biggest black newspapers, the *Chicago Defender* and the *Pittsburgh Courier,* with a circulation beyond their respective cities, gave fans across America the opportunity to vote for the starting lineups and a national stage for the players and their game.

Facing a lineup of the biggest names in the history of Negro League baseball, including Cool Papa Bell, Oscar Charleston, Josh Gibson and Judy Johnson, Bill Foster pitched a complete game, leading the West to an 11–7 victory in the inaugural contest. He gave up seven hits, struck out four and walked three to earn the victory.

Selected by the fans as the leading vote-getter to the 1934 East-West game, Foster figured heavily in the outcome of the game. Inserted in the seventh inning by manager Dave Malarcher, Foster battled Satchel Paige, with Paige and the East winning 1–0. Foster gave up four hits and one earned run in his three inning stint.

After pitching for Chicago in 1934 and 1935, Bill Foster's career ended with a year in Pittsburgh in 1936 and a return to the Chicago American Giants in 1937, his last in the highest level of black baseball.

"After retiring from baseball, Bill Foster moved to North Carolina as an insurance agent. He eventually settled in Lorman, Mississippi."[75] Bill returned to his alma mater, Alcorn State University, where he worked until his death.

By James Kastro

Floyd "Jelly" Gardner

Born September 27, 1896, Russellville, AK;
died 1977, Chicago, IL

Jelly Gardner enjoyed a fifteen year Negro League career with Detroit, Chicago, New York and Homestead. He started with the American Giants in 1920 and stayed with them for eleven seasons. During his years with them, the Giants won five pennants and played in the 1926 World Series. Though Gardner did not hit well in that series he played in all eleven games and scored eight runs.

He left Chicago in 1927 to join the Lincoln Giants but returned to the Windy City in 1928 and 1929. He finished out his career with the Detroit Stars, playing his final games with them in 1933.

As a player, Gardner was well-liked because he was a fierce competitor. He did not like to lose. At times his temper got away from him and he also had a reputation with opposing teams for being too aggressive. He was a free-swinging hitter, so his average fluctuated dramatically from season to season, but his speed kept him in the lineup and in the outfield. He covered

Floyd "Jelly" Gardner played in the outfield for the American Giants during most of the 1920s. He was a part of their World Champion team in 1926 and a member of the pennant winning clubs from 1920 to 1922. (Photograph courtesy of the National Baseball Hall of Fame Library, Cooperstown, New York.)

a lot of ground and helped his pitchers with his stellar defense. After his playing career ended Gardner continued to work hard for others. Along with a number of former Chicago players he helped form the Old Ball Players Association in 1949 to assist those in need.[76]

William "Big Bill Gatewood

Big Bill Gatewood was born August 22, 1881, in San Antonio, Texas. He was the epitome of the journeyman during his twenty-four year career in the Negro Leagues. Over that span, he played for no less than fifteen teams. Beginning with the Leland Giants in 1905, Gatewood finished his career with the Birmingham Black Barons in 1928. His career took him from Chicago to New York and Brooklyn, from Detroit and Milwaukee to Memphis and St. Louis. Big Bill stood six feet seven inches tall, weighed nearly 250 pounds and used his size to be one of the most dominating pitchers in the early years of the Negro Leagues. The hefty right-hander mastered both the spitball and the emery ball in an era when trick pitches were par for the course.

Pitching wasn't Bill's only skill, however. The lack of funds that plagued the Negro Leagues for much of their existence forced many players to fill multiple duties over the course of a season. Gatewood was no exception. While pitching his way to a 6–8 record with the New York Lincoln Giants in 1914, he tallied a .433 batting average and spent time patrolling the outfield as well. Not afraid to knock a batter down if he felt the hitter wasn't respecting his pitches, Gatewood rarely put together a winning season. On June 6, 1921, though, Big Bill hurled the first no-hitter in Negro League history, pitching the Detroit Stars past the Cuban Stars 4–0.

By 1922 he had made enough of a name for himself to be offered the manager's post with the St. Louis Stars in their first year in existence. While with the Stars in St. Louis, Gatewood was mentor to a young pitcher named James Bell. After seeing Bell remain calm enough to strike out legend Oscar Charleston in a tight spot, Gatewood gave the nineteen-year-old hurler the nickname "Cool Papa." Though the creation of the moniker was significant in its own right, perhaps the most lasting contribution to sports history came when Gatewood moved Bell into the outfield to give him a chance to play every day and moved him to the other side of the plate in order to maximize Bell's speed out of the box.

Gatewood pitched a game in the early 1920s for the Detroit Stars against the Cuban Stars. The Cuban players had never liked to play against Gatewood because of his reputation for throwing beanballs or "dusters," as some called his brushback pitches. The Cuban players complained all game to the umpire, who threw out two balls that appeared doctored and then found bottle caps in Gatewood's pockets. Gatewood completed the game as a no-hitter even amidst all the complaints. It was this kind of pitching that gained Gatewood a reputation as one of the early headhunters of the game.

The catcher and manager of the St. Louis Stars, Bruce Petway, knew that Gatewood was not averse to backing up a hitter. In one game Gatewood threw a couple under the chin of Joe Hewitt, and Petway stated, "Gatewood will never hit Joe Hewitt, but with some other batter at the plate I would not be so sure. You see, some players 'freeze' when that ball comes toward them."

Although he moved south to the Albany Giants of Georgia's Negro Southern League in 1926, Gatewood continued his role as a mentor to young talent. That year, he pitched another no-hitter against the Birmingham Black Barons, who later picked up his contract. His 1–2 record with the Black Barons was not stellar, but Gatewood helped a young Satchel Paige learn his famous hesitation pitch.

Big Bill Gatewood's statistics will never get him into the Hall of Fame. Few people outside the most serious fan of baseball and the Negro Leagues are likely to know his name. His career shows the impact a player and manager can have on the game even without gaudy numbers, however. Gatewood played before there was much call for an organized Negro League system, yet he helped develop players who would make an indelible mark on the game and on the towns in which they played.

By Shawn Selby

Napoleon "Nap" Gulley

Born August 29, 1924, Huttig, AR;
died August 21, 1999, Skokie, IL

Nap Gulley pitched for most of his Negro League career as a traveler. He moved around a lot, spending a year or two with a ball club before moving on. One of the teams he spent some time with was the Chicago American Giants in 1946. The previous season he had twirled for the Harlem Globetrotters baseball team and then in 1947 he left Chicago to join the Newark Eagles and San Luis in the Mexican League.

Gulley was a valuable addition to the pitching staff as a left-handed twirler. Late in his career he also played some outfield. He found his way to Chicago while playing out in California in a league there. The Chicago Brown Bombers came through town and Gulley caught on with them to come back to the Midwest and pitch for the Giants.

James Earl Gurley

Hailing from Memphis, James Gurley joined the Chicago American Giants in 1924 and quickly made an impact as both a top-notch fielder and a hitter with some pop in his bat.

Paul Hardy

Paul Hardy was signed by manager Winfield Welch to help bolster the American Giants' pitching in 1949. Hardy was being brought in to take over behind the plate for Quincy Trouppe and started catching in 1931 with the Montgomery Red Sox and joined the Detroit Stars in 1933. He traveled the league after that until he got drafted in 1943. He played for Camp Knight in Oakland until his discharge in 1945.[77]

Nathan "Nate" Harris

After playing third base for a number of years Nate Harris came to Chicago in 1905 and took over the second base job. He even got named captain of the squad by Frank Leland in 1910 before he retired in 1911. Harris was best known for his speed, which helped him lead the team in steals and runs scored. He was later described by one reporter as "one of the greatest second basemen of all time."[78]

Lemuel "Hawk" Hawkins

Playing first base for the Monarchs earned Hawkins a chance to play in the first Negro League World Series in 1924. Before joining the Monarchs he played for five years with the 25th infantry team in the U. S. Army. He also played for the Los Angeles White Sox and then Joe Green's Chicago Giants in 1921 before jumping mid-season to Kansas City.[79]

Albert "Buster" Haywood

Born January 12, 1910, Portsmouth, VA

Buster Haywood spent a long career with the Indianapolis Clowns, both as a player and as a manager. He guided the Clowns to the Negro American League Eastern Division title from 1950–52 and again in 1954. One of the players he managed for a short time before he went on to be a Hall of Famer in the major leagues was a teenager named Hank Aaron.

Haywood started playing baseball on the sandlots around Portsmouth.

While playing there he got a chance to join the Birmingham Black Barons in 1940. He left the Barons to try to find a team that would pay him better and ended up out in Denver trying to catch on with a team in the *Denver Post* Tournament. He joined the Miami Clowns and helped them win. He stayed with the Clowns for much of the remainder of his career, moving whenever they did. After he left the Barons he caught on for a short time as a backup catcher with the American Giants in 1940.

J. Preston "Pete" Hill

Pete Hill began his long and illustrious baseball career in 1899 with the Pittsburgh Keystones and played through 1926. He was described by his manager, Ben Taylor, as one of the most dangerous hitters a pitcher could face in a tough situation. Hill not only hit for power but patrolled centerfield, covering a lot of ground.

Hill came into the world in 1880 and died in Buffalo in December 1951. About his early life little is known, until he appeared on the baseball diamonds in 1899 with the Keystones. After two seasons in Pittsburgh, Hill joined the Cuban X-Giants before Foster enticed him away in 1903. He joined Foster on the roster of the Philadelphia Giants. While with

Pete Hill played for many years before the creation of the Negro National League in 1920. He learned the game from the great master, Andrew "Rube" Foster. Hill hit for power and had an incredibly strong arm in the outfield. (Photograph courtesy of NoirTech Research, Inc.)

Philadelphia, Hill helped the Giants win championships in 1905 and 1906. In 1907 he again joined Foster in Chicago, playing for the Leland Giants. After Foster broke with Frank Leland and formed the Chicago American Giants, Hill signed on as a Giant. One of their best years came in 1911 when the club sported a reported 106–7 record with Hill one of the leading hitters, batting over .400 for the year, according to the local press. Hill also proved a huge disruption on the base paths when he got on.

In 1909 the Leland Giants won the City League Championship, clinching the title in a victory over the Gunthers 2–1. Pat Dougherty got the win, which was saved by a superb catch by Hill in center field to preserve the score.[80] In a previous game that season Hill helped the Giants beat the Cuban Stars in an exhibition game 13–6. He contributed three hits, scored two runs and knocked in one. In that same game the club lost Foster for a few weeks after he broke his leg sliding into home plate in the first inning.[81]

Hill often helped out his club by knocking the opposing pitcher out of the game. For example, in a 1911 game he got to Smokey Joe Williams for a home run that helped knock him out of the box. The American Giants won that game 7–5. In a 1910 game for the Leland Giants Hill hit a two run homer that pushed Fred Bergmann of the Gunther's off the mound. Hill hit a two run blast off Perera that would have sent him to the showers but they had no one else to come in and pitch. The shot came in a 7–1 win over the Cuban Stars at Normal Park. The reporter claimed it was the longest ball ever hit in the stadium.[82]

Hill spent ten of his winters playing ball in Cuba. He continued to terrorize the pitching staffs south of the border just as he did in the states. During the winter of 1910–11 he got the opportunity to play against the Detroit Tigers and Philadelphia Athletics, hitting over .300 in the eleven games. In the winter of 1915–16 he went with the American Giants to play in a series of games in Cuba. The *Chicago Defender* reported in March that Hill hit .416 while there. He scored eight runs and had fifteen hits against a variety of Cuban opponents. He had the second highest average among the Giant hitters, behind only John Henry Lloyd, who hit .454.[83]

Hill also played out West when the American Giants participated in the California League. In one game against the San Diego–based Pantages team, Hill helped Dizzy Dismukes win 7–6 by driving in the tying and winning runs. They beat the Tacoma Tigers shortly before heading back to the Midwest and Hill had three hits, scored three runs and stole a base to lead the Giants to a 10–8 victory.[84]

One newspaper report claimed Hill never hit under .300 in his career, which also included time with Detroit, Milwaukee and Baltimore. In 1923, as player/manager of the Milwaukee Bears, Hill helped his club shut out the Logan Squares 7–0 with one hit and one run scored. He brought his last-place Bears to Schorling Park to play his former team and put on a better show than their record indicated. Hill's own knowledge and desire to beat his old nemesis always helped.[85]

Many newspaper accounts listed Hill with multiple hit games and often with multiple extra base hits. For example, in a 10–2 victory over the Gunthers in 1909, Hill went 6–6 and made a one-handed grab in center to save at least a triple.[86] Hill helped out his team in other ways as well. In an 11–3 loss to the Cuban Stars in 1909 he came in and pitched four no-hit innings to keep the game from getting completely out of hand. In a doubleheader against the Anson Colts, Hill had six hits and scored four runs. Four of the hits came in the opening contest. His hits included two doubles and a triple as Pat Dougherty and Walter Ball both came away with victories. In an 8–4 win over the Gunthers Hill went 3–4, including two doubles, and knocked in one run.[87]

Hill also had good base running skills and loved to try to take the extra base whenever possible. He often found himself involved in plays at the plate, when he even tried to steal home on more than one occasion.

In a 1952 poll by the *Pittsburgh Courier* to name the best players in the Negro Leagues, Hill received honorable mention. He was listed as the fourth outfielder behind Oscar Charleston, Monte Irvin and Cristobal Torriente. Owner Cum Posey named his All-Time All-Star team in 1944 and included Hill as one of the outfielders. Posey picked Hill because he contributed on such a consistent basis to every team he ever played for. A 1910 article talked about the Chicago players who would be stars in the majors if only they were white, and the first player discussed was Pete Hill. The reporter stated, "Hill can do anything a white player can do. He can hit, run, throw and is what could be termed a wise, heady ball player."[88]

After his baseball career ended, Hill went to work for Ford Motor Company. Ben Taylor once described Hill as being one of the most dangerous hitters you ever wanted to see at the plate in a tight spot.[89] Hill came back to Chicago in 1942 to visit his son, who was serving in the U. S. Army, and one of the *Defender* reporters caught up with him to ask him about the game and how it had changed. Hill said that the ball was livelier and easier to hit and that he believed one day a black player would be playing in the majors. He said he would love to play again so he could really hit this new ball and show the youngsters how it was supposed to be done.[90]

Samuel "Sam" Hill

Born November 24, 1929; died April 23, 1992, Dallas, TX

Sam Hill played basketball and football at Birmingham High School and then went on to enjoy a short baseball career. In one of his first games for the American Giants in 1947 he hit a long home run and a single as Chicago defeated Birmingham 13–6. Hill turned his solid play for the American Giants into an opportunity to play in the 1948 East-West All Star competition.

William "Billy" Holland

A strong left-handed pitcher, Holland got his baseball start with the Chicago Unions in 1894. He traveled the next couple of years before returning to Chicago in 1897 with the Unions, where he remained through the 1899 season. In 1900 Holland joined the outfield for the Columbia Giants before heading back to his native Minnesota until 1905. In 1905 Holland returned to the Windy City to join the newly formed Leland Giants.

William J. "Billy" Horne

Billy Horne played the infield for the American Giants in 1939 and 1941. He was known for his steady hands and for turning a quick double play. Horne got elected by the fans to two All Star games while playing in Chicago. In 1940 he was presented with a Gold Trophy by the Cross Roads Athletic Club of New Orleans during a doubleheader that involved the American Giants and the Birmingham Black Barons. Xavier student Jesse Russell presented Horne with the trophy as a former member of the club.[91]

David "Dave" Hoskins

Born August 3, 1925, Greenwood, MS

Dave Hoskins grew up in Greenwood, Mississippi, but his family moved to Flint, Michigan, where he went to high school. Hoskins starred in four sports while attending Northern High School. He got into baseball in 1942 with the Cincinnati Clowns and by 1945 was playing for the Homestead Grays. While with the Grays, Hoskins was supposed to get a tryout with the Red Sox but his manager, Cum Posey, refused him the time off and Marvin Williams attended in his place.[92]

Hoskins played for the Chicago American Giants in 1949, rounding out an outfield that included Lonnie Summers in left and Lloyd Davenport in center. He also pitched when they needed him. He went on to pitch for the Dallas Eagles in 1952 in the Texas League before starting as a rookie with the Cleveland Indians in 1953. The Eagles won the pennant and Hoskins helped with an 18–10 record. He got his first major league win against the St. Louis Browns, winning 12–3. He pitched three innings in relief and went 2–2 at the plate. He had a double and a two-run homer to help his own cause. During one stretch of his rookie season Hoskins won four straight games, giving him an 8–3 record in September. After a couple of seasons with the Indians, Hoskins found himself pitching for the San Diego Padres.[93]

Fred Hutchinson

Fred Hutchinson played shortstop for the American Giants in the 1910s and developed a reputation as having great hands in the field. He got to nearly every ball hit his direction and he turned a pretty double play with Monroe and Pierce. Rube Foster believed he never let anything get by that entered his territory. His name frequently appeared in the accounts of the games when they were lauding the fielding efforts. At the plate, Hutchinson did not have a strong bat and usually hit in the eighth spot in the order. On many occasions Foster himself would pinch hit for Hutchinson if the game was close in the late innings.

Cowan Fontella "Bubba" Hyde

Born April 10, 1908, Pontotoc, MS

Bubba Hyde played baseball from 1927 to 1950, patrolling the outfield and turning double plays at second base. He played for a number of clubs, including the Chicago American Giants and Memphis Red Sox. He played in two East-West classics while with the Red Sox. In his final season he played with the Negro League All-Stars in some exhibitions against the ML All-Stars.

Stanford "Jambo" Jackson

Stanford Jackson played for the American Giants from 1926 to 1930 and then with the Columbia Giants in 1931. It is reported that he had at least one run-in with his manager, Rube Foster, when he ignored a sign on the field.[94]

Joseph Gentry "Jeep" Jessup

Born July 4, 1914, Mount Airy, NC;
died March 26, 1998, Springfield, MA

Gentry Jessup pitched for a variety of ball clubs in his career, including spending a number of winters in Cuba. In fact, his play in Cuba got him nominated to the Cuban Hall of Fame in 1998. While pitching for the Chicago American Giants (1941–49), Jessup appeared in five East-West All Star games from 1944 to 1948. In his first appearance he pitched three innings and gave up only one run to earn the victory. In the 1947 game Jessup retired all nine batters he faced before yielding to Chet Brewer. All told, Jessup pitched in almost fifteen innings and had a 1.84 ERA as he gave up only 3 runs on nine hits. In 1946 Jessup barnstormed with Satchel Paige's All-Stars against Dizzy Dean and his crew.[95]

As a pitcher, Jessup developed a reputation for having great stamina but not the best control. He pitched a twenty-inning game in 1946 against the Indianapolis Clowns that ended in a tie. Hitters knew that it was not smart to dig in against Jessup, because he threw a lot of wild pitches and hit a number of batters.

Jessup helped his own cause whenever he pitched. He was a solid hitter who reportedly hit .300 in 1948 while posting a 6–9 record. In 1945 the papers reported his average as .267 by mid-season. He did not have a lot of power but made contact when he needed to. In a 1945 contest against the Monarchs, which Jessup won 6–3, he had a triple and a single and knocked in two runs.[96]

As a mainstay of the Giants pitching staff, Jessup often came out and pitched the Giants to victory. He won before a crowd of nearly 15,000 at Comiskey Park in 1944 and held the Cincinnati Clowns to only five hits as his club won 3–1. In a 1945 game against the Black Yankees Jessup threw a three-hit shutout as the Chicago squad won 1–0. He retired the first twenty-one batters he faced before the Black Yankees could muster any kind of threat. When the Giants came up against the 1944 World Champion Grays late in the season Jessup held them down and allowed the Giants to take a 4–3 victory. Two errors by the Grays in the ninth inning made the difference in the contest. He won the season opener in 1946 against the Kansas City Monarchs 9–2.[97]

Jessup's records in the mid–1940s included seasons at 8–7, 14–9, 15–10 and 7–8 in 1946. His ERA nearly always fell below 3.00, as consistency seemed to mark his twirling. If Jessup pitched, he would give his team a good strong outing, at least giving his offense the chance to win.

Late in the 1946 season Jessup got the chance to pitch in the South-

GENTRY JESSUP
PITCHER
CHICAGO AMERICAN
GIANTS

Gentry Jessup pitched for the American Giants during the 1940s and played in five East-West All-Star games. He once pitched a twenty inning game against the Indianapolis Clowns that ended in a 3–3 tie. (Photograph courtesy of NoirTech Research, Inc.)

North game. His team beat the south 8–2 at Comiskey Park. In addition to giving up only five hits and no earned runs, Jessup had two hits and drove in four runs to help his own cause. One of his hits came with the bases loaded. Jessup barnstormed in the fall with the Satchel Paige All-Stars. He pitched in a contest against Bob Feller's Major League All-Stars and lost 6–5. Jeff Heath of the St. Louis Browns tied the game with a bases loaded triple and then scored the winning run on another triple by Ken Keltner of the Indians. During the 1946–47 winter season Jessup played for Almendares in Cuba. In sixteen games Jessup compiled a 5–3 record with four complete games.[98]

One of the highlights of Jessup's career came in 1947 when he pitched a one-hitter against Indianapolis. About 7,500 fans got to see the Giants win 9–0 as Jessup took a no-hitter into the eighth inning before yielding the only hit of the game to Ray Neil. He also struck out four batters. At that time it was believed the White Sox were watching his progress.[99] In 1949 the Giants won the second half title by beating the Indianapolis Clowns in a doubleheader. Eugene Smith won the first game 1–0, while Jessup mopped up in the second with another shut-out at 2–0. Jessup gave up only five hits in that game, while Smith held the Clowns batters to only six hits in 10 innings.[100]

From 1950 to 1952 Jessup played some semipro ball and then minor league ball in the Man-Dak League. In 1950 he joined the staff of the Benton Harbor Cubs for the early part of the season. He pitched against the House of David in one contest. Then he pitched for the Carman team in the Man-Dak League, compiling a 10–4 and 9–6 mark his first two seasons. He also hit .278 and .298 respectively.[101]

Jessup remained involved in the game for many years. In 1957 he pitched in an All-Star game against the Skokie Indians. He appeared in the lineup for the Chicago Vets in 1961, pitching against the Skokie Indians in the Greater Chicago SemiPro League.[102]

Jessup came from an athletic family. His brother Sherman pitched for the Winston-Salem Pond Giants, a semipro club. His other brother Tom became a boxer and even had a bout with Hank Armstrong.

Don "Groundhog" Johnson

Born July 31, 1926, Covington, KY

Don Johnson's baseball career should never have happened according to the medical community. At the age of thirteen Johnson went to the grocery store for his mother and stopped to play a game of pickup football in the street. While playing, he got hit by a train, which tore the muscles in his left leg. The doctor at the hospital who worked on fixing his leg told him he would never play sports again.

Johnson started his baseball career in 1947 with the Pioneer League. He played one season in Ogden, Utah, before they released him. The following year he signed on with the Chicago American Giants. He played in the Negro Leagues through the 1952 season. While with Chicago, Johnson played second base alongside shortstop Larry Raines. They made an impressive keystone combination. He earned his nickname "Groundhog" because of his fine fielding skills. Any ball that came his way he gobbled up. Nothing got by him.[103]

George "Chappie" Johnson

Born 1876, Bellaire, OH

Although he started his career with the Page Fence Giants, Chappie Johnson played for Chicago teams from 1899 to 1902. He returned again in 1909–1910 for the Leland Giants. Johnson was considered by many to be one of the best catchers of the game at the time. He was an excellent pitch caller and he knew all the weaknesses of the opposing hitters. He later owned and managed a number of teams such as the Norfolk Stars and the Chappie Johnson All-Stars.

Louis "Dicta" Johnson

Johnson began his career in St. Paul in 1910, and moved to Chicago in 1912 to join Rube Foster's Chicago American Giants. He helped the Giants dominate the local scene as he joined a pitching staff that included Foster and Big Bill Gatewood. He spent part of the 1915 season and the 1916 season with the Giants. Before the close of the 1916 season he joined the ABCs and pitched for them against Chicago in the play-offs. He beat his former teammates in a complete game 1–0 shutout.

Thomas Johnson

Tom Johnson served in the U. S. military during the First World War and attained the rank of lieutenant with the 36th infantry. His military service interrupted a career in the Negro Leagues with the Chicago American Giants. He attempted a comeback playing with the Giants after the war but became ill and never really played full-time again. He also did a bit of umpiring and then came back to manage the Chicago Athletics. The Athletics were a semipro club in the city under the ownership of Jack Hunter. His club relied heavily on college ball players, especially from Howard University.[104]

Bert Jones

Bert Jones started his baseball career in 1896 in Kansas and was last listed on a baseball roster in 1923. In his nearly thirty-year career Jones pitched and roamed the outfield for a variety of clubs. He spent a number of seasons in Chicago, which was a hotbed for black baseball in the early part of the twentieth century. From 1898 to 1901 he pitched for the Chicago Unions and Union Giants.

Willis "Will" Jones

Will Jones patrolled right field for the Chicago Unions from 1895 to 1902. The team changed its name to the Chicago Union Giants and Jones remained with the club. He finished out his career playing for a variety of local teams in Minnesota.

Harry Kenyon

Harry Kenyon started his Negro League career with the Indianapolis ABCs and then joined Foster's American Giants in 1923.

John Henry "Pop" Lloyd

Bats left, throws right; born April 25, 1884, Palatka, Florida;
died March 19, 1965, Atlantic City, New Jersey;
inducted into Baseball Hall of Fame 1977

John Henry Lloyd's professional career lasted from 1905 until 1931. During his long career, Lloyd would be viewed as an outstanding fielder and an even better hitter. He would play all infield positions, but the legacy he left was as one of the greatest shortstops of all time, in any league.

In 1905, Lloyd began his professional career as a catcher for the Macon (GA) Acmes. It was while playing for the Acmes that Lloyd added a story to his legacy. After being hurt by foul balls while catching, Lloyd bought a wire basket to wear as a catcher's mask.

Word began to spread around Negro baseball about Lloyd's extraordinary skills on the field. He would play for the Philadelphia Giants for

One of the greatest ballplayers of any era, John Henry "Pop" Lloyd helped the American Giants to championships three out of his four years in Chicago. (Photograph courtesy NoirTech Research, Inc.)

three seasons before the father of black baseball would catch wind of this terrific player. For the 1910 season, Rube Foster brought Lloyd to Chicago to play for the Leland Giants. To say that the Leland Giants were good would be a massive understatement. With Foster's leadership and Lloyd's play the Leland Giants were able to amass a .953 winning percentage with a 123–6 record. During the 1910 season, Lloyd played shortstop for the Leland Giants.

For the 1911 season, Lloyd was lured away from Chicago by his Philadelphia Giants manager, Sol White, to play for the Lincoln Giants of New York under owner James Keenan. Lloyd would play for the Lincoln Giants through the 1913 season. While Lloyd was in New York, Rube Foster was back in Chicago, amassing possibly the greatest Negro League team ever.

To be the best Foster paid the best. It was quite lucrative for the great Negro League players to migrate to Chicago for the salary. "Wherever the money was, that's where I was," exclaimed Lloyd. Playing for the Chicago American Giants, Lloyd would make $250 a month.[105]

The crowds at Schorling Park were treated to excellent baseball. Among Lloyd's contemporaries were Oscar Charleston and Joe Williams. Later Lloyd would say that Smokey Joe Williams was the best pitcher ever in the Negro Leagues.[106] While Lloyd played for the American Giants, he batted cleanup and showed off his incredible fielding skills. While batting, Lloyd would hold his bat in the crick of his left elbow. Lloyd, wasn't a power hitter, but rather hit line drives and had the uncanny ability to stretch a single into a double and a double into a triple.[107]

John Henry Lloyd stood five feet eleven inches and weighed 180 pounds. His size made him a big man for the time and an even larger shortstop and he used his height as an advantage to cover more of the field. His range in the field may never be matched, but many people at the time compared Lloyd with the great Honus Wagner. Prior to playing in Chicago Lloyd got the nickname "El Cuchara" in Cuba, meaning "the shovel."

The American Giants with Lloyd were extremely successful throughout the short time that he played in Chicago. With the outstanding team that Rube Foster was able to mold and build, the American Giants claimed the unofficial black baseball title in 1914 and 1917. In the *Chicago Defender* article announcing his arrival in 1915, the reporter called Lloyd "the greatest shortstop in the country barring none."

In Lloyd's final game at Schorling Park he was able to get a double and a walk, and scored two runs in a 9–3 win over an all-white all-star team. After the 1917 season, Lloyd got a job with the postmaster general in Chicago and decided not to go to Florida during the winter. Rube Foster and Lloyd split amicably, but it is thought that Foster believed that Lloyd was a step slower and replaced him with Bobby Williams.

After Lloyd was finished playing in Chicago, his playing days were far from over. He would continue to play professionally until 1931. It was the later days of his career when Lloyd became known as a great mentor to many Negro ballplayers. He was a kind and compassionate manager who helped develop young talent.

Lloyd would eventually settle in Atlantic City, New Jersey. He became a janitor and helped develop youth baseball in the area and would eventually become the commissioner of the youth baseball league, and having the little league stadium named after him. Not only did the people of Atlantic City recognize the efforts of Lloyd, but the Baseball Hall of Fame did as well. In 1977, Lloyd was inducted into Cooperstown, twelve years after his death.

By Aric J. Smith

William "Bill" Lindsay

Bill Lindsay pitched for the American Giants during the early years before the Negro National League existed. He helped them win the California Winter League title in 1912–13 and became real popular with the Chicago fans. One reporter called him "a gentleman both on and off the diamond and all the time."[108] Rube Foster thought Lindsey had great stuff but occasionally he had to get on him to pitch his best. During one batting practice session, Foster told Lindsey anyone could get two hits off him the way he had been pitching. The next outing Lindsey had he had his best stuff again. Foster was a fine player in his own right but one of the things that made him stand out was his ability to work with his players and get the best out of them.[109]

Lester Lockett

Born March 26, 1912, Princeton, IN

A versatile infielder and outfielder, Lester Lockett enjoyed two short stints with the Chicago American Giants in 1937 and 1950. He played all sports at Lincoln High School but baseball was his real love. He got his start after moving to Chicago with Joe Green's Giants. While playing in Washington Park Lockett's hitting reputation became well-established and he got an offer to try out for the Chicago American Giants in 1937. After making the roster he played in the Negro Leagues until 1955, most often in Chicago.

One of Lockett's career highlights came when he was with the Birmingham Black Barons. For two straight years he helped lead his team into the World Series, where they lost in 1943 and 1944 to the Homestead Grays. Lockett played in four East-West Classics during his career.

Whether playing for the American Giants, the Barons or one of the teams in the Man-Dak League, Lockett hit in the heart of the order. He was there to hit the long ball and he often delivered. Some of his shots were especially memorable to those who saw him play because he hit them a long distance when he connected.

Lockett had the chance to finally win a championship in 1948 with the Fort Wayne Capeharts. They participated in and won the National Semi-Pro Championship in Wichita, Kansas. After his baseball career ended Lockett stayed in the city of Chicago and did a variety of work. He retired in the early 1980s after a final stint as a security guard.

Lester Lockett played for the American Giants in 1942 and again in 1950. Lockett was a versatile player who patrolled the outfield and could also play most of the infield. He played in four East-West All-Star contests and retired after the 1950 season. (Photograph courtesy of Dick Clark.)

Bernell Longest

Born July 15, 1917, Chicago, IL; died July 1984, Detroit, MI

Bernell Longest played in the infield for the American Giants in the mid–1940s. He developed a reputation as a fine fielder with a good bat. He later played alongside his brother on the Chicago Brown Bombers roster. The two made an excellent double play combination.

Clarence Lyttle

Clarence Lyttle pitched for the Union Giants from 1901 to 1905 and then moved to the Leland Giants in 1906. There is no record of him playing baseball after that season. He contributed to the incredible success of the 1905 club, which reported a record of 112–10 under manager William S. Peters. After leaving Chicago Lyttle pitched for the St. Paul Gophers for a number of years.

Jack Marshall

Jack Marshall started his professional baseball career with the Dayton Marcos in 1926. In 1928 he went to Chicago and joined the Gilkerson Union Giants. He moved to Canada to manage a club in Saskatchewan in 1929 and 1930. From 1931 to 1936 he returned to the Windy City and played second base for the American Giants. One of his highlights came in 1935, when he hit an inside-the-park home run in a 5–4 loss to the Homestead Grays. Midway through the 1936 season Marshall left to join the Philadelphia Stars and then returned again to Chicago in 1937 before joining the Monarchs in 1938. He left in 1936 because the owner, Robert Cole, was trying to cut salaries and save money to keep the team alive. In his first game with the Stars he had two hits and scored two runs.[110]

In 1944 Marshall found himself playing for a team calling themselves the Chicago Wonders. As described by a news reporter, the club appeared to be anything but wonderful, as they came together simply to provide an opponent for the Motor City Giants when they came to Chicago as part of the Negro American Baseball League.[111]

In 1950 Marshall opened a clinic for youngsters hosted by the Chicago Defender. He was assisted in this endeavor by Dave Malarcher. The clinic attracted about 40 youngsters to Washington Park four nights a week for about a month. In 1951 Marshall wanted to help more youngsters attend the Giants games and he created the Knot Hole Gang, which allowed boys under the age of 12 to attend games for free and those over 12 for 25 cents. He also organized a booster group to help encourage attendance at the Giants home games.[112]

In 1952 the Giants signed Marshall as a coach to help the club. He was popular with the Chicago players and the city.

Dell Mathews

Born Fox Lake, WI; died December 14, 1938, Chicago, IL.

Originally from Fox Lake, Wisconsin, Dell Mathews moved to Chicago with his family in 1903. He came to the Windy City after graduating from the University of Wisconsin at Madison. He pitched for the varsity baseball team and secured a number of victories against future major leaguers such as Fred Beebee, Jake Stahl and Cy Falkenburger. When he arrived in Chicago Frank Leland convinced him to join the Leland Giants. He was a part of the Giants club that won 56 straight games.

When Mathews died in December 1938, he had been serving in the state department of registration for fourteen years. His appointment to that department made him the only black working there. He belonged to the Berean Baptist Church and the Master Barbers Association. He was survived by his wife, Lulu Mathews.[113]

Walter "Real" McCoy

Candy Jim Taylor signed "Real" McCoy in 1945 as the newest lefty on the pitching staff. In his first outing McCoy pitched against the famed Kansas City Monarchs and beat the KC nine 7–2. McCoy gave up only three hits in the contest.[114]

James "Big Stick" McCurine

Born May 8, 1921, Clinton, KY; died May 24, 2002

Hailing from Clinton, Kentucky, originally, Jim McCurine played most of his Negro League career in Chicago. He patrolled the outfield from 1937 to 1949 for the Chicago American Giants and the Brown Bombers, among other teams. His hitting is what got him noticed while he played for the local semipro clubs like the Chicago Lincoln Giants. Manager Candy Jim Taylor liked what he saw when his club played the Lincoln team in an exhibition game in

Jim McCurine played in the outfield for the American Giants from 1946 to 1949. He was a strong defensive outfielder who hit with some power. (Photograph courtesy of NoirTech Research, Inc., and Marlin Carter.)

Racine, Wisconsin and he offered McCurine a contract with the American Giants.

McCurine quickly earned his nickname "Big Stick" because he hit in the heart of the lineup. Along with teammate John Miles, they gave Chicago a fearsome twosome who both averaged about twenty home runs a season. His first two years with the American Giants McCurine hit third and then Taylor moved him into the cleanup spot. McCurine recalls that one of his greatest homers came in a game against the Black Barons in 1948. With his team trailing by a score of 4–1 Big Stick came off the bench and hit a grand slam home run off Jehosie Heard over the head of the young outfielder Willie Mays.

In a game against the Indianapolis Clowns McCurine tied the game at 3–3 with a monster triple off the scoreboard at Comiskey Park. His manager, Candy Jim Taylor, held him at third with Mule Miles coming up next. Unfortunately, Miles struck out and the game went on for 23 innings before it got called due to darkness still tied at 3–3.[115]

Not only could McCurine hit but he had an incredible arm as well. He could throw out a runner at home with a throw on the fly from the outfield. He kept a lot of teams from manufacturing that extra run because they knew his reputation. Even after he hurt his shoulder he continued to play and his fierce desire to win kept him throwing long after he should have stopped.

McCurine's hitting got him noticed by the Boston Braves but he threw his arm out and never got a chance to pursue a major league career. With his baseball career at an end, McCurine worked for a couple of years for the Chicago Transit Authority and turned his hand to selling insurance, which he did until his retirement in 1985. He passed away due to kidney and heart failure in 2002.

Webster McDonald

Born January 1, 1900, Wilmington, DE; died June 12, 1982

Webster McDonald had an amazing array of pitches he used while on the mound. A bit like Satchel Paige, he had a variety of deliveries that made it tough on hitters. One writer claimed he had 56 varieties. McDonald helped the American Giants win the World Series in 1926 and 1927. Some claim that McDonald won two out of every three games he pitched with the Giants. He left Chicago after the 1927 series but returned again in 1929.

McDonald started his baseball career with a team called the Mason Stars in 1919 under manager Danny McClellan. In 1922 he left to join Chappie Johnson's All-Stars and then on to the Lincoln Giants and the Richmond

Giants. He settled in Philadelphia for the 1923–24 seasons before taking a chance on the Wilmington Potomacs in 1925. They folded mid-season and McDonald joined the American Giants and stayed until 1928.[116]

In 1928, he joined a team in Little Falls, Minnesota, and had the chance to pitch against the Minneapolis Millers of the American Association. He remained there for four seasons and won four championships with the club. In 1932 he acted as the player/manager of the Washington Pilots. In 1933 he came back to Philadelphia as their manager and led them to a pennant.

McDonald pitched a number of games during his career against major league all-star teams and beat them regularly. One of his favorite opponents to beat appears to have been Dizzy Dean, which he did on at least four occa-

Webster McDonald pitched for the American Giants in the 1926 and 1927 World Series. He had an amazing array of deliveries that made it tough for batters to hit him. He finished his baseball career as the manager of the Philadelphia Stars. (Photograph courtesy of NoirTech Research, Inc.)

sions. When asked by a reporter what his favorite game in his career was McDonald claimed it to be a game in 1927. He pitched against the Kansas City Monarchs and their twirler, Bill Bell. He won the game 3–1 on a two-hitter and struck out 16 batters along the way.[117]

When McDonald died in 1982 Monte Irvin stated that McDonald had been one of the best in the game.

Gread "Lefty" McKinnis

Born August 11, 1913, Union, AL; died March 8, 1991, Chicago, IL

Lefty McKinnis pitched for the Chicago American Giants in the 1940s and earned three appearances to the East-West Classic in 1943 and 1944 and again in 1949. When he appeared in the game in 1944 the papers reported that his previous record in the classic included four innings pitched, five strikeouts and two runs allowed.

McKinnis showed his stuff when he shut down the Kansas City Monarchs on two hits and won 15–0 in a 1945 contest. He never allowed a runner past first base. Unfortunately for the Giants, McKinnis decided to jump to Mexico with Pennington and Douglas in the mid–1940s and they lost his services for a while. In 1949 the *Chicago Defender* credited him with a 12–7 record by mid-season. The same reporter also said McKinnis had struck out 31 batters in the first 32 innings he pitched that season.[118]

Felix McLaurin

Born September 5, 1921, Jacksonville, FL; died May 1972

Felix McLaurin got his name in the record books for the Negro Leagues with his election to the 1952 West squad as a member of the American Giants. McLaurin played in the outfield for the American Giants, the Birmingham Black Barons and the New York Black Yankees during his career. He was highly sought after because of his fielding and his clutch hitting. In a 6–4 victory by the Yankees over the Cubans, McLaurin helped out with a game winning home run in the eighth inning. In an earlier contest, when he played for the Barons, McLaurin hit a bases loaded double off Satchel Paige to beat the Monarchs 4–2. In a 1951 contest with the New Orleans Eagles the Giants won both games. They won the first contest 1–0, with McLaurin scoring the only run when he walked and scored on a single and an error.[119]

Hurley McNair

Hurley McNair began his baseball career in 1911 with the Chicago Giants, and had a long career before turning to umpiring. He stayed in Chicago through 1916 and then joined the All-Nations club in 1917. Although he played through the mid–1930s it does not appear that he returned to Chicago until 1930 as an outfielder for the Gilkerson Union Giants. 1935 found him still playing for the Kansas City Monarchs as one of their star outfielders. McNair developed a reputation as a solid fielder and a good hitter with some real power. He was a small player with incredible range who surprised opposing teams with his power.[120]

Clyde Clifton "Junior" McNeal

Born December 15, 1928

Clyde McNeal played the infield for the American Giants from 1944 through 1950. He liked playing shortstop the best because he could take advantage of his range and strong arm. In a doubleheader against the Buckeyes in 1949 McNeal showed off his growing abilities at the plate. He hit a three-run homer to help Chicago win 7–5. He played in the 1950 East-West Classic as he slowly developed into a steady and reliable shortstop. He finally began to show some range and a stronger arm. McNeal later played some minor league ball for the Dodgers from 1953 to 1955 and again in 1957. He played in the Mexican League in 1956.[121]

Jose "The Black Diamond — el Diamante Negro" Mendez

Born March 19, 1887, Cardenas, Cuba; died October 31, 1928, Havana, Cuba

Jose Mendez started his Negro League career in 1908 with the Brooklyn Royal Giants. In 1909 he pitched for the Cuban Stars, where he is believed to have compiled a 44–2 record. He spent his longest stints with the All-Nations team of Kansas City and the Kansas City Monarchs. Mendez did spend the 1918 season with the Chicago American Giants after developing arm trouble and moving to the outfield. While playing with the Monarchs they won three pennants from 1923 to 1925. Mendez pitched in four games in the first World Series in 1924 and compiled a 2–0 record with a 1.42 ERA.[122]

Mendez had a variety of pitches he threw with deceptive speed. He was also an incredibly smart pitcher who knew how to pitch in all kinds of situations. Though fairly small in size, he threw with power. Mendez used his knowledge of the game to prolong his career with the Monarchs in the 1920s and piloted the club to pennant victories in 1923, 1924 and 1925.

Mendez's career and life were cut short when he died of pneumonia in 1928. He was elected to the Cuban Hall of Fame in 1939.

John "Mule" "Sonny Boy" Miles

Born August 11, 1922, San Antonio, TX

At six feet three inches and 230 pounds, John Miles played for the American Giants from 1946 to 1949, and in 1947 was among the league leaders in home runs with 26. That year he supposedly hit eleven home runs in

John "Mule" Miles, outfielder for the Chicago American Giants from 1946 to 1948. His manager Candy Jim Taylor gave him the nickname, saying Miles hit the ball like a mule kicks. (Photograph courtesy of the National Baseball Hall of Fame Library, Cooperstown, New York.)

eleven straight games. Before playing baseball Miles worked for his father at his gas station in San Antonio, Texas. He also played basketball in high school and at St. Phillips Junior College.

When World War II started, Miles heard about an opportunity at Kelly Army Airfield to be trained as a mechanic, so he signed on. In 1942, Miles and fifty other African Americans were sent to the Tuskegee Institute in Alabama as part of the first Aircraft Mechanics Journeyman Rating School for blacks called "The Black Wings." He spent two and a half years at Tuskegee and then learned he would be drafted; but his paperwork was apparently lost and after three months of waiting Miles returned home and went back to work at Kelly Airfield. While working there he played on the Kelly Field Brown Bombers. He drew the attention of the Chicago American Giants through a local scout named Webb, who knew the Giants manager, and he agreed to sign a contract and take a chance on a ball playing career. He did return home in the off-season to work as a sheet metal mechanic because he was married and had a family to take care of.

One of his coaches once said that Miles "hits as hard as a mule kicks" and the nickname stuck. It aptly described Miles' strength at the plate. He often hit in the cleanup spot and patrolled the outfield. In 1946 the Giants were counting on their new outfielder to take up the slack left by the loss of Pennington and Douglas to Mexico.[123] He remembers winning a number of games for the Giants with his home runs. For example, they played a white team in Connecticut and beat them 1–0 on Miles' homer in the late innings of the game. In 1948 Miles hit home runs in eleven straight games to lead his team.

In 1950 he decided to hang up his spikes and return to his family. He continued to work at Kelly Airfield until he retired in 1971. Miles also coached and played baseball in the San Antonio area. He never had any trouble on the local white teams with his teammates, just with the fans. As long as he hit the ball his teammates were happy with him. In 2003 Miles was honored by selection into the San Antonio Sports Hall of Fame.[124]

Joe Miller

As many early Chicago ballplayers did, Joe Miller started his pitching career with the Page Fence Giants. When the club disbanded he played with the new Columbia Giants in 1899–1900 before playing for three years with the Chicago Union Giants.

Henry Milton

Born Winona, MS; died July 2, 1943, Crown Point, IN

Henry Milton became a star athlete in the state of Indiana after moving there to live with his sister. He was born in Mississippi but lost both his parents at a young age and his sister brought him to East Chicago, Indiana, where he played baseball at Washington High School. He helped his team win the state championship from 1927 to 1929. He graduated in 1929 and went to Wiley College in Texas, where he graduated in 1933. His first professional baseball playing came with Joe Green's Chicago Giants. He also played with the ABCs, the Brooklyn Royal Giants, the Chicago American Giants and the Kansas City Monarchs, and he played and managed with the East Chicago Giants. He finished his career early because of poor health.

While with the Monarchs Milton married Rosetta Brooks and they had a daughter, Henrietta. During the winter months Milton worked for the recreation department.[125]

William "Bill" Monroe

Born 1878; died March 16, 1915, Chattanooga, TN.

Bill Monroe had a short but stellar career in black baseball. He died unexpectedly in 1915 before the Negro Leagues officially began, but he played with some of the best in the early days of the game. As a second baseman, Monroe captured the attention of many in the major leagues who said if he had been any other race he would have surely been a big leaguer. He covered a lot of ground in the infield. He could make the play between second and short and then turn right around and make the next one in short right field. Foster took great delight in testing his range and speed during infield practice by giving him tough chances.[126]

Growing up in Chattanooga, Bill Monroe got a lot of support from his parents, the Reverend and Mrs. A. S. Monroe. He loved the outdoors and all forms of athletic competition. His athleticism and knowledge of the game made him a hot commodity among the country's managers. He played for the Union Giants in 1899 and 1900, the Philadelphia Giants in 1903, the Quaker Giants in 1908, the Brooklyn Royal Giants and Rube Foster's American Giants from 1911 to 1914. In 1911–12 he batted cleanup for the Giants. He traveled with the Giants to California and south of the border in the winter months to continue playing. He did not make the trip in the winter of 1914 because he had fallen ill and he went home to be with his family. In 1914 Monroe hit .348 in a lineup that featured Bruce Petway, Pete Hill and Pop Lloyd.[127]

Harry "Mike" Moore

Playing first base around the turn of the century, Harry Moore got the chance to compete with some of the greats of the game as a member of the Leland and Chicago American Giants. He played for over fourteen years and reportedly hit over .300 during that time.

Leroy Morney

Leroy Morney played shortstop and the outfield for Chicago and New York during his career. He missed some time early in his career when he developed a sore arm playing the infield for New York. Morney played for the Monroe Monarchs when he first started and found himself on a team that, for a short time, boasted the services of later Negro League great Hilton Smith. Morney got noticed while playing with the Monarchs because of his heavy hitting.[128]

Sidney "Sy" Morton

Born 1920; died 1993

Sidney Morton played in the Negro Leagues from 1940 to 1947. He spent his final season with the Chicago American Giants as a part of their infield.

Clyde Nelson

Infielder Clyde Nelson played for the American Giants in the early 1940s and then left to join the Indianapolis Clowns. His career was cut short when he died unexpectedly in 1949. He played 10 innings against the Philadelphia Stars in a doubleheader and on the last play of the game he chased a foul ball which catcher Pigg caught just as Nelson collapsed on the field. He died en route to the hospital from an apparent heart attack. His mother was still living in Miami at the time, which is where Nelson was born on September 1, 1921. He finished high school in Florida in 1941 and then came north.[129]

In 1944 Nelson signed with the Giants and played until 1947, when his contract was sold to the Cleveland Buckeyes. In 1948 he led the league in hitting with a .395 average according to the Howe News Bureau. In 1949 he moved on to Indianapolis where he played in 50 games and was hitting .325 with 61 hits at the time of his death. Both J. B. Martin and R. S. Simmons of the American Giants remarked on what a wonderful young ballplayer Nelson had been.[130]

Will "Gabie" Owens

Born November 14, 1901, Indianapolis, IN; died May 5, 1999

Will Owens played the infield for 10 years in the Negro Leagues, from 1923 to 1933. Beginning his baseball playing as a catcher on the local sandlots, Owens got his chance to move up in 1923 with the Washington Potomacs. From there he went to the Chicago American Giants before returning to Indiana to play for the ABCs.

Owens generally batted near the top of the order because he got on base and he could bunt. He never hit for power or a high average but contributed mostly with his fielding. He even got involved in a triple play.

After leaving baseball Owens became a professional pool player and traveled all over the country to play. He also worked as a carpenter and general handyman.

Juan Padrone

Juan Padrone pitched for the Chicago American Giants and gained a reputation, while with Foster's club, of being a finesse pitcher who you had to get to early in a game. As the game progressed he always seemed to get stronger and his pitches more deceptive. A perfect example came in a game against the Cuban Giants which the Americans won 11–9. Padrone started and they got to him fairly early, knocking him out of the box and forcing him to yield to Owens, who kept the Giants in the game so they could win it in the final innings.[131]

Andrew H. "Jap" Payne

Born Washington, DC; died August 22, 1942,
New York City, NY

A right fielder of some renown, Payne played in Chicago from 1907 through 1913, changing teams with the fortunes of early Chicago baseball. Payne had the reputation of being speedy on the bases, a good hitter and one of the best at throwing runners out at the plate.

He started in Philadelphia and then came to Chicago as a nineteen-year-old and played for seventeen years before calling it quits. As was typical in these early years, he moved around a bit, as teams found his speed and his defense of great help. He left Chicago to join the Lincoln Giants in 1914 and in 1918 he signed on with the New York Central Red Caps and played there until he retired in 1922. His career allowed him to play with and against some of the greats of the game as he learned from the likes of Rube Foster, Bruce Petway and Pete Hill.[132]

Payne married Carrie Thomas and they had one son, Thomas. He lived his retired life in New York City.

James "Jim" Pendleton

Born January 7, 1924, St. Charles, MO

Jim Pendleton got his baseball start in the Negro Leagues but quickly caught the eyes of the Major League scouts and became the property of the Brooklyn Dodgers. During his one year with the American Giants he hit .301 and fielded well. Scouts were particularly impressed with his strong arm. It meant he could get to a ball deep in the hole and still have a play at first base. Dr. Martin sold Pendleton for the reported sum of $7,500.[133]

Pendleton joined the Dodgers team in Venezuela and hit .360 before moving up to St. Paul, where he led the St. Paul Saints in 1950 with 17 triples to keep him in the lineup. Ray Dandridge said that Pendleton could "hit, run and field with the best in the league."[134] By 1953 Pendleton found himself being converted to an outfielder because of a new crop of rookie players. They wanted to keep his speed and his bat in the lineup. In 1955 Pendleton was sent to the Toledo Sox by the Milwaukee Braves. The Sox used him primarily in the outfield.

Arthur David "Superman" Pennington

Bats switch, throws right; 5'11", 180 lbs.; born May 18, 1923, Memphis, Tennessee; Negro All-Star 1942 and 1950

Arthur David Pennington was born to Mr. and Mrs. Harry Pennington. His father, a school janitor, played baseball in his younger days and taught young Art to play the game. Pennington credits his father for his switch-hitting ability. "My Dad was quite a ballplayer and he saw that I was havin trouble hittin' 'em from the left side, left hand pitchers, so he told me to switch."[135] Art's mother would also play an intricate part in creating Pennington's baseball mystique. The family car got a flat tire when Pennington was only 10 or 11 and he picked up the car so that bricks could be placed underneath and the flat could be changed. After Pennington did this, his mother called him "my little Superman." Both his switch-hitting ability and his nickname made Art Pennington a superman for the Chicago American Giants in the 1940s.

Superman made his baseball debut in 1938 with the Zulu Clowns, a grass-skirt-wearing barnstorming team. While playing for this team he excelled in both hitting and fielding. In 1939, he moved to the West Indian Royals, a team he played with until his move to the Negro American League.

In 1941, Superman tried out for the Chicago American Giants in Memphis, Tennessee, and won a spot at shortstop. While playing for the American Giants Superman would play every position but catcher. The American Giants manager, Candy Jim Taylor, even used Superman as a relief pitcher in some instances. When playing, Superman would bat left handed for contact and right handed for power. He was so powerful from the right side of the plate that he couldn't even bunt.

Superman was confident in his ability, if not cocky. "Throw it and

duck," was what he said to pitchers as he went up to the plate. He even said this to Satchel Paige while playing in front of 44,000 people in Detroit. Paige turned out to be the victor in this battle, striking out Superman three times.[136]

Superman was not embarrassed too many times at the plate. He played in the Negro All-Star Game in 1942 and 1950. Undoubtedly he would have played in many more all-star games if Negro League star Buck Leonard had not played the same position in the same league as Superman. As an average while in the Negro Leagues, Superman batted .336 while belting out 18 home runs with Chicago.

Art "Superman" Pennington began his professional baseball career with Chicago in 1941 and got an opportunity to play in two East-West games in 1942 and 1950. (Photograph courtesy of NoirTech Research, Inc.)

Life was not totally great for Superman while playing with the Chicago club. His mother was white and his father was black. Superman experienced the sting of segregation while barnstorming down South with Chicago. While in the South the players had to go to segregated restaurants and nightclubs. Superman felt great resentment towards the people that perpetuated this segregation. This resentment would be elevated later as Superman played in Mexico and Latin America, where blacks were treated equally.

Another problem that Superman faced while playing in Chicago was his salary. The most that he got while playing for the Chicago American Giants was $600 a month. Problems with salary led to a confrontation with management in 1944. *The Chicago Defender's* July 22 edition read "Bad Boy Pennington is Indefinitely Suspended." Superman refused to play and demanded $200, which Dr. J. B. Martin, president of the club, refused, but rather gave him $100. Coincidentally, Pennington was overdrawn on his salary by $448 and the additional $100 brought the total to $548. Pennington responded in 1945 with one of his best seasons in the Negro Leagues. He batted .359 with 5 home runs and 24 RBIs.[137]

At the onset of the 1946 season, Superman would yet again rock the baseball world in Chicago. Along with two teammates, Lefty McKinnis and Jesse Douglas, he jumped to Mexico. Superman had been expected to play first base and bat cleanup for the American Giants. Upon the announcement of their departure, the three faced a five-year suspension from the league. The main reason for Superman's departure was monetary; he was able to earn $5,000 a summer while playing in Mexico. Another perk to playing in Mexico, Superman found, was that he could go anywhere and talk to any woman he wanted, regardless of her race. While playing in Mexico, Superman met and married a Spanish woman. But Superman's mother wanted him to return to the United States, so in 1949 he went back to the Chicago American Giants. Although all the players had been suspended when they returned, they were reinstated because the league needed them.

In 57 games of the 1949 season Superman was batting .348, but in July he was sold to the Portland Beavers of the Pacific Coast League. Superman was supposed to play in the all-star game that year, but since he was sold before the game he could not play. He went back to Chicago for one more go-round at Comiskey Park in 1950. In 43 games for the American Giants he had the highest batting average of his career at .370. He was leading all batters except Sam Hairston who was sold to the White Sox when he was hitting .424. After 1950, Superman would play in the Three-I League and again in Latin America and would even win the Three-I batting title in 1952.

Superman played at an exciting time for Negro ballplayers. He got to play against some of the greatest Negro League players who would eventually make it to the major leagues. He got to play against Jackie Robinson and Satchel Paige, and was teammates with Buck Leonard in Venezuela. He also got the chance to play in white organized ball for at least a short time in his career.

By Aric J. Smith

Bruce "Buddy" Petway

Born December 23, 1886, Nashville, TN; died July 4, 1941

Bruce Petway had a long and illustrious Negro League career. He learned a lot of his skills and tricks from one of the great minds of the game, Rube Foster. Petway started his career in Chicago and later moved on to manage the Detroit Stars for seven seasons. He caught for the Leland Giants from 1906 to 1910 and then moved to the American Giants from 1911–1918.

Bruce Petway caught for the Leland Giants and the American Giants during his long and illustrious career. Although he originally planned to be a doctor, Petway turned to professional baseball instead and made a name for himself as one of the best catchers ever. (Photograph courtesy of NoirTech Research, Inc.)

Though he originally planned to be a doctor, even getting accepted and attending Meharry Medical College for two years, Petway quit college in 1906 to begin his professional baseball career. He became one of the best catchers in the game, relying on his strong arm and superb defense. An example of just how strong an arm he had can be found in a 1910 exhibition series in Cuba against the Detroit Tigers. In that series Petway threw out Ty Cobb three times in three straight attempts. He also hit .390 against the Tigers. In another contest he threw out a runner leading off second base with what the reporter called a "mauser shot." The runner could not believe that anyone could throw like that and he even refused to leave the field until the umpire convinced him that Petway did indeed catch him that easily.[138]

After starting with the

Philadelphia Giants, Petway came to Chicago when Foster invited him in 1909. He stayed with Foster's club until 1920, when Foster gave him a chance to manage the new Detroit Stars. During the winter months Petway continued to play in Cuba, California and Florida.

Petway spent some time away from the game in 1914 and 1915 after he strained a ligament in his throwing arm. He returned to the Giants for the latter games in the 1915 season. In his absence Jones had taken care of the primary catching duties and had done quite well, but Petway's defense and strong arm had been sorely missed while he was out.

Petway knew how to call a game and enjoyed the confidence of his pitchers while he played. His durability kept him in the game over twenty seasons and he hit .254 over that time span. Petway, rather than Archer of the Chicago Cubs, is credited by some as being the catcher who taught so many others how to throw down to second without getting up.[139]

Petway married Emma Jefferson in 1919. They did not have any children but Petway had plenty of family, having grown up with four brothers and three sisters. After he stopped playing baseball in 1926 he managed an apartment complex in Chicago for fifteen years.[140]

Melvin "Putt" Powell

Born May 30, 1908, Edwards, MS; died February 1985, Chicago, IL

Mel Powell played in the 1934 East-West game for the American Giants. He also pitched for the other local Chicago clubs, including the Palmer House All Stars and the Brown Bombers.

Willie "Piggie" Powell

Willie Powell helped the American Giants to two World Series championships in 1926 and 1927. He pitched five games in the Series, winning two and losing one. Powell made the papers again in 1928 for an event that had nothing to do with baseball; he was shot by his father-in-law late in the season. The news report did not give any details as to what caused the shooting or how Powell faired.[141]

Marvin Price

Born April 5, 1933, Chicago, IL

Marvin Price began his professional baseball career as possibly the youngest player on a Negro League team. He traveled with the Chicago

American Giants in 1946 when he had barely turned 14 years old. Jimmie Crutchfield saw Price playing at Washington Park and encouraged the Giants' owner, J. B. Martin, to call Price and invite him to tryout. When Price showed up, Quincy Trouppe, the manager, thought he was a new bat-boy, at first. Price played only a short time with Chicago before heading back to finish school.

After graduating at sixteen, Price caught on with the Cleveland franchise before spending a year with Newark. After that he returned home to Chicago for two seasons and then went into the military in 1952–53. When he came back from the service Price got his chance to play in the white leagues, starting with the Texas League in San Antonio.

Price played first base during his career and established a strong reputation as a hitter. He displayed a good deal of power and could hit for average as well. In 1951 the *Chicago Defender* reported he hit .390 for the Giants that season.

Alexander "Alec" Radcliffe

Alexander "Alec" Radcliffe was born July 26, 1905, in Memphis, Tennessee. The brother of fellow Negro Leaguer Ted "Double Duty" Radcliffe, Alexander Radcliffe earned the repute as one of black baseball's finest third basemen, leading the Negro American League in home runs in 1944 and 1945. Alec lacked the showmanship of his elder brother (by three years), but was a solid .300 plus hitter for his career and had a very strong arm. Radcliffe appeared in eleven East-West All-Star Games, including seven straight, from 1933 to 1939. According to his manager, Dave Malarcher, "Radcliffe, in my estimation, became one of the truly great third basemen in baseball history."[142] Radcliffe did face his older brother Ted and the Pittsburgh Crawfords in 1932 as a member of the Chicago American Giants. Ted pitched a two-hitter, only to lose 1–0, due to a home run hit by his younger brother Alec.[143]

Radcliffe is best remembered as the slugger of the Chicago American Giants in 1936–39, 1941–44, and again in 1949. With his massive 40-ounce bat, Radcliffe set the record for most at bats and hits in the East-West All-Star game, and finished second behind Buck Leonard in RBIs. Radcliffe also played for the Chicago Giants and Cole's American Giants, as well as the Chicago Palmer House All Stars in 1940, serving as manager for the Illinois state semipro champions, which also included former American Giants stars such as Jack Marshall, Dick Byas, Norm Cross, Johnny Bissant, and Norm Lloyd.[144] After retiring from baseball, Radcliffe owned and operated a bar in Chicago, with his brother, Double Duty, serving as one of the bartenders.[145]

One anecdote exemplifying the historic prominence of Radcliffe was his matchup with the great Satchel Paige of the Kansas City Monarchs in July of 1944. While playing with the Chicago American Giants at Comiskey Park in the second game of a Sunday doubleheader, Radcliffe took advantage of Paige's long-timed windup and stole home. Monarchs manager Frank Duncan and secretary William "Dizzy" Dismukes (who was a former submarine-style pitcher of the Indianapolis ABCs) played both games under protest because of the Giants using Radcliffe at third base and Willie Wells, Jr., at shortstop, claiming that Radcliffe was still the property of the Cincinnati Clowns and that they could not loan a player to a team and take him back. Wells was with the Memphis Red Sox and they could not play because there was no formal notice of any such trade. Wells was hitless in four official at-bats in the doubleheader.[146]

Alec Radcliffe played third base for the Chicago American Giants for a number of years and was elected to 13 East-West Games. He hit .340 and drove in nine runs in those contests. (Photograph courtesy of NoirTech Research, Inc.)

After several years of semipro play with various clubs, his professional debut came in 1932 with the American Giants. Radcliffe committed an error in the first inning, drawing the immediate ire of coach Sam Crawford. Radcliffe remembers Crawford yelling from the dugout, "That boy will never make it." Though he was discouraged by such negativity, Radcliffe managed two hits that game, which prompted manager Dave Malarcher to assure Radcliffe that the error was meaningless and the young Radcliffe had plenty of potential.[147] Plenty of potential is a severe understatement, as Radcliffe is viewed as being among the top third basemen of all time, regardless of skin color or nationality. He enjoyed a stellar career as a brilliant defender at third base and was always able to hit for average and power. What most indicates his superior play was his selection and heroic performances in eleven East-West All-Star games. From 1933 to 1939, Radcliffe represented the American Giants by hitting for a .379 batting average. After a three-year hiatus from the all-star game, Radcliffe retuned once again in 1943 with the Giants. The following three years, from 1944 to 1946, Radcliffe played as a Cincinnati Clown. In his eleven appearances at the East-West All-Star game, Radcliffe batted an amazing .341, further showcasing his batting prowess against the elite pitchers of the league.[148] If there is any one way players can distinguish themselves from their peers, performing brilliantly in the showcase of the elite in the league is the way to do it.

By Michael Harkness-Roberto

Lawrence Glenn Hope "Lefty" Raines

Born March 9, 1930, St. Albans, WV;
died January 28, 1978, Lansing, MI

Lefty Raines came into the Negro Leagues in the later years but still was voted by the fans to play in the 1952 East-West All-Star game for Chicago.

Ulysses "Hickey" Redd

Born November 13, 1914, Baton Rouge, LA

Ulysses Redd started his baseball career in 1940 with the Birmingham Black Barons. What looked like a promising career got interrupted by the start of World War II. When he returned from the war, Redd played basketball and baseball for the Harlem Globetrotters. He stayed with them for nearly four years and then spent his final season, in 1951, with the Chicago American Giants. Redd had the chance to play alongside stars such as Parnell Woods, Dan Bankhead, Willie Wells and Theolic Smith.

After his ballplaying days ended, Redd worked for the United States Postal Service until he retired in 1982. He took on the steady work because he and his wife were raising a family and she wanted him home more often than he could be if he was playing basketball and baseball.

Richard "Dick" "Cannonball" Redding

Born 1891, Atlanta, GA; died 1948, Islip, NY

Looking at the roster of the opposing team, the last name a batter wanted to see in the pitcher's spot was Dick "Cannonball" Redding. Redding had seven no-hitters during one season in his career and in one he struck out 17 batters. According to at least one source he may have had as many as thirty no-hitters during his career, a phenomenal number. Redding was one of the hardest throwers in the league, who struck out hitters with great regularity.

Redding spent his career with a number of teams, including the Lincoln Giants, the Philadelphia Giants and the Chicago American Giants. After losing too often to the hard-throwing right-hander, Foster convinced Redding to join his club in 1917. He joined a roster that included the likes of John Henry "Pop" Lloyd, Pete Hill, Bingo DeMoss and Bruce Petway. During one stellar outing that year Redding showed why Foster wanted him on his roster. He beat Dizzy Dismukes and the Indianapolis ABCs 1–0. Not only did he pitch superbly but Redding also knocked in Lloyd with a single in the fourth to score the only run of the game. He left to serve in World War I shortly thereafter.

After the war Redding returned to baseball with the Bacharach Giants and then the Brooklyn Royal Giants. He finally retired from managing in 1938. While managing the Royal Giants, one of his players was future Hall of Famer Buck Leonard.

Wilson "Frog" Redus

Born January 29, 1905, Muskogee, OK;
died March 23, 1979, Tulsa, OK

When Candy Jim Taylor took over as manager of the Chicago American Giants in 1937 he found a club with a number of returning stars. He chose Wilson Redus to be his right-hand man and first base coach. Redus would retain that role as long as Taylor managed the ball team. Redus started his baseball career in 1924 with the St. Louis Stars, then joined the American Giants in 1935 along with Quincy Trouppe. Taylor wanted him in the outfield with Turkey Stearnes. Owner Robert Cole bought the services of Redus and Trouppe to help strengthen his club.[149] Redus rewarded Cole's judgment in 1936 and 1937 by being elected to the All Star games.

Cole wanted Redus because of his baseball knowledge, his speed and his bat. When he played in St. Louis he got the chance to learn from some of the best, Mule Suttles and Willie Wells. In 1940, when Taylor left the Giants, Redus took over the managerial reins and took his ball club to New Orleans for spring training.[150]

Donald "Soup" Reeves

Soup Reeves played for the American Giants and in 1940 the fans elected him to the All Star Game where he went 0–4 at the plate. At times,

Reeves starred at the plate, as he did in a 9–4 victory over a club from Council Bluffs. In that game Reeves had three hits, including a home run and a double to help the Giants. He led the Giants in 1940 with home runs. In 1939 the Giants won a series from the Memphis Red Sox and Reeves was the hitting and fielding star. He hit a grand slam home run in one of the games and then he robbed Charter of a triple with a one-handed grab at the fence. The Giants beat St. Louis 7–4 with seven runs, all coming in the fourth inning. Reeves had the big hit, a line drive double that knocked in two runs to tie the score.[151]

Harold "Lefty" Rhodes

Harold Rhodes played for the American Giants in the 1940s though his career was abbreviated because of World War II. He generally pitched for the Giants but also could play first base when needed. He finished the 1949 season with a 5–5 record and Double Duty Radcliffe decided that was enough to bring him back for his final season in 1950. One of Rhodes highlights came in 1948 when he beat the Indianapolis Clowns 1–0 in a twelve inning complete game. In addition to pitching the whole contest, Rhodes singled in the winning run in the twelfth inning.[152]

Edward Rile

Ed Rile pitched a one hit shutout over the St. Louis Stars in 1923 as one of his best outings of the season. He also struck out nine batters and Cristobal Torriente scored the only run he needed in the first inning. He walked and Brown drove him in with a triple to center.[153]

John Ritchey

John Ritchey had a short career with the Chicago American Giants in the 1940s before going out west to play for San Diego in the Pacific Coast League. The Cubs gave him a brief look at the end of the 1947 season before Ritchey decided to return to the West Coast. He had gotten his chance with the Chicago ball club because he had a friend on the team who got him a tryout. He also played for Portland, Vancouver, San Francisco and Sacramento during his seven year PCL career.

Ritchey's only season in the Negro Leagues was his rookie year of 1947 with the Giants. He hit .381 to lead the league as a rookie and then he returned home to play in the Pacific Coast League. Ritchey served in the signal corps during World War II after having spent one year at San Diego State College. His goal after baseball and college was to become a lawyer.[154]

Haywood Rose

Haywood Rose seems to have had a short career, playing only one season with the Leland Giants in 1907.

Tommy Sampson

Born August 31, 1912, Calhoun, AL

Tommy Sampson played for two championship teams in his career. The Birmingham Black Barons won the Negro American League (NAL) pennant in 1943 and 1944. Unfortunately, they lost the World Series both years to the powerful Homestead Grays. Sampson did not actually play in the 1944 series due to an automobile accident shortly before the series got underway. He spent the whole winter recuperating from his injuries.

Sampson played on a Birmingham club alongside Piper Davis in the infield. As a second baseman Sampson excelled in the field and his play earned him four consecutive trips to the East-West Classic. In the 1943 game, Sampson drove in the West's key run in a 2–1 victory over the East.

After many years with the Barons, Sampson spent the 1948 season with the New York Cubans and then finished his career with the American Giants in 1949, when he hit around .252. After finishing his baseball career he spent the rest of his life working a variety of jobs, including painting and construction work.

Charles "Lefty" Shields

Charles Shields pitched for the American Giants from 1941 to 1943. One of the highlights of his career came in 1942 when he got the nod to start against the Monarchs and the great Satchel Paige. The doubleheader was set up as a benefit for the South Side Boys Club. The group was chosen because Willard Brown of the Monarchs had once been a member of the club.[155]

Willie Simms

Born December 23, 1908, Shreveport, LA

Willie Simms played most of his career as a member of the famed Kansas City monarchs although he did spend three years with the Chicago American Giants. For much of his playing time he batted leadoff and used his excellent speed to create havoc for the opposing teams.

Simms started his baseball career on the sandlots around his hometown and eventually worked his way up to some of the local sawmill teams.

He got a late start in the Negro Leagues, being nearly thirty when he went to Cincinnati to play in 1936. He joined the Monarchs for his first stint with them in 1937 and then again in 1941. Simms spent the three seasons between 1937 and 1941 playing for the Giants in Chicago.

Simms' best memories of baseball all seem to revolve around his base stealing abilities. He tried to steal every chance he got, since that was why he got to play. Simms did not hit for power but he could steal that extra base. He could also field and throw, so he got his chances to play.

Herbert H. "Briefcase" Simpson
Born August 29, 1920, Hornville, LA

A left handed hitter, Herb Simpson appears to have hit over .300 for his career in the Negro Leagues and beyond. He played in the outfield and at first base. He generally hit in the heart of the batting order even though he had little power at the plate. He was a line drive hitter who could stretch a single into a double just about every time he hit. His ability to get on base and create havoc kept him in the lineup wherever he played.

Simpson started with Birmingham in 1941, left to serve in World War II in 1943 and, after he returned, he hooked up with the Globetrotters baseball squad in 1947. After a season of barnstorming Simpson joined the roster of the American Giants in the Negro American League (NAL). He remembers hitting .308 with the Giants while playing both first base and patrolling the outfield. He covered a lot of ground with his speed and helped his pitchers out of a number of jams by running down balls that looked like sure base hits. He finished his career in 1951 with the Giants.

Bazz Owen Smaulding
Born September 30, 1899, Fort Griffin, TX; died 1964

Bazz Smaulding grew up in Albuquerque, New Mexico, where he lived with his parents, sister and five brothers. He played a variety of sports while in high school until his graduation in 1919. Smaulding was not the only athlete in his family, as his brother Al went on to some boxing fame, fighting at least four matches with Sam Langford. Owen ran track and field, played football and basketball at the high school, and played sandlot baseball with the Albuquerque Grays. He helped his 1917 high school football team to an undefeated season, playing fullback most of the time. In a game against Santa Fe, Albuquerque won 101–0 and Smaulding scored seven touchdowns. In another victory Albuquerque beat Menaul 28–0 and three of the team's four touchdowns were scored by Smaulding.[156]

Gilkerson Union Giants of 1932. Bazz Owen Smaulding is second from the right in the front row. Pictured in the back row are (from left) Gill, Perry Hall, Akers, Martin, Clarence Coleman, Morris and Page. In the front row are (from left) Hicks, Alejandro Rogelio Crespo, Daniels, Smaulding and Saunders. (Photograph from the Bazz Owen Smaulding collection, Image no. 33571, New Mexico State Records Center and Archives, Santa Fe, New Mexico.)

In track and field Smaulding regularly led all performers with high scores at most track meets. For example, in one meet he qualified for so many finals that the officials were not sure he would be able to compete in them all. In another contest he won the 100 yard dash, the shot put, the pole vault, the 120 yard hurdles, the high jump, the running broad jump and the 220 yard hurdles. His athleticism helped him excel in so many different sports. In another meet held at the university he actually bested all the athletes present and set one state record. His high school seasons got interrupted in 1918 when he entered the U. S. Army for a short stint of five months. This delayed his graduation from 1918 to 1919.

Pitching for the Albuquerque Grays, the Aq Railroaders and the local Santa Fe nine, Smaulding gained a reputation as a solid, steady performer on the mound. He also handled the bat well and often helped his own cause with his hitting. In one article a reporter described his pitching in the following fashion, "Smaulding gave a near 100-proof exhibition of the moundsman's art."[157] In a contest against the Grays, Smaulding twirled for the Aq's and helped his team to a 4–3 victory. He gave up nine hits but also had to pitch out of a number of jams caused by his club's six errors. He struck out eight and walked only one to help himself out. In an 11–10 victory over the Grays, Smaulding played shortstop and went 4–6 at the plate with two runs scored. He also made two errors in the field, as part of the Aq's nine errors.

Smaulding played baseball and ran track at the University of Washington and then played baseball and football at the University of Idaho, which he attended on an athletic scholarship until he graduated. The University of Idaho played in the Pacific Coast League and during one season they defeated the University of Montana four straight times to take the lead in the league standing. They solidified their lead with a big victory over the Washington State Cougars in which Smaulding scored three of the club's seven runs and went 4–5 at the plate.[158]

Smaulding played local sandlot ball as well whenever he had the chance. For example, while in Seattle he played for a well-known local club called the Queen City All Stars who billed themselves as the city's "famous colored team."[159] He pitched the Stars to a thrilling 4–3 victory in 1921 over the Puget Sound Navigation. It was the first loss of the season for the Puget Sound club. The next night the Stars lost badly to the Navigation company (16–4) and Smaulding had to come in and pitch in relief to stop the scoring.

After college he worked for a bit and then joined the Kansas City Monarchs in 1928. He pitched three innings for the Monarchs in a rout of the Rock Island team at 17–5. He moved to Chicago in 1930 to play for the American Giants and then the Gilkerson Union Giants through the 1935 season. Smaulding often pitched and when he was not on the mound he patrolled the outfield. He was listed on the Gilkerson roster as the only player on the team with a college education.

After playing in Chicago, Smaulding took up teaching and coaching at the Piney Woods School in Mississippi. After five years in the South he moved back to Chicago to help manage the Palmer House baseball team until many of the players were drafted for the Korean War. He continued to work at the Palmer House until his retirement in 1961. At the same time Smaulding also ran his own tax business. In 1961 Smaulding returned to New Mexico to be honored by his high school for his athletic achievements as AHS All-time Athlete, Class of 1919. They renamed their gymnasium in his honor as the Smaulding Center in 1977 and created a yearly award to

be given out to an outstanding high school athlete called the Owen Smaulding Award. A number of sports reporters have claimed over the years in their
articles that Owen Smaulding may be the best athlete ever produced by the
state of New Mexico. A history of the Albuquerque High School says that
"It might not be amiss to digress here to mention that there is little if any
doubt that Owen Smaulding was the greatest of all athletes produced by
the AHS or the state of New Mexico."[160]

Theolic Smith

Theolic Smith pitched for the Chicago American Giants near the end
of the Negro Leagues. In 1951 the *Chicago Defender* reported he had a 9–2
record at mid-season, giving him the fourth best record in the league at the
time. Smith was known for the speed of his fastball and his quick temper.
While playing in Mexico in 1946 he was involved in an altercation with an
umpire over a disputed call and found himself in the middle of a near riot.
He later went on to pitch for the San Diego Padres in the major leagues.[161]

Norman "Turkey" Stearnes

Born May 8, 1901, Nashville, TN;
died September 4, 1979, Detroit, MI

Turkey Stearnes debuted with the Detroit Stars in 1923, playing in
nearly seventy games and hitting over .360. Quite the debut for the rookie
outfielder. It was a promise that he would live up to during the remainder
of his career with Detroit, Chicago and Kansas City. When he quit the game
after the 1940 season he left with a career average over .350.

Though Stearnes spent the majority of his career with the Stars he did
join the Chicago American Giants from 1932 to 1935 and again in 1938 for
two games. He spent his last three seasons with the Monarchs. As a Star,
Giant and Monarch, Stearnes generally led off even though he had a fair
amount of power. His speed and his high average made him a great choice
at the top of the order. He also could hit for power when needed as well.
In a game against the Wichita Black Spudders, Chicago won 10–2 and
Stearnes drove in half the runs with two long home runs. In the second game
Stearnes went 4–5 and scored three runs to secure a 7–1 victory for Ted
Trent. In a four game series with the Homestead Grays in 1935 Stearnes hit
solo homers in each of the first three games to help the Giants gain a split
in the series.[162]

Stearnes also played during the winter months in California and south of the border. One winter found him with the Royal Giants playing for the Winter League title. He helped Satchel Paige to a big victory over the White Kings, 7–1, with three hits in a 14 hit attack while Paige only yielded three.[163]

Stearnes was elected by the fans to play in five East-West All-Star games. He went only 4–19 at the plate but did knock in two runs. Stearnes played in the first three games from 1933 to 1935 as a representative of the American Giants. He returned to the game in 1937 from the Detroit Stars and then in 1939 as a member of the Monarchs.

After his career ended Stearnes returned to Detroit, where he went to work in the rolling mills until he retired in 1964. Stearnes received the highest recognition for his play in 2000 when he was posthumously inducted into the National Baseball Hall of Fame.

Theodore "Ted" Strong

Ted Strong was a player you wanted on your team because he could play so many different positions and play them well. Strong also had a powerful bat and could hit for average. All in all, Ted Strong was a superb athlete who played in the Negro Leagues and also for the Harlem Globetrotters during the off-season.

Ted Strong grew up in Indiana and became a well-known basketball star. He even captained the Globetrotters for a time because playing baseball did not earn him enough money to sit idle for months. Playing both sports also kept him in shape for each season. His brother Othello joined him in both sports.

Strong starred for the local Indianapolis Athletics as an infielder to start his career. He got his professional start with the Chicago club and then he signed with the Kansas City Monarchs where he played for a decade. His play with the Monarchs earned him five East-West appearances playing infield and outfield. He often led the Monarchs in hitting and home runs, using his power from both sides of the plate. His best season with the Monarchs came in 1942 when he reportedly hit .392 and led the team in runs scored, runs batted in and home runs. Strong also pitched one season for the American Giants in 1936. This was the same time he started playing basketball with the Globetrotters.[164]

Unfortunately for Strong's career it seemed he often let his outside activities take away from his playing. He loved to enjoy the life of the cities he traveled to and eventually this began to take a toll on his skills and he never became the star some thought he could have. He lost three years of playing time when he served in the Navy during World War II.

Tim Samuel Strothers

Born Kansas, 1868; died August 26, 1942.

Tim Strothers caught and played first base during his career for the American Giants and Joe Green's Chicago Giants. He was a part of the famous 1909 squad that won the Chicago Baseball League championship with a record of 66–28 and 2 ties. This included fifty exhibition games as well as the league contests.[165]

Lonnie Summers

Born August 2, 1915, Davis, OK;
died August 24, 1999, Inglewood, CA

Lonnie Summers played three seasons with the American Giants as a catcher and outfielder between 1948 and 1949 and again in 1951. He played a total of twelve seasons in the league and spent four years serving during World War II. Summers also played a number of winters in the Mexican League, hitting consistently in the .290s. In 1949 and again in 1951 Summers was elected by the fans to the All Star game, where he went 1–4 at the plate.

In 1952 Summers got the chance to play with San Diego in the Pacific Coast League. He ended his baseball career in 1954 with Yakima in the Northwest League.

George "Mule" Suttles

Born March 31, 1900, Brockton, LA;
died July 9, 1966, Newark, NJ

Mule Suttles could hit a ball a country mile, as the saying goes. When he approached the plate fans would yell "Kick, Mule, Kick" in anticipation of what heroic feat he might perform. He delighted fans for over thirty years, playing in the Negro Leagues beginning in 1918. One news reporter called him part of the Royal Giants' "murderers' row" in 1937, while another referred to him as the "Brown Babe Ruth."

Suttles remained a fan favorite during his career, and elected him on five different occasions to the East-West All-Star Classic at Comiskey Park. In 1933, during the inaugural contest, Suttles placed his name in the history books by cracking the first home run in all-star history. He hit a three-run blast off Pittsburgh's Sam Streeter. He hit another homer in the 1935 game to break open a tie in the eleventh inning to give the West an 11–8 victory. He went 7–17 with two homers and six RBIs while also walking six times. Opposing pitchers did not want to see Mule coming to the plate at any time.

Willie Foster pitched brilliantly in a game against the New York Cubans, which Chicago won 10–5. He got all the help he needed with two monster home runs from Suttles. Suttles helped Foster win another contest over the Brooklyn Eagles when he hit a two run homer. He followed that in the second game with a grand slam home run to give the Giants a 9–5 victory behind the strong pitching of Willie Cornelius.[166]

In a 1935 exhibition game Suttles rewarded the fans in the sixth inning against Des Moines. Suttles came up with two runners on base and smacked a ball beyond the center field fence. Chicago won the game 14–1. In the second contest the fans again wanted to see the Mule hit the long ball but he only tripled. Then in the tenth, with two runners on, the opposing pitcher walked him rather than take the chance and the fans booed. Fans came out whenever Suttles played because his reputation preceded him and they wanted to see him wallop the ball. His shots became legendary over the years, like the time he hit a

Mule Suttles played in five East-West games during his baseball career. He hit two home runs, including the first one ever in the inaugural game in 1933. He played for the American Giants in the 1930s with Turkey Stearnes and Willie Wells. (Photograph courtesy of NoirTech Research, Inc.)

double in a game against Kansas City that hit off the left field wall and bounced all the way back to the infield because he hit it so hard. True or not, this is what the fans came out hoping to see. In a four game series with the Pittsburgh Crawfords the Giants split the series with Willie Cornelius winning two games. He won the first game 1–0 on a monstrous home run by the Mule. It was all the hitting needed.[167]

Though a big man and a powerful hitter, Suttles came across as a gentle giant. He hit with a 50-ounce bat that looked more like a giant club. It was his hitting that earned him his fame but he could handle the plays at the first base bag as well. While he may not have had the grace of some others, he caught everything thrown his way and even showed off some excellent coverage in the outfield for a big man. Rarely did anything get hit by him.

In addition to his years in the Negro Leagues Suttles played in California and in Cuba. During two winters in Cuba in 1928–29 and 1929–30 he hit for average and led the league in home runs. Out west Suttles played against a variety of big leaguers where he reportedly hit .378 with 64 home runs in just 450 at bats.

Suttles played for a number of teams during his career, including the Birmingham Black Barons, the St. Louis Stars, the Baltimore Black Sox, the Detroit Wolves and the Newark Eagles. He also toiled with the New York Black Yankees, the Washington Pilots, the Indianapolis ABCs and Cole's American Giants out of Chicago. He managed the Eagles and spent many quality years with the St. Louis club.

While with the Washington Pilots, Suttles helped them defeat a group of former major leaguers 7–3 as he hit a double, triple and home run to lead the way.[168] He helped his Newark Eagles team defeat the Black Senators 7–5 without a single hit. In this contest the opposing pitcher, Yokeley, walked Suttles each time he came to bat; it was left to his teammates to drive him and they did. This illustrated how much pitchers feared facing the big man at the plate.[169] Suttles helped the Philadelphia Royal Giants defeat the San Diego Farleys 13–4 with two home runs and four RBIs. He had not played in two weeks because of illness but immediately came back and made up for lost time. Two years earlier Suttles helped the Royal Giants win the winter league title with an 8–3 victory over Pirrone's Café. He had two home runs to lead the hitting attack.[170]

George Alexander Sweatt
Born December 12, 1893; died July 19, 1983

A strong-hitting outfielder, George Sweatt joined the American Giants in 1926 and 1927, playing for them in the World Series both years. He brought with him a lot of experience, having played in the 1924 and 1925 series with the Monarchs.

After his playing career ended Sweatt took advantage of his college education and taught sixth grade and physical education in Coffeyville, Kansas. Sweatt graduated from Pittsburgh, Kansas Normal College. He played baseball, basketball, and football and ran track and field while attending the school. He also worked for the United States Postal Service until he retired in 1957.[171]

In 1957 Sweatt received a watch in honor of his baseball achievements from the Oldtyme Baseball Players Association. Joe Green made the presentation as an officer of the organization.

Danger Talbert

Danger Talbert played for the early Chicago ball clubs. In 1913 Rube Foster arranged to have a benefit game held for him. Two teams of nine were chosen from the four African American clubs in the city at the

George Sweatt played for the American Giants in the 1926 and 1927 World Series. He came to Chicago from Kansas City. Sweatt graduated from college and later went on to teach and coach. (Photograph courtesy of NoirTech Research, Inc.)

time. Foster's group lost 6–0 but they raised $300 to help Talbert with medical expenses.

Samuel "Sam" Thompson

A right-handed pitcher from Oklahoma, Sam Thompson joined the American Giants staff in 1942. He brought with him a lot of experience, having pitched for a number of years with the Philadelphia Stars. Thompson developed a reputation with the hitters as a pitcher with a lot of speed and a wicked curve ball. Candy Jim Taylor signed Thompson to help bolster a staff anchored by Leroy Sutton.[172]

Cristobal Torriente

Cristobal Torriente was born November 16, 1893, in Cuba. He is remembered throughout the United States as the home run king of baseball outside of the two major leagues, prompting his nickname as "the Babe Ruth of Cuba" as well as the "Cuba Strongman." Torriente was light skinned enough that he could have "passed" as a white player, except that he had frizzy hair. Torriente's career began with Tinti Molina's New York Cuban Stars in 1913, which barnstormed against the best black and semipro teams in the East and Midwest, but he is best remembered as a member of Rube Foster's Chicago American Giants (1919–1925) that dominated the Negro National League, moving Hall of Famer Oscar Charleston out of center field and into left.[173] The 1919 American Giants outfield consisting of Torriente, Charleston, and Jimmy Lyons is regarded as the fastest and best defensive outfield in Negro Leagues history. With the lefty power hitter leading the way, the Giants won the league championship three years in a row from 1920 to 1922. Torriente won the batting title in 1920 with a .411 average, which was followed up with averages of .338 and .342 the next two championship years.

Torriente was able to hit to all fields and was viewed as the solitary true power hitter in the legendary Giants lineup. He was also known for his bracelets, which he shook before going to bat, and a red bandana around his neck for his Cuban club, the *Rojos*, or Reds.[174] He also had a brutal temper that was rivaled by few players in any league. His rocky relationship with Sam Crawford, then a pitcher with the Chicago American Giants, was well known. In one instance, Torriente, while playing with the Cuban Stars in 1915, attempted to steal third base on Crawford and was called out by the umpire. Torriente exploded in anger, kicking the umpire, which Crawford responded to by punching Torriente in the mouth. Their opponents threw debris at the Giants players during the fray, which was eventually halted by police. The Giants prevailed 3–1, followed by another fracas between Torriente and Crawford, which was stopped by Rube Foster before any player was seriously injured.[175] Another incident showcasing the brazenness of Torriente was his brawl, once again, with current manager Crawford. Crawford was viewed by many as a strict authoritarian who did not allow his players to drink and strictly enforced a curfew. Few players had the bravado to truly challenge Crawford until Torriente did in a 1917 Detroit-Chicago American Giants game. The ensuing fight lasted twenty-five minutes on the field and continued even after the players left the ballpark. The brawl did not end until hours later, when both men were arrested for throwing bricks at one another.[176] One may believe that this was merely an extension of the fracas that started nearly two years earlier between two colorful personalities that never seemed to mesh.

Torriente's love of the nightlife led to his dismissal via trade by Foster

in 1925, when his batting production dipped as well. Torriente was traded for George Alexander Sweatt (who would become one of only two players to perform in all four of the Negro World Series played during the 1920s, playing in 1924–25 with the Kansas City Monarchs and in 1926–27 with the Chicago American Giants).[177] In 1926, as a member of the Kansas City Monarchs, Torriente led the Monarchs to a first-half league title with a .381 batting average, followed by a .407 average in the play-offs against his former American Giants teammates, eventually losing in seven games.[178] Torriente would also make a stop with the Gilkerson Union Giants, based in Spring Valley, Illinois, that spent most of the summer months traveling throughout the Midwest playing various league teams. This union was a vital foundation of talent for the leagues, as many of the members were independent.[179]

Cristobal Torriente came north to play in the Negro Leagues and starred for a number of ball clubs, including the American Giants from 1919 to 1925. He won the batting title in 1920 with a .411 average. (Photograph courtesy of NoirTech Research, Inc.)

Torriente died April 11, 1938, of tuberculosis (complications of alcoholism) in Bronx, New York, and was buried April 15 at Calvary Cemetery in Queens, New York. The burial line on his death certificate first listed City Cemetery (Potters Field) but this was crossed out and replaced with Calvary.[180] To the contrary, another report confirmed that Torriente's remains were disinterred from the Calvary Cemetery and sent to Cuba in the early 1940s. The head of the sports commission, Jaime Marine, obtained the approval and funding from the Batista government (then in power in Cuba) to have Torriente's remains transported from the U.S. and buried in heroic fashion, draped with the Cuban flag, at Colon Cemetery in Havana.[181]

By Michael Harkness-Roberto

Harold Treadwell

Harold Treadwell joined the American Giants pitching staff in 1923 after leaving the Bacharach Giants. Chicago fans were glad to acquire his services for their side since most remembered him from the 20 inning game with the Bacharachs in 1922. In another game with the Giants, Treadwell beat Foster's crew 3–2. In his first game to start the 1924 season Treadwell sprained a tendon in his arm, which kept him out of the early season. His arm never really recovered and in 1925 Foster sent him to Indianapolis.[182]

Theodore "Ted" Trent

Ted Trent was born Theodore Trent on December 17, 1903, in Jacksonville Florida. Among other aliases Trent went by were Big Florida and Stringbean, most likely ascribed in reference to his hometown in Jacksonville and his size as a ballplayer.[183] Trent stood at a staggering six feet three inches and weighed in at one hundred eighty-five pounds. Between his height, which translated into extra size standing on a pitcher's mound, and his weight, Trent was surely a force to be reckoned with.[184] Trent's career, lasting about thirteen years, was filled with splendor. With many different pitches in his arsenal and his ability at the plate, Trent lived up to all the hype surrounding him.

As far as can be determined, Trent's career began in 1924, when he played nonprofessionally in St. Augustine, Florida. Following this he played for Bethune-Cookman College, where he was most noted for helping to beat Clark University in Daytona Beach in 1926. This same year, Jimmie Reel, manager of the West Palm Beach Giants, scouted Trent and managed to get him to join his team, where he was successful in a rather quick time span. This led Reel, along with another man by the name of Marty Clark, to recommend that Trent play for the St. Louis Stars, where he officially started his professional career in 1927.[185]

Trent's career with the Stars started off strong as he pitched a 21 and 2 season his second year on the team. In 1930 he led the Stars to their second pennant winning season in a row, again winning the pennant in 1931.[186] However, while Trent seemed to be on top of the world playing for the Stars and performing exceedingly well his first half decade in the Negro Leagues, the Negro National League, which was the league the Stars were in, fell apart due to lack of money, mainly because of the Great Depression. For this reason, Trent spent the next five years floating from team to team simply to make a living the best he could.

He began his five-year hop with the Washington Pilots in 1932, where he didn't spend even one year with the team. He followed up that time with the Detroit Wolves again in 1932. Trent played for two more teams that same year, the Homestead Grays and the Kansas City Monarchs. This kind of changing was not unusual, as money was not always easy to make and players had to do what they needed to in order to make money and survive. Between 1933 and 1935 Trent slowed his travel somewhat, playing for only two teams, the Chicago American Giants and the New York Black Yankees. In 1936 Trent finally settled down with one team, the Chicago American Giants, which he played for until 1939 when his career ended due to health reasons. One of the highlights of his years in Chicago came in an 8–0 victory over the Mexicans when he held a no-hitter into the ninth inning and finally gave up a lone single to Marco.[187]

Trent's career, while lasting only a little over a decade, nevertheless was filled with accomplishment. On several occasions, he played in all-star games against white pro teams. "In 1930, Trent defeated a white all-star team composed of stars like Lefty O'Doul, Bill Terry, Paul Waner, Dick Bartell, and Billy Herman, 5–0."[188] He beat another white all-star team his last season with the Stars, 18–6, striking out 16 players.[189] Trent pitched in both halves of a doubleheader against the local Mills team, which had two former major leaguers pitching for them. He relieved Willie Cornelius in the first game and took the loss, while coming back in the second to beat Phil Collins 3–2. He also knocked in the winning run with a long triple. In addition to beating several white all-star teams, Trent played in several East-West All-Star games, including the one in 1934 in which he pitched three shutout innings to begin the game.[190]

Trent had several pitches in his repertoire that made him a spectacular ballplayer. He displayed a versatility that not too many players possessed. He had a good fastball, a nice slider, and three curve balls.[191] Cool Papa Bell said that Trent was "'the fastest pitcher [he] saw until [he] saw

Satchel,'" even adding that "'[he] wouldn't say Satchel was better than him.'"[192] One source contends that Trent's best year was his 1936 year, that he was 29–5 and batted .308; however, Larry Lester contends that his best year was in 1928, when "he posted a 21–2 record, and won three more games in the playoff against the Chicago American Giants, defeating Willie Foster in the final."[193]

As successful as Ted Trent's life was, it came to a bittersweet end at the age of forty, just four short years after he retired, his death attributed to his heavy drinking and the fact that he contracted TB. Trent no doubt could have had an even longer career had it not been for the drinking and the disease; but, even so, he posted a career 94–49 record over his twelve years in the Negro Leagues. It was a tragic end for such a young man and quality player as Trent; however, no matter what end he met, nothing can take away the fact that his career was filled with spectacular pitching, unimaginable victories against white all-star teams, and a career record that can't be ignored.

By Jason Norris

Ted Trent had one of the best curveballs in the game and he brought that expertise to the American Giants from 1936 to 1939. He played in four East-West games, from 1934 to 1937, pitching eleven innings and striking out five. (Photograph courtesy of NoirTech Research, Inc.)

Thomas "Highpockets" Turner

Born June 22, 1915, Olive Branch, TN

Tom Turner played sports all his life. He loved all athletic competition and passed that love on to the athletes he coached. His career started in baseball playing for his father's club as their second baseman. In high school he took up pitching and then, after graduation in Glendale, Ohio, he attended Tuskegee Institute for two years. He went there with the intention of playing football but the coach thought him too small to play.

In 1936 he began playing baseball in the Indiana-Ohio League. He played shortstop for four years before being drafted during World War II. He started playing first base on his service team and also played football and basketball. After the war Turner got an offer to play in Mexico and he played under manager Bob Lemon for the Hermosillo club. He stayed until

Thomas Turner (right) played first base for the American Giants in 1947. He went on to play on local ball clubs in southern Ohio for many years and coached in the area until 1996. (Photograph courtesy of Leslie A. Heaphy.)

1947 and then returned with his new wife to Ohio. He got an offer then to join the Chicago American Giants for $400 a month, so he went right after his daughter was born.

Turner spent only about four months with the Giants because they needed to make some budget cuts around mid-season. While with Chicago he hit around .332. However, Candy Jim Taylor told Turner they needed to cut him back to only $200, which Turner knew he could not take and still feed his family. He returned home, got a job and kept playing ball. He caught on initially with a local club called the Valley Tigers, which he played with and managed until 1954. He did get three offers for major league try-outs but none of them ever amounted to anything. He continued to coach at the local level until 1996.[194]

Roberto "Lefty" Vargas

Born May 29, 1929, Santurce, PR

Lefty Vargas came north to play in the Negro Leagues and pitched for the American Giants in the late 1940s and early 1950s. His skills got him elected by the fans to the All Star game in 1948.

Herman Warren

Herman Warren grew up in a church family, with his father as pastor of the Church of God in Evanston, Illinois. He and his brother Howard played baseball growing up and Herman tried to make a career of it. He played for the Evanston Giants and Joe Green's Chicago Giants. He also showed his athletic knowledge by managing the Evanston Wolverine football squad. In 1934 Warren won the 100 yard dash at the Chicago World's Fair, beating out Pug Rentner from Northwestern in the finals.

In 1941 Warren left behind Chicago and baseball to move to California to find employment. He went to work for the Pacific Parachute Company and eventually became its general manager.[195]

Willie "The Devil" Wells

Born August 10, 1904, Shawnee, OK;
died January 22, 1989, Austin, TX

A Hall of Fame shortstop, Willie Wells gained fame with Cole's American Giants in the mid–1930s and then rejoined them in 1944. He debuted in the Negro Leagues in 1925 with St. Louis and remained in the league until the end of the 1947 season. He teamed with Turkey Stearnes and other greats of the game in the mid–1930s on the roster of the Chicago American Giants.

Wells was elected to nine All Star games in his long career. He hit .325 with seven RBIs, two walks and one stolen base. He played in the first three games, representing the American Giants, and then came back in 1937–39 for the Newark Eagles. He returned his final two times in 1942 and 1945 as an Eagle.

In an exhibition game in late 1935, Wells showed the fans why Chicago had acquired him when he went 4–6 with three doubles in a 14–1 victory over Des Moines. The following month Wells went 2–4 in a 3–0 shutout over a team of barnstorming major leaguers that included Charley Gehringer and Schoolboy Rowe.[196] The Giants took a trip in the spring of 1935 to Austin, Texas, and beat the local Texas Steers 4–2 in 10 innings. Before the game began they honored hometown hero Willie Wells. A presentation was made by Dr. Givens, a local dentist. Wells then got the game off to a good start with a hit and scoring of the first run. He later made a great running catch of a line drive to keep the score tied. Mule Suttles also helped with a spectacular catch in the ninth at the base of the fence.[197]

Wells played a number of seasons south of the border and became a fan favorite there. He earned the nickname "El Diablo" while playing in Cuba. In 1935 he played for Santa Clara, enthralling the fans with his fielding, his hard hitting and his base-running.

Richard "Dick" Whitworth

Dick Whitworth pitched alongside Dick Redding for the Chicago American Giants in the second decade of the 1900s. According to the *Indianapolis Freeman* he often got solid run support in his games. He beat a club called the Ragens Colts 11–4 in one contest, with Jesse Barbour getting three hits and Bingo DeMoss stealing three bases, including home plate. He lost an earlier contest to the Cuban Stars in their ongoing rivalry to be the best colored team around. He lost 3–2 in a ten inning contest where he only gave up six hits but Padrone was even better on the winning side. He beat a team from Beloit, Wisconsin, 2–1 in which he had two hits and scored one run to help his own cause.[198]

In 1915 Whitworth helped the Giants in their effort to prove they were the best colored team in the country by shutting out the Cuban Stars. Whitworth pitched a masterful game, yielding only one hit, striking out five and walking four. His center fielder, Pete Hill, provided all the support he needed with two hits and one run scored.[199]

Foster finally let Whitworth go at the start of the 1925 season. Whitworth had been with Foster's team in the 1910s and then jumped east before joining Tenny Blount's Detroit Stars and then coming back to the Giants. Whitworth got hurt in a car accident in Indianapolis, but never fully recovered and always seemed to come back to Foster when he needed help.[200]

Frank "Red Ant" Wickware

Born 1888, Coffeyville, KS;
died November 2, 1967, Schenectady, NY

Frank Wickware was one of the early stars in black baseball. Most of his pitching career came before the creation of the Negro National League in 1920, although he pitched until 1925. Wickware got his start in 1909 with the Dallas Giants before moving on with Rube Foster and the 1910 Leland Giants. In 1915 he pitched for Chicago in the Black World Series. Wickware was mentioned in a 1915 article about three of the best pitchers in the game who could not pitch in the majors because of their color. The other two were John Donaldson and Jose Mendez.[201]

In 1916 Wickware traveled to Cuba with the American Giants for a series of games in which he dominated the Cuban opposition. He pitched a 2–0 shutout against Havana in one game. He allowed only two hits and struck out seven while walking five.[202] When the American Giants went out to California in the winter of 1915–16, Wickware enjoyed pitching against the West Coast teams. He took a no-hitter into the ninth inning of a game against the Pantages and still came away with a 4–0 shutout. He gave up only one hit, a Texas leaguer that fell between Pete Hill and Pop Lloyd. Wickware relied on the hitting of his own stars, Barber, Hill and Lloyd, to lead the Giants' scoring efforts.[203] Wickware beat another San Diego club on a three-hit shutout 4–0 and got all the run support he needed with Pete Hill's homer in the fourth inning. The Cline-Clines could not mount any real threat; even though Wickware walked six, he struck out six.[204]

Wickware's career outside of Chicago included a short stint with the Brooklyn Royal Giants and the Louisville White Sox in 1913 and 1914. He twirled for Indianapolis in 1916, the Detroit Stars in 1919 and the Lincoln Giants in 1925. In 1925 Wickware ran into a bit of trouble with the law, being accused of murdering Ben Adair in New York City. He was cleared of all the charges when the prosecution could not adequately prove its case.[205]

Frank Wickware pitched for fifteen years with a number of black teams, including the Leland Giants and American Giants. Wickware developed a reputation as a strike-out pitcher who could go the distance in every game. (Photograph courtesy of NoirTech Research, Inc.)

Maurice C. Wiggins

Born 1912, Water Valley, MS;
died March 23, 2002, Chicago, IL

At the age of twelve, Maurice Wiggins decided to leave his hometown of Water Valley, Mississippi, to move to Chicago. He wanted to visit his father, who had a barbershop on the south side of the city. He went north hoping to find a job and get an education. He attended high school through the ninth grade and then quit to start working at the Palmer House. His father had hoped to see him work at the hotel and play for the American Giants.

Wiggins married Artie Johnson in 1942, then joined the navy during World War II. He spent 23 months in the Pacific aboard the *Miami*. After the war he came back to the Palmer House to work as a waiter and to play baseball with the Palmer House All Stars. He played for a number of other local Chicago black teams, including the Gilkerson Union Giants and the Chicago Brown Bombers, all while still working at the Palmer House. When a player had a family it was sometimes easier to take a steady job and play baseball locally than to travel all over. Chicago made this possible because there were so many amateur and semipro teams, as well as industrial league clubs. After his playing days ended Wiggins and a number of other local ballplayers formed the Old Ball Players Club in 1949 to provide assistance to former players. His work at the Palmer House put him in contact with such dignitaries as President Jimmy Carter and Dr. Martin Luther King, Jr., during his nearly fifty years of service.[206]

Wiggins remained active in the local community after baseball. He was especially interested in promoting youth sports and founded the Antioch Missionary Baptist Church Athletic Association. He started his own ball playing career in a Sunday school league and wanted to provide those same opportunities for other youngsters. In 1972 Wiggins won an award from the Empire Professionals for his many years of community service.[207]

Jesse Sharon Williams

Jesse Williams played the 1944 season for the Chicago American Giants as an outfielder and first baseman.

John Williams

John Williams started at first base for the American Giants in 1944 and though a good fielder was not a strong hitter, compiling only a .234 average that season.[208]

Joseph "Smokey Joe" "Joe" Williams

Born April 6, 1886, Seguin, TX;
died February 25, 1951, New York, NY

Smokey Joe Williams had a long and distinguished baseball career. He pitched for nine different black baseball teams though his main team was the Lincoln Giants, where he played from 1911 to 1923. He got his start with the Leland Giants in 1910 and spent part of 1914 in the Windy City with the American Giants. He also twirled for the Mohawk Giants, the Atlantic City Bacharach Giants, the Hilldale Daisies, the Homestead Grays, the Detroit Wolves and the Brooklyn Royal Giants.

Williams dominated opponents easily with a hard fastball and wicked curve. Although records are incomplete it is believed that he pitched dozens of no-hitters against a range of talent and even beat five ML Hall of Fame pitchers in exhibition games. He came out on the winning side against Chief Bender, Walter Johnson, Rube Marquard, Grover Alexander and Waite Hoyt. One of the highlights of his career came in 1930 when he struck out 27 Monarchs batters in a 12 inning 1–0 shutout. In a poll taken in 1952 by the *Pittsburgh Courier,* Williams was named the "greatest pitcher" in the history of the Negro Leagues. He received further recognition with his election to the Baseball Hall of Fame in 1999.[209]

Robert "Bobby" Williams

Bobby Williams played shortstop for the Chicago American Giants and for the Santa Clara team in Cuba. In the winter of 1923 he joined the Santa Clara roster along with Oliver Marcell, and immediately the team started to climb in the standings. Williams' hitting was a big part of their rise and his numbers ensured that Rube Foster offered him another contract for the 1924 season. Williams left the Giants in 1926 along with Bingo DeMoss, who took Williams with him when he left to manage the Indianapolis ball club.

Thomas "Tom" Williams

Died January 1937, Chicago, IL

Tom Williams pitched for the Chicago American Giants in the 1910s and then again after the First World War. He helped lead the team in 1921, took time off and returned after playing ball all winter. Williams was best known for his snap throws to the bag to catch unsuspecting runners. He also could change pace with the best and had a wide assortment of pitches, including a nasty spitter. Foster once called Williams "the perfect machine twirler," because he could call pitches for Williams and he would throw exactly what was asked for every time. He also had incredible accuracy and control with his pitches. Unfortunately, after he came back from the war his pitching was never quite the same and Foster let him go at the start of the 1925 season to make room for some new, young arms.[210]

George Wilson

George Wilson starred in the early days of black baseball, making a name for himself as one of the best twirlers in the game. In 1899 and 1900 he pitched for the Chicago Columbia Giants and then in 1901 moved to the Union Giants for a couple of seasons. Sol White once compared him to the great major league pitcher Rube Waddell.

John "Jumpin' Johnny" Wilson
Born July 7, 1927, Anderson, IN

Better known as a member of the Harlem Globetrotters basketball team, Johnny Wilson did play for one year in 1949 with the Chicago American Giants. His athletic career was not all that long before he decided to go into teaching and coaching so he could be near his family.

As a youngster, basketball was Wilson's sport. He actually set the city scoring record as a sixth grader with 248 points in 13 games. He also played summer league and junior league baseball, mostly as a first baseman. His high school basketball coach, Charles Cummings, was the person responsible for making him believe he could go on to college after high school, which he did. At Anderson College he played baseball, basketball and football and ran track. Wilson was selected to the all–Indiana State College five for two straight years. His selection was based on the 515 points he scored as a freshman and the 565 points he added as a sophomore. He also broke the state scoring record both years. While still in school Wilson got a chance to try out for the White Sox but ended up playing for the Chicago American Giants. He signed with the Giants for $200 a month after hitting a pinch hit single in the tenth inning of a game against Philadelphia to win the game.[211]

Lewis Wolfolk
Born 1896, Providence, KY

Lewis Wolfolk pitched for the Chicago American Giants in the 1920s. Hailing from Kentucky, he moved to the Windy City to join Foster's club and bolstered their pitching staff with another strong right arm. He debuted in the Negro League pitching against Rogers Park and won 9–1. He gave up only two hits in his first game before being relieved by Rile and then Kenyon. The first run of the contest came with Gardner stealing two bases, including home plate. One impressive performance against the St. Louis Stars in 1923 saw Wolfolk pitching a three-hit shutout and striking out four to win 4–0.[212]

Wolfolk joined the Giants as a rookie in 1923 after playing for several years with the Providence Red Sox. When he did not pitch for the Sox he could be found in the outfield because the club wanted to keep his bat in the lineup. When he came to spring training in 1923 he immediately impressed Rube Foster with his size, speed and smarts.[213]

Parnell Woods

Parnell Woods played and managed in the Negro Leagues. Much of his career he spent in Cleveland. He managed the Buckeyes from 1942–44 after playing for the Jacksonville Red Caps and the American Giants. In fact, the Buckeyes held a day in his honor on June 25, 1944.[214] After a short stint playing ball outside the United States while in the service, Woods came back in 1948 to play third base for the Globetrotters baseball team. He joined the Strong brothers, Ted and Othello, on the Globetrotters club. The team was owned by Abe Saperstein but managed by another former Chicago player, Paul Hardy. Woods came back to Chicago in 1951 and hit .375 to take the batting crown.[215]

George Wright

George Wright played shortstop for a number of different teams during his career, including the 1909 Leland Giants. He had excellent hands and good range.

Ralph Arthur "Pepper" Wyatt

Born September 17, 1917, Chicago, IL;
died March 1990, Auburn Park, IL

Ralph Wyatt played for the famed Chicago American Giants in the 1940s, and in 1942 he joined five of his teammates on the roster for the west in that year's All Star Classic. He led the voting for all the shortstops on either squad that year. The following year he led the voting early but did not end up winning. As a result of his performance Wyatt found himself at the center of an attempt by the Homestead Grays to grab him for their team before the start of the 1943 season. At the start of the 1944 season Wyatt held out for $300 a month although the Giants were offering only $250, a $25 raise over his 1942 salary.

Candy Jim Taylor signed Wyatt to a Giants contract straight from the sandlots. Wyatt had been playing ball for the Wabash Avenue YMCA Industrial League. Taylor saw him play at Washington Park before offering him a chance as a professional ball player.[216]

Wyatt found himself on the market in 1946 after the Giants acquired a new young infielder named Clyde McNeal. When he did not like the idea of moving to the outfield, the Giants traded him to Cleveland. Wyatt had gotten himself in the doghouse in a game against Birmingham that the Giants had lost because Wyatt failed to run out a sacrifice hit and got thrown out to end a big threat. Wyatt's play seemed indicative of the Giants' overall lackadaisical style at the time and management thought they needed to shake up the team a bit.[217]

Edward "Pep" Young

Ed Young caught and played first base and the outfield for the American Giants in the late 1940s. He joined the club in 1946 after he got out of the army. In the off-season he worked in the stockyards to make ends meet. Young helped anchor a solid infield with his strong play at the first base bag.

At the plate Young had his ups and downs. In one game against a team from Council Bluffs, the Giants won 9–4 behind the hitting of Young and Donald Reeves. Young had four hits, including a homer and a double. In a come-from-behind victory against the Homestead Grays, Young tied the game in the ninth with a home run, allowing the Giants to come back in the tenth and score seven to win 9–4. Randolph Bowe picked up the save in relief of Hudson, the starter. In a losing contest with the Monarchs, Young provided the only real firepower for the Giants. They lost 6–3 and Young had a homer and a double to drive in two of the club's three tallies.[218]

4

Management and Owners

With the creation of the Leland Giants in 1905 the city of Chicago began a long tenure with black baseball that would last into the 1950s. In order to make that association possible there were many men who got involved with the various teams as owners, managers and even league personnel. What follows is an attempt to look at the contributions of some of these key figures over the years.

Frank C. Leland

Frank Leland got his start in baseball as a player himself before making his real mark as an owner in Chicago during the first two decades of the twentieth century. He played as an outfielder before starting the Unions and Chicago Unions in the late 1880s and 1890s. He combined the teams with the Columbia Giants in 1901 to start the Chicago Union Giants. Then in 1905 he founded the Leland Giants, which he managed until 1907 when he brought in a new manager. In 1910 he got in a dispute with his manager, Rube Foster, over the 1909 pennant and they split up, forming two new teams. Leland's club became the Chicago Giants and he stayed with them through 1912. Leland passed away on November 17, 1914, and is buried in Lincoln Cemetery in Chicago.

Leland was born in Memphis, Tennessee, in 1868. He graduated from Fisk University in Nashville, Tennessee, in 1886 and started playing baseball for the short-lived Washington Capital Citys in the League of Colored Baseball Clubs before playing for the Unions. After he came north to Chicago in 1887 he worked with manager William S. Peters of the Unions and then the Chicago Unions. In 1889 Leland even served in the role of umpire for the club as needed. They boasted a 100–10 record in 1896 and felt that they would be even better in 1897. Leland is shown in the team picture for the 1897 club, standing in the back in a suit and tie.[1]

Leland changed the name of his team to bear his moniker in 1905 and the club went on to win a reported 48 straight games. Their overall record was reported as 112–10. They battled the Union Giants for the championship and ended in a dead heat with two victories each and a tie in the fifth and deciding game. The club played at Seventy-ninth and Wentworth through the 1909 season. Leland had help in 1905 and 1906 from his traveling manager, William Brown, who assisted in travel arrangements and in booking games. In 1907 Leland decided to solidify his organization and incorporated the club as the "Leland Giants Base Ball and Amusement Association." In 1909 the club lost the colored championship to the St. Paul Colored Giants after Foster broke his leg and missed most of the season. When Foster returned he and Leland arranged for the club to play a four game series with the National League Chicago Cubs. They lost the series but none of the games were a runaway for the Major League stars. Mordecai Brown had the Giants number in the series and years later a news reporter wrote that when a pitcher regularly beats another they have that team's "Indian Sign." Brown had the "Indian Sign" when it came to the Giants.[2]

Leland's support of his Chicago ball clubs allowed a variety of well-known stars to develop their skills. One of his greatest pitchers was Walter Ball, who he enticed to join his club in 1903. In Leland's own records he recorded Ball sporting a 12–1 record in 1909. He brought in power hitting

This Chicago American Giants team features Rube Foster in the center of the back row. Foster came to the Giants in 1907 at the urging of Frank Leland and stayed until he became ill in 1926. (Photograph courtesy of NoirTech Research, Inc. and the National Baseball Hall of Fame, Cooperstown, New York.)

outfielder Pete Hill; his captain and first baseman, Nate Harris, who hit .255 in 1909; catchers Pete Booker and Bruce Petway; and pitchers Pat Dougherty and "Cannonball" Joe Miller. Petway was described in a 1910 article as "one of the best throwing catchers in the game today."[3]

In 1907 Leland made a decision that proved both good and bad for his club. He signed Rube Foster to the roster and made him the manager. Leland let Foster have a pretty free hand from the beginning in terms of player development. At first the two worked well together and developed the superb 1909 championship squad. Unfortunately, Foster began to feel that Leland was not sharing the proceeds fully with his players and decided to challenge his leadership. This led to the 1910 split between Foster and Leland. The problems had to be settled legally, and in the end Leland retained the right to the 1909 pennant and Foster kept the right to the team name.

Leland helped preserve the history of his involvement in the game and his various teams' stars by publishing a pamphlet entitled *Frank Leland's Chicago Giants Base Ball Club* after the 1910 season. It chronicled the history of Chicago baseball from 1887 to 1910. In addition to short biographies on the star players, Leland included statistics and photographs taken by Peter P. Jones, a local studio photographer. For legal advice Leland relied mainly on the expertise of local attorney Louis B. Anderson, who served the city in a variety of capacities. To ensure that his players got paid in a timely fashion, Leland employed the services of Al H. Garrett as his treasurer.[4]

In addition to his work in baseball Leland served as a clerk of the criminal court, a clerk for the circuit court, a deputy sheriff and on the board of the county commissioners for Cook County. Leland also used his ball club to help raise money for good causes. For example, in 1909 they played the Cuban Stars to help raise money for Provident Hospital. Over 5,000 fans came out for the doubleheader and $2,500 was raised for the hospital.[5]

After the split with Foster, Leland tried to keep his team alive. Unlike Foster, Leland did not enjoy a long tenure with the new teams. He died in 1914. He did, however, bring a number of other local Chicago businessmen and politicians into the baseball world. One of the men he worked with for the incorporation of the Amusement venture was Beauregard Moseley.

Beauregard Moseley

Ambition is a powerful motivator, causing people to work harder to achieve their view of success. Beauregard Moseley was one such individual. He wanted to be a success at everything he turned his hand to, whether it was the law, politics, business or baseball. Though born in Lincolnton, a small, rural town in Georgia, Moseley came north in the 1880s to better his chances. He eventually ended up in Chicago in the 1890s where he stayed until his death in 1919.

After spending a bit of time in Canada, Moseley decided to come back to the United States where he liked the weather a bit better. After arriving in Chicago he quickly made a name for himself in the newspaper business with the *Chicago Republic.* He also passed the bar in Illinois in 1896 and opened his own law offices at 6258 South Halsted Street. He got involved in the local political and social scene by chairing the Colored Committee of the Republican Party, where he became a huge supporter of Theodore Roosevelt. He also joined all the elite clubs, including the Appomattox Club, which he later served as president. The Appomattox Club attracted all the top businessmen and politicians in the black community, who were often referred to as the Chicago 400.

Moseley developed quite a reputation in Chicago and beyond as a superb orator and champion of the underdog. He did not sit idly by when he disagreed with something or thought a wrong had been committed. He often wrote editorials and letters for the Chicago *Broad Ax,* voicing his thoughts. For example, in 1901 a speech he gave at the South End Club entitled "What is the Best thing for the Negro to do for his Advancement and Success in this Country," ended up in its entirety in the paper. Moseley talked about the trouble with religion as he understood it. He felt everyone should worship together and not in segregated churches, because we would all go to the same heaven.[6] He wrote an editorial in 1911 after he had been refused accommodations at the Grand Pacific Hotel. He decided to press charges against the employee and the hotel in a civil suit which he won. He wrote about the case for the papers to urge others not to let such slights go by because nothing would ever change if people did not start to stand up for themselves. Waiting for someone else to do it would not work because no one else wanted to do it, either.[7]

Moseley married Carrie Hammond and they raised three children. Their daughter, Bertha, graduated with high honors from high school and went on to attend the state college for girls in Urbana. She later married local news writer Cary B. Lewis and became an elementary school teacher. Her husband proved to be a valuable addition to the family, as he regularly wrote about the Leland Giants and their adventures for the *Defender.* They also had two sons, Burton and Beauregard Junior. Moseley's law practice proved lucrative and he was able to support his family in style at 6248 Sangamon Street.[8]

As his business grew Moseley began to branch out into other ventures. For example, he got involved with a group of investors in running the

Idlewild Resort in Benton Harbor, Michigan. He also became an investor and stockholder in the Leland Giants baseball club during the early 1900s. With his investment, he helped create the Leland Giants Baseball and Amusement Association (LGBAA). The idea behind this association was twofold: to provide ongoing support for the Leland Giants in hopes of purchasing them a permanent home field and to create a variety of entertainment opportunities run by African Americans.

When the Association was incorporated in 1907, it was to include the baseball team, a roller skating rink, a dance pavilion, a restaurant and a bowling emporium. A call went out to the public to help name the venture, with three prizes being offered. The eventual name chosen was the Chateau de la Plaisance, as submitted by a Mr. Adams of Toledo. Professor William Emanuel's wife got second place even though he was involved with the investors.

Major Robert R. Jackson, who had been involved with the baseball team, was put in charge of the skating rink, while Frank C. Leland, the club manager, also had control over the dance pavilion. A. H. Hampton ran the Chinese restaurant and J. H. Bolden the bowling alley. The dance area and restaurant were often used over the ensuing years for special celebrations for the ball club as well as major social events in the city. Moseley served as the original secretary/treasurer of the group and helped bring in Rube Foster as a player and manager of the Leland Giants.

Some of the men brought in to help with the association had political or financial connections in the city that could help the club. Major Jackson, for example, was also the financial secretary of the Appomattox Club. Jackson grew up in Chicago, attending public school until he was twelve and then going to work in a variety of odd jobs before landing at the post office, where he spent fourteen years. In addition to belonging to the Appomattox Club, Jackson belonged to the Knights of Pythias and the Golden Fleece Lodge. Jesse Binga had some interests in the association and owned more real estate than any other African American in the city of Chicago. With men like this backing up the Giants they could count on excellent community support.[9]

The success of the Amusement Association led to additional features being added in June 1908. These included more gardens, a merry-go-round and a café. In addition to the music provided by Professor Armant and his band, new singers were added. This eventually led in 1910 to improvements being made to the park the Giants called home at Sixty-ninth and Halsted. There were 3,000 grandstand seats, 400 box seats and 1,600 bleachers to allow for 5,000 fans. The *Broad Ax* hailed the Leland Giants and the Association as the greatest business venture for the colored community in both the city and the state.

Moseley used the success of the ball club to enhance his political popularity, as he often attended the games and invited a variety of guests on a regular basis. When he ran for municipal court judge he could be seen in the box seats with prominent Republicans. When he campaigned for the circuit court he invited those in power to be his guest as the Giants beat up on the local competition. In 1912 he announced he would be voting for Teddy Roosevelt and the Bull Moose Party and he was chosen as a presidential elector, the first African American to receive that honor.[10]

By 1910 the Giants had become so successful that Moseley and Foster wanted to control the whole show, and they finally pushed Frank Leland out. They took him to court to enjoin him from using the name Leland Giants anymore and his club simply became known as the Chicago Giants. When it came time to declare the City Champion from 1909, Moseley and Foster claimed the title, as did Frank Leland. Both clubs had a flag raising ceremony, with the official pennant being given to Moseley's club in the presence of all the major city officials.

By the end of the 1910 season Moseley had decided that an association of Negro Baseball teams should be created. He issued a tentative plan in the *Broad Ax* in December. He wanted a league of ten ball clubs that paid $10.00 to be in the league. He proposed guarantees to the winning and losing teams, with clauses to deal with shortfalls in expenses. He wanted clubs to be suspended if they could not pay their debts and suggested paid umpires, half of whom were black. And finally he wanted players under contract to be left alone by other teams. Moseley believed these suggestions and others would create a professional atmosphere and allow black ballplayers to have a future outside the semipro ranks.

The first meeting of the newly proposed league was held at the Chateau, with Moseley, Frank Walker of New Orleans and Felix H. Payne of Kansas City being named to lead the effort. Eight teams were represented, including Chicago, Louisville, New Orleans, Mobile, Kansas City, St. Louis, Columbus and Kansas City (Kansas). Each city would be allowed only one team in the league and they had to pay $300 for the franchise.[11] This new league would provide opportunities for ballplayers that were currently denied to them in too many cities. Moseley urged each franchise to put together the best possible team they could to represent their city well.

Unfortunately, all Moseley's planning and appeals went for naught when the league failed. Two key problems seemed to hinder the league, the franchise fee and disagreements over transportation costs—who would pay and how they would be balanced so one team did not get overburdened. Moseley tried to answer the franchise issue by stating that each city needed only 30 investors to put up $10 each to secure the fee but this proved too difficult. Moseley's proposal was not the first for a colored league and it would not be the last. His 1910 proposal helped lay the groundwork for the eventual creation of the Negro National League in 1920, with Rube Foster of the Chicago American Giants leading the way. Mosley died December 1, 1919, in Fort Dearborn, Illinois

Andrew "Rube" Foster: Gem of a Man

Born September 17, 1879, Calvert, TX; died December 9, 1950, Kankakee, IL; 1981 Cooperstown Hall of Fame; 1998 Texas Sports Hall of Fame; 2004 Texas Baseball Hall of Fame

Genius touched his soul, for a black league was his goal. As a genius, Foster had answers to questions before they were asked. He had the vision to see the unforeseeable. Rube Foster became a symbol of hope, hope shared by a generation of hopefuls.

Rube Foster was an early day version of boxing promoter Don King. King smoked cigars and Rube puffed on a smelly pipe. King, aptly named, ruled boxing promotions, while Foster, aptly named, fathered the grown-up fairy tale of playing big-time sandlot baseball. You either loved them or hated them. Like King, Foster was flamboyant, full of braggadocio and ego-tistism, with a gift to capture a fan's fancies. This Rube was a diamond that scratched other pebbles with his influence.

Young Rube's career began in 1897 with the Austin (Texas) Reds of Tillotson College. The following year, he joined the semipro Yellowjackets in nearby Waco. The new century found Foster signing with Frank Leland's Chicago Union Giants for $40 a month and 15 cents meal money. Here, he developed a nasty screwball thrown from his somewhat unique submarine delivery.

A practitioner of slow play on the mound, Foster was described by the *Chicago Daily Tribune* in 1909 as "about as fast as a hippopotamus would run on skis." In 1905, the *Philadelphia Item* described the procrastinator as having "...an aggravating way of taking his time. He is a man of huge frame. His arms are like those of a windmill. He would swing them like the pendulum of a clock, looking the while, about the diamond. Suddenly he would twist up like a Missouri grasshopper about to make a spring and the ball would shoot from the pitcher's box. Time and again he struck out his man..."

Overall, the most descriptive visual of the famed hurler was written by Frederick North Shorey of the *Indianapolis Freeman* in 1907: "In appearance he is almost the typical stage darkie — husky, black as coal, with a halting stride, a head sunk between his shoulders, and without any ostensible neck. When he enters the box [pitcher's mound] he takes a calm survey of the field to see that his men are in place, sizes up the batter, and suddenly, before the batter realizes what has happened, the ball is over the plate for one strike. This is the most frequent of Rube's tricks, and he has plenty of them. He has the faculty of whipping the ball across the plate with or without the preliminary winding up [windup], which is the most painful performance of so many pitches, and he can do it underhand, with a side-wheel motion [side-arm], overhand, or apparently snap it with his wrist. And when he is in a tight place he seemingly can pitch so that the ball will be batted to a certain place."

From Slave Ship to Championship

In 1903, Rube headed East to play for the Cuban X-Giants. That fall, he posted four victories in a seven-game series against the Philadelphia Giants for the so-called Colored Championship of the World. The wandering Foster switched over to the Philly team the next season, 1904, and met some of his old teammates for bragging rights to the "colored" title. Foster accounted for both victories in the best-of-three series. He struck out 18 batters in one game, beating the current major league record of 15 set by Fred Glade of the St. Louis Browns. Foster give up seven hits and four runs to the defending champions before roughly 4,000 fans. He also got three hits, and stole a base in the game as the Giants from Philly won 8–5.

Earlier in the season he pitched his first recorded no-hitter against Mt. Carmel A.A. (PA), on July 7, in a four to nothing game that was called after seven innings because of rain. Foster had two hits and scored one run. His second no-hitter came on July 25, when he struck out 17 and walked four in beating Trenton YMCA 1–0. Foster also had three hits, scoring the Giants' only run.

Large and in charge, Foster's reputation as a fine pitcher continued to expand with a victory over Rube Waddell and the Philadelphia Athletics to finish the 1904 season, earning him the nickname of Rube.

On August 22, 1905, Foster pitched the third no-hitter of his career against the Camden (New Jersey) club. He struck out five and walked three batters, facing only 30 batters. By October the *Philadelphia Item* reported that the Giants had a "remarkable" 132–21–3 won-lost-tie record, noting that nine of the losses were by one run. The trio of Foster, Danny McClellan and Scotty Bowman was unbeatable. Soon after that article, the *Philadelphia Telegraph* wrote, "If Andrew Foster had not been born with a dark skin, the great pitcher would wear an American or National League uniform. Rube

Waddell, Cy Young, [Christy] Mathewson, [Joe] McGinnity and others are great twirlers in the big leagues and their praises have been sung from Maine to Texas. Foster has never been equaled in a pitcher's box. Out of 49 games pitched this season he has won 45. Aside from the twirling ability, he is a heavy hitter and a fine fielder and ranks among the foremost of the country." The *Indianapolis Freeman* echoed the sentiment, adding "Andrew Foster deserves every word of praise ever said of him. He is undoubtedly among the very best pitchers that America affords."

In 1907, he returned to Chicago and the Leland Giants, leading them to a 110–10 record, including 48 straight wins. It is believed Foster pitched his fourth no-hitter, defeating the South Chicagos and Homer Hillebrand 1–0. Lefty Hillebrand, from Princeton, had pitched for the Pittsburgh Pirates (1905–06, 1908) for three seasons. According to press accounts, "Four thousands five hundred witnessed the last game and enthusiasm was at an even higher pitch than when [Jude] Gans made his last fight. Rube Foster is now to baseball what Gans is to prizefighting, but the main feature that characterizes this battle of pitchers from the one of the fighters upon Labor Day is the fact that the white boy did not claim a broken wrist, neither did he quit when the Lelands landed the solar plexus blow in the sixth round, which really brought home the bacon. It was only one little score, but it looked as large as the Masonic Temple to the visitors because Foster had struck his gait and was striking them out so often that they kept up a regular procession [of] 'beatin' back to the bench.'"

At season end the Giants and Foster took on Mike Donlin's All-Stars. Donlin had vacated the New York Giants in 1906 after batting .356 and leading the National League with 124 runs scored. Other All-Stars included Jake Stahl, Jimmy Callahan and Jimmy Ryan, whose major league career ended four years earlier. With more hype than a heavyweight championship fight, on August 27 the teams took the field for the first of six games. Foster took the opener, holding the All-Stars to three hits and a run, winning 3–1. He struck out five, and walked one. At bat, he singled and scored a run that day.

After the game, Shorey, writing for the *Indianapolis Freeman*, wrote, "Rube Foster is the pitcher of the Leland Giants, and he has all the speed of a [Amos] Rusie, the tricks of a [Hoss] Radbourne, and the heady coolness and deliberation of a Cy Young. What does that make of him? Why, the greatest baseball pitcher in the country; that is what the best ball players of white persuasion that have gone up against him say. But his color has kept him out of the big leagues, and that is why the Leland Giants, the Philadelphia Giants, and other colored teams for the last ten years have had the advantage of a pitcher who otherwise would be a priceless boon to the struggling White Sox or the ambitious Highlanders just now."

When Shorey asked Foster what type of stuff he used to defeat the major league all-stars, he modestly replied, "I don't rely on any kind of ball, and I don't use any kind of system. I just kind of size up the batter and give them what I think he can't hit. Sometimes it's a curve, sometimes it's a straight ball, but I can most always tell, sort of by instinct, what's coming off behind me. Five or six years ago, I think, I'd have been a first-class pitcher, but I found then I'd got as far as I could go and that there was no hope of getting into the big leagues, so I kind of let myself go. I was playing with the Philadelphia Giants then."

After the 1907 season Foster was off to the island of Cuba. Playing for the Fe club, he won nine games against six losses in 16 starts. He pitched 15 complete games to lead the Cuban Winter League in that category.

The next season, 1908, Foster joined the Habana Reds and won eight games, losing five. He had nine complete games in 15 starts. On June 4, 1908, the *Chicago Daily Tribune* cried, "If Professor Rube Foster of the Leland Giants were a pronounced blond, he would be in one of the big leagues drawing a salary of his own prescribing."

In 1909, the Giants entered the tough integrated city league. In Foster's first eleven starts, he won eleven games, with four shutouts. Such a dominating force that season, after one commanding victory, that an *Indianapolis Freeman* newspaper's headlines simply stated: "FOSTER PITCHED, THAT'S ALL."

In fact, Spaulding's *Chicago Base Ball Guide of 1909*, claimed, "The colored wonders, the Leland Giants, are in a class by themselves, and their followers are justly entitled to be proud of them and claim whatever honors they think exist. For the greater part of the 1908 campaign the Lelands played ball as good as the major leagues, and none of the white clubs were able to do more than make a good showing against them, with the exception of Callahan's Logan Squares."

By 1910, the Leland Giants were the chatter of every clubhouse. They christened a ballpark in an all-white neighborhood near Sixty-ninth and Halsted as the Leland Giants Base Ball Park. Foster, now serving as player-manager, amassed, in his opinion, the greatest team of all time. Featuring such stars as John Henry "Pop" Lloyd, the notorious streak hitter Pete Hill, Grant "Home Run" Johnson, catcher extraordinaire Bruce Petway and great pitchers like Frank Wickware and Pat Dougherty, the Leland team won 123 of 129 games. This team compelled John McGraw of NY Giants fame to announce, "If I had a bucket of whitewash that wouldn't wash off, you wouldn't have five players left tomorrow."

The following season, Foster formed a partnership with John Schorling, a white businessman. Together they purchased Old Roman's, a ballpark at Thirty-ninth and Wentworth, from White Sox owner Charlie Comiskey.

The park became home to black baseball's finest team, the Chicago American Giants. Foster billed his team as "THE GREATEST AGGREGATION OF COLORED BASEBALL PLAYERS IN THE WORLD." The Giants normally played semipro teams for a guarantee of $60, rain or shine, with fifty percent of the gross receipts guaranteed if their ace, Rube Foster, would pitch.

Although an outstanding pitcher, a dependable team owner and a brilliant manager, perhaps Rube Foster's most impressive fulfillment came in 1920. With whites controlling the purse strings, black teams were often exempt from making the really big paydays. Foster sought alternative solutions. Owners of the most stable black teams gathered in Kansas City, Missouri, at the Paseo YMCA, to discuss a structured league, game schedule and player contracts.

On the eighth day, they drank the Kool-Aid and created the Negro National League of Colored Base Ball Professionals, better known as the Negro National League (NNL). It consisted of eight ships of hope to battle the sea of racism. The league's motto was "We Are the Ship, All Else the Sea." Going against the tide of segregation, Rube's voyage would become an obsession. Foster, the genetic Eve of black baseball, birthed a confederacy of clubs that embraced a permanent existence of quality baseball. It became the first league of color to survive a full season. Initially though, the new league barely caused a ripple in the ocean of recognition.

For years, Captain Rube struggled without a life preserver in his attempts to keep his boat afloat. The human anchor gave IOUs and advances, and sometimes loaned players to struggling franchises, attempting to balance the talent pool around the circuit. Foster argued that their exclusion from the National Pastime was a symbolic rip in the red-white-and-blue flag. His struggles became our successes, as black ball exploded in popularity and power, to boldly go where no black organization had gone before, ultimately becoming an integral part of baseball Americana.

As founder, secretary and president, Foster controlled the ATMs in the league. He set sail into his "home-of-the-brave" league with the aptly named Chicago American Giants. They captured the NNL title the initial three years. In 1923, along came the Eastern Colored League (ECL), creating competition for the country's top black players. Their raiding war of players instigated a fight for bragging rights in Black America that propelled both leagues to higher standards of quality play and management.

Nineteen hundred and twenty-four was a landmark year for both leagues, as they played their first world series. Rube's team lost out to the Kansas City Monarchs for the league title, and the Monarchs went on to defeat the Hilldale Giants in a thrilling ten-game series, with the final game played on Foster's home field in Chicago.

The Monarchs repeated as league champions in 1925, before yielding starboard control to Foster's American Giants in 1926 and 1927, now managed by a Foster protégé, "Gentleman" Dave Malarcher.

In a Dave Malarcher interview by author Charles Whitehead, Foster's successor recalled the memory of this genius with an example: "Jimmy Lyons might say, 'Jock, bring me pair of $20.00 spikes, Spauldings. Size 10-D.' Jelly would ask for 'jockey strap, size 30.' The Cuban would say, 'Me need new socks, Jock.' Then Bingo might say, 'A new black glove,' and so on. Rube Foster had neither pen nor pad, but when he returned, he had exactly what had been requested. Not only was his mind imaginative and creative," Malarcher added, "it was photographic as well." Rube's "rain man" mentality was like a Rubik cube: complex, colorful and incredibly systematic. Foster had an incredible memory that recalled every instance of a game with facts that escaped the common mind.

With brains and influence, Rolodex Rube seemed invincible, but in 1926, the czar-like dictator with the booming baritone voice succumbed to mental illness and was institutionalized in Kankakee, Illinois. Unable to float their boat, the entire league developed more seepage than the *Titanic.* Like a ship without a sail, or a compass without a needle, the league was lost at sea. The league struggled without Foster's life jacket, playing its last World Series in 1927, with several teams fading from existence.

Foster died four years after he was committed. One of baseball's most creative minds was extinguished. In November of 1930, renowned sportswriter Frank "Fay" Young, for *Abbott's Monthly,* testified on behalf of the late legend: "One of the most brilliant figures that the great national sport has ever produced. Rube knew every technicality of the game, how to play it, and how to make his men play it. A true master of the game."

Robert Peterson, in his required reading, *Only the Ball Was White,* wrote it best: "If the talents of Christy Mathewson, John McGraw, Ban Johnson and Judge Kenesaw Mountain Landis were combined in a single body, and that body was enveloped in a black skin, the result would have to be named Andrew "Rube" Foster. As an outstanding pitcher, a colorful and shrewd field manager, and the founder and stern administrator of the first viable Negro League, Foster was the most impressive figure in black baseball history. From about 1911 until 1926, he stood astride Negro baseball in the Midwest with unchallenged power, a friend of major league leaders, and the best known black man in Chicago. Rube Foster was an unlettered genius who combined generosity and sternness, the superb skills of a dedicated athlete and an unbounded belief in the future of the black baseball player. His life was baseball. Had he chosen otherwise, baseball would have been the poorer." And the meek shall inherit the earth.

As in all sports, it is the game's hero we hoisted on our jubilant shoulders in celebration of the ultimate victory. However, it was Rube Foster who shouldered the responsibility for carrying this sport to unprecedented heights, respectability, and reluctant recognition by major league gatekeepers.

Overall, his life history was a real page-turner. Rube was a phenomenal pitcher, a magnificent manager, a powerful organizer and an even greater humanitarian. He had the face of a koala bear, the heart of laborer John Henry, the smile of Billy Dee Williams, the essence of Malcolm X, the vision of Dr. Martin Luther King, the oratorical skills of James Earl Jones and the creative genius of Ray Charles. Rube Foster was the most robust blend of baseball expertise ever assembled.

After Foster left the Giants they would go through a number of different owners over the years. Some of them were local Chicago businessmen like Horace G. Hall, Robert A. Cole, William Little and William Trimble, while Dr. J. B. Martin came in from the south to take ownership of the club for a number of years. Robert Cole had the longest association and brought in Hall, who actually worked for him. Hall also served as the NAL vice president.

By Larry Lester

Cole's American Giants: Robert Alexander Cole

After 1926 the Chicago American Giants had some difficult years. Their longtime leader, Rube Foster, became ill that year and had to leave the team. He thought he would return but ended up spending his remaining years in an institution. The club was left without a strong leader and their fortunes declined, as did the Negro National League. The NNL actually disappeared before the end of the decade and there was some doubt as to what would be the future of black professional baseball. In Chicago the Giants got a significant boost when local businessman Robert A. Cole bought the club and renamed them Cole's American Giants.

Robert Cole was the founder and chairman of the board for Chicago Metropolitan Mutual Assurance Association. He also owned the Metropolitan Funeral Parlor, considered by some the largest funeral business in the nation. He started as a Pullman porter and rose to the ranks of the richest African Americans in the country. When he died in 1957 the worth of his company was estimated at over $75 million dollars. Over 2,000 people attended his funeral inside the church, while about 300 more gathered outside the Pilgrim Baptist Church. The list of attendees included all the prominent black politicians and businessmen in Chicago and from many surrounding areas, including some dignitaries from places like Fisk University.[12]

Cole came to Chicago in 1905 with a dream to become rich and famous. Born in 1882 in Covington, Tennessee, he left school after the fifth grade to get work to help his family. He was one of eight children. He eventually bought a train ticket in Mt. Carmel, Tennessee, and left home for the first time at the age of seventeen, determined to make his mark on the world. He took on a variety of jobs to make ends meet and did not really start to see a turn in his fortunes until after he was 40. Things did not turn around for him until he learned how to save some of the money he made. He worked for a year in Paducah, Kentucky, before coming to Chicago, where he started as a waiter. Cole got a break when he was hired as a Pullman porter and, before long, the company recognized his potential and made him a porter-in-charge.

With the first $500 Cole saved, he invested in a funeral business and the rest, as they say, is history. He went on to make his millions, married later in life and had two children. After incorporating in 1927, Chicago Metropolitan grew quickly. By 1932 the company had 30,000 policy owners.[13]

One of the other interests Cole developed was in baseball, and he owned the American Giants for five years before he turned over the reigns to his business manager, Horace G. Hall. Cole also served the Negro Leagues as the treasurer and as a member of the board of directors. In 1942 he threw out the first pitch at the East-West game as recognition of his involvement with getting the game for the city of Chicago. His catcher was William Little, a part owner of the Giants.

After Cole and Hall had done their part to keep the Giants alive, their interests were taken over by Dr. J. B. Martin. Martin had been involved with the league office for a number of years and had worked with his brothers to keep a franchise in Memphis before he moved to Chicago.

Dr. J. B. Martin

Dr. J. B. Martin originally came from Holly Springs, Mississippi, but grew up in Memphis. He attended Walden College and got his pharmacy degree from Meharry Medical School in Nashville. He owned a number of businesses in the area along with his three brothers. One of their joint ventures was to establish the Memphis Red Sox, with their own ball park. He married Lula in 1909 and they had two sons.

In addition to being a businessman and real estate dealer, Martin was heavily involved in the Republican Party. In fact, the local police and other city officials tried to force his drugstore out of business in 1940 because he had worked on the Republican presidential campaign of Wendell Wilkie. The effort appeared to be directed by "Boss" Edward Crump and police Chief Joseph Boyle. They set up officers outside his business to search everyone who went in on the charge that he was selling illegal drugs. Not all the police agreed with the plan and eventually a formal investigation vindicated Martin of all charges. To let the furor over the incident die down Dr. Martin decided to take a break and go to Chicago to visit his mother. While in the Windy City he received an offer to buy the Chicago American Giants, which he decided to accept. He saved the team from bankruptcy and later sold them in the mid–1940s to devote his time to politics. He also brought in R. S. Simmons as the club's traveling secretary to help with day-to-day arrangements. In 1949 Simmons became the team's general manager.[14]

Dr. Martin served as the president of the Negro American League (NAL) for nearly twenty years. He took over in 1940 and was still there at the end of the leagues in 1960. He was a huge supporter of the East-West game each year and in the end was also a supporter of the move to integrate major league baseball after meeting and discussing the issues with the new commissioner, Happy Chandler. He even considered an offer in 1960 from an American League team to subsidize the league to keep it in operation for the 1961 season. He had previously turned down other offers because he did not want to give one team a monopoly on players. Martin worked tirelessly over the years to improve the organization of the Negro Leagues by suspending and fining players when they broke their contracts, jumped to Mexico or harassed umpires. In 1956, in an effort to save the NAL, Martin came up with a plan to have the Negro League clubs play some of their league contests in cities where minor league teams had folded.[15]

In addition to being a prominent baseball man, Martin had a variety of important civic and political positions in Chicago. He belonged to the Republican Party and often held leadership roles within the organization. For a number of years he was a trustee of the Chicago Metropolitan Sanitary district. His election had made him the first African American to be elected to such a post in 1946. In 1959 he was elected to the Board of Directors of the Service Federal Savings and Loan Association.[16]

Dr. Martin died in 1973 while living in Jackson, Michigan. Services were held for him in Detroit.

While Dr. Martin owned the team, Candy Jim Taylor managed the club for him. Before Taylor, Dave Malarcher held the reigns after Rube Foster got sick. In addition to these three managers, the Giants operated under some others such as Winfield Welch, and Quincy Trouppe.

David "Gentleman Dave" Julius Malarcher

Bats switch, throws right; 5'7", 150 lbs; born October 8, 1894,
Whitehall, LA; died May 11, 1982, Chicago IL; cemetery near
covent, St. James Parish, LA; career 1916 to 1934, Indianapolis
ABC's, Detroit Stars, Chicago American Giants

Andrew "Rube" Foster's vision of quality play was passed on to "Gentleman" Dave Malarcher. Rube's star student had the gentle demeanor of a lap dog, but a rottweiler appetite to win. Malarcher had the purity of Black Moses, the tenacity of Black America, and sanctity of Black Madonna.

He was one of eleven children born to Martha and Henry Louis on Charbone's sugar and rice plantation near the Whitehall community in Ascension Parish, Louisiana. Whitehall is about 50 miles southeast of Baton Rouge, and 70 miles northwest of New Orleans, just down the road on Highway 22 and just south of Tiger Bluff Landing and Catfish Landing. While his Dad was a laborer, his mother was a midwife, teaching children, including her own, how to read, write and think.

Malarcher started his ball career in 1914 with the New Orleans Black Eagles while in college. He attended New Orleans University (now Dillard) before graduating in 1918. He expressed, in the true sprit of a philosopher, "Ever since I left the university in early spring of 1918, I've never ceased to read and build on my education by studying constantly in many subjects. My knowledge of history from school and such reading has made my life immune to the fears and frustrations and uncertainties which are derived from a lack of information of man's troublesome and sordid past."

Malarcher stated, "The education and mind and spirit discipline which I had acquired at New Orleans University enabled me to observe and absorb the baseball training techniques and strategy of the three greatest managers in baseball history — Charley Stevens [of the N.O. Eagles], C. I. Taylor of the Indianapolis ABCs; and the incomparable baseball genius, Andrew "Rube" Foster of the Chicago American Giants." Manager Stevens had taught the team captain how to steal signs, with Malarcher developing the art into a masterpiece.

He played with the Eagles two years before joining the Indianapolis ABCs in 1916. His three-year tour with the ABCs ended when he was drafted into the 809th Pioneer Regiment Baseball league during World War I. After the war, Malarcher returned to the States and played for the Detroit Stars in 1919 before being lured to the Chicago American Giants by Andrew Foster.

In a 1918 letter to Malarcher, discovered by Mike Kolleth, of Au, Switzerland, Foster offered an opportunity to enhance his sign-stealing abilities. The letter in part read, "My success has been to let my opponent know what I would do ... then reverse it. The signs that I knew you all knew I had — I started right in to use them ... the minute I saw you knew them, had been coached of them, it was then I take advantage of you. You played for them, as [if] you knew them. Where I so often made [a] sucker of your club, [and that's] why you had so many pitch outs, and [my] man did not start. I will learn you lots, give you the chance to do what you know, if you have an improvement [idea], I will be the first to adopt it." Foster closed the letter with, "Let me know if you will play, and I will send you a contract. I have heard nothing from C. I. [Taylor] since the season closed. Very Sincerely Yours, A. Rube Foster."

Joining the American Giants in 1920, Malarcher immediately made an impact. With Foster and Malarcher stealing signs, and with Dave's fine play around the hot corner, the Giants won NNL pennants in 1920, 1921, and 1922. Normally batting in the second slot of the lineup, he had the knowledge to protect the plate and move the runners to the next station. Despite being stuck in the sacrificial number 2 slot, he often hit over .300, meanwhile generally leading the team in steals.

"Malarcher has more than filled the shoes of [Bill] Francis," wrote Frank Young in the *Chicago Defender* in 1920. "All the dope saying he was the greatest third baseman playing ball that were advanced has really failed to do him justice. He is all that an infielder should be — a good hitter. His daring base running has opened the eyes of the fans. They have never seen his superior. On several different occasions he has electrified the fans by stealing home safely."

As one nugget knows another, Rube knew a gem when he discovered it. And so did Cum Posey, owner of the Homestead Grays. In 1924, Posey picked his All-American team and chose third baseman David Malarcher on his first team. Posey claimed, "Malarcher is better than [Oliver] Marcell, [Hall of Famer Judy] Johnson, or [Newt] Joseph on account of his ability to play for batters and his many ways to get on base. He is the fastest man on the club [American Giants], including [Oscar] Charleston."

Two years later, Andrew Foster was committed to a mental institution and Malarcher took command of the captain's ship. Malarcher was fortunate to have such fine tutors as Foster and C. I. Taylor. With more keys to knowledge than a high school janitor, the seasoned rookie led the Chicago American Giants to World Series titles in 1926 and 1927.

The road to the crown was not easy. In 1926, they had to win the second-half title to face the KC Monarchs, winners of the first-half. While the Monarchs needed one game to win the best of five, the Giants had to win both ends of a doubleheader to win a World Series trip. Willie Foster won the first game, beating the Monarchs' ace, Bullet Rogan. When Malarcher saw Rogan warming up for the second game, he inserted his ace

The 1926 World Champion Chicago American Giants were anchored by an incredible pitching staff. In addition to the six featured in this photograph Aubrey Owens and Robert Poindexter were also on the roster. The six here are (from left) Webster McDonald, George Harney, Willie Foster, Rube Currie, Edward Miller and Willie Powell. (Photograph courtesy of NoirTech Research, Inc., and the National Baseball Hall of Fame, Cooperstown, New York.)

into the lineup again and Foster came through with a deuce. It would be the first time in Rogan's career he had lost two games in a row.

The Chicago fellows went on to defeat the Bacharach Giants the next two years by winning five of eight games each time. For the first title, the American Giants had to overcome a no-hitter by Claude "Red" Grier in the third game of the series.

Malarcher also piloted the club to within one game of winning a league title in 1928, losing the play-offs to the mighty St. Louis Stars, who featured Willie Wells, "Mule" Suttles and "Cool Papa" Bell. In 1932, they won the Negro Southern League by defeating the New Orleans Crescent Stars for the Dixie Series crown. His club also claimed the 1933 NNL championship trophy, but league president Gus Greenlee made a fuss that his Crawfords were really league champions, stripping the American Giants of their glory. The following year, they lost a seven-game series to the tough Philadelphia Stars, led by "Biz" Mackey and "Slim" Jones, for the league title.

Overall, Malarcher, the beneficiary of Rube Foster's first mental scholarship, had one losing season (1930) in his career. Available records show
that the Giants, under Malarcher's management, won 379 games against
230 losses, a winning percentage of .622. In post-season competition, he
did slightly better, winning 30 of 48 games for a .625 winning percentage.
The ultimate strategist, the cerebral Malarcher often got on opposing managers' last medulla oblongata.

Hot corner man Alec Radcliffe sang, "He won so many one-run ball
game with 'inside' baseball. He was the type of fellow who played for one
run. He never played for the big inning. It could be the first inning, it was
just like the ninth inning. He'd sacrifice. He wanted that first run. I think
he's the greatest manager I've ever seen."

Ralph Waldo Emerson once said, "The only way to have a friend is to
be one." Gentleman Dave was that friend. Malarcher embraced another
Emerson saying, "The glory of friendship is not the outstretched hand, nor
the kindly smile, nor the joy of companionship; it is the spiritual inspiration that comes to one when he discovers that someone else believes in him
and is willing to trust him with his friendship."

If you mentioned Aristophanes, Pericles, Sophocles, Thucydides, Euri-
pedes, or Socrates, this scholar knew of their talents. Off the playing field,
Julius was known for his prose and philosophy. The nonsmoking teetotaler
was socially squarer than Pop Lloyd's jaw. Whether it be mo'nin' time or
nite' time, Malarcher preferred milkshakes to Michelobs. You never heard
dangits or darnits, frickin' or freakin,' or shoots, or any other disguised
expressions of profanity from this stately Gentleman. He would have Nun
of that. Any sailor worth his rum would have kicked Malarcher off his boat.

Neither did he allow the younger players any sassin' back to their mom-
mas, daddies, or elders. They were always greeted with a "Yes, sir or Yes,
ma'm." This gentleman was an early-day Heathcliff Huxtable. Gentleman
Dave could convert fornicators to fathers, sinners to saints, and chumps to
champions. Devotion was this Sunday schooler's first emotion when managing the American Giants. Radcliffe adds, "He was a deacon of his church,
and when I was a youngster and first started playing for Malarcher, he used
to come by, pick me up and take me to church Sunday morning. I love
Malarcher." As you may expect, emotionally balanced, Malarcher was never
bitter, vengeful or judgmental about his exclusion from white baseball.

Radcliffe also remembers Malarcher shouting, "'I don't want any profanity on my ball club.' He was always in the ball players' corner. He didn't
let the owners of the team abuse the ballplayers. If he thought you needed
a raise, he'd ask for you. That's right. Incidentally, I think that's why he
finally quit managing, because we wanted a raise and didn't get it. Malarcher

said to me, 'I'm giving it up because I don't like riding the buses all night.' But I couldn't see that. I think it [his retirement] was because of us."

His significant other, Mabel Eupora Sylvester, was equally adept at the fine arts, as she often sang the national anthem at American Giant games, including the opening hymn at the 1943 East-West game at Comiskey Park.

In his golden years, Malarcher was active in his real estate business and serving as a trustee for more than a quarter of century at the Woodlawn A.M.E. church in Chicago, Illinois. In 1982, Gentleman Dave got a box seat in the upper room. Haloed at 87 years old, he was still feisty as he got the call to the real Majors.

The world does not need Charles Barkley to be a role model — we have Gentleman Dave Malarcher.

The Thinker, with a deft use of dialogue, and lyrical prose, often composed poetry. Below are two of his creations.

By Larry Lester

Sunset Before Dawn (in 1948)

Thou wert among the best
Who wrought upon this earth,
O dead! Thine endless zest
Is merit of thy worthy ...

O mind of fleetful thought
O dead who lived too soon
What pity thou wert brought
To twilight ere the noon.

But sleep thou on in peace
As orchids which did bloom
Like pure unspotted fleece
Within the forest's gloom

Forevermore Asleep (To Ty Cobb)

Tyrus, the fearless at the bat:
Raymond, the fleetful on the base;
The Daring Cobb, whose skill begat,
The envy of the diamond race.

We honor thee in endless rest.
We here enshrine thy deathless fame!
The Brilliant star among the best,
The arch of baseball's thrilling game.

James "Candy Jim" Taylor

James "Candy Jim" Taylor was born February 1, 1884, in Anderson, South Carolina, and made his debut in professional baseball in 1904 with the Birmingham Giants, who were under the management of his brother, C. I. Taylor. Candy Jim became a member of the St. Louis Gophers in 1908, only to leave the following year for Rube Foster's Leland Giants, and winning a championship the same year. He would bounce between the St. Louis Giants, the Chicago American Giants, and the Indianapolis ABCs through his last year as a player in 1918.[17] Candy Jim Taylor spent an eon in black baseball, at times with his brothers, Ben, Johnny, and C. I. He peaked as a third baseman in 1916 as a key member of C. I.'s Black World Champion

Indianapolis ABCs. He was named to William Dismukes' "All Time team," placed as one of the best black third basemen ever, if not *the* best.[18] He had also been instrumental in the successes of the 1909 Black Western champion St. Paul Gophers and the 1913 Chicago American Giants, and gained a reputation as a master strategist, as he managed three Negro National League teams to pennants: the 1928 St. Louis Stars and the 1943–44 Homestead Grays, who won the championship both years.

Taylor is remembered for a comical but altruistic belief, "Try to understand your men. Know their abilities, and know when to change pitchers." He used to tell his players, "Do anything you want to do because I don't care if you hit standing on your head, as long as you hit." When the Negro National League, led by W. C. Hueston, in 1930 began to face severe difficulties, Taylor shared his tribulations with baseball in which he laid out the reasons for the league's declining public appeal. Sparing no one, he called out incompetent owners and "players that don't care enough for the game to stay in condition," appearing interested only when payday rolled around. Incompetent umpires and inconsistent press coverage also created problems, he claimed, and for the latter he blamed the teams, noting that the newspapers often were not given the necessary information.[19] Racism probably played a role in the lack of press accuracy, as many of the Negro Leaguers were as good if not better than quite a few of the white professionals. The result of inaccurate reporting of the exploits of the black players was that any threat to the white major leagues was extinguished. Taylor also played the role of player-manager. In one instance, his Crawfords were playing St. Louis and Taylor put himself into the game as a pinch hitter and broke up a no-hitter by Sam Streeter with two outs in the ninth inning.[20] Taylor was known to be very superstitious, not allowing his players to eat peanuts in the dugout. Opposing players took full advantage of such a belief, keeping their pockets full of peanuts and tossing them into Taylor's dugout.[21]

He would become manager of the Chicago American Giants in 1941, after a successful year with the Birmingham Black Barons. The Giants played that year in Comiskey Park because the bleachers at their park at Thirty-ninth and Wentworth had burned down.[22] No final standings were published for either half of the split season, although the Kansas City Monarchs were referred to as league champions in the years following. The Giants did send four players to the East-West game: Jimmie Crutchfield, Billy Horne, Pepper Bassett, and Henry Hudson.[23] As told by Larry Brown in *Colored Baseball & Sports Monthly* in 1934, "All the long list of Taylors who have participated in athletic sports have been great in their respective fields. That name Taylor is a valuable one. So if you are looking for sure success in sports, be a little superstitious and change your nomenclature to Taylor."[24]

In his last days of baseball leading up to his untimely death, Taylor had taken over as the manager of the Baltimore Elite Giants in 1948. He was scheduled to join the team for its spring training but fell ill and never improved. Since 1929, Taylor had been in the coaching vocation as manager of the Memphis Red Sox, the Indianapolis ABCs, the Baltimore Elite Giants, the Chicago American Giants, and the Homestead Grays, leading the Grays to the pennant and world title in 1943. He also managed hall of famers such as Josh Gibson, Satchel Paige and Cool Papa Bell, as well as many other great players.[25] For 45 years, the pudgy, colorful strategist left his mark not only as a great player but as a masterful manager as well.

On September 26, 2004, a Peoria, Illinois-area physician, Jeremy Krock, chose to honor Taylor along with Jimmie Crutchfield and John Donaldson by erecting headstones (similar to the plaques of major leaguers enshrined in Cooperstown) on the new resting places of these players at Burr Oak Cemetery in Alsip, Illinois. The graves of the three had been previously unmarked. Eight other players who also rest at Burr Oak, one of two Chicago-area cemeteries where African Americans were buried at the time, will receive headstones in the near future. Contributions came from former baseball commissioner Fay Vincent, former Cubs manager Don Zimmer, the Chicago White Sox and many other small donors and totaled $3,500, or enough for the three headstones.[26] What a fitting end for a player-manager that meant so much to black baseball for nearly a half century.

After Taylor's managerial days ended with Chicago, Quincy Trouppe, Double Duty Radcliffe, Winfield Welch, and Lucky Davenport all had short stints as the Giants field generals. None of them lasted for extended periods or enjoyed great success in the later years of the Giants and the Leagues.

By Michael Harkness-Roberto

Double Duty Radcliffe: 36 Years of Excellence!

Duty was a good one, just like what everybody says. He could catch, pitch, and he could do them both real well. He was a good hitter. He could hit the ball hard!
—Negro Leaguer William "Bobbie" Robinson[27]

Duty would talk your pants off. He was funny. Just as funny as he could be. He won. He always won. Duty was a star!
—Negro Leaguer Sam Hairston[28]

Theodore Roosevelt Radcliffe was born on July 7th, 1902, in Mobile, Alabama, to James and Mary Radcliffe. James was a carpenter, and Mary spent most of her time taking care of Ted and his nine siblings. It is said that kids who grow up in large families usually have to make noise to get attention. The squeaky wheel gets the grease, you know. Well, Radcliffe started squeaking (talking) at age one and did not stop until he passed away in 2005 at the age of 102.

He is known to many Negro League fans as "Double Duty" (or just plain "Duty"), and within minutes of meeting him you would usually find out who he considered the greatest player he ever saw — himself! It is true that Double Duty talked a good game; it is equally true that he played a great game. "How many men you know could do what I did?" he often asked.

Radcliffe received his nickname from famed playwright-sportswriter Damon Runyon, who bestowed the moniker on Radcliffe after watching him catch Satchel Paige in the first game of a doubleheader, then toss a shutout in the second. Runyon wrote in the *New York American* the next day that "Double Duty Radcliffe was worth the price of two admissions to see him pitch and catch." Radcliffe took to the larger-than-life nickname and for the rest of his career was one of the top drawing cards in black baseball; he still is today at card shows and Negro League celebrations.

Radcliffe grew up in Mobile, only a few miles from Satchel Paige, and they were an airtight battery when only kids. Another neighbor who played in those early sandlot games, Bobbie Robinson, became a star third baseman in the Negro Leagues and was one of Radcliffe's closest friends for 90 years until his death on May 2, 2002.

In 1919, Radcliffe hitchhiked to Chicago where an older brother was living and soon the rest of the Radcliffes followed. Radcliffe lived for years within a Josh Gibson homer of that first Chicago home on the South Side. As a teenager, he hung out at White Sox Park, pitching batting practice for the handsome pay of a Coca-Cola, and was awed by the great Chicago American Giants team of Rube Foster's. In the spring of 1920, Radcliffe was playing sandlot ball when the Illinois Giants, a black traveling team, spotted the strong-armed youngster and offered him a contract on the spot: $50 for every 15 games and 50¢ a day meal money. Duty jumped at the offer.

"We had a tough time, but the reason we kept playing was mostly 'cause there wasn't no work," Duty remembered. "You couldn't make over a dollar a day working. I was making good money — it was good at that time, and I could get the girls 'cause they came looking for you even way back then!"

After a few seasons playing with the Giants throughout the Midwest, Radcliffe jumped to Gilkerson's Union Giants, a top-notch traveling team, and then, in 1928, to the Detroit Stars of the Negro National League — considered "The Show" in black baseball circles. Radcliffe was an immediate success and would continue to be for years.

Double Duty Radcliffe (left) and Candy Jim Taylor got the honor of being pictured here with a local beauty queen before a game with the Memphis Red Sox. Taylor and Radcliffe both had long and illustrious careers as players and managers. (Photograph courtesy of NoirTech Research, Inc.)

As enamored with money as he was with winning, he brought the idea of free agency to an art form by "jumping" whenever more money was offered elsewhere. In all, Radcliffe played for more than 40 teams in his career, seven in one season. As a result, he played with and against almost every Negro Leaguer you could name, and was around for some historic moments in Negro League history.

In the Negro Leagues, players who were good at only one position were not very valuable. With rosters as small as 12 men during the depression years, pitchers needed to be able to play outfield, third basemen needed to be able to pitch in an emergency, and everyone needed to be able to hit. It is no wonder that Double Duty was in high demand for 36 years. Besides being one of the best catchers in the Negro Leagues, he usually won about 70 percent of his decisions on the mound and was a dangerous power hitter, often belting 20–25 homers per season.

As a pitcher, Duty was a combination of Don Drysdale, Gaylord Perry and Deion Sanders. He had a good fastball and would knock you down if you dug in too deep, but it was his repertoire of illegal pitches that made him especially tough. His pitch of choice was the emery ball, and he usually had an emery board or other scuffing tool with him at all times. With a properly placed scuff on a new ball, Radcliffe could make a ball break in, out, up or down!

"Double Duty had an emery board," remembered batboy Tony Carlascio. "He'd keep it inside his waistband. If an umpire came out to check him, he'd tug on his belt, the board would slide into his pants, and when he got back to the dugout he'd get it and put it back."[29]

What most ex–Negro Leaguers remembered about Duty's playing, though, was that he never shut up. On the mound he would yell, "Here it comes. Here's the fastball. See if you can hit it!" He had enough on the ball to hurl two no-hitters in his career (he also caught at least two no-hitters). While behind the plate, Duty would taunt batters, throw dirt on their shoes, and tease them about their girlfriends. He also wore a chest protector that read "Thou Shalt Not Steal," and would dare runners to test his cannon-like arm.

"Hey, I know [Duty] was in his late fifties," recalled teammate Slick Surratt, "and he would get back there and he'd tell you, 'Go ahead and steal if you think you can make it,' and he would gun you out!"[30]

Duty played on what many consider the three greatest teams in Negro League history — the '30 St. Louis Stars, the '31 Homestead Grays, and the '32 Pittsburgh Crawfords. The '32 Crawfords featured Hall of Famers Satchel Paige, Josh Gibson, Oscar Charleston and Cool Papa Bell, and they breezed through the season, then beat the Monroe, Louisiana, Monarchs and Chicago American Giants in what was billed as a roving "Negro World Series." To cap the season off properly, they then throttled a major league all-star team led by Hall of Famer Hack Wilson.

Duty also had some unique opportunities to play on teams that were integrated for tournament play and barnstorming. In 1934, he was player-manager of the integrated Jamestown (North Dakota) Red Sox. In what was considered a short season for Negro Leaguers, Duty batted .355, with 17 wins, three losses, and three saves.[31] After the season, Duty managed a North Dakota semipro team that beat Jimmie Foxx's Major League All-Star team three straight games, in Valley City, Jamestown and Bismarck. In the final game Duty went the distance on the mound and ripped a double and two singles in an 11–3 win.[32]

In 1935, Duty and Satchel Paige led an integrated Bismarck, North Dakota, team to the first National Semipro Championship in Wichita, Kansas. The team also featured Negro Leaguers Chet Brewer, Hilton Smith, Barney Morris and Quincy Trouppe, as well as white stars Moose Johnson and Joe Desiderato. Desiderato, a Chicago native, was awed by the skill of Double Duty, and believed he could pitch with Satchel or anyone.

The Bismarck team won seven straight games to win the tournament, which consisted of the top 32 semipro teams in America. Double Duty batted a combined .309 with four wins and no losses while with Bismarck for about two months. He would return to Bismarck in late 1936 to bolster Bismarck's team in an attempt to repeat as semipro champs. Radcliffe performed well, batting .375, but, without Satchel Paige, Bismarck fell short of its goal.[33]

In the late 1930s, Radcliffe played for the Claybrook (Arkansas) Tigers, for whom he threw his second career no-hitter, and for the Memphis Red Sox. The Red Sox, a perennial loser for decades, were turned around by Radcliffe, who pitched, caught and managed. In 1938, Radcliffe led the Sox to the Negro American League first-half pennant, and two play-off wins over the Atlanta Black Crackers — after which the series was suspended because the two teams could not agree on a park to play the games in. Typically, the Negro League World Series rotated between four cities in order to maximize the attendance and money that could be made.

Radcliffe played in six East-West All-Star games in Chicago, representing the Cincinnati Tigers in 1937, the Memphis Red Sox in '38, '39 and '41, the Chicago American Giants in '43 and the Black Barons in '44. Radcliffe, showing his versatility, caught in the '37 classic, pitched and saved the game in '38, pitched and won the '39 game, then pitched in relief in '41. The game in '41 was possibly Radcliffe's lowest moment as a professional. He gave up a home run to Hall of Famer Buck Leonard and the black baseball press openly wondered if the great star was past his prime.

Radcliffe turned 40 during the '42 season and he spent the year as player-manager of his hometown Chicago American Giants. When he and his team underachieved, Radcliffe set out to show that he was not finished yet.

In 1943, he was his usual hustling self, and not only did he bat over .300 and pitch magnificently, as well as catch the entire East-West game representing the Chicago American Giants, but he also copped the Negro American League MVP award, the oldest player to ever do so!

After the season, Radcliffe was "borrowed" by the Birmingham Black

Barons for the Negro League World Series against the Homestead Grays. The Grays whipped the Barons, but Radcliffe made his presence known, getting the only hit off the Grays' Raymond Brown in game four.

Radcliffe stayed with the Black Barons in 1944, and had his greatest baseball thrill during that season's East-West game. With a runner on base, in front of almost 50,000 fans, including his mother, Radcliffe homered off Barney Morris into Comiskey Park's upper deck and that sealed the victory for the West. Radcliffe was showered with money from the crowd and his mother was allowed on the field to hug her son, the hero of the day!

In 1945, Radcliffe started with the Birmingham Black Barons, jumped to the Kansas City Monarchs where he spent two months as teammate and sometime roommate of Jackie Robinson, caught Satchel Paige in a game for the East Chicago Giants against Dizzy Dean's All-Stars, then spent July, August and September as player-manager of the brand new Harlem Globetrotters baseball team, owned by Abe Saperstein, who had started the Globetrotter basketball team years before.

In one game with the Globetrotters, Radcliffe inserted himself into the game as a pinch hitter against the House of David. The David's pitcher was future Major Leaguer Cliff "Rube" Chambers, on leave from the Army, who was throwing a no-hitter with two outs in the ninth inning when Radcliffe dug into the batter's box. He hit a double, and Chambers swore at him as he was doubled over with laughter on second base.[34]

Most baseball fans know that Jackie Robinson integrated the International League in 1946 with the Montreal Royals, and the Majors in 1947 with the Brooklyn Dodgers. Often overlooked are the other pioneers who integrated teams and leagues all across the United States and Canada.

In 1948, Radcliffe integrated two semipro leagues. The first, the Southern Minnesota League, was one of the longest-running leagues in the country. Radcliffe was signed by the Rochester Aces as their "featured hurler," meaning he would pitch every game. Radcliffe's team, one of the worst in the league, was especially weak defensively, and they booted away some great pitching performances.

Radcliffe had one win, five losses, and a 2.54 ERA when he left the team; he left not because of his team's lack of success, but because of the terrible treatment he suffered in the town of Albert Lea. Radcliffe had played for more than 25 years, in every town from sea to shining sea, in "every town a black man could play," but it was that little town in the progressive state of Minnesota that Radcliffe remembers as the worst. Radcliffe's wife, who was at the game in the stands, demanded Radcliffe leave the team and return to Chicago.

When Radcliffe returned to Chicago, a telegram was waiting for him with an offer from the South Bend Studebakers for him to integrate the Michigan-Indiana League, the strongest semipro circuit at the time, and considered to be a shade below the major leagues in strength.

Radcliffe immediately became the team's regular catcher, batted .312 and led his team in homers and RBIs.[35] He was such a success that two other black players were added to the team, third baseman Howard Easterling, and pitcher Gread McKinnis.

Back in the Negro Leagues in 1950, Radcliffe, as player-manager of the Chicago American Giants again, signed two white players named Louis Chirban and Louis Clarizio. When his American Giants traveled to Birmingham to play the Black Barons, he was met at the park's entrance by police chief Bull Connor, who would not allow a "mixed" team to play in "his city."

After 1950, the Negro Leagues became more of a semipro circuit than a black major league, and Double Duty traveled north of the border and became player-manager of the Elmwood Giants in the Manitoba-Dakota League, where he batted .459 with a 3–0 pitching record. The following year he hit .364 with a 1–0 pitching mark at age 50.[36]

After playing briefly in 1953 and '54, his 35th and 36th professional seasons, Radcliffe hung up his cleats, catcher's gear and two gloves for good. He worked several jobs after baseball, including running a Chicago saloon with his brother Alec, one of the best third basemen in Negro League history. Eventually, Radcliffe served as a bird dog scout for the Cleveland Indians and Chicago White Sox.

Starting in the 1980s, when the Negro Leagues gained popularity with modern baseball fans, Radcliffe became a favorite at card shows and hot stove league functions, where he usually brought down the house with his colorful stories of days gone by.

In 1999, Double Duty "came out of retirement" and took the mound for the Schaumburg, Illinois, Flyers of the Northern League. Less than a month shy of his ninety-seventh birthday, Duty threw one pitch (low and outside), and became the oldest player ever to appear in a professional game.

In all, Duty played 36 summers and 22 winters of baseball, retiring in 1954 at the age of 52. In a 1952 *Pittsburgh Courier* newspaper poll of Negro League experts, Double Duty was named the fifth greatest catcher in Negro League history and the seventeenth strongest pitcher.[37]

In 22 games against major leaguers in exhibitions, Duty batted .406 with three wins and no losses on the mound,[38] and in East-West All-Star games, where he was chosen three times as a pitcher and three times as a catcher, he batted approximately .308 with a home run, won one game pitching, saved another and had a 2.35 ERA.[39]

Radcliffe's career lasted so long that he played against both Honus

Wagner, whose rookie year was 1897, and Hank Aaron, who retired after the 1976 season. One can estimate that Radcliffe belted more than 400 homers and 4,000 hits in his long career, and probably won more than 400 games on the mound.

Most of the more than fifty Negro Leaguers that the author has interviewed over the last 15 years believe that Double Duty belongs in the Hall of Fame. "He could do everything but run!" remarked one teammate.[40] "He bragged a lot, but he could back it up. He should be in the Hall of Fame!" said another.[41]

In an online poll in 1999, Duty came in first among Negro Leaguers deserving induction, far outdistancing Cristobal Torriente and Biz Mackey.[42] It is a testament to Double Duty's uniqueness that there is no one major leaguer that historians can compare him to. Five maybe, but not one!

"I don't like to brag," remarked Double Duty, thinking back on his glory days, "but my career was fantastic! I played against the best and held my own. Nobody ever played like I did 'cause I'm Double Duty."

Double Duty had a short stint with the Giants as their manager, as did Quincy Trouppe. Trouppe had a long career as a catcher in the Negro Leagues but during the latter stages of his career he also managed.

By Kyle McNary

Quincy Trouppe in Chicago

During the Depression era 1930s, Chicago was the capital of black baseball. The city's black population tripled between 1910 and 1930, largely due to arrivals from Alabama and Mississippi. Most of them lived on the city's South Side, specifically in what was nicknamed "Bronzeville." Louis Armstrong and others had helped usher in the Jazz Age at local clubs such as the Savoy. The *Chicago Defender* was America's leading black newspaper. And one of the nation's best-known touring basketball teams, the Harlem Globetrotters, was really based in the City of Big Shoulders. Moreover, the father of black organized baseball, former pitcher Andrew "Rube" Foster, founded the Chicago American Giants in 1911. The American Giants became one of the most storied clubs in the history of black baseball, winning the first three pennants in the Negro National League (established in 1920). They played some of their home games in the former ballpark of the White Sox at Thirty-ninth Street and Wentworth Avenue. A variety of stars joined the club's roster over the years and one of those players was catcher Quincy Trouppe.

Quincy Thomas Trouppe was born the youngest of ten children in Dublin, Georgia, on Christmas Day 1912. (The name was spelled with one "p" until Trouppe added a second because of the way Puerto Rican fans pronounced it). The family is said to have moved from Dublin after Quincy's older brother Albert, then a teenager, threatened to kill a white man who had addressed him with racial slurs.

Quincy Trouppe emerged as a strapping sandlot star in St. Louis, hailing from a section of town that produced black stars such as Ross "Satchel" Davis, "Cool Papa" Bell, and Elston Howard. Trouppe began his professional baseball career as a teenager in 1930, his first major team his hometown St. Louis Stars. By 1933, the 20-year-old Trouppe was a switch-hitting reserve catcher for one of black baseball's premier outfits, the Chicago American Giants.

Under new owners Robert A. Cole and Horace G. Hall, the team won the Negro Southern League pennant in 1932 and, when the second Negro National League was organized in 1933, they captured the new league's first title. The year 1933 was a significant year in the Windy City because it was the inaugural year for the social highlight of black American summers, the Negro League East-West game. In that first classic, seven players in the starting lineup for the West squad came from the Chicago roster, including future Hall of Famers Turkey Stearnes and Mule Suttles, and Willie Wells. The others were third baseman Alec Radcliffe, leftfielder "Steel Arm" Davis and catcher Larry Brown, an underrated receiver who started for the Chicago American Giants in front of young Trouppe. Another teammate was Joe "The Midnight Express" Lillard, a former University of Oregon running back and Chicago Hottentot basketball player-coach.

In 1934, Cole's American Giants won the first-half title in the league, but a controversial seven game play-off loss to the Philadelphia Stars prevented a third straight crown. Trouppe split the 1935 season between Kansas City and Chicago.

Trouppe was also an accomplished amateur boxer, a Golden Glover who won a major heavyweight tournament title in 1936. Listed at six feet two inches and 215 pounds, he was bigger than most major league catchers of the time and even some today. He used a heavy bat, and was a pull hitter who had more power from the right side of the plate. Among his monikers were "Baby Quincy" and "Big Train."

Like many catchers, the burly Trouppe was a leader of men. He managed the Cleveland Buckeyes to Negro American League titles in 1945 and 1947. There he signed Eddie Klepp, black baseball's first white everyday player. On the social scene, he made lifelong friends with musicians such as Lionel Hampton, who was an avid baseball fan.

Trouppe's services behind the plate were always in demand. He played in the Mexican League, where he first managed. Employed in a defense job during the height of World War II, he had trouble securing a passport to play in Mexico. The league's president, Jorge Pasquel, intervened, making arrangements for Trouppe's services (and those of hurler Theolic Smith) in exchange for those of 80,000 Mexican workers. He saw action in the Canadian Provincial League, and for the crack semipro Bismarck, North Dakota, club, which also featured Satchel Paige, Hilton Smith, and Ted "Double Duty" Radcliffe, Trouppe's contemporary as a catcher-manager.

He started for the West team in five black East-West games, four of them between 1945 and 1948. In 1948 Trouppe returned to Chicago; here the 35-year-old backstop hit .342 for the city's entry in the Negro American League. It was his second-highest seasonal batting average, and he belted 10 homers. By this time he was the premier handler of pitchers in black baseball.

Trouppe played 14 winters in Latin America. At the age of 39, he appeared in six games for the 1952 Cleveland Indians and 84 games for their Triple-A farm club. He died in Creve Coeur, a suburb of St. Louis, in August of 1993. His son Quincy is an accomplished poet, and a biographer of musician Miles Davis.

By Bijan C. Bayne

5

The Ballparks, the East-West Classics, Integration and the Great Lakes Naval Team

Chicago's ties to black baseball encompass more than just the usual games and teams. In order to get a complete picture one needs to explore some of the other aspects of the game. A fan or a researcher can get a better feel for the type of ballplayers in the Negro Leagues by knowing about their opponents and the parks in which they played their games. These parks hosted a variety of teams and special events, including being the scene of the eventual integration of Chicago's two major league clubs, the White Sox and the Cubs. Integration came about in the 1940s, in part because of the experiences and events surrounding World War II, when many African Americans served their country in the Armed Services, finding themselves fighting and playing alongside their fellow Americans.

Chicago Ballparks

While the City of Chicago's Negro League teams and their history are well known by baseball historians and fans, the places these teams plied their trade have been obscured by the mists of the past. Even those most knowledgeable about the annals of black baseball in the Windy City are not aware that over thirty different ball fields[1] in the city limits served as home fields for Chicago area Negro League teams. In addition to such legendary parks as Old Comiskey Park, Wrigley Field, and Soldier Field, home of the Monsters of the Midway, the Chicago Bears (all served as home field for the Chicago American Giants), places with such unassuming names as Normal Park, Logan Square Park, Tortenson Park, McNichols Park and Brotherhood Park are part of the history of black baseball.

Lake Front Park, which sat at the corner of State Street and Twenty-

third Street, and Ogden Park on the city's north side share the distinction
of being the earliest known home fields for all black teams in the city. Both
played home to the Chicago Excelsiors in 1868, each park being used by the
team into the next decade. By the 1880s, with the steadily increasing popularity of baseball, the number of black teams had grown and as a result
so had the number of ballparks in the city. In that decade alone, the Chicago
Unions used five different parks,[2] the locations of which spanned the city
as their home fields at various times. The clubs played wherever they could
find a willing owner who allowed them to lease or rent their stadium.

Historically speaking, two parks, one of great importance and one of
great interest to baseball historians made their appearances in the 1890s.
The one of great interest was Grand Crossing Park, which sat at Seventy-
first Street and Cottage Grove. The Chicago Unions used this as a home
field in 1890 and 1892, with lesser black teams of the era using it in 1891,
while the Unions played at the Athletic Grounds at Seventy-sixth and Langley Streets. Grand Crossing Park is of interest to baseball historians because
it is the oldest known "Negro League" park that still exists in the city, with
a baseball field currently occupying the spot.[3]

At Thirty-ninth Street and Wentworth Avenue, the year 1899 marked
the first time a major league-level black team played at the Thirty-ninth
Street grounds, which would be the home of the Chicago White Sox from
1900 to 1910. Located four blocks south of Old Comiskey Park, the field was
owned by John Schorling, future business partner of Andrew "Rube" Foster. Schorling purchased the park from the White Sox when Charles
Comiskey wanted it torn down, and he remained involved until his retirement in 1928.[4] The Columbia Giants, Leland Giants, and Chicago Giants
all used the field between 1899 and 1910 but it was not until the 1920s, by
which time it was known as Schorling Park, that its name was immortal-
ized in the pages of black baseball.

In 1920 the Chicago American Giants first used the park as their home
field. The wooden structure, which at various times seated anywhere from
nine thousand to eighteen thousand fans, would remain the home of the
American Giants throughout the 1920s, witnessing the legendary World
Championship teams of 1926 and 1927. The true significance of the park is
the fact that so many Negro league World Championship teams played in
it. Games eight, nine, and ten of the 1924 Negro League World Series
between the Hilldale Daisies and the Kansas City Monarchs were played at
Schorling Park, as were games seven through eleven of the 1926 World Series
between the American Giants and the Atlantic City Bacharach Giants and
games one through four of the 1927 series, which was once again between
the American and Bacharach Giants.

A fire destroyed this legendary park on December 25, 1940, and rebuilding efforts were abandoned the following spring. In 1947 a housing project was built on the site and remains there to this day. Looking at the Wentworth Garden Apartments, no one would imagine the storied past of the land they sit upon.[5]

Normal Park, located at Sixty-ninth and Halstead Streets, which hosted its first black teams in 1907, went on to become home to several Negro League teams over the next two decades. Both the Chicago Giants and the Leland Giants used the park as a home in 1910 as they tried to work out their differences. While the Chicago Giants moved elsewhere the following season, the Leland Giants continued to use the park as a home until about 1919. The park became so synonymous with the Leland team that for a period of time it was known as Leland Giants Field. With 400 box seats, 3,000 grandstand seats, and 1,000 bleacher seats,[6] the field promised the possibility of good gate receipts and no doubt this was part of the appeal for the best Negro League teams to use this park. In fact, in the 1920s it attracted the best black team Chicago had to offer: Rube Foster's Chicago American Giants used it as a home field at various times throughout the decade. The park was condemned in the early 1940s and torn down and replaced with a recreation center for the local community.[7]

When the Leland Giants and, later, the American Giants played in the Chicago City League, one of their regular opponents was the Gunther nine. The Gunthers had their own ballpark at Clark, Leland and Ashland, which opened in 1905 and served as the venue for many great Chicago rivalries. The park was dedicated in April 1905 with the Gunthers playing their first game against the Spaldings and winning 4–3. The park remained in operation until 1913 and then was abandoned as bigger parks took its place. The wooden grandstands that Billy Niesen envisioned held approximately 5,000 fans. A wooden fence surrounded the outfield and a small section of the grandstand was covered, which cost a bit more to sit there. Chase Park later was built on the site of the original Gunther Park. One of the more memorable games that took place there came in 1910, when the Gunthers finally broke the 35 game winning streak of the Leland Giants, defeating them 3–1 behind the strong right arm of Rugar, with Foster on the losing end. When the Chicago Cubs played a three game series against the Leland Giants in 1909 the games were played at Gunther Park.[8]

In 1907 some local residents living near Gunther Park staged a protest to get rid of the park. They objected to the loud noise coming from the stands on Thursday, Saturday and Sunday nights during the season. Lawyer Jonas Hoover was enlisted to help by filing an injunction against the park owner, J. D. Cameron, claiming that the park was a public nuisance.[9]

Another regular opponent of the Leland and American Giants in the first decades of the twentieth century was the Logan Squares. Jimmy Callahan's team had two different parks over the years that hosted games with the Giants. Their new park opened in 1925 and was located at Elston and Kedzia avenues. Callahan estimated that $25,000 was spent to take the old park there and turn it into a new facility for his team. The original ballpark appears to have been close to the new ballpark since they did not expect to lose many local fans.[10]

While a great number of local or city league parks were used in the early half of the century, the use of major league parks by Negro League teams continued as well. It was in 1910 when what would become the best known park in Chicago to Negro League enthusiasts first welcomed black teams. The first Chicago White Sox game to take place at Old Comiskey Park occurred on July 1, 1910[11] and exactly forty-seven days later the first game between two black teams took place.[12] This game would mark the start of an association between the park and black baseball that would span

Comiskey Park not only served as a venue for many Negro League contests over the years but hosted the largest event of the season with the start of the East-West Classic in 1933. (Photograph courtesy of NoirTech Research, Inc.)

over four and a half decades. From 1933 to 1955, Old Comiskey was the site of the annual Negro League East-West All Star game, sometimes even outdrawing its major league counterpart. One such example was 1942, when major league baseball's All Star game held at the polo Grounds in New York drew 34,178 fans[13] compared to the East-West classic of that year, which drew 45,179.[14] All Star games were not the extent of Comiskey Park's role in black baseball, however. Game three of the 1943 World Series between the Birmingham Black Barons and the Homestead Grays was played there, as was game five of the 1946 series between the Kansas City Monarchs and the Newark Eagles, and game four of the 1947 series between the New Cubans and the Cleveland Buckeyes. Although those facts alone would be enough to immortalize it in Chicago baseball lore, the park was also the home of the Chicago American Giants from 1941 through 1950.

Tales abound about Old Comiskey in the storied past of black baseball in Chicago. Hall of Famer Josh Gibson is credited with having struck

Five of the hitting stars of the mid–1940s. From the left are John Smith, Lloyd Davenport, Ralph Wyatt, Jess Douglas and Art Pennington. The photograph was found in Art Pennington's scrapbook. (Photograph courtesy of NoirTech Research, Inc., and the National Baseball Hall of Fame, Cooperstown, New York.)

the clock that sat atop the scoreboard in center field with one of his count-
less home runs. According to Negro League legend Ted Page, a home run
by slugger George "Mule" Suttles left the park, going "between the decks
and out the other side."[15] Destroyed in 1991, this piece of land so steeped
in black baseball history is now a parking lot for the new Comiskey Park.

While its Negro League history cannot compare to that of its American League counterpart, the friendly confines of Wrigley Field was the site
of Negro League games as well. The park was the home field for two different
Negro League teams, the Chicago American Giants from 1943 to 1946 and
the Chicago Brown Bombers of the short lived Negro Major League from
1943 to 1944 and the United States League in 1944 and 1945.

It was at Wrigley Field in 1934 that the Satchel Paige All Stars met the
Dizzy Dean All Stars in a game before 30,000 fans and ended with Paige's
team winning a 1–0 game. During the early 1940s, a number of Satchel Paige

Wrigley Field was home of the Chicago Cubs, who played a few series with
some of the black clubs in the city. Later, the Cubs integrated, with Ernie Banks
and Gene Baker as players and Buck O'Neil as a scout. (Photograph courtesy
of NoirTech Research, Inc.)

Days were held at the park to honor the legendary pitcher and it was these events that resulted in great pitching duels between Paige and Verdell "Lefty" Mathis at the park. As talked about as these games were in the press of the day, the most important Negro League event at the park did not occur until 1955.

While playing for the Chicago Cubs, former Negro League pitcher "Toothpick" Sam Jones became the first African American to pitch a no-hitter in the major leagues. The game, which took place on May 12, 1955, was a pitching masterpiece until the ninth inning, when it appeared as though Jones's luck had run out. He walked the bases loaded to start off the inning but apparently regained his composure when it was needed the most. He proceeded to strike out Dick Groat, Roberto Clemente, and Frank Thomas to win the game and secure the no-hitter.

While there is abundant information available about the ballparks used by Negro League teams in Chicago, that is not to say the story is complete. The truth is that there is much work still to be done. While we may know of the park's existence, that does not automatically mean we know everything else. Researchers know the location of eight different parks used as home fields by black teams in Chicago but do not know the names of any of them. In some cases, this is because the fields were used by teams in the late nineteenth century and the names are simply lost to time — but not always. At the corner of Thirty-seventh and Butler Streets was a park that was used as a home field by the Chicago American Giants during the 1920s. We know the park was average sized, with the foul lines running 355 in left and 353 in right and that center field at its deepest point was 400 feet from home plate, information which was found in various box scores and game accounts. What we don't know is the name of the park. In many cases the newspapers that covered the game knew there was only one ballpark at Thirty-seventh and Butler, so to name the park would have been unnecessary.

In addition, there is much we do not know about parks that were used for games in which the field was not home to either of the teams playing. There are over twenty of these "neutral" sites in Chicago. While newspapers of the time were more apt to give the names and locations of these parks, very little other pertinent information was included. With a team playing at one particular park for years, information that does not appear in print can be gleaned from the recollections of former players. With neutral parks, this is not the case, so information on these sites is extremely difficult to come by.

As an example, a news article talked about the grandstands burning down twice in three weeks at a park on Polk and Lincoln streets. No name was given for the park but the amount of damage to the grandstands was estimated at $19,000. This park likely was used by the Chicago Unions and maybe some of the other semipro black clubs of the time. The Leland Giants played the West Ends at McNichols Park but no other details about the park have been found. They regularly played the Anson Colts, and the Colts had their own park called Anson Park. The Chicago Giants played a series of All-Star contests at Red Sox Park in Chicago.[16]

Of the twenty-two neutral sites in the city, we know the locations of twenty-one of them, the names of fourteen, the seating capacity of three, and the dimensions and history of none of them.[17] Due to the fact that they were city parks and not home to "organized" baseball teams, they can not be found in the tomes that record the history of major and minor league ballparks. City sports directories, which were prevalent at one time, list the home fields of the area teams but not the names or dimensions of the neutral sites. While no doubt the missing information is out there somewhere, the difficulty lies in the finding. As with all other aspects of Negro League baseball history, the search for information is like trying to walk through a maze in the dark; you are going to run into just about every obstacle there is to run into. At the same time, however, the information available on ballparks

The 1948 East-West game at Comiskey Park saw the West triumph over the East 3–0. The West squad included (back from left): Neil Robinson, Willard Brown, Spoon Carter, Willie Grace, Gentry Jessup, Sam Hill, Bill Powell, Lefty Lamarque, Chet Brewer, Piper Davis and Quincy Trouppe. Front Row (from left): Nat Rogers, Leon Kellman, Sam Hairston, Bob Boyd, Ray Neil, Jim Cohen, Verdell Mathis, Herb Souell, Artie Wilson and Roberto "Lefty" Vargas. (Photograph courtesy of NoirTech Research, Inc.)

used by the Negro League, lacking though it is in some cases, is of the utmost importance as it aids further research.

One of the greatest known events for black baseball each year after 1933 was the staging of the East-West Classic. The game was played at Comiskey Park, which allowed the crowds to really grow for these games. Fans of all colors came out to watch the stars of the Negro Leagues play in a big league park.

By Sammy Miller

The East-West Classic

The pinnacle of any Negro League season was the East-West All-Star Classic. It was an all-star game and World Series all wrapped up in one spectacle. Starting in 1933, the game was played annually at Chicago's Comiskey Park, with additional appearances in other cities, some years. It brought thousands of fans to the Grand Hotel in Chicago, becoming the single most important continuous black sporting event in America. Horrendous economic conditions of the thirties and disagreement among league officials on a World Series format from 1928 to 1941 precluded an annual championship series, making the All-Star game black baseball's grandest attraction.

Eventually, all-star attendance grew to over 50,000, often outdrawing its major league counterpart in the early to mid-forties. Many historians, players, and fans argued that the overall smashing success of the Chicago All-Star games was one of the most important factors in the integration of baseball. So many scouts and managers came out to see the stars of the Negro Leagues in these games.

Fans chose the teams by voting in the nation's two largest black newspapers, the *Chicago Defender* and the *Pittsburgh Courier*. Both papers were national weeklies that owed much of their success to excellent political and sports coverage. These papers and others promoted the East-West classics, allowing fans across the country to discover many unheralded stars—the batting power of Buck Leonard, Mule Suttles, and Turkey Stearnes; the lightning speed of Cool Papa Bell, Willie Wells, and Sam Jethroe, and the pitching magic of Leon Day, Hilton Smith, and Satchel Paige. This abundance of talent assembled on the field raised optimism that black players were ready for the white major leagues. With league play normally ignored by the white press, the East-West attraction offered an opportunity for white America to see black baseball's best performers under one tent.

Except for a radio-broadcasted Joe Louis championship fight, this game was the biggest sporting event in black America. In 1995, at the seventy-fifth anniversary dinner given by the Negro Leagues Baseball Museum in

Kansas City, Monte Irvin, in 1941 a 22-year-old outfielder for the Newark Eagles, recalled the tingle that surrounded the game:

One of Kansas City's greatest was Satchel Paige. Satchel and I became great friends after a lot of turmoil in the beginning. Satch was the center of attention, and he knew it. As we stood around the batting cage, he'd say, "Fellas, the East-West Game belongs to me. I don't have to pitch but two or three innings, so I'm gonna be very stingy today. In fact, I'm givin' up nothin'. When I get around to the Grand Hotel tonight, I'll buy you a beer. But today, nothin'. Zero!" You know something. He was right!

On a hot Sunday afternoon, around the eighth inning, the whole stadium started chanting, "Satchel, Satchel, we want Satchel!" Satchel got up and warmed up and took that long loping stride of his across the outfield grass to the pitcher's mound. My buddy and teammate, Len Pearson, was the first hitter. I leaned over to him and said, "Lenny, I feel sorry for you!" He said, "Why?" "You're the first hitter and you know what Satchel wants to do to the first hitter?" He went and took his swings and came back and sat down. I said, "How did he look?" Lenny replied, "I don't know, I haven't seen him yet." Satchel pitched the eight and ninth, and the only hit we got off of him was a swinging bunt by Roy Campanella.

In the 1939 East-West all-star game, the bases were loaded and we were behind by a couple of runs. Up comes Mule Suttles, a big home run hitter just like Babe Ruth. He came to the plate and on a 3–2 pitch, he popped the ball up for the third out. At the Grand Hotel that night, about four o'clock in the morning, Mule said, "If I had that pitch just one more time, I'm sure I could do something with it." After another four or five more beers, he said, "I wish I had that pitch one more time."

Sam Lacy, a writer for the *Baltimore Afro-American* fondly remembered his days at black baseball's biggest event. At 94, Lacy recalled,

It was a holiday for at least 48 hours. People would just about come from everywhere. Mainly because it was such a spectacle. It was better than our present all-star game because the interest was focused purely on black folks.

Train, bus, automobile, very little flying, somehow fans managed to get there. I would go on my vacation during all-star week so that I could be there the entire week. I didn't want to miss anything.

In those days we played ball to win. It was not an exhibition game like it is today. It wasn't just a case of showing up. Guys would vie for positions on the team. And the audience participation was much more rabid than it is now. Much more rabid! Now days, attention is so divided among so many people.

For example, there was a game played here recently in Washington [DC] and Bill White [National League president] had me in his box. It was different! Just different! People didn't go overboard and get excited about the play on the field. At the East-West game, we just raised hell from the first pitch, right on through to the end of the game.

It was a case where it was much more enjoyable. More like a picnic. It was typical of a Joe Louis fight. People came from everywhere. They came in to

New York and settled in around the Hotel Theresa. And made a ball of it all. They didn't give a damn whether they went to the fight or not. Another thing! All the old time musicians would hang around there. All of that added color to the whole affair.

Until recently, even the most avid fan knew little of Negro League history or the rich culture of black baseball that preceded the Jackie Robinson Era. Few fans knew that for more than a half a century, some of the greatest ballplayers excelled behind an artificial, but solid, socioeconomic color line. Hidden behind the color barrier were championship quality teams like the Kansas City Monarchs, the Homestead Grays, the Pittsburgh Crawfords, the Chicago American Giants, the Newark Eagles, the Cleveland Buckeyes and other top professional teams. Out of the shadows came players with catchy names like Buck and Mule, Turkey and Rabbit, the Rev and the Devil, Cool Papa and Pop, Schoolboy and Sonnyman, Smokey and Satch, coming in all shades and sizes to play a game between the white foul lines. Now, we can examine their true greatness without racial blinders.

In 1949, at Ebbets Field in Brooklyn, Jackie Robinson, Roy Campanella, Don Newcombe and Larry Doby became the first African Americans to play in the major leagues' Mid-Summer Classic. The historic event, attended by 32,577 colorful fans, was won by the National Leaguers 11–7.

Since that barrier breaking year, several hundred African Americans, dark-skinned Hispanics, and Latin Americans have dotted the rosters of the American and National Leagues. The East-West Classic really did pave the way for so many others that came afterward.

The East-West Classic gave the best players a chance to show people their talents. Fans came by the thousands to Comiskey Park to watch these talented athletes play each August. The game became so successful that some years they tried a second game in New York City. There was also an effort for a few years to have a North-South Classic as well. Chicago's Gentry Jessup had some success pitching against the southern stars.

Comiskey was not the only big league park in Chicago. While Wrigley never hosted an event as large as the All Star game it did host a number of Negro League games there. In addition, Wrigley became the scene of a historical event in 1947 when Jackie Robinson and the Dodgers came to town.

By Larry Lester

Jackie Goes to Wrigley

All of baseball celebrated 1997 as the Golden Anniversary of Jackie Robinson crossing the color barrier. Fifty years before that May, Jackie and the Dodgers visited Wrigley Field. Reports from the conservative *Chicago*

Tribune and the African American–based *Chicago Defender* offer interesting perspectives on the event.

A look at the attendance charts shows when this game was played. May 18, 1947, featured the largest paid crowd for any single game in Wrigley Field history. The *Chicago Tribune* explains the gate of 46,572: "There was no doubt that the new paid record was set because Robinson, the much discussed Negro athlete, was making his first baseball appearance in Chicago, as a big leaguer." The only larger crowd was in 1930 when 51,556 saw the Cubs. However, there are two other facts to that game. First, over 30,000 of those fans were women who came in for free for Ladies Day. Second, that was back in the days when the fire department allowed management to let overflow crowds take the outfield. The *Defender* noted that over 20,000 were turned away, and then went on to toot its own horn. Quoting a Cubs official, the *Defender* claimed that the fans were "the most orderly large crowd in the history of Wrigley Field ... We were pleased to note that the Negro fans behaved better than our average Sunday fans, for which we thank the *Defender* for its part in this."

The Dodgers handed the Cubs a 4–2 loss, their fifth in a row. However, Jackie would see his 14-game hitting streak snapped when he went 0–4 in the second slot. As he did many times in 1947, Robinson played first base, committing his second error of the year, resulting in no runs.

The Cubs had scored two runs in the fourth when they were able to bunch several base hits. In the seventh Peewee Reese led off with a walk, and Tom Brown, pinch-hitting for Joe Hatten, singled off of Johnny Schmitz. Eddie Stanky then beat out a bunt to load the bases for Jackie. He managed to battle his way to a full count, but then watched a called strike three. Pete Reiser doubled to left, tying up the ballgame. Carl Furillo was given an intentional walk, but when Dixie Walker grounded to second the Dodgers put the go-ahead run on the scoreboard. Cookie Lavagetto was given a free pass, but then Bruce Edwards drew a walk, forcing in the fourth run. That was it for Schmitz; Hank Wyse came in to pitch. He was able to retire Reese to end the inning.

And that was it, an exciting ballgame for one of the largest crowds in Wrigley Field history. The newspaper accounts tell of only one incident of racism. According to the *Defender,* "Other than Robinson [the fans] paid attention to one Dixie Walker, who was the recipient of plenty of boos."

Robinson's experience at Wrigley brings to light the larger issue of integration and the ballplayers given that opportunity to play in Chicago. Ernie Banks and Gene Baker integrated the Chicago Cubs as players, while John "Buck" O'Neil did the same as a scout. Minnie Minoso became the first from the Negro Leagues to star for the Chicago White Sox.

By David Marasco

Bingo & Bango Break the Cubs' Color Line

Ernie Banks and Gene Baker were not the first African Americans to play major league baseball in Chicago. The two infielders integrated the Chicago Cubs in 1953, more than two years after Minnie Minoso joined the White Sox on Chicago's South Side, but they rapidly became two of the most beloved players in the city. They came from the Kansas City Monarchs (the Yankees of the Negro Leagues) and, although Gene was actually signed to a Cubs' contract before Ernie, they became fast friends during their brief time together in the Cubs clubhouse. Both went on to groundbreaking careers in professional baseball, Ernie setting records for his hitting and Gene opening the managerial ranks to blacks across the country.

When Ernie Banks stepped onto the field with the Chicago Cubs for the first time on September 17, 1953, he was the ninth African American to play in the major leagues. During his nearly 18 years with the Cubs, his talent on the field and his modesty and great personality combined to make him arguably the best-loved athlete in Chicago sports history. A stellar infielder with unexpected pop in his bat, Banks was born January 31, 1931, into a lower class family in Dallas and was the oldest boy out of 12 children. His father, Eddie Banks, worked for the Works Progress Administration (WPA) and Essie, his mother, stayed at home to care for the large family. Banks was introduced to baseball by his father, who had played for the Dallas Green Monarchs, a Sundays and holidays Negro baseball team in the city. Ernie and his brother, Benjamin, had served as the Green Monarchs' bat boys.

Ernie became a standout softball player once he entered high school, and quickly branched into football and basketball. His skill on the Booker T. Washington High School softball team brought him to the attention of J. W. Worlds, who owned a fast-pitch team that played around town. Worlds made Banks his starting shortstop and Ernie spent the next few summers touring the Dallas area with the team. At one game, he impressed a former pitcher with the Indianapolis Clowns who was scouting for a local Negro team, the Detroit Colts. Contrary to the name, the Colts were actually based in Amarillo and were essentially a barnstorming team which played throughout the Southwest. The scout, Bill Blair, hoped that Ernie's skill in fast-pitch would carry over to baseball and gave him a tryout. In his first game with the team (even before he'd been offered a spot) Banks hit a home run. After rounding the bases and returning to the dugout, several of the other players told him to take his hat into the stands. A confused Banks did so and returned to the bench with six dollars and change from fans who wished to show their appreciation for his homer. The barnstorming tradition would have paid off handsomely in the big leagues if Ernie could have passed the hat after each of his 512 home runs!

Banks spent two years with the Colts and when he was a senior in high school was given the greatest opportunity of his young life. Negro League legend "Cool Papa" Bell of the Kansas City Monarchs had seen Ernie play with the Colts and suggested to Tom Baird, the Monarchs' owner, that the organization send a representative to the Banks home. Baird sent two and before the day was out Ernie had agreed to join the team as soon as he finished high school. If he made the club, Ernie would earn $300 a month doing what he loved. At one point, after making the squad, Ernie had the honor of playing on an All-Star team organized by Jackie Robinson. The team consisted of blacks who had recently broken into the majors as well as standouts from the Negro Leagues. In the midst of his time with the Monarchs, Ernie was drafted and served in the U.S. Army, where the knee problems that would plague his time at shortstop first developed. Upon his discharge in March 1953, Ernie returned to the Monarchs. The next few months would be the most important of his life.

While in Chicago with the Monarchs, he and a friend, pitcher Bill Dickey, were taken to Wrigley Field to meet with the Cubs' vice-president of personnel, Wid Mathews. Wid first offered Bill a minor league contract and then moved on to a wide-eyed Banks. He said that the Cubs' scouts thought of Banks as a player ready to join the majors without the need for any minor league tryout. He then offered Banks a contract worth $800 a month. Ernie had to hold his right hand steady with his left as he signed the contract. After leaving Wrigley, Monarchs manager Buck O'Neil told Banks that Ernie better write him by the start of the next season with news that he'd doubled his salary. Buck realized what a steal the Cubs had gotten and didn't want Ernie selling himself short for a shot at the bigs. Although the Cubs had paid a total of $20,000 for both Bill and Ernie, later it came out that Ernie was not the organization's first choice. The Cubs initially wanted Jim Gilliam, a second-baseman and outfielder for the Baltimore Elite Giants who had already signed as a free agent with the Dodgers in 1951.

Although Ernie did not join the Cubs until seven years after Jackie Robinson broke the color barrier with the Dodgers, the delay in Chicago was not racially motivated. Phil Wrigley, the beloved owner of the team, did not want to sign a black player simply for financial or fashionable reasons. While some teams seemed to sign the first prospect they could, often with little thought to the player's fit with the team, Wrigley wanted to be sure that he was getting the best possible player for the deal.[18] Wrigley's father, William Wrigley, Jr., had foreseen the days when blacks would be in the majors but recognized during the 1940s that there were many people "in high places" who did not want integration.[19]

When Banks arrived with the club in September 1953, he met the man who was to join him in breaking the color line in Chicago, Gene Baker. Together the two formed the first all-black double-play combination in major league history. Baker had already signed with the Cubs as a free agent in 1950, and as such had been to the Cubs spring training earlier that season. In fact, it was Baker who was the first African American to wear a Cubs uniform. When Gene joined the team from the West Coast a few days after Ernie arrived, many in the Cubs clubhouse already knew him and were on good terms. Ernie had replaced Gene as the Monarchs' starting shortstop when Baker left for the Los Angeles Angels. The Angels were part of the Pacific Coast League and served as a quasi-independent minor league system for the Cubs. The two men became fast friends and Ernie always said he owed a great deal to Gene's help in his transition to the big leagues.

Gene Baker was born June 15, 1925, in Davenport, Iowa, and had attended college at St. Ambrose University in his hometown. He had distinguished himself at shortstop with the Monarchs before signing with the Cubs, but when Ernie joined the Chicago club, Baker shifted to second base. Together the two made a formidable infield combination. Although Baker had little of the slugging ability of the younger Banks, the Chicago fans loved them both and the press took to calling them "the Bingo and Bango twins," with Gene being Bango and Ernie as Bingo. The two were the focus of a fan club whose monthly paper was called *Keystone Capers*.[20] Gene's transition to the majors was rough, and he led National League second basemen in errors during each of his first three seasons.

Eventually, Baker's troubles in the field and nagging injuries to his knees led the Cubs to trade him to the Pirates early in the 1957 campaign. After a series of signings and releases, Baker left the Bucs in June 1961. In a curious twist of fate, however, it was Baker and not Ernie Banks who managed to play in a World Series, getting three at bats against the hated Yankees in the memorable 1960 Series. Gene Baker subsequently scouted for the Pirates throughout the Midwest and even served as manager of their Batavia, New York, farm team for a short time. In so doing, he was the first black manager in professional baseball history.[21] So impressed was Banks with Baker's leadership abilities and his knowledge of the game that he suggested Baker's name often as a good candidate for the first black manager in major league baseball.

The integration of Cubs baseball in Chicago was relatively smooth and lacked much of the antagonism and bitterness that accompanied Jackie Robinson's breaking of the color line in Brooklyn in 1947. This is not to say that everything was easy for Ernie or Gene. However, many of the problems the two did face developed in National League cities further south, such as St. Louis, where racial discrimination was still a facet of everyday life and the two were turned away from a white's only movie theatre. This was due partially to the lateness of their arrival with the Cubs.

When Gene and Ernie broke through in 1953, baseball's great experiment had already been underway for six years. Much of the anti-integration vitriol had already been expended and even the most ardent supporters of the color line recognized that theirs was a losing battle. In addition, the success of players like Jackie Robinson and Larry Doby on the field silenced many critics who expected the quality of the game to decline when blacks took the field. Ernie Banks and Gene Baker, admittedly to different degrees, helped reinforce the idea that African Americans (and an increasing number of Latin Americans) could play on a par with, and often outperform, many whites in the majors. Although Ernie describes in his autobiography an incident during spring training in 1970 when a death threat was phoned in to Cubs management, he never makes it clear what motive the individual might have had for wanting him dead. While it certainly may have been racial (Hank Aaron's problems as he chased Ruth's home run record three years later are evidence enough of the lingering effects of racial tension), it may also have been a fan disgruntled over the Cubs' collapse during the 1969 season, or a person reacting to Ernie's status as a Chicago icon. In the end, Ernie's integration of the Cubs is largely forgotten by fans, who remember his amazing production on a largely unspectacular club or his sunny disposition regardless of the circumstances. Gene Baker's role is almost completely unknown. Both men, however, deserve recognition for their ability to play during a time of great change in baseball and to earn the respect of their peers. They helped to move baseball into a modern era where athletes are rewarded for their ability irrespective of skin color.

The Chicago Cubs not only integrated the ranks of their players but they also took the step to end segregation in their coaching ranks. They called upon a knowledgeable and popular baseball man, Buck O'Neil of the Kansas City Monarchs, to be their first.

By Shawn Selby

Buck O'Neil Integrates the Coaching Ranks

When looking at the Negro Leagues it is difficult to escape a conversation on the topic without talking about John Jordan "Buck" O'Neil. Initially, one might be apt to discuss his time as a player and even his time as a coach. The discussion would inevitably lead into his time with the Kansas

City Monarchs as a player and later scout and coach. However, by discussing Buck O'Neil in this light, while his career was impressive as a player, scout and coach in the Negro Leagues, a major piece of Mr. O'Neil's career, and more importantly, a major piece of baseball history, would be left out. As great as Buck O'Neil's career was in the Negro Leagues, his career in the major leagues was stunning and filled with many historical triumphs, not only for himself but also for black baseball and integration. Mr. O'Neil's time with the Chicago Cubs brought about perhaps more historically profound events than any other African American player's career in the history of major league baseball. Although Jackie Robinson might have been the first Negro Leaguer to play in the major leagues, Buck O'Neil held several firsts himself in integration.

It goes without saying that oftentimes there are people who have the capability to inspire those around them to pursue careers and ideas never thought imaginable. Buck O'Neil was inspired by such an outstanding person in his life. Indeed, Mr. O'Neil had many people influence him in his life; but two people stand out more so than the others. Andrew "Rube" Foster and Ox Clemons seem to have had a major impact on the life that Buck O'Neil led as well as the career that he went on to have. To begin with, Rube Foster was one of the great managers in the Negro Leagues when O'Neil was a child. Buck recalls that Foster "was one of the reasons that [he] wanted to be a manager before [he] played organized baseball."[22] Little did the young John O'Neil know that he was not only bound to become a great player, coach and manager, but also to make history on more than one occasion because of the drive that he developed in watching Rube Foster. More important than perhaps even that drive were the skills that O'Neil learned from watching Rube Foster, how to evaluate talent and lead a team to success— skills that undoubtedly aided in Buck's scouting years with the Cubs.

The other person who passed on some simple yet certainly profound knowledge was Ox Clemons. In Buck O'Neil's book, *I Was Right on Time,* he makes the claim that Ox Clemons was influential to Mr. O'Neil both on the field and off.[23] When asked exactly what he meant by that, Buck responded that the best lesson Ox Clemons ever taught him was that "in whatever you do, be the best that you can be." Mr. O'Neil said "that was enough for me."[24] Buck O'Neil took this information seriously, as his career indicates. He had nothing but praise for Ox Clemons and the lessons he taught Buck about both baseball and life. These lessons, which seem simple, had a profound impact on Mr. O'Neil, and surely helped him when he finally made it to the big leagues. Those simple words mattered more than ever with all eyes on the African American scout and coach, just waiting for him to slip up.

With two great men of such profound inspiration present in Buck O'Neil's life it seems as if he were destined for greatness. Greatness asserted itself throughout his entire career as Buck set records, such as his league-leading batting average of .353 in 1946.[25] However, the accolades that he accumulated in the Negro Leagues, as impressive as they are, do not compare to two achievements that not only put Buck O'Neil in the history books, but also held deep meaning for the integration of black baseball with white baseball. The year was 1956, and with the civil rights movement raging on the domestic scene, John Jordan "Buck" O'Neil made history on the baseball front. That year, following the sale of the Monarchs, Wid Matthews offered Buck O'Neil a job with the Chicago Cubs as a scout. Buck happily accepted and in doing so he became the first African American to ever be a scout in the major leagues.[26]

As a new scout with the Chicago Cubs, Buck's first assignment was to sign Ernie Banks, a task that was not foreign to Buck O'Neil. While he was with the Monarchs he had the opportunity to meet and help sign Ernie Banks to a contract with them. Bell found Ernie in Dallas, Texas, following a tip that told him that there was a player he should go and investigate for shortstop.[27] Wid Matthews told him that his first job as a scout for the Cubs was to get Banks to sign a contract with them, consequently Buck O'Neil had the opportunity to see Ernie Banks sign with two different teams.[28] In doing so, it was almost as if Buck O'Neil was singularly responsible for advancing Ernie Banks's career as a baseball player. While Ernie had the talent, no doubt, it was Buck who encouraged him and helped him in to the big leagues.

O'Neil also had the privilege of finding other talent besides Ernie Banks. O'Neil recalls that some of the other great players he scouted for the Cubs and signed were Lou Brock and Joe Carter, who are in the Hall of Fame, as is Ernie Banks. In reference to Lou Brock, O'Neil notes in his book that Brock "was a good example of a kid with tools and no polish. He must have hit .150 that first year at Southern, but I could see his speed and his power."[29] O'Neil ended up signing Brock after talking to him and encouraging him to finish college before going pro, and instructing him to let the Cubs have a shot at countering any offer he might get. Brock evidently remembered that, because while he was trying out for the White Sox he got in touch with the Cubs and O'Neil topped the Sox offer and signed Lou

Opposite: Buck O'Neil played for many years with the Kansas City Monarchs and often came to Chicago to play. Later he became the first black scout when the Chicago Cubs hired him to find new players for their organization. (Photograph courtesy of NoirTech Research, Inc., and Buck O'Neil.)

Brock.[30] Joe Carter was slightly different. Buck had to promise Carter and his coach at Wichita State that Carter would get more money than the first round draft pick if he did not return to college for his senior year, a promise that Buck did keep. As Buck recalls, "It was just a little more, maybe a thousand dollars, but it worked."[31] Another player Mr. O'Neil scouted and signed was Lee Arthur. Buck is optimistic about Arthur being inducted into the Hall of Fame as well.[32]

Buck recalls that scouting evolved over time and remembers when scouts really had to work to find and sign players. This seemed to be the case with Lou Brock, for example. Buck found him, saw the potential and watched him grow until he signed him. However, with Joe Carter, other people knew about him and wanted to sign him. O'Neil recalls, "When I first started you could hide a guy out, so nobody knew about this guy but you."[33] Lou Brock is a good example. The advantage this gave O'Neil, as a black scout, was that he could get into places that oftentimes the white scouts could not go, or would not go. Buck says, "With me, when I was scouting, the reason the Cubs hired me to scout, was the fact that they wanted me to scout the black players. The Cubs did not have any black players, and so they wanted me to scout the black players because so many of the white scouts actually would not go into the black neighborhoods to scout the black players."[34] Therefore, Buck had an advantage over the white scouts. He also took families to dinner and went to church with them. Often he would stay at the coach's home. The reality is that Buck did more than just scout the players; he mingled with them and almost became part of the family. Buck says that, currently, "everybody knows where everybody is." He states that because of current reports and technology it is easier to find players.[35] Thus scouting, according to Buck O'Neil, has changed. Whether for better or worse he did not say, but it is clear that when Buck O'Neil made history in 1956 by becoming the first black scout he had a clear advantage.

It was during his tenure with the Cubs that he made history for a second time. On May 29, 1962, the Chicago Cubs named Buck as an official coach with the team. He was fifty years old at the time and made a second monumental leap in major league baseball.[36] This second historical event came with a bittersweet twist because Buck O'Neil was never going to be permitted to coach on the field as a third base coach. However, the main reason for that, as Buck recalls, was "because Charlie Grimm, who was more or less the general manager at the time, said, 'Don't you ever let Buck coach third base 'cause if he does some of you guys will lose your job because he knows what he is doing at third base, and so he might be a better coach than you are.'"[37] Outside of baseball the political and social atmosphere of the U.S. was still hostile toward black people. Segregation in northern cities like Detroit, Cleveland, and other areas was deeply imbedded. The South, in states like Mississippi and Alabama, still had its racially charged problems as well. Yet, inside baseball there were clear victories for integration. Buck O'Neil's monumental steps with the Cubs are two good examples.

His career was filled with so many achievements as he grew from a small boy in a celery field who saw the opportunity to play baseball as a career, to a scout and coach with the Cubs, making monumental leaps for integration and consequently making history in the process. While it is clear that O'Neil advanced as a scout as scouting advanced with baseball, it is interesting to see the benefits that went along with his being the only black scout in baseball at the time of his appointment. In addition to that, Buck's tactics for recruiting — such as sitting down with families and going to church with them — while unorthodox to the league, were extremely effective. By his getting to know the family, Buck notes, "it was easier for families and players to say good-bye to home and move away," often to places like Chicago which were often far from their homes.[38] Buck recalls that his most fond memory as a scout was just

> Seeing the baseball players and seeing the black baseball players that were excelling in the major leagues. I knew that the players were good enough. I saw Willie Mays as a kid. I saw Hank Aaron as a kid, all of them playing Negro League baseball. When I got to organized baseball it was just everything I could hope for.[39]

As a player, a scout, and a coach Buck O'Neil was, and remains, an important person in baseball. While he might be remembered more for his time with the Kansas City Monarchs, there is no doubt that his time as a scout and coach with the Cubs is an important component of Buck O'Neil's long history in baseball.

By Jason Norris

Orestes "Minnie" Minoso — Integrating the White Sox

On May 1, 1951, the White Sox made history in Chicago as they integrated their team by signing Orestes "Minnie" Minoso. Minoso, better known as the "Cuban Comet," came to the Major Leagues as a rookie at the age of 26, although he already had a lot of baseball experience in the Negro Leagues and south of the border. He played in two East-West games in 1947 and 1948 and even hit leadoff for the New York Cubans in the 1947 Negro League World Series. In 1946 he hit .309 for the Cubans.[40]

Minoso came to the White Sox in 1951 through a three-team deal with the Indians and As. In his first at bat for the Sox, Minoso hit a home run off Vic Raschi at Comiskey Park. He went on to lead the American League in stolen bases with 31 and triples with 14 as a rookie while hitting .326, and was named the *Sporting News* Rookie of the Year. He led the AL in stolen bases in 1952 and 1953 and tied for the lead in 1956. Minoso used his speed to get on base and to cause havoc once he got there.

The Indians signed Minoso and a nineteen-year-old shortstop named Jose Santiago from the New York Cubans in 1948. They were immediately assigned to Cleveland's Dayton club. Alex Pompez of the Cubans supposedly asked for $25,000 for the two players but Bill Veeck did not pay that amount.[41]

In 1957 Minoso got traded by the White Sox to Cleveland for Early Wynn and Al Smith. Though he did not get to help the White Sox win the pennant in 1959, Bill Veeck gave him an honorary ring, anyway. Minoso returned to the White Sox in 1960 and led the AL in hits with 184. He also hit over .300 and knocked in 105 runs. He finally retired at 42 after the 1964 season, when he was used by the Sox as a pinch hitter, but he went on to play for another decade in Mexico.

Minoso returned for a short stint as a DH in 1976, when the Sox played the Angels. He came up to hit against Frank Tanana and did not get on base. The next game he got the last hit of his career. From 1976 to 1978 Minoso worked for the Sox as a coach, then came to the plate one last time in 1980 as a pinch hitter, going 0–2. Over the course of his career, Minoso hit .298 and had 1,962 hits. He scored over 1,100 runs and drove in just over 1,000. He won a Gold Glove three times for his outfield play and was elected to the AL All Star team seven times. He was incredibly popular during his time with the White Sox, winning the hearts of the fans from his first at bat; after his retirement he was named "Mr. White Sox" by the team president. Those who have met Minoso have always described him as a true gentleman. He never turns down a request for an autograph and is always gracious to everyone he meets.[42]

Minoso was born in Perico, Cuba, on November 29, 1922, as Saturnino Orestes Arrieta Armas Minoso. He played baseball every chance he got, always hoping that one day he would get the chance to be a professional player. He learned a lot of his early skills from his brothers, who also played baseball. Although Minoso quit school at age twelve to go work in the sugar cane fields, he never gave up his dream of playing baseball. Eventually, his father gave him $100 and he headed off to Havana to play. As he was growing up, his baseball idols were Ted Williams and Hank Greenberg.[43]

Integration in major league baseball happened for a variety of complicated reasons and had been a long time coming. One of the things that helped open the doors for people like Larry Doby, Monte Irvin, Ernie Banks,

Gene Baker and Minnie Minoso was World War II. During the war, a number of Negro Leaguers served and found themselves playing baseball for various service teams. One of those clubs found their home at the Great Lakes Naval Training Center.

Great Lakes Naval Team

After seeing success on the basketball court in the winter of 1943–44 the navy decided to expand its sporting activities for its new African American recruits. In 1944 the Great Lakes Training Center established a new baseball team under the direction of Ensign Elmer Pesek. Pesek was given the responsibility of putting together a team of African American athletes to play in the Midwest Servicemen's League (MSL). The navy hoped this team would be as successful as the white team was under the leadership of Mickey Cochrane. Cochrane's club played one game against a Negro League

The 1944 Great Lakes Varsity Club included the following on their roster. Back (from left): William Randall, Chuck Harmon, John Wright, Andy Watts, Herb Bracken, Isaiah White, Jim Brown, Larry Doby and William Campbell. Middle (from left): Earl Richardson, Howard Gay, Stephen Summerow, Luis Pillot, unknown, Leroy Clayton, Jeff Shelton, Wyatt Turner. Seated (from left): Lt. Luke Walton, Ens. Elmer Pesek and Lt. Comm. Paul Hinkle. (Photograph courtesy of NoirTech Research, Inc.)

club in 1943 and lost. Gentry Jessup pitched the Chicago American Giants to a 7–3 victory with Double Duty Radcliffe, Lloyd Davenport and Ralph Wyatt leading the hitting attack.

Pesek received the honor of leading the new ball club because of his own baseball background. A graduate of Capitol University, he had played for three years on the varsity baseball team, and also played in the Ohio State League with a club from Mansfield after graduation. The Great Lakes team, a mix of veterans and new players, would play Negro League clubs, semipro teams, Midwest league games and other service teams. The one team they never played with a complete roster was the training center's white ball club.

Most of the club's games were played at Constitution Field on the naval base, and could be broadcast over three different stations, with more stations added if needed. It appears, however, that the *Great Lakes Bulletin* covered the white games but not the black bluejackets games.

Leading the team to its overall success was its pitching staff. Herbert "Doc" Bracken led the staff with a reported 13–1 record. Doc Bracken made the MSL All Star squad along with teammates Larry Doby, Chuck Harmon, Sonny Randall, John Wright, Brown and Clayton. John Wright is the same pitcher most came to know as the player signed to room with Jackie Robinson when Branch Rickey inked him to a contract at the close of the 1945 season. Wright had played for the Homestead Grays for three seasons before joining the Great Lakes squad. In fact, his reported record in 1943 was 30–5 and he pitched in the East-West classic that year. The third member of the pitching staff came from Guayama, Puerto Rico, but he had started playing ball in the United States in 1939. Luis Pillot twirled for the Cuban Stars and the New York Black Yankees before joining the Cincinnati Clowns in 1943. At age twenty-two, when he became a seaman second class, Pillot brought a great deal of experience to the mound.

Catching duties were shared by Wyatt Turner and Leroy Clayton. Turner brought seven years of playing with the Pittsburgh Crawfords with him, while Clayton had a year's experience with the semipro Chicago Brown Bombers. Clayton hit .340 with the Bombers in 1943.

Arguably the most well-known of the players on the team to fans today was Larry Doby. Hailing from Paterson, New Jersey, Doby had played for the Newark Eagles before joining the navy. He was joined in the infield by four other Negro League players and two newcomers. Chuck Harmon came to the team straight from the University of Toledo, where he played first base, and Andrew Watts had played for the Glen Rogers Red Sox in West Virginia as a utility player. The four veterans included Stephen Summerow and Art Grant from the Cleveland Buckeyes, Alvin Paschal from the Columbus

Buckeyes and James Brown from the Birmingham Black Barons. Brown had also played basketball at Southern University in 1942.

Patrolling the outfield for the Great Lakes squad were three veterans and two newcomers. Leroy Coates and William Randall both came from the Homestead Grays and Howard Gray from the Ethiopian Clowns. Joining them were Isaiah White from the Baltimore Bees and William Campbell of the New Kensington Elks.

Peshek worked with Lt. John Griffith to set up a twenty-five game schedule, played from May 3 through August 13. Griffith was the training base assistant athletic officer. Between league games, the team played barnstorming games with Negro League and semipro clubs in the Midwest. One of the more valuable people associated with the team due to their heavy playing schedule was trainer Francis Drumgolf.

With Bracken and Wright leading the pitching staff, the Great Lakes club won the MSL title with a 32–10 record. To mark their achievement, each member of the club got a ring. One of the highlights along the way to the title was a seven inning no-hitter by John Wright against the Naval Aviation squad in July.[44]

Appendix A

Time Line of African American Achievements in Chicago Baseball*

1901 Frank C. Leland combines the Chicago Unions with the local Columbia Giants to create the Chicago Union Giants.

1905 The Chicago Union Giants are renamed the Leland Giants, reportedly win 112 games against only 10 losses.

1910 Andrew "Rube" Foster takes over control of the Leland Giants.

1911 Andrew "Rube" Foster, the "Father of Black Baseball" organizes the Chicago American Giants.

1914 Frank C. Leland, pioneer club owner, dies in Chicago, Illinois, and is buried in Lincoln Cemetery in Chicago.

1920 The American Giants join the newly organized Negro National League and take the title.

1921 The American Giants win their second league championship.

1922 The American Giants win their third straight league championship.

1926 In the World Series, Claude "Red" Grier for the Bacharach Giants pitches a no-hitter against the Chicago American Giants, the first in Negro League series play. The Chicago club rebounds to win the black World Series, five games to three.

1927 The Chicago American Giants repeat as winners of the Negro World Series, beating the Bacharach Giants five games to three.

1928 The Chicago American Giants, of the Negro National League, put numbers on their jerseys, a year before the New York Yankees do the same.

1930 The godfather of black baseball, Andrew "Rube" Foster dies in a mental institution and is buried in Lincoln Cemetery.

1933 The first East-West All-Star game is played in Chicago at Comiskey Park. American Giants pitcher Willie Foster is the winner of the game.

*Compiled by Larry Lester

1937 The Radcliffe brothers, the Chicago American Giants' Alec (3b) and the Cincinnati Tigers' Ted (c), become the first siblings to appear in the same East-West All-Star game.

1939 The Negro Leagues play two all-star games, one in New York and the other in Chicago. This is 20 years before the major leagues would play two all-star games in the same season, one in Pittsburgh and the other in Los Angeles (1959).

1942 Wrigley Field hosts "Satchel Paige Day." Paige, of the Kansas City Monarchs, pitches against Verdell Mathis of the Memphis Red Sox.

1943 Alec and Ted Radcliffe became the first brothers to represent the same team, the Chicago American Giants, in the East-West all-star classic.

1951 Catcher Sam Hairston becomes the first African American player signed by the White Sox.

1951 White Sox star Minnie Minoso becomes the first black American League player to lead the league in stolen bases, with 31 steals.

1952 The American Giants make their last appearance in the Negro American League.

1953 Gene Baker becomes the first African American to sign with the Chicago Cubs. Ernie Banks becomes the first black player to take the field.

1953 Cubbies Ernie Banks at shortstop and Gene Baker at second base become the first African American keystone combination in major league baseball.

1955 Chicago Cubs' "Toothpick" Sam Jones becomes the first African American to pitch a no-hitter in major league baseball.

1956 Buck O'Neil becomes the first black scout in the major leagues for the Chicago Cubs.

1957 Minnie Minoso (lf), of the White Sox, and Willie Mays (cf) become the first former Negro Leaguers to make major league baseball's first Gold Glove team.

1958 Ernie Banks becomes the first African American Cub to be named the most valuable player in the National League. He would win the MVP award again the next season.

1960 Ernie Banks, Chicago Cubs, becomes the first black player in either league to win the Gold Glove Award at shortstop.

1960 Minnie Minoso, of the White Sox, becomes the first black American League player to lead the league in hits, with 184.

1962 Buck O'Neil becomes the first black coach in major league baseball with the Chicago Cubs.

1971 Vida Blue, with the Oakland As, and Ferguson Jenkins, with the Chicago Cubs, become the first black pitchers to win Cy Young Awards in the same year.

1987 Andre Dawson, outfielder for the Chicago Cubs, becomes the first MVP winner from a last place team.

1993 Bo Jackson becomes the first major leaguer to play with an artificial hip; he homers in the Chicago White Sox opener.

1993 Frank Thomas (1b), is the first African American White Sox player to win the American League's Most Valuable Player Award. He is a unanimous choice by the writers. He would win the MVP award again the next season.

1994 The Chicago White Sox sign NBA legend Michael Jordan to a minor league contract. He is assigned to their Class AA Birmingham Barons.

2000 Jerry Manuel of the Chicago White Sox and Dusty Baker of the San Francisco Giants become the first black managers from both leagues to be named manager of the year in the same year. Baker becomes the first black manager in the NL; he wins the award three times.

2000 Ken Williams becomes the first black general manager in the Chicago White Sox's 100-year history.

Appendix B
Rosters*

All rosters were compiled by the editor from a variety of sources. The rosters are not intended to be seen as being all-inclusive and complete but the best effort by the editor to see who played black baseball in Chicago.

Chicago American Giants

Adkins, Stacy — p (1950)
Alexander, Ted — p (1941)
Allen, Todd — 3b
Allison, Moody — ss (1915)
Anderson, Robert "Andy" — inf/of (1924–25)
Anderson, Curt — p (1951)
Andrews, Herman — of (1940)
Armour, Alfred "Buddy" — of (1947)
Ball, Walter — p (1912, 1915)
Bankhead, Dan — p (1940)
Barbour, Jess — of/1b (1912, 1915–18)
Barnes, Theodore "Ted" — p (1937–40)
Barnhill, Herbert — c (1944–45)
Bassett, Lloyd "Pepper" — c (1936, 1939–41)
Bauchman, Harry — inf (1915–16)
Bayliss, Hank — util (1948–49)
Beckwith, Stan — of /1b (1922–23)
Bell, James "Cool Papa" — of/1b (1942)
Benson, Cleo "Baldy" — c (1942)
Beverly, William "Fireball" — p (1952)
Bibbs, Junius "Rainey" — 2b (1938, 1944)
Bissant, John — of (1939, 1942–47)

Blackman, Clifford — p (1937–38)
Blackwell, Charles — util (1910s)
Bond, Theodore "Tim" — 3b (1940)
Boone, Oscar — c (1940–41)
Bostock, Lyman, Sr. — 1b (1947, 1949)
Bowe, Randolph "Lefty" — p (1939–41)
Bowman, George — 2b (1915–16)
Bradford, William — util (1942)
Bragg, Eugene — c (1925)
Branahan, Finis — p (1923)
Branham, Luther — 2b (1950)
Bray, James — c/of (1925–27)
Brazelton, Clarkson — c (1916)
Brewer, Chet — p (1946, 1948)
Britt, George "Chippy" — p (1918)
Brooks, John — p (1944)
Brown, David — p (1921–22)
Brown, James "Jim" — c (1920–26, 1928–29, 1935)
Brown, John — p (1946)
Brown, Larry "Ironman" — c (1933–35)
Brown, O. — p (1935)
Brown, T. J. — ss (1944)
Bruce, Lloyd — p (1940)
Bumpus, Earl — p (1946–47)
Burris, Samuel James "Speed" — p (1940)

*Compiled by Leslie A. Heaphy

Buster, Herbert — 2b (1943)

Byas, Richard Thomas "Subby" — c/1b (1930–31, 1935–41)

Cannaday, Jesse "Hoss" — 2b (1942)

Carswell, Frank — p (1949, 1951)

Carter, Marlin — ss/3b (1948–50)

Charleston, Oscar — of (1919)

Charter, William M. "Bill" — 1b/2b (1943, 1946)

Chirban, Lou — p (1950)

Clayton, Leroy "Zack" — 1b (1935)

Clifton, Nat — 1b (1949)

Coachman, James — c (1945)

Cornelius, William McKinley "Sug" — p (1933, 1935–41, 1943, 1945–46)

Crawford, Sam — p/trainer (1915, 1925–26)

Cross, Norman — p (1932, 1936–37)

Crutchfield, John William "Jimmie" — of (1941, 1944–45)

Cunningham, Larry — of/1b (1952)

Currie, Rube — p (1926)

Dalton, Rossie — util (1940)

Dandridge, Ray — 3b (1934)

Davenport, Lloyd "Ducky" — of (1943–44, 1949)

Davis, Lonnie — 1b (1952)

Davis, Walter C. "Steel Arm" — of (1927–29, 1935)

Dawson, Johnny — c (1940)

DeMoss, Elwood "Bingo" — inf (1917–18, 1920–25) mgr — 1924, 1936, 1944

Dial, Wilbur — of (1936)

Dials, Lou — of (1936)

Dismukes, William "Dizzy" — p (1916)

Dixon, Herbert "Rap" — c/p (1916–18)

Dixon, George "Tubby" — c (1924–25)

Donaldson, John — p (1917)

Dougherty, Charles "Pat" — p (1913–17)

Douglas, James "Jim" — p (1951)

Douglass, Jesse — 2b/ss/3b (1944–45, 1949–50)

Duff, Ernest — of (1925)

Dukes, Tommy — c (1945)

Duncan, Frank, Sr. — of (1912, 1915–16, 1918)

Duncan, Frank, Jr. — c (1938–40, 1946)

Dunlap, Herman — of (1936–38)

Durham, Joseph Vann "Winn" — of (1952)

Dyll, Frank — ss (1950)

Ellis, Bill "Speak" — p (1944)

Etheridge, — p (1911) Evans, William — of (1924)

Farrell, Luther "Fats" — p (1923)

Felder, Kendall "Buck" — 2b (1944)

Ferrell, Willie Hendrick — p (1941–42)

Ferrer, Efigenio "Coco" "Gene" — of/inf (1951)

Fields, Romey "Buddy" — p (1920)

Folkes, Erwin — ss (1947)

Forrest, Percy — p (1939)

Foster, Rube — p/mgr (1905–1926)

Foster, Willie — p (1923–30, 1932–37)

Francis, William — 3b (1915–18, 1920, 1925)

Gans, Edward "Jude" — of/p (1915–16, 1918, 1920)

Gardner, Floyd "Jelly" — of (1920–26, 1928–29)

Gatewood, William "Big Bill" — p (1912–13, 1915)

Gerard, Alphonso "Al" — of/inf (1948)

Giles, George — of (1936)

Gilliard, Luther — of (1938–40)

Gillyard, Luther — 1b (1937–39)

Gipson, Alvin — p (1941–42, 1949–50)

Golden, Clyde — p (1952)

Grant, Leroy — 1b (1916–18, 1920–24)

Gray, G. E. (1923)

Gray, Roosevelt — 2b (1943)

Guice, Lacey — of (1952)

Gurley, James Earl — p (1924–25)

Hamilton, Gene — 3b (1952)

Hardy, Paul — c (1937–38, 1949, 1951–52) mgr (1952)

Harney, George — p (1923–29)

Harris, Victor — of (1924–25)

Hatten, Rufus — c (1944)

Hawkins, Lemuel — 1b (1924, 1928)

Hayes, Melvin — c (1937)

Haywood, Albert "Buster" — c (1940)

Henderson, Curtis — inf (1941)

Hewitt, Joseph "Joe" — 2b (1924)

Hill, J. Preston "Pete"— of (1911, 1915–18, 1920)

Hill, James— of (1948)

Hill, Samuel "Sam"— of (1947–49)

Hines, John "Mexican"—c/of (1924–29)

Horne, Billy J.— 2b (1938–41)

Hoskins, Dave — p/of (1942, 1949)

Houston, Jess— p (1938–39)

Howard, Herman "Red" "Lefty"— p (1939–40, 1945–46)

Huber, John "Schoolboy"—c (1942, 1944–45, 1950)

Hudson, William Henry "Lefty"— p (1939–41)

Hundley, John —c (1946)

Hunt, Grover —c (1946)

Husband, Vincent — p (1952)

Hutchinson, Fred — ss (1915)

Hyde, Cowan "Bubba"— of (1950)

Ivory, Kay Bee — p (1936)

Jackson, Samuel — 1b (1944)

Jackson, Sanford — 3b/of (1926–28, 1936)

James, Tice "Winky"— ss (1941)

Jefferson, Willie — p (1942)

Jeffries, Harry —c (1944)

Jenkins, Harry — p (1915)

Jessup, Gentry "Jeep"— p (1940–49)

Johnson, Dicta — p/coach (1923–25)

Johnson, Don — 2b (1952)

Johnson, Fred — p (1947)

Johnson, Tom "Schoolboy"— p (1912, 1915–16, 1920–21)

Johnson, Tom "Tommy"— p (1938–40)

Johnson, William "Bill"— p (1938–39)

Jones, Al — p (1944)

Jones, Edward —c (1915)

Kenyon, Harry — of (1923)

King, Wilbur — 2b/ss (1945–46)

Kober, George —(1927)

Lebaux, Wilbert — ss (1936)

Leonard, James— of (1924)

Lillard, Joe — of (1934)

Lindsay, Bill — p (1911–13)

Listach, A.— util (1940)

Lloyd, John Henry "Pop"— ss (1915–17, 1922)

Locke, Clarence — p (1945–49)

Lockett, Lester — 2b (1939–40, 1950)

Longest, Bernell "Berney"— 2b (1946–47)

Lyles, John —(1941)

Lyons, James "Jimmie"— of (1915, 1920–24)

Malarcher, David Julius "Gentleman Dave"— inf (1920–22, 1924–26) mgr (1927–34)

Marshall, Jack — p (1920, 1923, 1928–29)

Marshall, Jack — inf (1935–37)

McAdoo, — 1b (1915–16)

Mcallister, George — 1b (1925)

McBride, Fred — 1b (1940)

McCall, William "Bill"— p (1924–25)

McCall, Henry — 1b (1936–37)

McCord, Butch — 1b

McCoy, Walter Loreo "Real"— p (1945–48)

McCurrine, Jim "Big Stick"— of (1945–48)

McDonald, Luther —(1930–31, 1935)

McDonald, Webster — p (1925–29)

McDougal, John — of (1952)

McKinnis, Greade "Lefty"— p (1944–45, 1949–51)

McLaurin, Felix — of (1949, 1951–52)

McMeans, Willie — p (1945)

McNair, Hurley — of (1915, 1924)

McNeal, Clyde Clifton — ss/2b/3b (1947–50)

Mendez, Jose — p (1918)

Merchant, Henry — p (1940–42)

Miarka, Stanley — 2b (1950)

Miles, John "Mule"— of (1945–46)

Miles, Zell — of (1951–52)

Miller, Eddie — p (1924–25)

Miller, James— p (1927)

Miller, — p (1940)

Milton, Henry — of (1942)

Minor, George — of (1944)

Mitchell, George (1925)

Monroe, William "Bill"— 2b (1911–12)

Morney, Leroy — of/ss (1940)
Morris, Barney — p (1949)
Morton, Sidney "Cy" — ss/2b
Nelson, Clyde — 1b/2b/3b (1943–46)
Newberry, "Schoolboy" — p (1944)
O'Neil, Steve "Buck" — c (1914)
Ortiz, Rafaelito — p (1948)
Owens, Alphonso — 2b (1951)
Owens, Aubrey — p (1923–25)
Owens, William "Bill" — (1925)
Padrone, Juan — p (1924–25)
Paige, Satchel — p (1951)
Parks, William — 1b (1915)
Patterson, Willie Lee "Pat" — of (1952)
Payne, Andrew "Jap" — of (1912)
Pendleton, James "Jim" — ss (1948)
Pennington, Arthur David "Art"
    "Superman" — of/inf (1941–45,
    1949–50)
Petway, Bruce — c/of (1915–18, 1920)
Pierce, William "Bill" — c/1b (1912)
Pierre, Rogers — p (1939)
Pitts, Curtis — c (1950)
Poindexter, Robert — p (1926)
Powell, Mel — p (1935–37)
Powell, Willie — p (1925–26, 1928–29)
Preston, Al — p (1952)
Prince, Buster — p (1944)
Prince, John — 3b (1936)
Radcliffe, Alexander "Alec" — 3b
    (1933–39, 1941–43)
Radcliffe, Theodore "Ted" "Double
    Duty" — p/mgr (1943–44, 1950)
Raines, Lawrence Glenn "Larry" — ss
    (1951–52)
Randolph, Percy — p (1939)
Redd, Ulysses — 3b (1952)
Redding, Dick "Cannonball" — p
    (1917–18)
Redus, Wilson "Frog" — (1935–40)
    capt. (1940)
Reeves, Donald "Soup" — of (1939–41)
Rhodes, Harry — p/1b (1942–50)
Rile, Edward — p (1922–24)
Ritchey, John — c (1947)
Robinson, Charles — of (1939)
Robinson, Jacob — 3b (1947)

Rodriquez, Bienvenido — of/c (1948)
Rogers, William — lf (1928)
Ross, Harold — p (1925)
Roth, Herman — c (1923–25)
Russ, Pythias — c (1926–28)
Russell, Ewing — c (1939)
Sampson, George — ss (1938)
Santop, Louis — c (1915)
Saunders, Leo — p (1940)
Sayler, Al — p (1944)
Scott, Joe — (1950)
Seagraves, Samuel — (1945–46)
Sharpe, Robert — p (1944)
Sheelor, James — 2b (1951–52)
Sheppard, Fred — p (1948)
Shields, Charley "Lefty" — p (1941–43)
Simms, Willie — of (1938–40)
Slaughter, James "Jim" — p (1920s)
Smith, Ernest — of (1939)
Smith, Eugene — p (1949)
Smith, Henry — 2b (1942–43)
Smith, Hilton — p (1943)
Smith, John — rf (1944–45)
Smith, Robert — c (1944)
Smith, S — of (1951)
Smith, Theolic — p (1951)
Smith, Wardell — p (1946)
Sparks, Joseph — 2b (1938–40)
Spearman, Clyde — of (1941–42)
Starks, Otis — p (1920–21)
Stearnes, Norman "Turkey" — of
    (1932–35, 1938)
Stevens, Frank L. — p (1925)
Stewart, Riley — p (1946–48)
Stratton, Leroy "Felton" — 3b (1925)
Strong, Othello — p (1949–51)
Strong, Theodore "Ted" — p (1936)
Strothers, Samuel — (1912)
Summers, Lonnie — c/3b (1949, 1951)
Suttles, George "Mule" — 1b (1933–35)
Sutton, Leroy — p (1942–44)
Sweatt, George — (1926–27)
Talbot, James — c (1947)
Tate, William — 1b (1944)
Taylor, Candy Jim — mgr (1937–38,
    40–41, 1943–44, 1946)
Taylor, Leroy R. — of (1925)

Taylor, R —c (1942)
Thomas, Alfred — p (1949)
Thomas, Dan "Banch" — p (1935–36, 1940)
Thomas, Hazel — (1935)
Thomas, Lacey "Banch" — p (1935–36)
Thomas, Walter — of (1946)
Thompson, Leonard — p (1947)
Thompson, Samuel — p (1942)
Thompson, Sandy — of (1926–27)
Torriente, Cristobal — of (1919–25)
Treadwell, Harold — p (1923–24, 1927)
Trehearn, Bundy "Lefty" —1b (1944)
Trent, Ted "High pockets" — p (1935–39)
Trouppe, Quincy Thomas "Big Train" —c/mgr (1935, 1948)
Turner, E. S. — inf (1930–31)
Turner, Tom (1b)
Tyler, Roy — of (1925–26)
Vargas, Roberto "Lefty" — p (1948)
Vines, Eddie — p (1940)
Walden, Allie — (1944)
Ward, Ira — of (1924)
Ware, Willie Lee —1b (1924–26)
Warren, Jesse — 2b (1947)
Washington, — p (1916)
Watts, Jack —c (1915)
Welch, Winfield — mgr (1949, 1951–52)
Wells, Willie James "Devil" — ss (1933–35)
West, Ollie — p (1944–45)
White, Burlin — C (1916)
White, Eugene "Lawrence" — 2b (1950–51)
White, George — p (1938)
Whitworth, Richard "Dick" — p (1915–18)
Wickware, Frank — p (1911–12, 1914–21)
Wiggins, Maurice — ss
Williams, Bobby — inf (1920–25, 1928–29)
Williams, Charles— 2b (1926–28)
Williams, Frank — of (1946)
Williams, G — 2b (1928)

Williams, Henry — p (1939)
Williams, John — 1b (1948, 1951–52)
Williams, Robert L.— ss (1924–25, 1928)
Williams, Roy — 3b (1952)
Williams, Smokey Joe — p (1914–15)
Williams, Thomas "Tom" — p (1920–21, 1923–24)
Wilson, Emmett — of (1936)
Wolfolk, Lewis— p (1923)
Woods, Parnell — 3b (1942 — mgr (1951)
Wright, —c (1915)
Wright, Danny — p (1952)
Wyatt, Ralph Arthur "Pepper" — ss (1942–46)
Young, Edward "Pep" —1b/c (1938–46)

Chicago Blue Stockings (19th century team)

Adams, F.— of
Briddle, J.— of
Brown, George —c
Brown, T.— 3b
Carter, —1b
Clery, B.— 2b
Daniels, Zack — ss
Hamilton, Thomas— 3b
Hampton, — of
Johnson, — 2b
Shiner, — of
Smith, H.— of
Wing, Charles— p

Chicago Brown Bombers

Bassett, Pepper — (1942)
Bowen, Chuck — of (1943)
Boyd, —1b (1943)
Brock, "Bomber" —c/of (1942–43)
Burch, Walter — p (1943)
Byrd, Ollie — (1944)
Chretian, Rollin — 2b (1943)
Clayton, Leroy —c (1943)
Coles, Ralph — (1942)

Davis, Roosevelt — mgr/p (1942–44)
DeMoss, Bingo— mgr (1942–43, 1946)
Drake, "Double Duty"— p/c (1943)
Evans, Ulysses— p (1943)
Fagen, Gervis— of (1942–43)
Harris, Charles— inf (1943)
Howard, Percy— c (1943)
James, Trice — of/c (1942)
Jefferson, Bernie — mgr (1946)
Jeffrey, — c (1942)
Lewis, Jim — p (1943)
Longest, Bernell — 2b (1942–43)
Longest, Jimmy — 1b (1942–43)
Merchant, Henry — 1b (1942)
Mitchell, George — mgr (1945)
Morehead, Albert — c (1943–46)
Neil, Ralph — (1942)
Nelson, Clyde — inf (1942–43)
Parisee, George — of (1942)
Parker, "Sonny"— p (1942–43)
Petway, Shirley— c (1942–43)
Pierson, — of (1942)
Powell, Melvin "Putt"— p (1943)
Prelo, J. C.— of (1943)
Ray, Richard — inf/of (1943)
Reed, Johnny— p (1942–43)
Rhodes, Armstead — of (1943)
Rowe, William "Schoolboy"— inf/p (1943)
Saylor, — p (1942)
Smith, — 3b (1943)
Stracham, — (1942)
Strong, George — 1b (1942)
Thomas, William — of (1943)
Thompson, Eddie "Buddy"— p (1942–43)
Turner, Oliver— p (1943)
Tyler, Eugene — c/inf (1942–43, 1946)
Tyler, William "Bill"— c (1942)
Walker, Jesse — (1942)
Waller, George — inf (1943)
Wiggins, Maurice — ss
Williams, Bilbo— of (1942–43)
Williams, F. B.— c (1942)
Williams, Johnny "Stringbean"— p/1b (1942–43)
Wilson, Fred — (1942)

Chicago Dominos

Bissant, John — of (1942)
Drake, — p (1942)
Knight, — (1942)
Lewis, — p (1942)
Lockett, Fletcher — ss (1942)
Mathews, — 1b (1942)
Morehead, — c (1942)
Spearman, Clyde — of (1942)
Turner, Thomas— 1b (1942)
Waller, — 3b (1942)
Webb, — 2b (1942)

Chicago Giants

Alexander, — p (1923)
Bachman, Harry — 2b (1923)
Ball, Walter — p (1910–11, 1923–24)
Barbour, Jess— of/1b
Barron, — of (1911)
Beckwith, — ss (1925)
Booker, James— c (1916)
Bray, — c (1923, 1925)
Brewer, Luther — 1b/0f (1918–19)
Buckner, — of (1915)
Clarkson, — c (1915)
Coleman, Clarence — p/c (1919)
Crawford, Sam — p (1913)
Davis, James— p (1920)
Davis, S.— of (1935)
Davis, W.— ss (1935)
Dixon, — p (1915–16)
Donaldson, John — p (1935)
Dougherty, Charles "Pat"— p (1915)
Gatewood, Bill — 1b/p (1911)
George, — ss (1923)
Grace, — of (1937)
Green, Charles— of (1910–11)
Green, J.— of (1915–16)
Green, Joe — 3b (1923)
Green, W.— 3b (1915–16, 1923)
Hall, Perry — 2b (1935)
Harris, Nate — capt. (1910)
Hawkins, Lemuel — 1b (1921)
Hayes, — 3b (1937)
Jackson, — ss (1915)

Jenkins, — of (1916, 1923, 1925)
Jennings, — 2b/ss (1915–16, 1923, 1925)
Johnson, — p (1923)
Jones, —c (1916)
Kelly, — p (1916)
Lane, — 3b (1911)
Lyons, James "Jimmie" — of
Macklin, — ss (1925)
Marshall, Bobby — (1910)
Martin, — p (1913)
Milton, Henry — inf
Mitchell, — p (1935)
Moore, H. — (1910)
Nance, — 2b (1935)
Neal, — 2b (1911)
Norman, William — p (1910)
Ousley, — ss (1935)
Parks, — ss (1911)
Pettus, William — (1910–11)
Radcliffe, "Double Duty" —c (1937)
Saunders, 3b (1935)
Smallwood, — 2b (1925)
Smith, —c (1935)
Smith, K. — ss (1937)
Strothers, Tim — 1b (1915–16)
Sweatt, George — inf/of
Talbert, Danger — (1910)
Taylor, James — (1910)
Taylor, "Steel Arm" — p (1910)
Toney, — 3b (1916)
Turner, Oliver — p (1937–38)
Wallace, Felix — (1910)
Waller, — of (1937)
Ward, — 1b (1925)
Warren, Herman
Waters, — ss (1916)
White, — 1b (1923)
Wiggins, Maurice — ss
Williams, Cyclone Joe — p (1911, 1925)
Wilson, — of (1925)
Winston, Bobby — of (1910–11, 1915–16, 1923)
Wright, George (1910)
Ziegler, — of (1935)

Chicago Keystones (19th century team)

Callahan, — p
Craig, — of
Davis, — of
Glenn, — of
Hanley, —c
Lyons, — 2b
McNamara, — 1b
Selden, — ss

Chicago Monarchs

Braxton, Sonny — (1946)
Byas, Richard "Subby" —c/mgr
Humble, John — p (1946)
Jackson, Horace — p (1946)
Lockett, Fletcher — ss (1946)
McKinnis, Gread "Lefty" — p (1946)
Noble, Gip — P (1946)
Porter, R. —c (1944)
Spearman, Alvin — p (1944)
Thomas, W. — ss (1944)
Tyson, Armand Sr. — owner

Chicago Union Giants

Bachmann, Harry — inf
Binga, William — 1b
Bingham, "Bingo" — of (1915–18)
Bluett, — 2b (1916, 1918)
Brown, E. — 3b (1915, 1918)
Brown, Theo — 3b (1911)
Buckner, Harry — p (1902)
Burch, — p (1915–16)
Coleman, Clarence "Pops" —c (1909, 1915, 1918)
Crawford, Sam — p (1918)
Easley, — of (1924)
Ford, — of (1918)
Foster, Andrew "Rube" — p
Francis, — 3b (1916, 1918)
Glyer, — of (1924)
Graham, — of (1916)
Green, — of (1918)

Hamilton, — p (1924)
Hawks, — 3b (1915)
Hill, — 2b/p (1915)
Jones, Bert — p/of (1901)
Jones, Willis — of (1901–02)
Kelley, — p (1918)
Lee, — of (1918)
Lynch, — of/p/2b (1915)
Lyttle, Clarence — p (1902)
Mann, —1b (1918)
Matthews, — 2b (1924)
McNair, — of (1916)
Means, Thomas — p (1904)
Miller, Joe — p (1902, 1904, 1907)
Monroe, William "Bill" — 2b
Norman, Billy — p (1907)
Payne, Andrew — of (1915–16)
Peters, — ss (1915–16, 1918, 1924)
Ramsey, — of (1907, 1915)
Reeds, —c (1924)
Ross, — p (1904)
Sard, — 3b (1915)
Scotland, —1b (1916)
Simpson, Samp "Slick" — p (1915–16)
Strothers, Tim — c (1918)
Thompson, — 3b (1924)
Treadwell, — p (1924)
Turner, — 2b/1b (1915–16)
Walker, — p (1915)
Washington, —c (1907)
White, —c (1916)
Wilson, — of (1924)
Wyatt, — of (1904)

Chicago Unions

Holland, Billy — p/of (1894, 1897–99)
Hyde, Harry —capt.
Jackson, Robert —c
Jones, Bert — p/of (1898–1900)
Jones, Willis — of (1895–1900)
Means, Thomas — p (1900)
Peters, W. S. — owner
Wyatt, David — of

Cole's American Giants

Brown, Larry —c (1935)
Byas, Dick —c (1935)
Malarcher, Dave — mgr
Redus, Wilson — of (1935)
Suttles, Mule —1b/of (1935)
Trent, Ted — p (1935)
Wells, Willie — ss (1935)

Columbia Giants/ Columbia Union Giants

Ball, Walter — mgr (1938)
Barton, Sherman — of
Binga, William —1b
Brown, — of (1939)
Buckner, Harry — p
Burns, Pete —c/of (1899–1900)
Childs, — 3b (1940)
Davis, Sol — 2b (1939)
Goff, — p (1940)
Grant, Charlie
Hall, —1b (1939)
Hoffman, — of (1940)
Holland, William "Billy" — p/of (1900)
Johnson, George "Chappie" — inf (1899–1900)
Lillard, Joe —c (1939)
Patterson, John W. — mgr (1899–1900)
Powell, Wee Willie — p/of (1938)
Reed, —c (1939)
Roach, — of (1939)
Simmons, Oze — 3b (1939)
Thomas, — ss (1939)
Wiggins, Maurice — ss (1940)
Wilson, George — p

Gilkerson Union Giants

Akers, — ss/of (1930–33)
Anderson, Robert — ss
Brewer, Chet — p (1924)
Brown, David "Lefty" — p (1926)
Byas, Dick —1b (1933)
Campbell, —c (1933)

Coleman, Clarence "Pops"—c
  (1920–30)
Crespo, — 2b (1930)
Donaldson, John — p (1917)
Dwight, — of (1930)
Evans, William — of (1923)
Farrell, Luther — p (1922)
Fernandez, —c (1930)
Gray, —c (1928)
Haley, — 3b (1930)
Hall, —1b (1930)
Harney, George — p (1922)
Harrison, — p (1930)
Henderson, E.— of (1933)
Henderson, R.— 2b (1933)
Johnson, — p (1930)
Mack, —c (1923)
Marshall, Jack — ss (1928)
McDonald, — of (1933)
McNair, — of (1930)
Morris, — p (1930)
Paige, Satchel — p (1933)
Sims, — p (1928)
Smaulding, Owen — p (1930–35)
Torriente, Cristobal — p (1930)
Webb, — 3b (1933)
Wiggins, Maurice — ss (1933)

Great Lakes Naval Team

Bracken, Herb — p
Brown, James— inf
Campbell, William — of
Clayton, Leroy —c
Coates, Leroy — of
Doby, Larry — inf
Grant, Art — inf
Gray, Howard — of
Harmon, Chuck — inf
Paschal, Alvin — inf
Pesek, Elmer — mgr
Pillot, Luis— p
Randall, Leroy — of
Summerow, Stephen — inf
Turner, Wyatt —c
Watts, Andrew — inf

White, Isaiah — of
Wright, John — p

Leland Giants

Baker, Howard —(1910)
Ball, Walter — p (1907–09)
Barton, Sherman —(1905–06)
Becker, —1b (1910)
Binga, Jesse — 3b (1905)
Boles, —1b (1911)
Booker, James—1b (1907–10)
Bowman, Emmett — inf (1909)
Braddick, — 2b (1911)
Campbell, —c (1906)
Davis, Dago— p (1905, 1908)
Dougherty, Charles "Pat" — p (1909–11)
Duncan, Frank — of (1910)
Foster, Andrew "Rube"— p (1907–10)
Gatewood, Bill — p (1906–10)
Gilkerson, — 2b (1909)
Green, Joe — of (1905–06, 1909)
Hardy, — of (1911)
Harris, Nate — 2b (1905–11)
Hill, Pete — of (1908–10)
Hutchinson, Fred — util (1910)
Irwin, — ss (1906)
Johnson, Grant — 2b (1910)
Lindsay, Bill — p (1910)
Lloyd, John Henry — ss (1910)
Lyttle, Clarence — of (1906)
Matthews, Dell — p/of (1905)
Mill, — of (1910)
Mooney, — p (1910)
Moore, Harry "Mike"—1b (1907–11)
Norman, William "Billy" — p (1907–09)
Payne, Andrew — of (1907–10)
Petway, Bruce —c (1908–10)
Pryor, — 3b (1910)
Robinson, —c (1905)
Rose, —c (1908)
Smith, — 3b (1905–06)
Strothers, Samuel "Tim"—1b/c
  (1908–11)
Talbert, Danger — 2b (1906–11)
Taylor, —1b (1905–06)

Taylor, Johnny "Steel Arm" — p
  (1907–09)
Wickware, Frank — p (1910–11)
Williams, Smokey Joe — p (1910)
Winston, Robert "Bob" — of (1907–09)
Wright, Jess — ss (1907–09)

Mounds Blues

Curd, G. — of (1936)
Hayes, T. — of (1936)
Johnson, Allen — owner
Lyles, J. "Hook" — ss (1936)
McCallister, Chip — p (1936)
McNeary, S. — of (1936)
Merritt, R. B. — c (1936)
Mims, R. — p (1936)
Mitchell, George — mgr (1936)
Newman, William — c (1936)
Scott, Robert "Rabbit" — p (1936)

Palmer House All Stars

Abbott, Langston — p (1939)
Alexander, — p (1940)
Bibbs, Rainey — 3b (1939)
Bissant, John — of (1940–41)
Brown, James "Jim" — c/mgr
Byas, Richard "Dick" — 1b/c (1939–40)
Campbell, Buddy — c (1939)
Cross, Norman — p (1939–41)

Davis, Roosevelt — p (1940)
Davis, Walter "Steel Arm" — 1b (1941)
Dial, Kermit — 1b (1938–39)
Donaldson, — p (1940)
Drake, Andy — c (1939–40)
Duncan, Frank — c (1939–40)
Henderson, Robert "Wimpy" — 2b
  (1939–41)
Johnson, Tom — p (1940–41)
Jones, Hank — p (1939)
Listach, A. — p (1940)
Livingstone, — of (1939)
Lloyd, Curtis "Bingo" — of (1939–40)
Longest, Bernell — (1941)
Markham, John — p (1939–40)
Marshall, Jack — inf (1939–41)
Mitchell, — p (1941)
Ousley, Guy — 3b (1939)
Parker, Lefty — p (1939)
Powell, Malvin — p/of (1940–41)
Radcliffe, Alec — mgr/p (1940–41)
Radcliffe, Theodore "Double Duty" —
  c (1940)
Reed, John — p (1939–40)
Rogers, Nat — inf (1939)
Smaulding, Bazz Owen — sec (1941)
Stearnes, Norman "Turkey" — of
  (1941)
Thompson, Sandy "Lefty" — p
  (1939–41)
Wiggins, Maurice — ss (1939)
Williams, — p (1941)

Appendix C
Chicago Players in the Major Leagues*

Listed below are representatives from Chicago-based teams who would later play in the major leagues.

Future major leaguers who played with the American Giants

1. Dan Bankhead, debut 1947 — Brooklyn Dodgers
2. Leroy "Satchel" Paige, 1948 — Cleveland Indians—**HOF**, *All-Star*
3. Quincy Trouppe, 1952 — Cleveland Indians
4. Jim Pendleton, 1953 — Milwaukee Braves
5. Dave Hoskins, 1953 — Cleveland Indians
6. Joe "Pop" Durham, 1954 — Baltimore Orioles
7. Joe Taylor, 1954 — Philadelphia Athletics
8. Roberto Vargas, 1955 — Milwaukee Braves
9. Larry Raines, 1957 — Cleveland Indians

Former Negro Leaguers who played for either the White Sox or the Cubs

CUBS
1. George Altman — 1b, of — 1959–62, 1965–67, *All-Star*
2. Ernie Banks — ss, 1b — 1953–71, *All-Star*, **HOF**
3. Gene Baker, 2b, 1953–57, *All-Star*
4. Mike Gonzalez — c — 1925–29
5. Monte Irvin — of — 1956, *All-Star*, **HOF**
6. "Sweet" Lou Johnson — of — 1960, 1968
7. "Toothpick" Sam Jones — p — 1955–56, *All-Star*

*Compiled by Larry Lester

8. Luis Marquez — of —1954
9. Willie Smith — of —1968–70

WHITE SOX

1. Jose Acosta — p —1922
2. Bob Boyd —1b —1951, 1953–54
3. Larry Doby — of —1956–57, 1959, *All-Star,* **HOF**
4. Sam Hairston —c —1951
5. Connie Johnson — p —1953, 1955–56
6. Minnie Minoso— of —1951–57, 1960–61, 1964, 1976, 1980, *All-Star*
7. Hector Rodriquez — 3b —1952
8. Harry "Suitcase" Simpson — of, 1b —1959, *All-Star*
9. Al Smith — of —1958–62, *All-Star*

Players who played blackball in Chicago and are now members of a National Hall of Fame (with induction years)

CHICAGO GIANTS
Smokey Joe Williams, U.S.—1999

CHICAGO AMERICAN GIANTS
James "Cool Papa" Bell, U.S.—1974
Oscar Charleston, U.S.—1976, Cuba —1997
Jose Fernandez, Cuba —1965
Andrew "Rube" Foster, U.S.—1981
Willie Foster, U.S.—1996
John Henry "Pop" Lloyd, U.S.—1977
Jose Mendez, Cuba —1939, U.S.— 2006
Rafaelito Ortiz, Puerto Rico—1992
Leroy "Satchel" Paige, U.S.—1971, Puerto Rico—1996
Norman "Turkey" Stearnes, U.S.— 2000
Cristobal Torriente, Cuba —1939, U.S.— 2006
Willie "Devil" Wells, U.S.—1997
Smokey Joe Williams, U.S.—1999

LELAND GIANTS
Andrew "Rube" Foster, U.S.—1981
John Henry "Pop" Lloyd, U.S.—1977

CHICAGO UNION GIANTS
Andrew "Rube" Foster, U.S.—1981

Appendix D
East-West Game Highlights, 1933–1953[*]

Highest Attendance

1943: 51,273. West 2, East 1. Satchel Paige — WP; Dave Barnhill — LP

Lowest Attendance

1933: First game 19,568. West 11, East 7. Willie Foster — WP, Sam Streeter — LP

Career Batting

Most Game Appearances: 13, Buck Leonard and Alec Radcliffe
Most At Bats: 50, Alec Radcliffe
Most Runs Scored: 9, Buck Leonard
Most Hits: 17, Josh Gibson
Most Doubles: 7, Willie Wells
Most Triples: 2, Sam Jethroe
Most Home Runs: 3, Buck Leonard
Most RBIs: 14, Buck Leonard
Most Total Bases: 27, Buck Leonard
Most Stolen Bases: 4, Pat Patterson and Henry Kimbro
Highest Batting Average: .500, Neal Robinson, 9 games
Highest Slugging Percentage: .941, Mule Suttles, 5 games.

Career Pitching

Most Games Pitched: 9, Leon Day
Most Games Won: 2, Dan Bankhead, Bill Byrd and Satchel Paige
Most Games Lost: 3, Vibert Clarke
Most Innings Pitched: 21⅓, Leon Day
Most Hits Allowed: 18, Hilton Smith and Bill Byrd
Most Strikeouts: 23, Leon Day
Lowest ERA: 0.00, Jonas Gaines, 11⅓ innings

Participants in the East-West All-Star Game from the Chicago American Giants

1933

Brown, Larry "Iron Man" c
Davis, Walter C. "Steel Arm" lf
Foster, Willie Hendrick "Bill" p
Radcliffe, Alexander "Alec" 3b
Stearnes, Norman Thomas "Turkey" cf
Suttles, George "Mule" 1b
Wells, Willie James "Devil" ss

1934

Brown, Larry "Iron Man" c
Foster, Willie Hendrick "Bill" p

*Compiled by Larry Lester

Radcliffe, Alexander "Alec" 3b
Stearnes, Norman Thomas "Turkey" cf
Suttles, George "Mule" 1b
Trent, Ted "Highpockets" p
Wells, Willie James "Devil" ss

1935

Cornelius, William McKinley "Sug" p
Radcliffe, Alexander "Alec" 3b
Stearnes, Norman Thomas "Turkey"
  rf
Suttles, George "Mule" lf
Trent, Ted "Highpockets" p
Wells, Willie James "Devil" ss

1936

Byas, Richard Thomas "Subby" c
Cornelius, William McKinley "Sug" p
Dials, Oland Cecil "Lou" rf
Dunlap, Herman lf
Radcliffe, Alexander "Alec" 3b
Redus, Wilson R. "Frog" rf
Trent, Ted "Highpockets" p

1937

Byas, Richard Thomas "Subby" ph
Radcliffe, Alexander "Alec" 3b
Redus, Wilson R. "Frog" rf
Trent, Ted "Highpockets" p

1938

Cornelius, William McKinley "Sug" p
Duncan, Jr., Frank c
Radcliffe, Alexander "Alec" 3b

1939

Bassett, Lloyd "Pepper" c (2)
Horne, William "Billy" 2b (2)
Radcliffe, Alexander "Alec" 3b, ss (2)

1940

Morney, Leroy ss
Reeves, Donald "Soup" lf

1941

Bassett, Lloyd "Pepper" c
Crutchfield, John William "Jimmie" lf
Horne, William "Billy" ss
Hudson, William Henry "Lefty" ph

1942

Bell, James Thomas "Cool Papa" cf, rf
  (2)
Pennington, Arthur David "Superman" ph, cf (2)
Wyatt, Ralph Arthur "Pepper" ss

1943

Davenport, Lloyd "Ducky" rf
Radcliffe, Alexander "Alec" 3b
Radcliffe, Theodore Roosevelt "Dou-
  ble Duty" c

1944

Davenport, Lloyd "Ducky" rf
Jessup, Gentry "Jeep" p
McKinnis, Gread "Lefty" p

1945

Jessup, Gentry "Jeep" p

1946

Jessup, Gentry "Jeep" p
Nelson, Clyde 3b

1947

Armour, Alfred "Buddy" p, rf (2)
Jessup, Gentry "Jeep" p

1948

Hill, Samuel "Sam" rf (2)
Jessup, Gentry "Jeep" p
Trouppe, Quincy Thomas "Big Train"
  c (2)
Vargas, Roberto Enrique p

1949

McKinnis, Gread "Lefty" p
Summers, Lonnie "Carl" c

1950

Douglas, Jesse Warren 3b
McNeal, Clyde Clifton "Junior" ss
Pennington, Arthur David "Super-
    man" cf

1951

Anderson, Andy lf
Woods, Parnell 3b

1952

Beverly, William "Fireball" p
Durham, Winn lf
McLaurin, Felix lf

Patterson, Jr., Willie Lee "Pat" 1b
Raines, Lawrence Glenn Hope
    "Larry" ss

Most Appearances by a Chicago American Giant

9, Alec Radcliffe, 3b
5, Gentry Jessup, p
4, Ted "Highpockets" Trent, p

Chapter Notes

Chapter 1

1. *New York Clipper*, 3 September 1870.
2. *Chicago Tribune*, 17 September 1870; *New York Clipper*, 24 September 1870.
3. *Chicago Times*, 21, 23, 25 and 28 September 1870.
4. *Chicago Tribune*, September 1896.
5. Ibid., June and September 1897.
6. "Chicago Unions," *Chicago Tribune*, 2 September 1899.
7. "Lost to Columbia Giants," *Chicago Tribune*, 4 September 1899.
8. "Unions 13, Joliet Standards 10," *Chicago Tribune*, 31 July 1899.
9. "Unions 11, Rochester 1," *Chicago Tribune*, 5 June 1899; "Unions Defeat Cuban Giants," Ibid., 12 June 1899.
10. "Hold Last Rites for Major R. R. Jackson," *Chicago Defender*, 20 June 1942.
11. *Chicago Tribune*, 26 May 1902 and 4 August 1902.
12. "Union Giants Reorganized," *Chicago Tribune*, 2 March 1902; "Union Giants 17, Eclipse 5," Ibid., 26 May 1902; "Union Giants are Champions," *Chicago Tribune*, 4 August 1902.
13. "Interstate League Meets," *Chicago Tribune*, 23 February 1903; "Union Giants 6, Clinton 1," Ibid., 21 August 1903; "Giants Down the Standards," Ibid., 14 September 1903;
14. "Three Game Series," *Chicago Tribune*, 11 September 1904.
15. "Cuban Giants are Winners," *Chicago Tribune*, 19 September 1904; "Chicago Colored Team Wins," Ibid., 26 September 1904.
16. "Fight for the Union Giants," *Chicago Tribune*, 7 June 1904.
17. Larry Lester, et al., *Black Baseball in Chicago* (Chicago: Arcadia Publishing, 2000), 18.
18. "Games of 'Semi-Pro' Teams," *Chicago Tribune*, 3 September 1907, 11 and 10 July 1905; *Decatur Review*, 13 July 1905; *Fort Wayne Journal Gazette*, 28 May 1905.
19. *Chicago Broad Ax*, 8 August 1908.
20. "Contests on the Semi-Pro Field," *Chicago Tribune*, 16 September 1907.
21. "Support Presidential Candidate," *Chicago Tribune*, 7 June 1908.
22. "Beat Gunthers 2–1," *Chicago Tribune*, 13 September 1909.
23. "Beat Cuban Stars 13–6," *Chicago Tribune*, 13 July 1909.
24. "Lost to Cuban Stars," *Chicago Tribune*, 16 July 1909.
25. Fay Young, "Through the Years," *Chicago Tribune*, September 1909; *Chicago Defender*, 21 August 1948, 11.
26. "Club in Court," *Chicago Tribune*, 3 March 1910; "Show Split," Ibid., 18 April 1911.
27. "Beat Oklahoma Giants," *Chicago Tribune*, 6 September 1910.
28. "Again the Leland Giants Take Measure of Gunthers," *Chicago Tribune*, 14 August 1910, C2.
29. *Chicago Tribune*, 8 May 1911 and 5 July 1911.

Chapter 2

1. *Indianapolis Freeman*, 8 September 1917, 4.
2. Ibid., 15 September 1917, 7.
3. Ibid., 25 August 1917, 6 and 20 October 1917.
4. *Indianapolis Recorder*, 25 September 1926.
5. "Jim Taylor Signs as Manager of Am. Giants," *Chicago Defender*, 13 January 1945, 7.
6. *Indianapolis Freeman*, 14 June 1913; *Chicago Daily Tribune*, 12 June 1913.
7. Harry Williams, "Mighty Foster Fans in Pinch," *Los Angeles Times*, 9 November 1912, I9.

8. *Chicago Defender,* 14 December 1912, 5 April and 5 July 1913.

9. "Foster Anxious to Tackle Tinks," *Chicago Tribune,* 19 September 1914.

10. *Chicago Defender,* 25 September 1915; "Negro Clubs in Title Play," *Indianapolis Star,* 1 August 1915, 9; "Riot on Field as Fosters Beat Cuban Team, 3–1," *Chicago Tribune,* 24 August 1915.

11. *Chicago Defender,* 16 September and 21 October 1916.

12. "American Giants Rap Ball to All Corners of Park for Victory," *The Decatur Review,* 17 July 1921, 6; "American Giants on Top," *Chicago Tribune,* 14 June 1921.

13. *Chicago Defender,* 4 September 1948.

14. Ibid., 2 June 1923.

15. "Torriente Hits Home Run with 3 on in Wild 9th," *Chicago Defender,* 22 September 1923.

16. *Chicago Defender,* 23 August 1924.

17. "Giants Sweep Six Straight Games," *Chicago Defender,* 13 June 1936.

18. *Chicago Defender,* 22 May 1937.

19. Ibid., 27 August 1938.

20. Ibid., 14 August 1943; "Chicago Giants Beat Sailors," *Chicago Daily Tribune,* 8 August 1943.

21. "American Giants Split Even with Cincinnati," *Chicago Defender,* 17 July 1943; "Chicago is Shut Out By Memphis Sox," Ibid., 11 September 1943.

22. "Huber's 1–0 Victory wins League Title," *Chicago Defender,* 25 September 1943.

23. "Alex Radcliffe Steals Home to Beat Paige," *Chicago Defender,* 15 July 1944, 7.

24. "Birmingham Defeats Chicago Twice, Even One-handed Southpaw Wins," *Chicago Defender,* 16 June 1945; "Am. Giants Win Three from Memphis Red Sox," Ibid., 21 July 1945.

25. *Chicago Tribune,* 5 May 1946, A2; "Openers Divided," Ibid., 6 May 1946, 24.

26. *Pittsburgh Courier,* 18 May 1946, 16; "Gibson Homers as Giants Lose," *Chicago Defender,* 27 July 1946.

27. "Chicago Divides Two with Memphis," *Chicago Defender,* 17 May 1947.

28. "Elite Giants Take NAL Title in Four Straight," *Chicago Defender,* 1 October 1949; "American Giants End Season by Beating Indianapolis Twice," *Chicago Tribune,* 6 September 1949, B3.

29. *Chicago Defender,* 15 July 1950.

30. "Monarchs Win 2 Games from Chicago Giants," *Chicago Defender,* 22 July 1950.

31. "Fire Destroys American Giants Ball Park Seats," *Chicago Defender,* 4 January 1941, 24.

32. *Cleveland Call and Post,* 11 May 1939, 11; *Chicago Defender,* 20 May 1939 and 6 September 1941; "Kansas City Is Here Aug. 24," Ibid., 25 August 1945; "Chicagoans Test Bucks," *Syracuse Herald-Journal,* 4 June 1949.

33. "Kansas City Wallops Chicago Giants 13–3," *Chicago Defender,* 10 May 1947.

34. *Chicago Defender,* 16 May 1936 and 3 December 1949.

35. Ibid., 28 April 1962.

36. Ibid., 13 January 1951.

37. Ibid., 11 April 1942.

38. *Chicago Defender,* 25 April, 6 June, 18 July and 19 September 1942; "Winklers and Bombers Play 2 Games Today," *Chicago Tribune,* 2 August 1942.

39. "Nate Shyer's Semi-pros Beat Brown Bombers," *Chicago Tribune,* 27 September 1943; *Chicago Defender,* 16 May and 27 June 1942, 12 June and 3 July 1943 and 22 July 1944.

40. "Bombers vs. E. C. Giants here Sunday," *Hammond Times,* 18 May 1943, 9.

41. *Chicago Defender,* 26 May 1945; "Chicago Brown Bombers, Cuban La Palomas Play Tuesday Night," *Council Bluffs Nonpareil,* 16 June 1946, 19; "La Palomas Top Brown Bombers," *New York Times,* 4 July 1946.

42. "Chicago Nine Wins Illinois Semi-pro Title," *Chicago Tribune,* 2 August 1939, 24.

43. David Condon, "Negro Baseball: Scars are Fading," *Chicago Tribune,* 20 September 1977, C3.

44. "Paige is Here on Sept. 22," *Chicago Defender,* 21 September 1940, 22.

45. "Palmer House Nine Wins; Changes Name," *Chicago Defender,* 5 July 1941.

46. *Chicago Defender,* 10 and 17 June 1939; 28 September 1940, 22; "Toledo Crawfords Won the Trophy," Ibid., 24 June 1939, 10; *Chicago Tribune,* 7 and 22 July and 11 August 1940.

47. *Chicago Defender,* 10 June 1939, 14 June 1941.

48. "Joe Green's Giants Drop Double Header," *Chicago Defender,* 20 June 1936; "Chicago Giants Win," Ibid., 16 July 1938.

49. "Walter Ball Will Manage Columbia Giants Ball Team," *Chicago Defender,* 9 April 1938.

50. "Union Giants Win 7–1 Game," *Chicago Defender,* 28 September 1940.

51. "Mounds Blues Lighting System Second to None," *Chicago Defender,* 7 May 1938.

52. *Chicago Defender,* 3 June 1944 and 15 June 1946.

53. *Merrill Daily Herald,* 19 June 1923.

54. *Portage Register Democrat,* 29 August 1923.

55. *Park Falls Herald*, 17 August 1923.
56. *Tomahawk Leader*, 28 June 1923.
57. Gilkerson Union Giants File, National Baseball Hall of Fame, Cooperstown, New York.
58. Smaulding Papers, New Mexico State Archives.
59. "Gilkerson Union Giants Return Here for Three Games with St. Paul," *Bismarck Tribune*, 21 June 1930, 10.

Chapter 3

1. *Chicago Tribune*, 28 July 1947.
2. "Close Game to Colored Men," *Chicago Tribune*, 1 August 1909, C2.
3. "Cubs Trim Giants in Final Game, 1–0," *Chicago Tribune*, 23 October 1909, 14.
4. "American Giants Victors against Chicago Giants," *Chicago Tribune*, 21 August 1911, 6.
5. *Chicago Defender*, 21 December 1946, 11; Merle Kleinknecht, "Ball, George Walter," *Biographical Dictionary of American Sports* (Westport, CT: Greenwood Press, 2000), 59–60.
6. "Walter Ball, Famous Pitcher, Dies in Chicago," *Chicago Defender*, 21 December 1946, 11.
7. *Chicago Defender*, 27 May 1916.
8. Brent Kelley, *The Negro Leagues Revisited*, 70–78.
9. Larry Lester, Sammy J. Miller and Dick Clark. *Black Baseball in Chicago* (Chicago: Arcadia, 2000), 62.
10. John B. Holway wrote in his book that Bassett batted .295 in 1937, and in a short paper written by Holway that was unpublished he wrote that Bassett batted .414 in that same year.
11. John B. Holway, *The Complete Book of Baseball's Negro Leagues: The Other Half of Baseball Histor* (Fern Park, FL: Hastings House, 2001), 406.
12. William Brashler, *Josh Gibson: A Life in the Negro Leagues* (Chicago: Ivan R. Dee, 2000), 104.
13. Larry Lester, *Black Baseball's National Showcase: The East-West All-Star Game, 1933–1953* (Lincoln: University of Nebraska Press: 2001), 321.
14. Ibid., 106, 128, 133, 164–65, 412.
15. Ibid., 106, 133.
16. William F. McNeil, 94–95.
17. Art Carter, "Baseball's Fastest," *Chicago Defender*, 30 March 1974, B8.
18. *Chicago Defender*, 18 July 1942.
19. Lester, *Black Baseball's National Showcase*, 57.

20. *Chicago Defender*, 31 December 1938, 16 and 2 September 1939.
21. Ibid., 24 June 1939.
22. Ibid., 10 August 1940.
23. Ibid., 24 June and 29 July 1939 and 13 July 1940.
24. Larry Lester, "Chester Brewer," *Biographical Dictionary of American Sports*, 143–144.
25. Lester, *Black Baseball's National Showcase*, 35.
26. *Chicago Defender*, 18 May 1935 and 13 February 1943.
27. *New York Age*, 11 April 1931, 6.
28. *Chicago Defender*, 15 June 1935.
29. David Bernstein, "Larry Brown," *Biographical Dictionary of American Sports*, 157–58.
30. Kenan Helse, "Richard 'Subby' Bayas [sic] Star of Negro Baseball," *Chicago Tribune*, 15 October 1985, A6.
31. *Chicago Defender*, 20 December 1944; Lester, 58.
32. Ibid., 25 July 1936, 14.
33. "Chairmakers Drop 8–5 Tilt to Chicago American Giants," *Sheboygan Press*, 17 June 1939; *Chicago Defender*, 25 April 1942.
34. *Chicago Defender*, 14 April 1945, 7, and 1 September 1945, 7.
35. "Chicago Negro Team Defeats Blues, 10–7," *Oshkosh Northwestern*, 9 June 1938, 17.
36. Lester, *Black Baseball's National Showcase*, 35.
37. *Chicago Defender*, 26 March 1955, 11.
38. *Chicago Tribune*, 2 August 1939, 24.
39. James A. Riley, *The Biographical Encyclopedia of the Negro Leagues* (NY: Carroll and Graf, 1994).
40. Ross Forman, "Jimmie Crutchfield: Walking, Talking Baseball History," *Sports Collectors Digest*, 4 September 1992; Riley, 202.
41. Riley, 202.
42. Lawrence Shulruff, *AARP Journal*, n.d., n.p.; Obituary for Julia Crutchfield, *Chicago Defender*, 10 December 1996.
43. *Chicago Defender*, 14 August 1943.
44. Ibid., 1 October 1949.
45. Ibid., 24 May and 13 December 1941.
46. John B Holway, "BINGO," unpublished manuscript, 3.
47. "Elwood DeMoss" unknown encyclopedia entry with afterword by Larry Lester, 420–21.
48. "Gas Nearly Kills Andrew Rube Foster," *Chicago Defender*, 6 June 1925.
49. "Chairs Meet American Giants Here Tonight." *The Sheboygan Press*, 23 June 1936.
50. Al Monroe, "DeMoss, Ballplayers 'Best'

Choice Dies." *Chicago Defender,* 1 February 1965; "Old Ball Players Set Date for Installation," *Chicago Defender,* 7 March 1964.

51. Lou Dials, *Life in Baseball's Negro Leagues,* Self published, 1987, 8.

52. Dials, 9, 23, 25.

53. Tom Mortenson, "The Coach's Box: Ex-Negro League Player, Hobby Dealer, Lou Dials Remembered." *Sports Collectors Digest,* 6 May 1994.

54. Holway, *The Complete Book of Baseball's Negro Leagues.*

55. Ron Agostini, "Lou Dials: A Rich Baseball Life," *The Modesto Bee,* 20 August 1989.

56. Ibid.; Lester, *Black Baseball's National Showcase*

57. The Wentworth Club was formed by Dials and some of his teammates, such as Walter Davis and Jelly Gardner, in Chicago. When someone hit a ball out of the old American Giants' ballpark at Thirty-ninth Street and Wentworth, they were admitted into the club. A 450-foot blast was required to join the club, which Dials did once (*Kansas City Call,* 20 May 1955).

58. Agostini, 27.

59. *Chicago Defender,* 23 September 1916.

60. Ibid., 23 September 1916.

61. Ibid., 23 September 1911 and 22 July 1939.

62. Ibid., 7 May, 17 June and August 26 1950.

63. "Chicago American Giants Play Chairs Here Tonight," *Sheboygan Press,* 1 September 1938, 14.

64. Moffi and Kronstadt, 109.

65. *Chicago Defender,* 11 July 1942, 19.

66. Riley, *The Biographical Encyclopedia of The Negro Baseball Leagues,* 292.

67. John Holway, *Voices From The Great Black Baseball Leagues,* 191.

68. Ibid, 191.

69. Ibid, 191.

70. Ibid, 192.

71. Ibid, 189.

72. Robert Peterson, *Only The Ball Was White,* 210.

73. Phil S. Dixon, *The Monarchs 1920–1938,* 63.

74. Holway, *The Complete Book of Baseball's Negro Leagues,* 250.

75. Holway, *Voices,* 189.

76. "Funeral Rites Held for Old Ball Player," *Chicago Defender,* 5 December 1953.

77. *Chicago Defender,* 12 February 1949.

78. Ibid., 2 November 1935, 14.

79. Ibid., 27 September 1924.

80. "28–7 Record So Far," *Chicago Tribune,* 13 September 1909.

81. "Beat Cuban Stars 13–6, Gunther Park," *Chicago Tribune,* 13 July 1909.

82. "Easy for Lelands to Win," *Chicago Tribune,* 1 August 1910; "Stars Fall 7–1 before Lelands," *Chicago Tribune,* 23 May 1910.

83. *Chicago Defender,* 18 March 1916.

84. Ibid., 1 January 1916 and 29 April 1916.

85. "Milwaukee Club Beat Logan Squares 7–0," *Chicago Tribune,* 18 and 22 April 1923; "Pete Hill with Detroit Club," Ibid., 14 June 1919.

86. "Half Game out of First Place," *Chicago Tribune,* 6 July 1909.

87. "Lost to Cuban Stars," *Chicago Tribune,* 16 July 1909; "Again the Leland Giants Take Measure of Gunthers," Ibid., 14 August 1909; "Giants Win Double Header," Ibid., 3 October 1909.

88. "Colored Baseball Players Are Good," *The Mansfield News,* 1 December 1910, 9.

89. William F. McNeil, 99.

90. "Pete Hill, Retired Ball Player Visits Soldier Son," *Chicago Defender,* 12 December 1942, 21.

91. *Chicago Defender,* 20 April 1940.

92. Larry Moffi and Jonathan Kronstadt, *Crossing the Line* (Iowa City: University of Iowa Press, 1994), 95–98.

93. *Chicago Defender,* 23 May 1953 and 7 June 1952; *Chicago Tribune,* 4 September 1953.

94. Lester, 49.

95. *Chicago Tribune,* 28 July 1947, 29.

96. *Pittsburgh Courier,* 8 July 1944; *Chicago Defender,* 1 September 1945.

97. "Chicago Giants Top Clowns, 3–1," *Chicago Tribune,* 17 July 1944, 15; *New York Times,* 20 August 1945, 15; *Chicago Defender,* 18 August 1945, 7; *Chicago Tribune,* 6 May 1946, 24.

98. *Chicago Defender,* 28 September 1946, 11; "Feller's Nine Edges Negro All-Stars," *Traverse City Record-Eagle,* 3 October 1946, 10.

99. *Chicago Defender,* 21 June 1947; "Strong Negro League Teams Play Thursday," *Syracuse Herald-Journal,* 12 August 1947, 21.

100. *Chicago Tribune,* 6 September 1949.

101. Gentry Jessup File, National Baseball Hall of Fame; "Cubs to Meet Sox Saturday," *St. Joseph Herald-Press,* 2 June 1950, 10.

102. *Chicago Tribune,* 8 September 1957.

103. Brent Kelley, *Voices from the Negro Leagues* (Jefferson, North Carolina: McFarland, 1998), 254–58.

104. *Chicago Defender,* 14 April 1923 and 30 May 1925.

105. Robert Peterson, *Only the Ball Was*

White (New York: Oxford University Press, 1992), 77.

106. 20 May 1955, *Kansas City Call.*

107. Ibid.

108. *Chicago Defender,* 19 July 1913.

109. Harry Williams, "Negro Ball Stars Shine," *Los Angeles Times,* 30 October 1912.

110. *Chicago Defender,* 9 May 1936.

111. Ibid., 29 July 1944.

112. Ibid., 8 and 29 July 1950; 9 June 1951.

113. Ibid., 17 December 1938.

114. Ibid., 2 June 1945, 7.

115. Kelley, *The Negro Leagues Revisited,* 190.

116. *Chicago Defender,* 20 April 1935, 17.

117. Ibid.

118. Ibid., 11 June 1949.

119. *New York Times,* 27 August 1945, 14; *Chicago Defender,* 8 May 1943; *Chicago Tribune,* 3 September 1951.

120. *Chicago Defender,* 27 September 1924.

121. *Chicago Tribune,* 6 June 1949; Lester, 71.

122. Riley, *Biographical Dictionary,* 1043–44.

123. *Pittsburgh Courier,* 27 April 1946, 17.

124. Capt. Becky Colaw, "In the Game," *Airman* (February 1993), 39–41; Kelley, *Voices from the Negro Leagues,* 206–209.

125. *Chicago Defender,* 10 July 1943.

126. Ibid., 20 March 1915; Harry Williams, "Negro Ball Stars Shine," *Los Angeles Times,* 30 October 1912.

127. Riley, *Biographical Dictionary,* 1069–70.

128. *Chicago Defender,* 20 April 1035.

129. *New York Times,* 27 July 1949, 32.

130. "Ball Player Dies During Game," *Chicago Defender,* 26 June 1948 and 6 August 1949, 14.

131. *Chicago Tribune,* 14 July 1924.

132. *Chicago Defender,* 5 September 1942.

133. Ibid., 5 March 1949, 14.

134. Ibid., 20 May 1950, 19.

135. Kelley, *Voices from the Negro Leagues,* 76.

136. Tony Salin, *Baseball's Forgotten Heroes* (Masters Press, 1999.), 172.

137. "Bad Boy Pennington is Indefinitely Suspended," *Chicago Defender,* 22 July 1944.

138. *Los Angeles Times,* 2 November 1912.

139. *Chicago Defender,* 21 January 1950.

140. Ibid., 12 July 1941; 21 January 1950.

141. Ibid., 26 September 1928; Lester 48.

142. "Alex Radcliffe," in *Baseball, The Biographical Encyclopedia,* eds. David Pietrusza, Matthew Silverman, and Michael Gershman. (Kingston, New York: Total Sports Publishing, 2000), 912.

143. Phil Dixon with Patrick J. Hannigan, *The Negro Baseball Leagues: A Photographic History* (Mattituck, New York: Amereon, 1992), 257.

144. "Paige, Monarchs Battle Illinois Champs Today." *Chicago Daily Tribune,* 22 September 1940.

145. Larry Lester, et al., *Black Baseball in Chicago,* 60.

146. "Alex Radcliffe Steals Home to Beat Paige," *Chicago Defender,* 15 July 1944.

147. 1972 interview with Alec Radcliffe by unknown source.

148. Robert Peterson, *Only The Ball Was White* (New York: Oxford University Press, 1970), 288–305.

149. *Chicago Defender,* 9 March 1935 and 27 February 1937, 13.

150. Ibid., 6 April 1940.

151. Ibid., 9 September 1939 and 5 April, 10 May and 7 June 1941.

152. *Chicago Tribune,* 19 July 1948.

153. *Chicago Defender,* 16 June 1923.

154. Ibid., 27 September 1947.

155. Ibid., 18 July 1942, 21.

156. Bazz Owen Smaulding Papers, New Mexico State Archives.

157. Scrapbook, Smaulding Papers.

158. Ibid.

159. Ibid.

160. Ibid.

161. "Mexican Umpire Loses a Decision," *Washington Post,* 19 July 1946.

162. *Chicago Defender,* 20 April and 8 June 1935.

163. "Paige Conquers Thurston," *Los Angeles Times,* 11 December 1933, 12.

164. "Three Cage Games Sunday at Carroll College," *Helene Independent Record,* 3 December 1960.

165. *Chicago Defender,* 8 September 1945.

166. Ibid., 1 June and 20 July 1935.

167. Ibid., 25 May, 1 and 28 September 1935.

168. "Pilots Win, 7 to 3, On Suttle's Homer," *Washington Post,* 11 August 1932, 10.

169. "Eagles Trim Senators, 7–5," *Washington Post,* 3 July 1938, X4.

170. "Big League Stars Bow to Giants," *Los Angeles Times,* 30 October 1935, 20; "Royal Giants Win 13–4," Ibid., 29 November 1937, A13.

171. *Chicago Defender,* 27 September 1924 and 23 June 1956.

172. Ibid., 13 June 1942, 19.

173. John B. Holway, "Cristobal Torriente," *Baseball Historical Review* (1981), 73.

174. "Cristobal Torriente," in *Baseball, The Biographical Encyclopedia,* eds. David Pietrusza, Matthew Silverman, and Michael

Gershman (Kingston, New York: Total Sports Publishing, 2000), 1140.

175. "American Giants Beat Cubans Who Start Trouble," *Chicago Defender*, 28 August 1915.

176. Dixon with Hannigan, *The Negro Baseball Leagues*, 76.

177. Ibid., 108.

178. Mike Shalin and Neil Shalin, "Cristobal Torriente," in *Out by a Step: The 100 Best Ball Players Not in the Baseball Hall of Fame* (Lanham, MD: Diamond Publications, 2002), 115–117.

179. Dixon with Hannigan, *The Negro Baseball Leagues*, 144.

180. Robert Bailey, in an e-mail to Larry Lester on 15 November 2003, titled "New York City Findings."

181. Jorge S. Figueredo, in a letter to Dick Clark on 12 December 2003.

182. *Chicago Defender*, 22 December 1923, 19 April 1924 and 7 March 1925.

183. John Holway, "The Florida Stringbean," unpublished paper, n.d.; Larry Lester, "Trent, Theodore 'Ted' 'Highpockets' 'Big Florida," *Encyclopedia:* 211–212.; Riley, *The Biographical Encyclopedia of the Negro Baseball Leagues*, 789–790.

184. Riley, 790.

185. "Theodore Trent," *Colored Baseball and Sports Monthly* (Oct., 1934): Baseball Hall of Fame Archives.

186. Encyclopedia article from Larry Lester.

187. Ibid; "Just Missed," *Chicago Defender*, 21 August 1937.

188. Article from Baseball Hall of Fame Archives

189. "Theodore Trent," *Colored Baseball and Sports Monthly*, October 1934, Baseball Hall of Fame Archives.

190. Ibid; "Giants and Mills Split a Pair of Games," *Chicago Defender*, 25 July 1936, 14.

191. Monte Irvin, *The Biographical Encyclopedia of the Negro Leagues* (New York: Carroll and Graf, 1994), 790.

192. Holway, "The Florida Stringbean,."

193. Irvin, 790.

194. Art Hunter, "Georgetown Man Plays, Coaches Sports over 70 Year Span," *Brown County Shopper*, 26 July 1998, 1, 4.

195. *Chicago Defender*, 26 June 1943.

196. Ibid., 1 September 1935 and 19 October 1935.

197. Ibid., 13 April 1935.

198. *Indianapolis Freeman*, 13 July 1918, 7.

199. *Chicago Defender*, 4 September 1915.

200. Ibid., 7 March 1925.

201. "Great Pitchers are Barred from Majors," *Mansfield News*, 12 June 1915.

202. *Chicago Defender*, 11 March 1916.

203. Ibid., 15 December 1915.

204. Ibid., 27 November 1915.

205. Larry Lester, "Frank Wickware," *Biographical Dictionary of American Sports*, 1673–74; "Colored Pitching Stars to Twirl Against Bush's Team," *Indianapolis Star*, 16 October 1914, 6.

206. David Condon, "Negro Baseball Scars are Fading," *Chicago Tribune*, 20 September 1977, C3; Roi Ottley, "Former Negro Ball Players Pitch in to Help Needy," *Chicago Tribune*, 19 May 1947, SW 23.

207. Marion B. Campfield, "'Writing Waiter' Wins Award," *Chicago Defender*, 8 July 1972, 3.

208. Lester, 74.

209. Hall of Fame Bio, National Baseball Hall of Fame Web site.

210. *Chicago Defender*, 12 May 1923, 7 March 1925 and 30 January 1937, 17.

211. "Johnny Wilson Makes Indiana All-State 5," *Chicago Defender*, 3 April 1948.

212. *Chicago Defender*, 28 April and 16 June 1923.

213. Ibid., 7 April 1923.

214. Ibid., 24 June 1944, 9.

215. Ibid., 14 May 1949.

216. Ibid., 24 April 1943.

217. Ibid., 8 June 1946.

218. *Chicago Defender*, 11 May 1940 and 7 June 1941; 27 April 1946.

Chapter 4

1. "Chicago Unions," *The Chicago Inter Ocean*, 2 September 1897.

2. "Brown of Cubs Had 'Indian Sign' on the Leland Giants," *Chicago Defender*, 17 December 1932.

3. "Colored Baseball Players Are Good," *The Mansfield News*, 1 December 1910, 9.

4. Frank Leland File, National Baseball Hall of Fame and Library, Cooperstown, New York.

5. Linda Ziemer, "Chicago's Negro Leagues," *Chicago History* (Winter 1994–95), 49.

6. *Chicago Broad Ax*, 28 September 1901.

7. *Chicago Defender*, 18 February 1911.

8. Ibid., 30 January 1954.

9. *Chicago Broad Ax*, 27 December 1902.

10. *Chicago Defender*, 9 November 1912.

11. *Chicago Broad Ax*, 31 December 1910;

Fay Young, "Some Baseball History," *Chicago Defender,* 30 January 1954, 22.

12. "Cole Death Not to Affect Met; Thousands at Rites," *Chicago Defender,* 11 August 1956, 1–2.

13. Denton J. Brooke, Jr., "From Cabin to Riches is Cole Success Story," *Chicago Defender,* 19 December 1942.

14. "Dr. J. B. Martin in Chicago; Silent on Persecution," *Chicago Defender,* 7 December 1940; Roi Ottley, "Memphis Row is Boon to Chicago," *Chicago Tribune,* 26 September 1954; "Chicago Giants to Observe 61st Birthday Today," *Chicago Tribune,* 25 July 1948, B5.

15. "Martin Cracks Down on Players Who Strike or Shove Umpires," *Chicago Defender,* 30 June 1945, 7; "Major League Subsidy Offered to Negro Loop," *New York Times,* 31 July 1960, S2; Russ Cowans, "NAL Starts Big Program to Swell Coffers," *Chicago Defender,* 7 April 1956.

16. "J. B. Martin on Service Fed. Board," *Chicago Defender,* 28 February 1959, 9; Vernon Jarrett, "First Sanitary District Trustee Wins Acclaim," Ibid., 21 June 1947.

17. "Comments on East West Game; Candy Jim Taylor," *Colored Baseball and Sports Monthly* (1934).

18. "The World Series That Never Was Played," *Chicago Tribune,* 18 October 1970.

19. "Taylor Tells What's Wrong in Baseball," *Chicago Defender,* 1 February 1930.

20. Phil Dixon with Patrick J. Hannigan, *The Negro Baseball Leagues: A Photographic History* (Mattituck, New York: Amereon, 1992), 166.

21. Ibid., 214.

22. Ibid., 251.

23. Robert Peterson, *Only The Ball Was White* (New York: Oxford University Press, 1970), 276–297.

24. "Comments on East West Game; Candy Jim Taylor," *Colored Baseball and Sports Monthly* (1934).

25. "Candy Jim, Ace Pilot, Succumbs," *Chicago Defender,* 1948.

26. "A Fan's Tribute to Legends of Negro Leagues," *Chicago Tribune,* 25 September 2004.

27. Interview with William "Bobbie" Robinson, November 22, 1992.

28. Interview with Sam Hairston, April 1, 1995.

29. Interview with Tony Carlascio, August 15, 2000. Text in possession of author.

30. Interview with Slick Surratt, February 2, 1993. Text in possession of author.

31. McNary, 256–7.

32. *Bismarck Tribune,* 9 October 1934.

33. McNary, 260.

34. Author's interview with Sam Wilson, November 1, 1994. Text in possession of author.

35. McNary, 261.

36. Ibid., 230, 235.

37. John B. Holway, *Blackball Stars,* (New York: Carroll & Graf, 1988), 384.

38. McNary, 254.

39. Ibid., 264.

40. Author's interview with Tommy Demark, May 15, 1993. Text in possession of author.

41. Author's interview with Slick Surratt, February, 2, 1993. Text in possession of author.

42. Web site, *www.negroleaguebaseball.com,* June 8, 1999.

Chapter 5

1. Sammy J. Miller, *Negro League Ballparks,* Database on file at Baseball Hall of Fame Library

2. Ibid.

3. Larry Lester, Sammy J. Miller, & Dick Clark. *Black Baseball in Chicago* (Chicago: Arcadia, 2000), 33.

4. "John Schorling, Former Ball Park Owner, Dies at 74," *Chicago Defender,* 30 March 1940, 9.

5. Ibid., 53.

6. Miller.

7. "Normal Park to Be Recreational Center," *Chicago Defender,* 17 January 1942.

8. "Way Back When Semi-pros Really Prospered," *Chicago Tribune,* 31 May 1936, B5; "Lelands Defeated at Last," Ibid., 12 June 1910, C2; "Cubs Trim Giants in Final Game, 1–0," Ibid., 23 October 1909; "Begin at Gunther Park," Ibid., 24 April 1905.

9. "Plan War on Gunther Park," *Chicago Tribune,* 24 December 1907.

10. "Logan Squares Open at New Park Today," *Chicago Tribune,* 17 May 1925.

11. Philip J. Lowry, *Green Cathedrals* (Reading, Massachusetts: Addison -Wesley, 1992), 131.

12. Ibid.

13. Chris Roewe, Larry Wigge, and Joe Marcin, eds.; *Official 1977 Baseball Dope Book* (St. Louis, Missouri, *The Sporting News*), 148.

14. Larry Lester, *Black Baseball's National Showcase: The East West All Star Game, 1933–1953.* (Lincoln, Nebraska, University of Nebraska Press), 199.

15. John Holway, *Blackball Stars: Negro League Pioneers* (Westport, Connecticut, Meckler), 274.

16. "Grandstand in Ashes," *Boston Globe,* 30 August 1894; "Semi-Pro Parks to Be Busy," *Chicago Tribune,* 19 August 1911, 10; "Giants Win Fifth Contest of All-Star Series, 6 to 2," Ibid., 27 August 1910, 10.

17. Miller.

18. Ernie Banks & Jim Enright, *Mr. Cub* (Chicago: Rutledge, 1971), 165.

19. Robert Peterson, *Only the Ball Was White: A History of Legendary Black Players and All-black Professional Teams* (New York: Oxford University Press, 1970), 179.

20. Larry Moffi and Jonathan Kronstadt, *Crossing the Line: Black Major Leaguers, 1947– 1959* (Jefferson, NC: McFarland, 1994), 84.

21. Ibid., 84.

22. Interview by Jason Norris with Buck O'Neil, Thursday August 18, 2005, Kent State University Stark Campus.

23. Buck O'Neil with Steve Wolf and David Conrads, *I Was Right on Time: My Journey from the Negro Leagues to the Majors* (New York: Simon and Schuster, 1997).

24. Personal Interview, August 18, 2005.

25. Mike Shatzkin, *The Ballplayers: Baseballs Unlimited Biographical Reference* (New York: Arbor House, 1990), 827.

26. Personal Interview, August 18, 2005; also see Buck O'Neil with Steve Wolf and David Conrads, *I Was Right on Time.*

27. Ibid.

28. Ibid.

29. O'Neil, 204.

30. Ibid., 205.

31. Ibid., 217–218.

32. Personal Interview, August 18, 2005.

33. Ibid.

34. Ibid.

35. Ibid.

36. Richard Dozer, "Cubs Sign Negro Coach," *Chicago Daily Tribune,* 30 May 1962.

37. Personal Interview, August 18, 2005.

38. Ibid.

39. Ibid.

40. William Hageman, "Minnie the Giant," *Chicago Tribune,* 2 October 2005, 1, 6.

41. "Cleveland Indians Sign Oresta Minoso and Jose Santiago," *Chicago Defender,* 4 September 1948, 10.

42. Larry Moffi and Jonathan Kronstadt, *Crossing the Line,* (Iowa City: University of Iowa Press, 1994) 41–44.

43. Alfred Duckett, "Marvelous Minnie Sets Fast Pace with Sox," *Chicago Defender,* 17 July 1954, 23.

44. All information gathered from Great Lakes Naval Training Center Publicity brochure and Jerry Malloy, "Black Bluejackets," *The National Pastime,* (Winter 1985), 72–77.

Bibliography*

Avendorph, Julius

Avendorph, Julius. "Chicago Men Are Chided for Not Being Gallant." *Chicago Defender*, 27 February 1915.

Ball, George Walter

"Ball Blanks Anson's Colts." *Chicago Tribune*, 23 August 1908, B2.

Kleinknecht, Merl F. "Ball, George Walter 'Georgia Rabbit.'" In *Biographical Dictionary of American Sports, Baseball*, edited by David L. Porter. Westport, CT: Greenwood Press, 2000, 59–60.

Banks, Ernie

Enrigh, James. "Ernie Banks." *The Sporting News*, 31 December 1958, 8.

Horn, Barry. "Baseball Hero Ernie Banks Recalls Dallas Roots." *Dallas Morning News*, 19 September 1997.

Hoskins, Alan. "Banks Recalls Playing Days in Kansas City." *The Kansan*, 3 July 1977.

Simms, Gregory. "Ernie Banks Recalls His Days in the Old Negro Leagues." *Jet* (10 February 1977): 54–55.

Bassett, Pepper

Washington, Chester. "Interview with Johnnie Craig." *Pittsburgh Courier*, 24 April 1937.

Binga, Jesse C.

"Jesse C. Binga the Real Estate Wizard." *Chicago Defender*, 5 November 1910.

Brown, Larry

Bernstein, David. "Brown, Larry." In *Biographical Dictionary of American Sports, Baseball*, edited by David L. Porter. Westport, CT: Greenwood Press, 2000, 157–158.

"Former Baseball Great, Larry Brown, Succumbs." *Appleton Post-Crescent*, 9 April 1972, D2.

Chicago

"Baseball Doings in the Windy City." *Indianapolis Ledger*, 18 October 1913, 4.

"Base Hits for Chicago." *Indianpolis Freeman*, 25 July 1908, 7.

"Half a Million Fans Will Root for Favorites in 1,000 Baseball Games in Chicago Today." *Chicago Tribune*, 5 September 1909, H1.

Heaphy, Leslie, ed. *Negro Leagues in Chicago*. Jefferson, NC: McFarland, 2005.

Jackson, Major R. R. "No Baseball War for Chicago." *Indianapolis Freeman*, 18 December 1909, 7.

Lerner, Daniel J. "Visions of a Sporting City: 'Shadowball' and Black Chicago, 1887–1952." PhD diss., Michigan State University, 2002.

Lester, Larry, Sammy J. Miller, and Dick Clark. *Black Baseball in Chicago*. Chicago: Arcadia, 2000.

Lomax, Michael E. "Black Entrepreneurship in the National Pastime: The Rise of Semiprofessional Baseball in Black Chicago, 1890–1915." *Journal of Sport History* 25, no. 1 (Spring 1998): 43–64.

Ottley, Roi. "Former Negro Ball Players Pitch in to Help Needy." *Chicago Tribune*, 19 May 1957, SW23.

*Compiled by Leslie A. Heaphy

"Semi-Pros Enjoy Prosperous Year." *Chicago Tribune*, 10 October 1909, D1.

Travis, Dempsey J. *An Autobiography of Black Chicago.* Chicago: Urban Research Institute, 1981.

Wyatt, David. "Baseball War for Chicago." *Indianapolis Freeman*, 4 December 1909, 7.

Zeimer, Linda. "Chicago's Negro Leagues." *Chicago History* (Winter 1994): 36–51.

Chicago American Giants

"A. B. C.'s Beat the American Giants." *Chicago Defender*, 4 November 1916.

"A.B.C. Club to Engage Colored Champs in Series." *Indianapolis Star*, 12 September 1914, 7.

"A. B. C.'s Confident Before First Game with Giants." *Indianapolis Star*, 17 July 1915, 10.

"A. B. C.'s Drop Two Straight to Fosterites." *Chicago Defender*, 10 June 1922.

African-American Ball Players. *Chicago Daily News* Negatives Collection, Chicago Historical Society.

"Am. Giants in 3–2 Win Over K. C." *Chicago Defender*, 20 September 1924, 12.

"American Giant Shortstop Tops East-West Poll." *Chicago Tribune*, 13 July 1952, A2.

"American Giants." *Chicago Defender*, 15 and 29 June 1912.

"American Giants." *Wisconsin Daily Rapids Tribune*, 1 August 1934, 5.

"American Giants and Bull Moosers in Tie." *Chicago Defender*, 9 September 1916.

"American Giants and Henry Grays Split." *Chicago Defender*, 23 September 1916.

"American Giants and Kansas City Split; Third Game Off." *Chicago Defender*, 4 October 1924.

"American Giants Annex Three Out of Four Games in Series with Cubans." *Chicago Defender*, 27 June 1925.

"American Giants at St. Louis, Monarchs at Detroit Sunday." *Chicago Defender*, 19 May 1923.

"American Giants Beat Black Barons." *Indianapolis Recorder*, 12 May 1928.

"American Giants Beat City Champs." *Chicago Defender*, 16 September 1916.

"American Giants Beat Cleveland Buckeyes Twice, 7–5 and 8–3." *Chicago Tribune*, 6 June 1949, B4.

"American Giants Beat Cubans Who Cause Trouble." *Chicago Defender*, 28 August 1915.

"American Giants Beat Great Lakes Navy Team of Ex-Major Leaguers." *Chicago Defender*, 14 August 1943, 11.

"American Giants Beat Pittsburgh Team, 4 to 0." *Chicago Tribune*, 23 May 1932, 23.

"American Giants Beat Portland, P. L. Champions." *Chicago Defender*, 3 April 1915.

"American Giants Beat West Ends." *Chicago Defender*, 10 June 1911.

"American Giants, Cleveland Buckeyes Split Double Bill." *Chicago Tribune*, 30 May 1949, C2.

"American Giants Defeat A. B. C.'s." *Baltimore Afro-American*, 10 August 1923, 14.

"American Giants Defeat Cleveland." *Pittsburgh Courier*, 19 June 1943.

"American Giants Defeat Former Big Leaguers." *Chicago Defender*, 15 May 1915.

"American Giants Defeat New York Black Yankees." *Chicago Tribune*, 10 September 1934, 20.

"American Giants Defeat Taylor's A. B. C.'s." *Chicago Defender*, 2 September 1916.

"American Giants Deliberately Robbed." *Chicago Defender*, 1 April 1916.

"American Giants 18 Hit Attack Beat Birmingham." *Chicago Tribune*, 30 April 1951, C1.

"American Giants End Season by Beating Indianapolis Twice." *Chicago Tribune*, 6 September 1949, B3.

"American Giants Find K. C. Monarchs a Tough Bunch." *Chicago Defender*, 13 May 1922, 10.

"American Giants Gain Negro League Finals." *Chicago Tribune*, 8 September 1949, B2.

"American Giants Games." *Chicago Defender*, 19 July 1913.

"American Giants Given Scare." *Chicago Defender*, 31 May 1913.

"American Gaints Go Down in Defeat." *Chicago Defender*, 7 June 1913.

"American Giants Hand A. B. C.'s Game." *Chicago Defender*, 26 June 1915.

"American Giants Hit Texas on Spring Trip." *Chicago Defender*, 8 March 1924.

"American Giants in Detroit for Five Games." *Chicago Defender*, 14 August 1926.

"American Giants in Fierce Riot at Hoosier City." *Chicago Defender*, 24 July 1915.

"American Giants in Shut-Out Games." *Chicago Defender*, 14 June 1913.

"American Giants Invade Indianapolis for Five Games." *Chicago Defender*, 7 July 1923.

"American Giants Knock K. C. Monarchs Into Third Place." *Chicago Defender,* 15 July 1922.

"American Giants Leading in Lincoln American Series." *Chicago Defender,* 7 August 1915.

"American Giants Leave Saturday for Memphis." *Chicago Defender,* 25 March 1944, 9.

"American Giants Lose." *Chicago Defender,* 5 July 1913 and 22 April 1916.

"American Giants Lose to City Champions." *Chicago Defender,* 17 June 1916.

"American Giants Lose to Winning Chicago Giants." *Chicago Defender,* 18 September 1915.

"American Giants Make it 5 Straight Over Dayton as Curry Hurls Record Game." *Chicago Defender,* 17 July 1926.

"American Giants Meet Chairs Thursday Night." *Sheboygan Press,* 29 June 1938, 14.

"American Giants Meet Chairs Tonight." *Sheboygan Press,* 29 June 1938, 14.

"American Giants on Top in Long Pitcher's Battle." *Chicago Defender,* 14 August 1915.

"American Giants on Top in Twelve Inning Game." *Chicago Defender,* 26 June 1915.

"American Giants Open 11 Day Tour of East." *Chicago Tribune,* 26 July 1934, 21.

"American Giants Open Season at Kay Cee's Park." *Chicago Defender,* 28 April 1923.

"American Giants Open Today." *Chicago Defender,* 29 April 1916.

"American Giants Play Paige and Kansas City in Detroit August 6." *Chicago Defender,* 5 August 1944, 7.

"American Giants Rally at Finish." *Chicago Tribune,* 15 July 1912, 13.

"American Giants Rally to Defeat Barons, 10–8." *Chicago Tribune,* 24 July 1945, 16.

"American Giants Rap A's for 4 Straight." *Chicago Defender,* 7 August 1926.

"American Giants Rap Ball to All Corners of Park for Victory." *The Decatur Review,* 17 July 1921, 6.

"American Giants Resume Tour in Wichita Today." *Chicago Tribune,* 20 April 1941, B2.

"American Giants Ring Down Curtain with a Win." *Chicago Defender,* 16 October 1915.

"The American Giants Rout Jack Ryan's Romeos." *Chicago Defender,* 9 October 1915.

"American Giants Show This Evening." *Appleton Post-Crescent,* 31 July 1939, 13.

"American Giants 6, East Chicago 1." *Chicago Defender,* 24 May 1913.

"American Giants 6, St. Louis 3." *Chicago Defender,* 22 July 1916.

"American Giants Shut Out." *Chicago Defender,* 26 June 1915.

"American Giants Take 8–6 Game from the Pyotts." *Chicago Defender,* 14 April 1923.

"American Giants Take the Ft. Wayne Team into Camp 14–1; Gardner Proves Star." *Chicago Defender,* 31 May 1924.

"American Giants Take 3 Out of 4 Games from St. Louis Stars in National League." *Chicago Defender,* 15 May 1926.

"American Giants 13, Hammond 6." *Chicago Defender,* 10 May 1913.

"American Giants to Go to Memphis for Spring Training." *Chicago Tribune,* 2 January 1949, A3.

"American Giants to Play Cleveland Nine Sunday." *Chicago Tribune,* 17 April 1948, A2.

"American Giants to Play 5 Games This Week-End." *Chicago Tribune,* 3 June 1936, 26.

"American Giants to Play in Negro World Series Today." *Chicago Tribune,* 8 September 1934, 21.

"American Giants to Play Papermakers Friday Night." *Appleton Post-Crescent,* 11 June 1940.

"American Giants to Play Staley's Here." *Decatur Review,* 21 June 1921, 10.

"American Giants to Start Practice April 1 Bobby Williams to Indianapolis." *Chicago Defender,* 27 March 1926.

"American Giants Took Opener from Monarchs." *Chicago Defender,* 2 June 1923.

"American Giants Top Winter League." *Chicago Defender,* 1 January 1916.

"American Giants Transfer Game with New York." *Chicago Tribune,* 5 May 1935, A2.

"American Giants Trim Portland." *Chicago Defender,* 15 April 1916, 8.

"American Giants Trim West, Ends in Double Bill." *Chicago Defender,* 22 July 1916.

"American Giants 20; Detroit 0." *Chicago Defender,* 30 June 1923.

"American Giants Victors Against Chicago Giants." *Chicago Tribune,* 21 August 1911, 6.

"American Giants vs. Pyotts Saturday; Chi. Giants, Oct. 5." *Chicago Defender,* 4 October 1924.

"American Giants Whale LaPorte Team 7 to 1." *Chicago Defender,* 29 May 1915.

"American Giants Will Appear Against Chairs on Wednesday Afternoon." *Sheboygan Press,* 9 August 1938, 3.

"American Giants Will Start Practice Wednesday Morning." *Chicago Defender,* 28 March 1925.

"American Giants Win." *Chicago Tribune,* 5 July 1935 and 6 September 1937, 21; *Chicago Defender,* 11 and 18 March and 13 May 1916.

"The American Giants Win Again." *Chicago Defender,* 4 December 1915.

"American Giants Win Final from Cubans." *Chicago Defender,* 15 and 29 July 1916.

"American Giants Win First Sunday in Two Months." *Chicago Defender,* 28 August 1915.

"American Giants Win Four Straight From Cleveland." *Chicago Defender,* 17 May 1924 and 29 May 1926.

"American Giants Win in the Ninth." *Chicago Defender,* 5 June 1915.

"American Giants Win No Hit No Run Contest." *Chicago Defender,* 25 September 1915.

"American Giants Win Opener in Los Angeles." *Chicago Defender,* 6 November 1915.

"American Giants Win Opener from Detroit." *Chicago Defender,* 30 June 1923.

"American Giants Win Opener from Staleys by Score of 4 to 1." *The Decatur Review,* 15 July 1921, 12.

"American Giants Win the Opening Game, 6000 Fans." *Chicago Defender,* 1 May 1915.

"American Giants Win the Pennant." *Chicago Defender,* 8 January 1916, 7.

"American Giants Win Three and Lose One to Cubans; Tie Saint Louis for 2d Place." *Chicago Defender,* 24 July 1926.

"American Giants Win Three Games from Milwaukee." *Chicago Defender,* 12 May 1923.

"American Giants Win Three Out of Four Games from Birmingham Black Barons." *Chicago Defender,* 20 June 1925.

"American Giants Win Three Out of Four Games from the Memphis Red Sox." *Chicago Defender,* 13 June 1925.

"American Giants Win Two and Lose 1." *Chicago Defender,* 21 October 1916.

"American Giants Win Two from Buckeyes." *Chicago Tribune,* 21 June 1943, 22.

"American Giants Win Two Out of Three in Tacoma Series." *Chicago Defender,* 24 April 1915.

"American Giants Win Uphill Game 10–8." *Chicago Defender,* 29 April 1916.

"American-Lincoln Giants Games in New York." *Chicago Defender,* 26 July 1913.

"Argentine Nine to Face Mills in Two Games Today." *Chicago Tribune,* 4 July 1935, 17.

"Barons Defeat Chicago Giants 5 to 3 and 7 to 2." *Chicago Tribune,* 8 May 1944, 23.

"Baseball Season Opens." *Chicago Defender,* 27 April 1912.

"Batting Paves Way for Foster's Men to Halt the League Leaders." *Chicago Defender,* 3 July 1926.

"Battle Royal to the American Giants." *Chicago Defender,* 11 September 1915.

"Birmingham Here for Five Foster Games." *Chicago Defender,* 20 June 1925.

"Birmingham, Negro Giants to Play Today." *Chicago Tribune,* 7 May 1944, A3.

"Bismarck Tackles Chicago National Colored League Champions Tonight." *Bismarck Tribune,* 13 August 1934, 6.

"Black Yankees Lose, 4–3, Before 20,000." *New York Times,* 10 September 1934, 21.

"Black Yanks Halted, 1–0." *New York Times,* 20 August 1945, 15.

"Brains and Hits Beat St. Louis Giants." *Chicago Defender,* 15 July 1916.

"Butler Brothers Beat American Giants in Ninth." *Chicago Defender,* 19 June 1915.

"Carl Zinth Hurls Locals to Victory Over Negro Stars." *Oshkosh Northwestern,* 6 June 1935, 14.

"Chairs Meet Chicago American Giants Tonight." *Sheboygan Press,* 9 August 1938, 10.

"Chairs Meet Colored Team from Chicago." *Sheboygan Press,* 22 June 1936, 12.

"Chairs to Battle Chicago Colored Stars Here Sunday." *Sheboygan Press,* 3 June 1939, 14.

"Chairs to Meet American Giants Friday Night." *Sheboygan Press,* 15 June 1939, 28.

"Chairs to Meet Chicago Stars Here Sunday." *Sheboygan Press,* 2 June 1939, 14.

"Champions Lose 2 to American Giants." *Pittsburgh Courier,* 24 July 1943.

"Champs Visit Town." *Twin City Herald,* 11 August 1934, 3.

"Chicago American Giants Defeat Chairmakers." *Sheboygan Press,* 24 June 1936, 12.

"Chicago American Giants Have Won 17 Colored World's Championships." *Bismarck Tribune,* 19 July 1938, 6.

"Chicago American Giants, Louisville Here Thursday." *Newark Advocate and American Tribune,* 6 July 1949, 8.

"Chicago American Giants Play Chairs Here Tonight." *Sheboygan Press,* 1 September 1938, 14.

"Chicago American Giants to Meet Chairs Tuesday Night." *Sheboygan Press,* 8 August 1938, 10.

"Chicago American Giants Win from Memphis Sox, 11–5." *Stevens Point Daily Journal,* 14 August 1935, 6.

"Chicago at Cleveland; Kay Cees in Birmingham." *Chicago Defender,* 6 June 1942, 19.

"Chicago at Home, Loses to Monarchs." *Indianapolis Recorder,* 2 June 1928.

"Chicago Beats Cleveland in Fourteenth, 6 to 5." *Chicago Defender,* 3 July 1943, 11.

"Chicago Faces Memphis Next." *Chicago Defender,* 2 June 1945, 7.

"Chicago Colored Nine Will Not Join League." *Washington Post,* 14 February 1921, 10.

"Chicago Giants and Kansas City Play Two Today." *Chicago Tribune,* 30 May 1943, A3.

"Chicago Giants and Toldeo Team Booked in Lima." *Lima News,* 19 July 1943, 11.

"Chicago Giants Beat Sailors, 7–3, at Great Lakes." *Chicago Tribune,* 8 August 1943, A2.

"Chicago Giants Collect 18 Hits; Beat Clowns 11–2." *Chicago Tribune,* 14 July 1944, 20.

"Chicago Giants Divide with Indianapolis." *Chicago Tribune,* 16 June 1947, 33.

"Chicago Giants Play Buckeyes 2 Games Today." *Chicago Tribune,* 3 September 1945, 34.

"Chicago Giants Play Four Games with Memphis." *Chicago Tribune,* 2 July 1944, A3.

"Chicago Giants Play Monarchs Twice Today." *Chicago Tribune,* 26 August 1945, A2.

"Chicago Giants Play Toledo Team Here Monday Night." *Lima News,* 17 July 1939.

"Chicago Giants Top Clowns, 3–1; Lose Second, 9–1." *Chicago Tribune,* 17 July 1944, 15.

"Chicago Negro Giants Boast Leading Hitter." *Lima News,* 7 September 1947, 28.

"Chicago Signs Hardy as Regular Catcher." *Chicago Defender,* 12 February 1949, 14.

"Chicago vs. Memphis in New Orleans." *Chicago Defender,* 21 August 1943, 19.

"Chicago Wins World Series from East." *Indianapolis Recorder,* 23 October 1926.

"Circus Game to Giants 8 to 1." *Chicago Defender,* 26 June 1915.

"City Team-American Giants Game Ends in Argument." *Wisconsin Rapids Daily Tribune,* 7 August 1934, 5.

"Clever Fielding Wins for the Giants." *Chicago Defender,* 15 July 1916.

"Colored Baseball Championship." *Chicago Defender,* 5 August 1911.

"Cornelius or Trent to Hurl for Visitors." *Sheboygan Press,* 16 June 1939, 14.

"Critical Series." *Chicago Defender,* 26 August 1916.

"Cubans Hand American Giants a Lacing." *Chicago Defender,* 9 September 1916.

"Cubans Here for Five Games with American Giants." *Chicago Defender,* 2 June 1923.

"Cubans Shut Out Giants." *Chicago Defender,* 13 July 1912.

"Cubans Toy with American Giants." *Chicago Defender,* 19 August 1916.

"Cubans Treated to Some Defeats by Foster's Men." *Chicago Defender,* 9 June 1923.

"Cubans Win in the Twelfth on Error." *Chicago Defender,* 4 September 1915.

"Cubans Win Two." *Chicago Defender,* 26 August 1916.

"Cubs Bow to Chicago Nine." *Herald-Press (MI),* 12 June 1950, 11.

"Curtain Rings on Baseball Season." *Chicago Defender,* 7 October 1916.

"Detroit Stars Here for Five-Game Series with Foster's American Giants." *Chicago Defender,* 16 May 1925.

"Diamond Dust." *Chicago Defender,* 20 and 27 May, 3 June and 8 July 1911.

"Dick Kerr and Gang Face Am. Giants Saturday." *Chicago Defender,* 3 June 1922.

"Dicta Johnson to Coach American Giants Slabmen." *Chicago Defender,* 28 March 1925.

Donaldson, John. "All-Nations Tackle the American Giants." *Chicago Defender,* 30 September 1916.

Donough, John. "Giants Look at Other Half of Baseball's History." *Chicago Tribune TV Week,* 26 January 1992, 5, 7.

"18,000 Fans See Giants Win in 12th." *Chicago Defender,* 16 May 1925.

"Eleven-Inning Game to American Giants." *Chicago Defender,* 9 September 1916.

"Errors Defeat American Giants." *Chicago Defender,* 8 July 1916.

"Falcons Meet Colored Giants in Ball Game." *Oshkosh Northwestern,* 13 July 1934, 9.

"Foster Team Wins Another." *Chicago Defender,* 25 September 1915.

Foster, Rube. "The American Giants, Champions—In Los Angeles." *Indianapolis Freeman,* 9 November 1912, 7.

"Fosterites Are Ready for Start." *Indianapolis Recorder*, 17 April 1926.

"Fosterites Lead as Game is Called in 7th Inning." *Chicago Defender*, 20 May 1922.

"Foster's All-Stars Lose to the La Porte Beavers." *Chicago Defender*, 14 October 1916.

"Foster's American Giants." *Chicago Defender*, 23 September 1911.

"Foster's Gang Too Much for 6th Army Corps." *Chicago Defender*, 29 April 1922.

"Foster's Giants to Play Series Here." *Indianapolis Freeman*, 21 October 1916, 7.

"Foster's Men Go 11 Innings to Beat St. Louis Stars 8–7." *Chicago Defender*, 20 May 1922.

"Foster's Men in 5 to 4 Win from St. Louis in 9th." *Chicago Defender*, 16 June 1923.

"Fosters Spank Lowedermilk for an 8–2 Win." *Chicago Defender*, 7 July 1923.

"Fosters Win 4 to 3 from Kansas City." *Chicago Defender*, 16 May 1925.

"Games Here Sunday Count in Standings." *Bismarck Tribune*, 22 July 1938, 14.

"Giants Again Champions of Negro League." *Chicago Tribune*, 7 September 1952, A2.

"Giants Annex First Game; Langford's Triple Wins 2nd Game." *Chicago Defender*, 12 August 1916.

"Giants Battle Birmingham in Two Games Today." *Chicago Tribune*, 14 September 1947, A3.

"Giants Cop Final." *Chicago Defender*, 10 June 1916.

"Giants Drop Home Night Opener 11–2." *Chicago Defender*, 15 June 1946, 11.

"Giants Drub U. of O." *Chicago Defender*, 15 April 1916.

"Giants Hosts to Clowns in Game Tonight." *Chicago Tribune*, 26 July 1945, 18.

"Giants Invade Memphis for Loop Opener." *Chicago Defender*, 8 May 1937.

"Giants Make it 2 Straight Over Indianapolis A's." *Chicago Defender*, 23 June 1923.

"The Giants Move into First Place as A. B. C.'s Lose." *Chicago Defender*, 16 June 1923.

"Giants Off to Jackson, Miss." *Chicago Defender*, 30 March 1946, 11.

"Giants Onslaught Buries Lincoln Stars." *Chicago Defender*, 26 August 1916.

"Giants Rally in Eighth Beats Cuban Stars, 5 to 4." *Chicago Defender*, 15 July 1916.

"Giants Spot Kerr's Crowd 4 Runs and Then Beat Them." *Chicago Defender*, 10 June 1922.

"Giants Win from Beavers." *Chicago Defender*, 21 October 1916.

"Giants Win Game in the Eleventh Round." *Chicago Defender*, 8 July 1916.

"Giants Win Opening Series." *Indianapolis Recorder*, 6 May 1933, 2.

"Giants Win Pair." *Chicago Tribune*, 22 May 1939, 19.

"Grant's Home Run Features Twin Bill." *Chicago Defender*, 5 August 1916.

"Grays Beat Giants." *Chicago Defender*, 1 July 1916.

"Grays Face Giants in Stadium Today." *Washington Post*, 12 August 1945, M7.

"Grays To Face Chicagoans in Sox Park Today." *Chicago Tribune*, 21 July 1946, A2.

"Great Array of Twirlers Here Sunday." *Davenport Democrat and Leader*, 23 June 1927, 9.

"Grocers to Tangle with Colored Giants Tonight." *Herald-Press (MI)*, 27 July 1943, 7.

Hoekstra, Dave. "Two 'Giants' Remember Days of Black Baseball." *Chicago Sun-Times*, 30 January 1992, 140.

"Holland's Flying Dutchmen Meet Strong Colored Outfit Thursday." *Holland Evening Sentinel*, 14 July 1948, 2.

"Indianapolis Beaten 5 to 1 by the American Giants." *Chicago Defender*, 30 May 1925.

"Indianapolis Here for 5 Games and Fight for First Place." *Chicago Defender*, 16 June 1923.

"Indianapolis Here for Four Game Series." *Chicago Defender*, 14 June 1921.

"Indianapolis Plays Great Baseball, But Drops Three Games to American Giants." *Chicago Defender*, 10 July 1926.

"Invading Squad Originally was Union Giant '9.'" *Appleton Post-Crescent*, 22 June 1937, 12.

"Ivy Play Spoils No-Hit Game." *Chicago Defender*, 11 December 1915.

"Jeffries Single Beats Wickware One to Nothing." *Chicago Defender*, 28 October 1916.

"Jenkins Pitches American Giants to Victory." *Chicago Defender*, 4 September 1915.

"Johnson Blows and the Giants Lose." *Chicago Defender*, 19 August 1916.

"Johnson's Miscues Cost Foster Game." *Chicago Defender*, 15 July 1916.

"Joliet Nine Trims Foster's Crew, 7 to 4." *Chicago Defender*, 6 May 1922.

"Jones' Error Paves Way for Giant Victory." *Chicago Defender*, 27 May 1922.

"Kansas Citians Beat Chicago." *Chicago Defender,* 17 July 1948.

"Kansas City Here for Games Starting Memorial Day Morning with Fosters." *Chicago Defender,* 31 May 1924.

"Kansas City Rally Beats Fosters, 2–1." *Chicago Defender,* 16 May 1925.

"Kansas City Takes Five Straight from Rube Foster's American Giants." *Chicago Defender,* 6 June 1925.

"Kansas City vs. Am. Giants." *Chicago Defender,* 5 June 1926.

"Kaws Will Meet Colored Giants." *Appleton Post-Crescent,* 23 June 1937, 14.

"Kenyon's Rap in Tenth Wins 3–2 Game for Rube." *Chicago Defender,* 2 June 1923.

"Leading Colored Team Plays Toledo Team Under Lights Monday Night." *Lima News,* 20 July 1943, 8.

Levy, Scott J. "Chicago's Forgotten Giants of Negro League Baseball." *Chicago Cubs Magazine Scoreboard* 9 (January 1990): 34–35, 39–42.

Lewis, Billy. "The American Giants!" *Indianapolis Freeman,* 6 March 1915, 7.

Lewis, Cary B. "American Giants Take Four Out of Five in Series from Plutos." *Indianapolis Freeman,* 7 June 1913, 4.

_____. "Foster's Giants Capture a Title." *Indianapolis Freeman,* 26 August 1916, 4.

"Lincolns Defeat American Giants." *Chicago Defender,* 19 August 1916.

"Local Sports." *Chicago Defender,* 19 and 26 April 1913.

"Marquard's Record Beaten." *Chicago Defender,* 20 July 1912.

"Miller 'Bunted' Off Third-Base." *Baltimore Afro-American,* 31 August 1923, 14.

"Mills Defeated by Chicago in Doubleheader." *Chicago Tribune,* 3 May 1937, 19.

"Mills to Face Firemen in Two Games." *Chicago Tribune,* 8 September 1935, B6.

"Monarchs Face Negro Giants in Opener Today." *Chicago Tribune,* 9 May 1948, A6.

"Monarchs, Negro Giants Meet Today." *Chicago Tribune,* 3 July 1949, A5.

"Monarchs to Play Fosters 4-Game Series." *Chicago Defender,* 26 June 1926.

"Monarchs Win Over American Giants, 4–3." *Chicago Tribune,* 31 May 1943, 22.

"Montalvo Hits Three Homers Over Fence, Torriente One, As American Giants Beat Cubans." *Chicago Defender,* 24 May 1924.

"More about Foster's Baseball Team." *Half Century Magazine* (June 1919): 8, 13.

"Negro American League Game at W. Frankfort, June 16." *Harrisburg Daily Register* (IL), 10 June 1948, 7.

"Negro Clubs Here Tonight." *Newark Advocate and American Tribune,* 7 July 1940.

"Negro Giants and Cleveland Battle Today." *Chicago Tribune,* 18 June 1944, A3.

"Negro Giants and Memphis Play 2 Today." *Chicago Tribune,* 16 May 1948, A7.

"Negro Giants, Barons Start Series Today." *Chicago Tribune,* 12 September 1943.

"Negro Giants Bid for Title in Last Games." *Chicago Tribune,* 5 September 1943, A2.

"Negro Giants, Black Barons Play Two Today." *Chicago Tribune,* 2 June 1946, A5.

"Negro Giants, Clowns Meet Twice Today." *Chicago Tribune,* 16 July 1944, A4.

"Negro Giants Face Memphis Red Sox Today." *Chicago Tribune,* 20 August 1944, A3.

"Negro Giants, Indianapolis Play 2 Today." *Chicago Tribune,* 9 July 1950, A2.

"Negro Giants Lose 2; Barons Get Triple Play." *Chicago Tribune,* 14 July 1952, B3.

"Negro Giants, Memphis Sox to Meet Today." *Chicago Tribune,* 14 May 1944, A3.

"Negro Giants Open Home Card Today." *Chicago Tribune,* 7 May 1950, A3.

"Negro Giants Play Two Today with Memphis." *Chicago Tribune,* 6 July 1952, A5.

"Negro Giants Seek 2d Half Crown Today." *Chicago Tribune,* 2 September 1951, A2.

"Negro Giants to End Night Home Card Tomorrow." *Chicago Tribune,* 28 August 1946, 29.

"Negro Nines Open Today in Sox Park." *Chicago Tribune,* 5 May 1946, A2.

"Negro Teams Get Unasked Guest-Rain." *Chicago Tribune,* 2 May 1949, C4.

"Negro Teams to Play 2 Games in Comiskey Park." *Chicago Tribune,* 23 August 1942, B4.

"New American Giants to Open Season Today." *Chicago Tribune,* 1 May 1949, A2.

"No-Hit, No-Run Games to American Giants." *Chicago Defender,* 9 September 1916.

"Omaha Giants Beaten in Poor Game, 11 to 2." *Chicago Defender,* 12 June 1915.

"Openers Divided." *Chicago Tribune,* 6 May 1946, 24.

"Padron Beats Giants, 4–0." *Chicago Defender,* 22 July 1916.

"Paige Agrees to Pitch for Negro Giants." *Chicago Tribune,* 8 May 1951, C6.

"Paige to Pitch for Chi. Giants." *Portland Press Herald,* 8 May 1951, 12.

"Players Anxious to Start Practice." *Chicago Defender,* 20 March 1926.

"Pyotts Take Beating by American Giants." *Chicago Defender,* 7 July 1923.

"Rain Halts Giants Game in Fourth Inning." *Chicago Defender,* 8 May 1915.

"Rhodes Hurls, Bats American Giants to Split with Clowns." *Chicago Tribune,* 19 July 1948, B2.

"Roselands Blanked by American Giants in Hot Fight, 2 to 0." *Chicago Tribune,* 6 May 1918, 13.

"Rube Foster and His American Giants." *Chicago Defender,* 5 April 1913.

"Rube Foster's Giants Holding Their Own in California." *Chicago Defender,* 14 December 1912.

"Rube Foster's Team Opens Here Thursday." *Decatur Review,* 13 July 1921, 5.

"Satchel Paige Faces Chicago Giants Today." *Chicago Tribune,* 9 July 1944, A4.

"Satchel Paige, Using 'My Nuthin' Ball,' Tames Chicago Giants in 4-Inning Stint." *New York Times,* 21 May 1951.

"Six Chicagoans Picked on Negro All-Star Squad." *Chicago Tribune,* 25 July 1943, A3.

"Six Run Rally Beats Gary: Giants Beat Cubans in Opener." *Chicago Defender,* 12 August 1916.

"6,500 See Benefit Game." *Chicago Defender,* 15 July 1939.

"Skokie Indians Meet Chicago Vets Today." *Chicago Tribune,* 27 August 1961, A4.

"Snow and Cold May Force Foster to Take Team South Until League Season Opens." *Chicago Defender,* 10 April 1926.

"Southside Junior Giants vs. Young American Giants." *Chicago Defender,* 27 June 1919.

"Sporting World." *Chicago Defender,* 18 and 31 August and 14 September 1912.

"St. Louis 4, American Giants 3." *Chicago Defender,* 27 July 1912.

"St. Louis Loses 2–0 Game When Riley Yields One Hit." *Chicago Defender,* 16 June 1923.

"St. Louis Stars Win Two, Lose Two, in Four Game Series with Foster's Club." *Chicago Defender,* 4 July 1925.

"Stars Defeat Giants, 9 to 5." *Hammond Times,* 28 June 1937, 11.

"Sunday's Tilt with A. B. C.'s to Chicago Team." *Chicago Defender,* 28 October 1916.

"Take Game in the Ninth." *Chicago Defender,* 22 April 1916.

"Tie Broken in Ninth Frame with 4 Runs." *Lima News,* 21 July 1933, 8.

"Toledo Club Is Here Sunday for Game with Jints." *Chicago Defender,* 14 July 1923.

"Too Much Mullin, Giants Lose 5 to 0." *Chicago Defender,* 29 July 1916.

"Trouppe and McNeal Homer as Chicago Wins 2." *Chicago Defender,* 18 September 1948, 10.

"Two Home Runs Beat Pantages." *Chicago Defender,* 11 December 1915.

"West Ends Outbat American Giants in Hitting Bee, 8–6." *Chicago Tribune,* 20 May 1918, 11.

"Wickware Shuts Out the Cuban Stars." *Chicago Defender,* 26 August 1916.

Williams, Harry A. "Giants Lose First Game." *Los Angeles Times,* 2 November 1921, 17.

"Win Saturday, Tie Sunday, Win Again Monday, Only to Get Shut Out on Tuesday." *Chicago Defender,* 8 May 1926.

"Winklers to Play Giants in Doubleheader Today." *Chicago Tribune,* 20 September 1942, A5.

Wyatt, David. "American Giants and All Nations Pull Largest Crowd of the Season." *Indianapolis Freeman,* 7 October 1916, 7.

Young, Fay. "Through the Years." *Chicago Defender,* 8 May 1948, 11.

"Young Named Secretary of American Giants Club." *Chicago Tribune,* 27 April 1951, C3.

"YWCA Benefit Game Sunday at Am. Giants Park." *Chicago Defender,* 23 June 1923.

"YWCA Day Sunday, June 24." Chicago Defender, 16 June 1923.

Related Terms: Chicago Baseball, Andrew "Rube" Foster, Frank Leland, NNL

Chicago Ball Parks

"Dedicate New Park on Sunday." *Chicago Tribune,* 9 May 1911, 10.

Chicago Baseball

"Baseball in Chicago." *Chicago Tribune Magazine,* 20 June 2004, Section 10.

"Chicago League Books Week's Twilight Games." *Chicago Tribune,* 24 June 1924, 19.

"Colored Baseball League Next." *New York Times,* 18 November 1913, 9.

"Colored Baseball Players Are Good." *Mansfield News,* 1 December 1910.

"Form League for Negroes." *Chicago Tribune,* 18 November 1913, 16.

Heaphy, Leslie, ed. *Negro Leagues in Chicago Commemorative Booklet.* 8th Annual Jerry Malloy Negro League Conference, Chicago, Illinois. Jefferson, NC: McFarland, 2005.

"New League Stops Sunday A. M. Ball." *Chicago Tribune,* 26 May 1909, 8.

"Opposed to Visiting Teams." *Chicago Tribune,* 21 July 1908, 7.

Schmidt, Ray. "The Golden Age of Chicago Baseball." *Chicago History,* (Winter 2000).

Terry, Don. "Pride and Prejudice." *Chicago Tribune Magazine,* 20 June 2004, Section 10.

Wyatt, David. "Baseball War for Chicago." *Indianapolis Freeman,* 4 December 1909.

_____. "Chicago to Have New Baseball Club." *Indianapolis Freeman,* 30 October 1909.

Chicago Brown Bombers

"Bombers, LaPalomas in Bluffs." *Council Bluffs Nonpareil,* June 1946.

"Brown Bombers to Meet Giants." *Hammond Times,* 23 May 1943, 15.

"Chicago Brown Bombers, Cuban LaPalomas Play Tuesday Night, American Legion Park." *Council Bluffs NonPareil,* 16 June 1946, 19.

Chicago Giants

"'Bugs' Beats Chicago Giants." *Chicago Tribune,* 20 August 1911, C2.

"The Chicago Giants Base Ball Club." *Chicago Defender,* 22 January 1910, 1.

"Chicago Giants Clout Ball." *Chicago Tribune,* 17 July 1911, 9.

"Chicago Giants Forfeit, 9–0." *Chicago Tribune,* 7 July 1911, 11.

"The Chicago Giants in their New Home." *Chicago Defender,* 25 June 1910, 1.

"Chicago Giants Lose." *Chicago Defender,* 5 June 1915.

"Chicago Giants Lose Ten-Inning Affair." *Chicago Defender,* 29 July 1916.

"Chicago Giants Lose to Joliet Rivals in Great Game." *Chicago Defender,* 7 August 1915.

"Chicago Giants Record." *Chicago Defender,* 1 July 1911.

"The Chicago Giants Show Class." *Chicago Defender,* 29 October 1910.

"Chicago Giants Take First." *Chicago Tribune,* 14 August 1911, 11.

"Chicago Giants Victors, 3 to 2." *Chicago Tribune,* 30 May 1910, 15.

"Chicago Giants Win Ball Game." *Los Angeles Times,* 26 November 1915, III4.

"Chicago Giants Win 15th, 6–3." *Chicago Tribune,* 17 September 1911, C2.

"Chicago Giants Win Greatest Game of Season." *Chicago Defender,* 14 August 1915.

"Giants Down Cards Again." *Chicago Tribune,* 1 August 1911, 12.

"Giants Take Joke Victory." *Los Angeles Times,* 31 December 1910, 16.

"Late Rally Gives West Ends Game." *Chicago Tribune,* 7 August 1911, 8.

Leland, Frank. *Frank Leland's Chicago Giants Baseball Club.* Chicago: Fraternal, 1910.

"Leland's Chicago Giants on Tour." *Indianapolis Freeman,* 30 April 1910.

"Lone Homerun Wins 1–0 Game." *Chicago Tribune,* 6 September 1910, 15.

"Milwaukee Drops Two Games Here to Kansas City." *Chicago Defender,* 14 July 1923.

"Normals Beat Chicago Giants." *Chicago Defender,* 21 August 1915.

"Reiger Loses to Giant Team." *Los Angeles Times,* 7 January 1911, 16.

"Squares and Giants in Even break." *Chicago Tribune,* 20 August 1928, 25.

"Toledo to Play Chicago Giants Sunday, April 29." *Chicago Defender,* 28 April 1923.

"Upset Giants in 1 to 0 Clash." *Chicago Defender,* 24 June 1916.

Chicago Keystones

"Lincoln Life Team Loses to Chicago Keystones." *Fort Wayne News and Sentinel,* 21 July 1919, 13.

"Seldon to Take Field with Chicago Club against Lifers." *Fort Wayne Journal-Gazette,* 18 July 1919, 8.

Chicago Union Giants

"Amateurs to Begin Play." *Chicago Tribune,* 17 April 1904, 10.

"Aurora Joins the Interstate." *Chicago Tribune,* 15 March 1903, 15.

"Camp Nine Trims the Union Giants." *Chicago Tribune,* 20 May 1918, 11.

"Chicago Colored Team Wins." *Chicago Tribune,* 26 September 1904, 4.

"Chicago Unions." *Chicago Inter Ocean,* 2 September 1899.

"Clinton 19, Union Giants 5." *Chicago Tribune,* 30 June 1904, 8.

"Cragins Defeat Union Giants." *Chicago Tribune,* 1 April 1918, 13.

"Cuban Giants are Winners." *Chicago Tribune,* 19 September 1904, 6.

"Fight for the Union Giants." *Chicago Tribune,* 7 June 1904, 8.

"Flag Day at Auburn Park." *Chicago Defender,* 14 May 1910.

"For 'Colored' Championship." *Chicago Tribune,* 11 September 1904, A2.

"Fourteen Errors Made in One Game." *Chicago Defender,* 5 August 1916.

"Games of Semi-Professionals." *Chicago Tribune,* 14 July 1902, 6.

"Games of the Amateurs." *Chicago Tribune,* 28 April 1902, 6.

"Games on Local Diamond." *Chicago Tribune,* 25 August 1902 and 2 May 1904, 8.

"Games on Other Ball Fields." *Chicago Tribune,* 1 August 1904, 8.

"Giants Down the Standards." *Chicago Tribune,* 14 September 1903, 6.

"Huge Attendance See Union Giants Lose to Henry Greys." *Chicago Defender,* 16 October 1915.

"Joliet Standards 4, Union Giants 3." *Chicago Tribune,* 1 June 1902, 11.

"Lively Day on Local Diamonds." *Chicago Tribune,* 23 May 1904, 6.

"Mills Launch Season; Defeat Union Giants." *Chicago Tribune,* 6 April 1931, 30.

"Niesens Pound Double Win from Union Giants." *Chicago Tribune,* 6 October 1924, 30.

"No Hit Made Off Koukalik." *Chicago Tribune,* 22 August 1904, 10.

"On Diamonds Around Chicago." *Chicago Tribune,* 29 August 1904, 8.

"On the Amateur Field." *Chicago Tribune,* 15 September 1902, 6.

"Open the Semi-Pro Season." *Chicago Tribune,* 15 April 1907, 10.

"Other Local Games Today." *Chicago Tribune,* 18 September 1904, A2.

"Pittsburg Wins and Loses." *Chicago Tribune,* 22 August 1903, 9.

"Racine 6, Union Giants 4." *Chicago Tribune,* 30 May 1904, 12.

"Rogers Parks in Slugging Bee." *Chicago Tribune,* 3 July 1910, C4.

"Rogers Parks Play Sunday." *Chicago Tribune,* 29 April 1913, 15.

"St. Louis Defeats Champions." *Chicago Tribune,* 29 April 1903, 7.

"Semi-pro Card Today Offers Both Quality and Quantity." *Chicago Tribune,* 5 June 1927, A2.

"Snow Prevents Ball Game Between Semi-Pro Teams." *Chicago Tribune,* 13 March 1911, 19.

"South Chicago Team Wins." *Chicago Tribune,* 13 June 1904, 8.

"Spauldings Beats the Giants." *Chicago Tribune,* 21 April 1902, 6.

"Taylor's Team Wins Out in a Close Game." *Indianapolis Star,* 28 May 1916, 18.

"Union Giants are Champions." *Chicago Tribune,* 4 August 1902, 6.

"Union Giants Beat Dubuque Team, 13 to 9." *Chicago Tribune,* 28 April 1928, 21.

"Union Giants Capture Game." *Chicago Tribune,* 5 August 1907, 11.

"Union Giants Defeat Joliet." *Chicago Tribune,* 18 August 1902, 4.

"Union Giants Divide Omaha Double Header." *Chicago Defender,* 5 August 1916.

"Unions Giants 8, Gowrie 5." *Chicago Tribune,* 18 August 1916, 9.

"Union Giants 11, Joliet 3." *Chicago Tribune,* 26 June 1918, 11.

"Union Giants 4, Artesians 0." *Chicago Tribune,* 8 July 1907, 8.

"Union Giants 4; East Side Maroons 5." *Chicago Defender,* 12 June 1915.

"Union Giants Lose." *Chicago Defender,* 15 April 1916.

"Union Giants on Top at Des Moines." *Chicago Defender,* 3 July 1915.

"Union Giants Open Season." *Chicago Defender,* 27 March 1915.

"Union Giants Reorganized." *Chicago Tribune,* 2 March 1902, 20.

"Union Giants Schedule." *Chicago Tribune,* 3 April 1921, A2.

"Union Giants 6, Clinton 1." *Chicago Tribune,* 21 August 1903, 4.

"Union Giants 13, Hyde Park 6." *Chicago Tribune,* 16 April 1902, 10.

"Union Giants Too Fast for All-Stars." *Chicago Defender,* 9 October 1915.

"Union Giants 12–5 Victors Over Cunneas." *Chicago Tribune,* 13 April 1931, 26.

"Union Giants Whip the All Nations Club." *Chicago Defender,* 25 September 1915.

"Union Giants Win Two." *Chicago Defender,* 29 July 1916.

"Union Giants Winners as Sullivan Weakens." *Chicago Defender,* 12 August 1916.

"Unions are Defeated Again." *Chicago Tribune,* 26 June 1899, 4.

"Unions Defeat the Giants." *Chicago Tribune,* 19 June 1899, 4.

"Want Post-Season Play." *Chicago Tribune,* 11 October 1903, 11.

"West Ends Beat Union Giants." *Chicago Tribune,* 15 September 1907, C2.

Chicago Unions

"Amateur Games for Today." *Chicago Tribune,* 4 May 1902, 11.

"Chicago Unions 5, Cuban Giants 4." *Chicago Tribune,* 13 June 1900, 4.

"Colored Ball Clubs at War." *Chicago Tribune,* 8 April 1899, 6.

"Unions are Defeated Again." *Chicago Tribune,* 26 June 1899, 4.

"Unions Defeat Cuban Giants." *Chicago Tribune,* 12 June 1899, 4.

"Unions Defeat the Giants." *Chicago Tribune,* 19 June 1899, 4.

East-West Classic

"All-Star Baseball Game in Memphis, Oct. 4." *Chicago Defender,* 3 October 1942.

"All Star Diamond Game to Be Staged at Yankee Stadium, September 18." *New Jersey Herald News,* 10 September 1938, 11.

"All Star East-West Game at Yankee Stadium, Aug. 27." *New Jersey Herald News,* 19 August 1939, 8.

"All-Star Negro Baseball Teams to Clash Today." *Chicago Tribune,* 26 August 1934, A5.

Barry, Howard. "Negro League All-Stars to Clash Today." *Chicago Tribune,* 22 August 1954, A3.

_____. "West Negro All-Stars Deal East 3d Straight Loss, 8 to 4." *Chicago Tribune,* 23 August 1954, C3.

"Baseball's Dream Game." *New York Amsterdam News,* 26 July 1947.

Bostic, Joe. "The East-West Classic, Top Sports Event." *The People's Voice,* 14 August 1943.

Burley, Dan. "Confidentially Yours." *New York Amsterdam News,* 24 August 1946.

Cattau, Daniel. "Baseball Strikes Out with Black Fans." *Chicago Reporter,* 1 April 1991, 1, 6–9, 13.

"Chandler to Open East, West Game." *Chicago Tribune,* 14 August 1949, A3.

"Charleston, Posey Lead East's Poll on Colored Pilot." *Chicago Tribune,* 30 July 1937, 20.

"Chicago Gets West vs. East Negro Contest." *Chicago Tribune,* 18 July 1954, A4.

"Chicago Prepares for '35 East-West Baseball Game." *Indianapolis Recorder,* 20 July 1935.

Clark, James C. "All-Star Players Made Two Dollars a Game." *Orlando Sentinel,* 23 February 1990.

Clark, John L. "Chicago Awaits All Star Baseball Classic." *Indianapolis Recorder,* 9 September 1933, 2.

_____. "E-W Game Seen as Economic Boom." *Pittsburgh Courier,* 18 August 1934.

_____. "Game to Inspire Players, Plan to Aid League." *Pittsburgh Courier,* 28 July 1934.

_____. "Interest Running High in National All Star Baseball Classic During World Fair." *Indianapolis Recorder,* 19 August 1933, 8.

_____. "Umpires, Managers and Coaches in East-West Contest." *Indianapolis Recorder,* 11 August 1934, 7.

"Colored Nines Due Tomorrow; Plan Workouts." *Chicago Tribune,* 15 August 1940, 21.

"Colored Stars Assemble for Annual Game." *Chicago Tribune,* 10 August 1935, 15.

"Colored Stars Meet Today in Annual Game." *Chicago Tribune,* 6 August 1939, B2.

"Colored Teams Play Today for Baseball Title." *Chicago Tribune,* 10 September 1933, A2.

"Comiskey Park Is Scene of 14th Annual Classic." *Chicago Defender,* 17 August 1946.

"Crawfords with East in Big Game." *Chicago Defender,* 21 July 1934.

Cummiskey, Joe. "Baseball's Biggest Drawing Card." *Negro Digest* 1 (August 1944): 69–70.

Day, John C. "Buck Leonard's Homerun and Pitching of Paige Feature Game." *Chicago Defender,* 2 August 1941.

Drebinger, John. "Sports of the Times." *New York Times,* 14 August 1961, 18.

Dial, Lewis E. "The Sport Dial." *New York Age,* 10 August 1935, 8.

Dixon, Randy. "The Sports Bugle." *Pittsburgh Courier,* 5 September 1942.

Downer, Fred. "Chicago Gay for East-West Game." *New York Age,* 17 August 1935, 5.

"East and West Colored Stars to Play Aug. 21." *Chicago Tribune,* 24 July 1938, A6.

"East Is Out to Beat West in Big Game." *Indianapolis Recorder*, 3 August 1935, 12.

"East Favored in Tomorrow's A — Star Game." *Chicago Tribune*, 17 August 1940, 18.

"East Plans to Switch Fielders for Contest." *Chicago Defender*, 1 August 1942.

"East Selects 21 All-Stars for Colored Game." *Chicago Tribune*, 1 August 1939, 23.

"East vs. West Today in 14th Negro Game." *Chicago Tribune*, 18 August 1946, A2.

"East-West All-Star Game to be Played in Chicago." *New York Age*, 13 July 1935, 8.

"East-West Baseball Classic in Chicago Attracts National Attention." *New York Age*, 26 August 1933, 6.

"East-West Classic Play by Play." *New York Amsterdam News*, 24 August 1946.

"East-West Contest to Stimulate Interest in Negro National League." *New York Age*, 20 July 1935, 8.

"East-West Game Coverage." *NewYork Amsterdam News*, 12 August 1944.

"East-West Game Now Takes Spot." *New York Amsterdam News*, 10 August 1935.

East-West Games File. Research Library, National Baseball Hall of Fame and Museum, Cooperstown, New York.

"East-West Line-up Is Completed." *New York Amsterdam News*, 12 August 1939.

"Eastern Negro Stars Defeat West Team, 4–0." *Chicago Tribune*, 15 August 1949, B1.

"Expect 30,000 at All-Star Game Sunday." *Chicago Defender*, 10 August 1935.

"Fans Again to Pick Players for 2nd Classic East vs. West Baseball Game." *Indianapolis Recorder*, 7 July 1934, 2.

"Fans' Dream Comes True." *Pittsburgh Courier*, 17 August 1935.

"Fans Spend $247, 500 to See Classics." *Pittsburgh Courier*, 31 July 1943.

"Fernandez to Pilot East Team in Annual Negro Baseball Game." *Chicago Tribune*, 4 August 1948, B2.

"50,000 to See Negro Teams Clash Today." *Chicago Tribune*, 13 August 1944, A2.

"Final East-West Game Voting." *New York Amsterdam News*, 10 August 1935.

"49,500 to See Negro All-Star Game Today." *Chicago Tribune*, 29 July 1945, A2.

Galbreath, Elizabeth. "The Women Take to East vs. West Baseball Classic." *Chicago Defender*, 2 Agust 1941.

"Game at Stadium Was Second Loss for West Outfit." *Cleveland Call and Post*, 22 August 1942.

Gant, Eddie. "Cover the Eastern Front." *Chicago Defender*, 12 July 9141; 25 July 1942.

Harris, Ed. "At It Again." *Philadelphia Tribune*, 29 August 1935.

Hawkins, Dave. "Hawkins Picks Argument Over East-West Voting." *Chicago Defender*, 25 August 1934.

Hayes, Marcus. "East-West Game was Jewel of Negro Leagues." *Los Angeles Daily News*, 7 July 1996.

_____. "Ten Times, Negro Leagues East-West Game Drew Bigger Crowds Than All-Stars." *Knight-Ridder Newspapers*, 4 July 1996.

"Heavy Hitting Beats East in Classic." *Kansas City Call*, 15 September 1933.

"Here's Your Chance to Pick the 1933 All Star Baseball Team and Get $100.00 in Cash." *Indianapolis Recorder*, 12 August 1933, 2.

"Indications Point to Record Vote in Negro Stars' Game." *Lincoln Sunday Journal and Star*, 21 July 1940, 3-B.

Irvin, Monte. "The Time of a Lifetime." *Sports Illustrated*, 19 July 1993, 106.

"Jessup, Hill Picked to Play for West in Negro All-Star Game." *Chicago Tribune*, 6 August 1948, B2.

"Jim West, Gangling First Baseman of the Elites." *Chicago Defender*, 22 August 1936.

Johnson, Lee A. "23,000 Watch 'Big' Bill Foster Defeat East." *Indianapolis Recorder*, 16 September 1933, 1.

Jones, Lucius. "East-West Game Interest Again High as American League Stars Seek Revenge." *Pittsburgh Courier*, 10 July 1943.

"Josh Gibson May Lead Explosive Lineup for East against West in Big Classic." *Pittsburgh Courier*, 24 July 1943.

Kleinknecht, Merl. "Cleveland and the East-West All-Star Game." In *All Star Baseball in Cleveland*, 57–60.

_____. "East Meets West in Negro Games." *Baseball Research Journal* 1 (January 1972): 78–79.

Lacy, Sam. "All-Star Classic Delayed by West's Pay Demands." *Baltimore Afro American* 24 (August 1946).

Lester, Larry. "Baseball: Some New Books That Look at the National Pastime." *Chicago Tribune*, 7 July 2002.

_____. *Black Baseball's National Showcase.*

Lincoln: Bison Original, University of Nebraska Press, 2002.

"Managers Named for All-Star Colored Game." *Chicago Tribune*, 31 August 1933, 22.

Monroe, Al. "20,000 See West Beat East in Baseball 'Game of Games.'" *Chicago Defender*, 16 September 1933.

_____. "Suttles' Homerun Wins It for the West." *Chicago Defender*, 17 August 1945.

_____. "Willie Foster Loses Contest to S. Paige." *Chicago Defender*, 1 September 1934.

"Name West Nine for 14th Negro All-Star Game." *Chicago Tribune*, 11 August 1946, A5.

"Name West's All-Stars for Negro Game." *Chicago Tribune*, 20 July 1947, A2.

"National League Picks Team for Annual 'Dream Game.'" *Pittsburgh Courier*, 19 July 1947.

"Negro All-Star Game Listed for August 18." *Washington Post*, 21 July 1940, SP5.

"Negro All-Star Nines Assemble for 14th Game." *Chicago Daily Tribune*, 17 August 1946, 17.

"Negro East-West Game Today May Attract 40,000." *Chicago Tribune*, 16 August 1942, B2.

"Negro East-West Tickets Go on Sale Today." *Chicago Tribune*, 16 July 1949, A2.

"Negro National League Power Crushes West 10–2." *New York Amsterdam News*, 2 September 1939.

"Negro Nines Assemble for All-Star Game." *Chicago Tribune*, 25 August 1934.

"Negro Stars Clash Today in Sox Park." *Chicago Tribune*, 12 August 1951, A6.

"Negro Stars for East-West Game Chosen." *Chicago Tribune*, 5 August 1951, A4.

"Negroes Meet in All-Star Game Sept. 10." *Chicago Tribune*, 15 August 1933, 18.

"North vs. South Negro Baseball Carded Today." *Chicago Tribune*, 22 September 1946, B2.

Nunn, William. "Powerful Attack Masterful Mound Work Beats West." *Pittsburgh Courier*, 24 August 1940.

_____. "Satchel Paige Is Magnet at E-W Game." *Pittsburgh Courier*, 29 August 1936.

_____. "'Satch' Stop 'Big Bad Men' of West Team." *Pittsburgh Courier*, 1 September 1934.

_____. "West's Satellites Eclipse Stars of the East in Classic." *Pittsburgh Courier*, 16 September 1933.

"One Big Inning Routs East in Classic." *Chicago Defender*, 19 August 1944, 7.

"Padden to Hurl First Ball for Negro All-Stars." *Chicago Tribune*, 23 August 1934, 18.

"Paige to Pitch for East vs. West Game." *Chicago Defender*, 26 July 1941.

"Pitching Duel Is Assured by Colored Stars." *Chicago Tribune*, 19 August 1936, 27.

"Players of 10 Teams Eligible for 2nd East-West Classic at Chicago, Aug. 26." *Indianapolis Recorder*, 14 July 1934, 2.

"Popularity Contest to Determine Teams of East-West Game at Chicago Aug. 11 Enters Final Week." *New York Age*, 3 August 1935, 8.

"Promoters in Move to Foil Hit at Game." *Chicago Defender*, 22 August 1936.

Rapoport, Ron. "Negro Leagues Stars Sparkled at Comiskey." *Chicago Sun-Times*, 10 July 2003.

"Report Heavy Early Vote on Colored Nines." *Chicago Tribune*, 9 July 1939, B7.

"Satchel Paige to American League." *Chicago Defender*, 29 June 1940.

"Satchel Paige Tosses East to 1–0 Victory over West before 25,000 Roaring Baseball Fans." *Indianapolis Recorder*, 1 September 1934, 7–8.

"Scalpers Take Good Beating." *Chicago Defender*, 4 August 1945.

Smith, Wendell. "Americans Too Good for Spiritless East." *Pittsburgh Courier*, 4 August 1945.

_____. "Dream Game Star Dust." *Pittsburgh Courier*, 24 August 1946.

_____. "Smitty's Sports Spurts." *Pittsburgh Courier*, 19 August 1944.

_____. "East-West Game Star Dust," The Sports Beat. *Pittsburgh Courier*, 4 August 1945.

_____. "There's Only One," The Sports Beat. *Pittsburgh Courier*, 17 August 1946.

_____. "What a Difference a Year Makes." *Pittsburgh Courier*, 17 August 1946.

Spellman, Mike. "Negro League All-Star Game 'an Instant Hit,' Event Was Bigger Deal Than the League's World Series." *Daily Herald*, 14 July 2003.

Sullivan, Brad. "The Patriot Game, 2. The Negro Leagues Benefit Game." In *All-Star Baseball in Cleveland*, 61–63.

"Teams All Set for Big Tilt Tomorrow." *Los Angeles Times*, 10 November 1922.

"35,000 to See Negro Baseball Contest Today." *Chicago Tribune*, 20 August 1950, A4.

"Top Candidates for Big 'Dream Game' at Comiskey Park." *Pittsburgh Courier*, 24 July 1943.

"20,000 Fans Will Watch Series Start." *Washington Post*, 15 August 1946.

"20,000 See East Colored Stars Beat West, 7 to 2." *Chicago Tribune*, 9 August 1937, 21.

"Two All-Star Negro Nines Clash Today." *Chicago Tribune*, 27 July 1947, A3.

"Two Great Rival Teams Await Calling of the Big East-West Baseball Classic in Chicago." *Indianapolis Recorder*, 25 August 1934, 7.

"Umpires, Managers and Coaches in East-West Game Contest." *Indianapolis Recorder*, 11 August 1934, 7.

Vanderberg, Bob. "Sox Footnote Provides Rich Anecdote." *Chicago Tribune*, 23 September 1990, Sec. 3, 2.

"West Defeats East All-Star Negro Nine, 4–1." *Chicago Tribune*, 19 August 1946, 27.

"West Defeats East, 5 to 1, in All-Star Play." *Chicago Tribune*, 17 August 1953, C5.

"West Defeats East's Negro Stars, 5–2." *Chicago Tribune*, 28 July 1947, 29.

"West Tops East, 5–3, in Negro Baseball." *New York Times*, 21 August 1950, 23.

"West Wins, 11–8, as Suttles Hits Homerun in 11th." *Chicago Tribune*, 12 August 1935, 17.

"West's Negro Stars Win, 5–3." *Chicago Tribune*, 21 August 1950, C1.

"West's Pitchers Face Problem in East's Mighty Bats." *New York Amsterdam News*, 5 August 1939.

Young, Fay. "Ace West Hurlers Beat East 4–1." *Chicago Defender*, 24 August 1946.

_____. "East vs. West Game Gets a Fanning." *Kansas City Call*, 27 July 1934.

_____. "Gibson, Suttles and Leonard Held Hitless." *Chicago Defender*, 12 August 1939.

_____. "Let's Get This Straight." *Chicago Defender*, 15 August 1942.

_____. "Paige Threatens Not to Hurl in All-Star Classic." *Chicago Defender*, 5 August 1944.

_____. "Through the Years." *Chicago Defender*, 2 August 1947, 11.

_____. "Through the Years: Past — Present — Future." *Chicago Defender*, 27 August 1938; 2 August 1941; 1 August 1942; 22 August 1942; 7 August 1943; 4 August 1945.

_____. "Through the Years: Time to Call a Halt." *Chicago Defender*, 28 August 1944.

Young, Frank A. "48,000 See East All-Stars Beat Paige and West." *Chicago Defender*, 22 August 1942.

_____. "Satchel Paige Not Eligible for 1940 East-West Baseball Classic." *Chicago Defender*, 3 August 1940.

_____. "West Beats East in Classic Thriller, 5 to 4." *Chicago Defender*, 27 August 1938.

_____. "West Ready to Halt East's Bats." *Chicago Defender*, 8 August 1942.

Foster, Andrew "Rube"

Adams, Sam. "Celebrating Black Baseball Leagues." *Rocky Mountain News*, 13 February 2003, 2C.

Allard, Jenny. "Rube Foster." Research Prospectus. National Baseball Hall of Fame and Library. Cooperstown, New York.

"Andrew Jackson "Rube" Foster Celebrates His Fortieth Birthday Anniversary." *Chicago Defender*, 7 December 1912.

"Andrew Rube Foster." *Chicago Defender*, 6 September 1916, 6.

Avendorph, Julius N. "Rube Foster and His American Giants." *Chicago Defender*, 5 April 1913, 8.

_____. "'Rube' Foster's Giants Hold Their Own in California." *Chicago Defender*, 14 December 1912, 7.

"Baseball War Becomes Bitter." *Baltimore Afro-American*, 16 March 1923.

Beckwith, Carl. "Rube Foster Leads New NNL." *Kansas City Call*, 2 January 1925, 1.

Brennan, Gerald E. "Foster, Andrew 'Rube.'" In *Biographical Dictionary of American Sports, Baseball*, edited by David L. Porter. Westport, CT: Greenwood Press, 2000, 489–491.

Broeg, Bob. "Mize, Foster to Enter Hall." *The Sporting News*, 28 March 1981, 32.

Broughman, Royal. "'Rube' Thinks Black Men Will Play in Big Leagues." *Seattle Post Intelligencer*, 5 April 1914, 1.

"Bury Rube Foster." *Chicago Defender*, 13 December 1930.

"Cosmopolitan Throng Pays Final Tribute to Organizer of Negro Baseball League." *New York Amsterdam News*, 17 December 1930.

Cottrell, Robert. *The Best Pitcher in Baseball: The Life of Rube Foster, Negro League Giant.* New York: New York University Press, 2001.

_____. "A Season of Courage." In *Blackball, the Black Sox and the Babe*. Jefferson, NC: McFarland, 2002, 141–153.

"Daguerreotypes." *The Sporting News*, 1 January 1990, 23–24.

"First Inning Spurt by Foster's Giants Beats Chicagos, 4–2." *Chicago Tribune*, 21 May 1917, 13.

Floto, James. "Profile — Rube Foster." *Diamond Angle* 4, no. 2 (1 February 1993): 21–23.

Foster, Andrew, File. Research Library, National Baseball Hall of Fame and Museum, Cooperstown, New York.

Foster, Andrew "Rube." "Come Fans Rally Round the Flag." *Indianapolis Freeman*, 13 November 1909.

_____. "A Few Facts Relative to the National Negro League." *Indianapolis Freeman*, 24 December 1910.

_____. "Pitfalls of Baseball, Part I-III." *Chicago Defender*, 29 November 1919, 3 January 1920, 17 January 1920, 10 December 1921 and 29 December 1921.

_____. "The Season of 1917 Closes." *Indianapolis Freeman*, 20 October 1917, 7.

_____. Series of Articles in *Baltimore Afro-American* 1921 and 1922.

_____. "Success of the Negro as a Ball Player." *Indianapolis Freeman*, 16 April 1910, 9.

"Foster Argues; Schulte Scores." *The Chicago Daily Tribune*, 19 October 1909, 12.

"Foster Asks Patience." *Chicago Defender*, 19 April 1919, 11.

"The Foster Banquet." *Indianapolis Freeman*, 30 August 1913, 4.

"Foster Faces the 2 Waner Brothers." *Chicago Defender*, 8 October 1932, 11.

"Foster, Father of Negro Ball League, Dies." *Chicago Tribune*, 11 December 1930, 24.

"Foster Gives Reasons for Firing Umpires." *Kansas City Call*, 21 August 1925.

"Foster Pitches Hitless Contest." *Minneapolis Tribune*, 29 August 1908, 15.

"Foster to Give Fans Chance to Look Them Over." *Chicago Defender*, 7 April 1923.

"Foster Wins His Games." *Indianapolis Freeman*, 3 August 1912, 4.

"Foster's Crew are on Their Training Trip." *Chicago Defender*, 18 March 1922.

"Foster's Crew Back in First Place Again." *Chicago Defender*, 29 July 1922.

"Foster's Giants to Make Bow." *Chicago Tribune*, 25 April 1911, 20.

"Foster's Speed Frightens." *Union Times*, 26 July 1904.

"Foster's Team Downs Rivals." *Chicago Tribune*, 30 July 1911, C2.

"Fosters Win 4 to 3 from Kansas City." *Chicago Defender*, 16 May 1925.

"Gas Nearly Kills Andrew Rube Foster." *Chicago Defender*, 6 June 1925.

"Giants Honor Rube Foster in 2 Games Today." *Chicago Tribune*, 25 May 1941, A4.

Greene, A. C. "Two Famed Pitchers Claimed for Little Town of Calvert." *Dallas Morning News*, 27 December 1998.

Grimsley, Will. "Veterans Committee Elects Mize, Foster." *The Times*, 12 March 1981, 11.

Hall, John. "Hall of Shame." *Los Angeles Times*, 28 February 1974.

Heaphy, Leslie. "Foster, Andrew ('Rube')" in *Encyclopedia of Ethnicity and Sports in the United States of America*, edited by George Kirsch, et al. Westport, CT: Greenwood Press, 2000, 166–167.

Holway, John B. "Andrew Rube Foster." *Black Sports Magazine*, 1 November 1977, 58 60.

_____. "The Negro League's Winningest Pitcher Wins Hall Backing." *Baseball Weekly*, 13 March 1996.

_____. "The Rube and Smokey Joe." *Dawn Magazine*. (1 September 1977): 12, 14–15.

_____. "Rube Foster and the League." *Chicago Sun-Times*, 29 March 1981, 25.

_____. "Rube Foster: Father of the Black Game." *The Sporting News*, 8 August 1981, 19–20.

_____. "Texas Smokey: Negro Leaguer Ranks as One of Top Pitchers." *Dallas Morning News*, 23 July 1999.

_____. "Rube Foster." Unpublished manuscript, Chicago Historical Society.

"In the Wake of the News." *Chicago Tibune*, 17 December 1930, 25.

Jarrett, Vernon. "Black Baseball's 'Father.'" *Chicago Tribune*, 5 August 1981, 23.

_____. "Years Ago Many Blacks Were Achievers." *Chronicle-Telegram*, 16 August 1981, D-5.

"Kansas City Club Here for 5-Game Series with Foster." *Chicago Defender*, 8 July 1922.

"Kansas City Takes Five Straight from Rube Foster's American Giants." *Chicago Defender*, 6 June 1925.

Koenig, Bill. "Bound for Cooperstown." *USA Today Baseball Weekly*, 31 July 1996.

_____. "Reveling—and Reviling: New In-
ductees Speak Out." *USA Today Baseball
Weekly*, 7 August 1996.

Lewis, Billy. "Rube Foster in the City." *Indianapolis Freeman*, 16 July 1916.

_____. "Rube Foster Invades Kentucky." *In-
dianapolis Freeman*, 1 August 1914.

_____. "Rube Foster Setting the Baseball
Pace." *Indianapolis Freeman*, 25 March
1916, 7.

"Logans Unkind to 'Rube.'" *Chicago Tribune*, 31 August 1908, 7.

Madden, Bill. "At Long Last, Mize Is in Hall
of Fame." *New York Daily News*, 12 March
1981.

Malloy, Jerry. "Rube Foster and Black Baseball in Chicago." In *Baseball in Chicago*,
1986, 24–27.

Mason, George E. "Rube Foster Chats About
His Career." *Chicago Defender*, 20 February 1915.

Mims, Linda. "The Vision of Andrew 'Rube'
Foster." *Sacramento Observer*, 23 August
1995.

"Mize, Foster Elected into Hall." *New York
Times*, 12 March 1987.

Nance, Rahkia. "Foster Little-Known Force
in Negro League." *Capital Outlook*, 3 January to 9 January 2002.

"National Negro Baseball League Is Automatically Disbanded as Foster Resigns."
New York Age, 3 January 1925.

O'Toole, Andrew. "Now is the Time: Rube
Foster." In *The Best Man Plays, Major
League Baseball and the Black Athlete,
1901–2002*. Jefferson, North Carolina: Mc-
Farland, 2003, 7–24.

Peterson, Robert. "Men Who Changed
Baseball." *Boy's Life* 72 (August 1972):
14–17.

_____. "Rube Foster, Best of the Black Man-
agers." *Sport*, May 1975, 38–40.

"Resentment Felt Over Domination of Eastern and Western Leagues by 'Rube' Foster and Nat Strong." *New York Age*, 23
January 1926.

Cottrell, Robert Charles. *The Best Pitcher in
Baseball: The Life of Rube Foster*. New
York: New York University Press, 2001.

"Rube Wants Championship Without
Fighting for It." *Indianapolis Freeman*, 11
November 1916.

"Rube Foster and Fate Beats Cuban Stars."
Chicago Defender, 10 June 1916.

"Rube Foster Back in Form." *Chicago Defender*, 5 February 1910, 1.

"Rube Foster Beat Gunthers 3 to 2." *Chicago
Defender*, 22 May 1915.

"Rube Foster Beaten by the Pantages."
Chicago Defender, 20 November 1915.

"Rube Foster Breaks Leg in Game Against
Cubans." *Chicago Tribune*, 13 July 1909, 8.

"Rube Foster Chats about His Career."
Chicago Defender, 20 February 1915.

"Rube Foster Goes Eastward; Giants to
Train in Texas." *Chicago Defender*, 3 February 1923.

"Rube Foster Heads Big Negro League." *Decatur Review*, 30 January 1922.

"Rube Foster in Come Back Role." *Chicago
Defender*, 20 May 1916.

"Rube Foster in Psycho-Pathic Hospital."
Indianapolis Recorder, 4 September 1926,
6.

"'Rube' Foster in Star Role," *Indianapolis
Freeman*, 28 September 1907, 6.

"Rube Foster Launches Out Against East-
erners." *New York Amsterdam News*, 17
January 1923.

"Rube Foster, Negro Diamond Star, Dies."
Oakland Tribune, 11 December 1930, 33.

"Rube Foster Off for the Coast." *Indianapolis Freeman*, 22 January 1916, 5 and
Chicago Defender, 22 January 1916.

"Rube Foster Praised!" *Indianapolis Freeman*, 26 September 1914.

"Rube Foster Returns to Chicago." *Indianapolis Freeman*, 19 September 1914.

"Rube Foster Saves the Day." *Indianapolis
Freeman*, 25 July 1908, 5.

"Rube Foster Signs 7 Colored Umps." *Baltimore Afro-American*, 27 April 1923.

"Rube Foster Speaks." *Chicago Defender*, 18
and 25 November 1916, 9.

"Rube Foster Takes Club to Monarch's Lair
for Battle that Eliminates the Giants."
Chicago Defender, 30 May 1925.

"Rube Foster Takes First Game." *Indianapolis Freeman*, 28 October 1916, 7.

"Rube Foster Tells a Few Things of Interest." *Chicago Defender*, 11 November 1916,
10.

"Rube Foster to Be Honored with Stag."
Philadelphia Tribune, 14 September 1912,
7.

"Rube Foster vs. George Mullin." *Chicago
Defender*, 22 July 1916.

"Rube Foster Will Invade the East." *Indianapolis Freeman*, 25 December 1909, 7.

"Rube Foster's Day." *Indianapolis Freeman*,
28 May 1910, 4.

"Rube Foster's Signed Statement of the

Giants-ABC Mixup." *Chicago Defender,* 31 July 1915.

"Rube Foster's Team Opens Here on Thursday." *Decatur Review,* 13 July 1921, 5.

"Rube's Team Taking in Everything!" *Indianapolis Freeman,* 29 April 1916, 7.

Shorey, Frederick North. "A Historical Account of a Great Game of Ball." *Indianapolis Freeman,* 14 September 1907, 6.

"St. Louis Stars Drop 2 Games to Fosterites." *Chicago Defender,* 8 July 1922.

"Stars of Baseball Coming to Aid 'Rube Foster Day.'" *Chicago Defender,* 25 July 1936, 14.

Streur, Russell. "Rube Foster, Father of Negro League Baseball." *Sports Collectors Digest* 8 (February 1991): 186.

"Success of Negro on Diamond Told by 'Rube' Foster." *Chicago Tribune,* 21 December 1913, B1.

Thorn, John. 'Tales of the Hudson Valley League." *Saugerties Old Dutch Post Star,* 23 July 1981.

Vecsey, George. "Welcome to the Hall." *New York Times,* 3 August 1981, C1, C7.

Wade, Shirley. "A League of Their Own." *Michigan Chronicle,* 10 October 1995.

Whitehead, Charles E. *A Man and His Diamonds.* New York: Vantage Press, 1980.

Williams, Harry A. "Negro Ball Stars Shine." *Los Angeles Times,* 30 October 1912, III2.

Wilson, Lyle K. "Mr. Foster Comes to Washington." *The National Pastime* 17 (1998): 107–111.

Wyatt, Dave. "Players Developed, Need Trained Officials Now." *Chicago Defender,* 7 January 1922.

_____. "Rube Foster, as I Knew Him." *Pittsburgh Courier,* 10 January 1931.

Young, A. S. "Doc." "Baseball's Hall of Fame: How Bob Gibson and Rube Foster Made It." *Sepia,* 1 June 1981, 38.

_____. "Rube Foster: Baseball's Negro Pioneer." *Hue Magazine* (August 1957).

Young, Frank. "More About Foster's Baseball Team." *The Half Century,* June 1919, 8, 13.

_____. "Rube Foster: The Master Mind of Baseball." *Abbott's Monthly,* November 1930, 42–49, 93.

_____. "Rube Foster Challenges the Cubs." *Chicago Defender,* 18 October 1913, 8.

Related Terms: Chicago baseball, Chicago American Giants, Frank Leland, Hall of Fame, Owners

Foster, Willie "Bill"

Brennan, Gerald E. "Foster, Willie 'Bill.'" In *Biographical Dictionary of American Sports, Baseball,* edited by David l. Porter. Westport, CT: Greenwood Press, 2000, 492–493.

Holway, John B. "Historically Speaking ... Bill Foster." *Black Sports Magazine* (March 1974): 58–59, 62.

Johnson, Lee A. "23,000 Watch 'Big' Bill Foster Defeat East." *Indianapolis Recorder,* 16 September 1933, 1.

Monroe, Al. "Willie Foster Loses Contest to S. Paige." *Chicago Defender,* 1 September 1934.

"Negro League Pitcher William Foster Inducted in Baseball Hall of Fame." *Jet* (26 August 1996): 49.

"Rube's Brother in Win for Memphis." *Chicago Defender,* 31 May 1924.

Hill, J. Preston "Pete"

"Baseball Today." *Chicago Tribune,* 14 June 1919, 14.

Baxter, Terry. "Hill, J. Preston "Pete." In *Biographical Dictionary of American Sports, Baseball,* edited by David l. Porter (Westport, CT: Greenwood Press, 2000), 675–676.

"Pete Hill." In *Baseball, The Biographical Encyclopedia,* edited by David Pietrusza, Matthew Silverman, and Michael Gershman. Kingston, New York: Total Sports Publishing, 2000, 501.

Riley, James. "Pete Hill, the Greatest Black Outfielder of the Deadball Era." *Oldtyme Baseball News,* 1 September 1991, 9, 31.

"Squares Jolted by Colored B. B. Club, 7 to 0." *Chicago Tribune,* 22 April 1923, A3.

Jessup, Joseph Gentry

"Black Yanks Halted 1–0." *New York Times,* 20 August 1945, 15.

"Chicago Giants Top Clowns 3–1; Lose Second 9–1." *Chicago Tribune,* 17 July 1944, 15.

"Chicago Plays Memphis Sunday." *Chicago Defender,* 5 April 1947, 11.

"Giants, Clowns Tie, 3 to 3, in 20 Inning Game." *Chicago Tribune,* 13 May 1946, 29.

"Jessup Hurls North to Win." *Chicago Defender,* 28 September 1946, 11.

"Jessup to Pitch." *Chicago Tribune,* 15 May 1947, 39.

"No Worry for Jim Taylor." *Chicago Defender,* 13 April 1940.

Obituary, *Sports Collectors Digest*, 1998.
"Semi-Pros to Play All-Star Contest Today." *Chicago Tribune*, 8 September 1957.
"Skokie Indians Meet Chicago Vets Today." *Chicago Tribune*, 27 August 1961, A4.
Smith, Wendell. "Jessup's Three-hit Hurling Silences Red Sox' Big Guns." *Pittsburgh Courier*, 8 July 1944.
"West Wins , 5 to 2, in All-Star Game." *New York Times*, 28 July 1947, 20.
"Y Industrial League Play Will Close Today." *Chicago Tribune*, 30 August 1942, A5.

Johnson, George "Chappie"

"George Johnson, Catcher of the Long Prairie 1909 Baseball Team." *Long Prairie Leader*, 16 July 1909.
Hart, Larry. *Schenectady's Golden Era, 1880 and 1930*. Schenectady, NY: Old Dorp Books, 1974, 63–65.
Kleinknecht, Merl F. "Johnson, George 'Chappie.'" In *Biographical Dictionary of American Sports, Baseball*, edited by David L. Porter. Westport, CT: Greenwood Press, 2000, 752–753.
"Too Much Johnson." *Upper Des Moines Republican* (IA), 9 July 1902, 1.

Leland, Frank

"Frank Leland." In *Baseball, The Biographical Encyclopedia*, edited by David Pietrusza, Matthew Silverman, and Michael Gershman. Kingston, New York: Total Sports Publishing, 2000, 657.
"Frank C. Leland Resigns." *Indianapolis Freeman*, 2 October 1909, 7.
"Frank Leland's Chicago Giants." *Indianapolis Freeman*, 18 June 1910.

Leland Giants

"Again the Leland Giants Take the Measure of Gunthers." *Chicago Tribune*, 14 August 1910, C2.
"All Stars Beat Colored Men." *Chicago Tribune*, 29 August 1907, 6.
"Another for Leland Giants." *Chicago Defender*, 3 September 1910.
"Another Game to Lelands." *Chicago Tribune*, 26 September 1908, 9
"Anson's Defeat Giants." *Chicago Tribune*, 5 July 1909, 6.
"Ball Blanks Anson's Colts." *Chicago Tribune*, 23 August 1908, B2.
"Banquet and Reception in Honor of Rube Foster and His Leland Giants." *Broad Ax*, 26 November 1910.
"Ball's Hit Wins for Giants." *Chicago Tribune*, 23 June 1907, A2.
"Batting Bees in Chicago League." *Chicago Tribune*, 6 September 1909, 10.
"Black Champs are Trimmed." *Los Angeles Times*, 20 November 1910, 16.
"Brown of Cubs Had 'Indian Sign' on the Leland Giants." *Chicago Defender*, 17 December 1932.
"Bush League Results." *The Decatur Review*, 13 September 1905, 3.
"Champion Leland Giants to Go South for Spring Training." *Indianapolis Freeman*, 20 February 1909, 7.
"City Champs Win from Lelands, 4–1." *Chicago Daily Tribune*, 19 October 1909, 8.
"Close Game to Colored Men." *Chicago Tribune*, 1 August 1909, C2.
"Colored Baseball Championship." *Chicago Defender*, 5 August 1911.
"Crowd Sees Semi-Pros." *Chicago Tribune*, 14 August 1905, 8.
"Cubs Beat Leland Giants, 4–1." *Chicago Tribune*, 19 October 1909, 8.
"Cubs 4, Lelands 1." *Atlanta Constitution*, 20 October 1909, 6.
"Cubs' Rally Beats Leland Giants, 6–5." *Chicago Tribune*, 22 October 1909, 12.
"Cubs Trim Giants in Final Game, 1–0." *Chicago Tribune*, 23 October 1909, 14.
"Cuban Stars and Leland Giants." *Chicago Defender*, 31 July 1909, 1.
"Cubans Evade Court Order." *Chicago Tribune*, 8 August 1910, 15.
"Defeat for League Leaders." *Chicago Tribune*, 29 August 1909, C2.
"Defeat for Leland Giants." *Chicago Tribune*, 1 September 1907, C2.
"Diamond Dust." *Chicago Defender*, 6, 20, 27 May and 3, 10, 17, 24 June and 8 July 1911.
"Donahue Becomes a Magnate." *Chicago Tribune*, 1 February 1910, 14.
"Double Victory for the Giants." *Chicago Tribune*, 7 September 1909, 17.
"Easy for Lelands to Win." *Chicago Tribune*, 1 August 1910, 11.
"Felix Colts win in Eleventh." *Chicago Tribune*, 10 August 1908, 14.
"For Colored Championship." *Chicago Tribune*, 11 September 1904, A2.
"Games in the City League." *Chicago Tribune*, 18 May 1908, 10.

"Games of Semi-Pro Teams." *Chicago Tribune,* 3 September 1907, 11.

"Games of the Amateurs." *Chicago Tribune,* 19 May 1907, A2, and 1 July 1908, A2.

"Giants and Dodgers Split." *Chicago Tribune,* 1 July 1909, 10.

"Giants Lose Two Contests." *Los Angeles Times,* 5 December 1910, 18.

"Giants Shut Out Logan Squares." *Chicago Tribune,* 16 August 1909, 10.

"Giants Take Benefit Game." *Chicago Defender,* 27 August 1910.

"Giants Win Double Header." *Chicago Tribune,* 3 October 1909, C2.

"Gunthers Again Take the Lead." *Chicago Tribune,* 1 June 1909, 8.

"Gunthers Head Chicago League." *Chicago Tribune,* 7 June 1909, 12.

"Gunthers Land Hard Fight." *Chicago Tribune,* 19 September 1909, C2.

"Gunthers Trim Leland Giants." *Chicago Tribune,* 14 September 1908, 15.

"Last Season Greatest for Baseball." *Indianapolis Freeman,* 15 February 1908.

"Lawndales Capture Game, 5–2." *Chicago Tribune,* 8 July 1907, 8.

"League Determined to Open this Season." *Indianapolis Freeman,* 7 March 1908.

"League Rules to Be Distributed." *Indianapolis Freeman,* 14 March 1908.

"The Leland Chicago Giants." *Chicago Defender,* 16 April 1910, 1.

"Leland Chicago Giants Winners." *Chicago Defender,* 2 April 1910, 1.

"Leland Giants." *The Decatur Review,* 10 July 1905, 3.

"Leland Giants Again Win." *Indianapolis Freeman,* 8 August 1908, 5.

"Leland Giants Against Ridgewood." *New York Times,* 1 October 1910, 11.

"Leland Giants Apply Brush to Ryan's Rogers Park Nine." *Chicago Tribune,* 11 October 1909, 12.

"Leland Giants Are Victors." *Chicago Tribune,* 6 July 1909, 16.

"Leland Giants Beat Logan." *Chicago Tribune,* 5 August 1910, 8.

"Leland Giants Beat Sullivan." *The Decatur Review,* 13 July 1905, 3.

"The Leland Giants, Black Stars of the Baseball Firmament Outshine All Competitors." *Broad Ax,* 21 May 1910.

"Leland Giants Clinch Lead." *Chicago Tribune,* 5 September 1909, C2.

"Leland Giants Club in Court." *Chicago Tribune,* 3 March 1910, 9.

"Leland Giants Complete a Successful Southern Trip." *Indianapolis Freeman,* 15 May 1909, 7.

"Leland Giants Continue." *Chicago Tribune,* 10 July 1905, 8.

"Leland Giants Defeat Spaldings in Ninth." *Indianapolis Freeman,* 1 August 1908, 5.

"Leland Giants Defeated Aurora." *Chicago Tribune,* 22 April 1907, 10.

"Leland Giants Down Logan Squares, 7 to 4." *Chicago Tribune,* 23 August 1909, 7.

"Leland Giants Drub All Stars." *Chicago Tribune,* 28 August 1907, 6.

"Leland Giants Favor Taft." *Chicago Tribune,* 7 June 1908, 2.

"Leland Giants 4, Spaldings 1." *Chicago Tribune,* 5 August 1907, 11.

"Leland Giants Get Revenge." *Chicago Tribune,* 15 August 1908, 10.

"Leland Giants of Chicago." *Indianapolis Star,* 30 August 1911.

"Leland Giants on Top, 3 to 2." *Chicago Tribune,* 11 July 1908, 12.

"Leland Giants Reorganized." *Chicago Tribune,* 6 December 1907, 10.

"Leland Giants 6, Mutuals 5." *Chicago Defender,* 29 April 1910.

"Leland Giants Take a Game from Garrett." *Fort Wayne Journal-Gazette,* 28 May 1905, 3.

"Leland Giants Take Cubans into Camp by Score of 6 to 3." *Chicago Tribune,* 11 September 1910, C2.

"Leland Giants Take Game." *Chicago Tribune,* 6 July 1908, 15.

"Leland Giants Take Game, 4–1." *Chicago Tribune,* 22 August 1910, 12.

"Leland Giants Take Third." *Chicago Tribune,* 9 August 1907, 7.

"Leland Giants 10, Aurora 2." *Chicago Tribune,* 22 July 1907, 8.

"Leland Giants Tighten Grip." *Chicago Tribune,* 25 July 1909, C2.

"Leland Giants to Make Great Southern Tour." *Indianapolis Freeman,* 15 January 1910, 7.

"Leland Giants Victors Over All Star Players." *Chicago Tribune,* 7 August 1907, 6.

"Leland Giants Win 8–1." *Chicago Tribune,* 27 June 1910, 8.

"Leland Has Great Bunch." *Chicago Tribune,* 20 March 1910, C2.

"Lelands Capture Third of Series." *St. Paul Pioneer Press,* 27 July 1910, 7.

"Lelands Defeat Cubans." *Chicago Defender,* 30 July 1910.

"Lelands Defeat Ridgewood." *Chicago Defender*, 15 October 1910.

"Lelands Defeat Sprudels, 9–0." *Chicago Tribune*, 18 July 1910, 9.

"Lelands Defeated at Last." *Indianapolis Freeman*, 18 June 1910, 4.

"Lelands Draw 10 to 0 Blank." *Chicago Tribune*, 8 May 1911, 10.

"Lelands Land Game on Jump." *Chicago Tribune*, 11 July 1910, 9.

"Lelands Make Triple Play." *Chicago Defender*, 10 September 1910.

"Lelands Off to Good Start." *Chicago Tribune*, 15 May 1910, C2.

"Lelands Record 33 in Row." *Chicago Tribune*, 31 May 1910, 15.

"Lelands 3, All Stars 1." *Chicago Defender*, 13 August 1910.

"Lelands Trim Stars of Cuba." *Chicago Defender*, 17 September 1910.

"Lelands Win at Moquoketa." *Chicago Tribune*, 25 July 1907, 6.

"Lelands Win by Stickwork." *Chicago Tribune*, 20 September 1908, B2

"Lelands Win from West Ends." *Chicago Tribune*, 14 October 1907, 10.

"Local Fans Disappointed." *Chicago Tribune*, 9 July 1910, 10.

"Logan Squares and Leland Giants to Play." *Chicago Tribune*, 25 August 1908, 7.

"Logan Squares 5, Leland Giants 4." *Chicago Tribune*, 21 July 1907, A2.

"Logan Squares Lose Twice." *Chicago Tribune*, 31 May 1907, 10.

"Logan Squares Top City League." *Chicago Tribune*, 31 May 1909, 14.

"Logan Squares Victorious Over Leland Giants, 7 to 6." *Chicago Tribune*, 26 July 1908, B2.

"Long Game to West Ends." *Chicago Tribune*, 24 May 1908, B2.

"Mendez Weakens, Giants Win." *Chicago Tribune*, 11 July 1909, C2.

"Millers Beat Colored Nine." *Chicago Tribune*, 22 September 1908, 8.

"Moseley's Leland Giants to Have New Park." *Chicago Defender*, 12 March 1910, 1.

"Negro Baseball League." *The Standard Post*, 27 December 1910.

"New Home for Colored Nine." *Chicago Tribune*, 14 June 1910, 12.

"New Owners at Rogers Park." *Chicago Tribune*, 31 July 1907, 7.

"Normals Down Rogers Park." *Chicago Tribune*, 21 September 1908, 10.

"Pennant is Won by the Lelands." *Chicago Tribune*, 13 September 1909, 14.

"Portland Plays the Leland Giants." *The Fort Wayne Journal-Gazette*, 17 August 1906.

Pot, Jack. "Bars Alien Colored Clubs." *Chicago Defender*, 23 July 1910.

"Rally Saves the White Rocks." *Chicago Tribune*, 10 September 191, C2.

"River Forest Takes Game, 9–4." *Chicago Tribune*, 16 July 1911, B2.

"Scare the Leland Giants." *Chicago Tribune*, 9 August 1908, B2.

"Semi-Pros Book Many Games at Meeting of Managers." *Chicago Tribune*, 10 May 1910, 13.

"Semi-Pros Play Tomorrow." *Chicago Tribune*, 26 August 1907, 11.

"Shut-out by Leland Giants." *Chicago Tribune*, 5 June 1910, C3.

"Stars Fall, 7–1, Before Lelands." *Chicago Tribune*, 23 May 1910, 10.

"Stars Slaughter Giants in Opener." *Chicago Tribune*, 29 June 1909, 12.

"Stop Anson Rally in Nick of Time." *Chicago Tribune*, 30 August 1909, 10.

"Strong Semi-Pro Card Today." *Chicago Tribune*, 10 July 1907, 7.

"Take Third Straight from Leland Giants." *Indianapolis Freeman*, 15 August 1908, 5.

"Tries to Score With Broken Leg." 1907.

"Trim the League Leaders." *Chicago Tribune*, 4 July 1909, C2.

"Two Big Ball Games." *Sheboygan Press*, 10 August 1910.

"Victory for Cuban Stars." *Chicago Tribune*, 16 July 1909, 11.

"Victory for Leland Giants." *Chicago Tribune*, 3 August 1908, 10; 24 April 1911, 18.

"Victory for the Oak Leas." *Chicago Tribune*, 15 July 1907, 8.

"West End Rally Wins Game." *Chicago Tribune*, 24 September 1911, C2.

"West Ends Trounce Lelands." *Chicago Tribune*, 20 August 1911, C2.

"West Ends Win a Lively Game." *Chicago Tribune*, 22 September 1907, C2.

"What the Royals and Leland Giants Did at Palm Beach." *Indianapolis Freeman Supplement*, 16 April 1910, 9.

"Winter Games Begin Today." *Los Angeles Times*, 19 November 1910, 18.

"Withdraws from League." *Indianapolis Freeman*, 21 March 1908.

Lockett, Lester

"Clowns, Monarchs Continue Series; Get Lester Lockett." *Chicago Defender,* 27 July 1946, 11.

Dickson, Albert. "Lester Lockett." *Sporting News,* 14 April 1997, 34.

Radcliffe, Ted, Lester Lockett and Jerry Malloy. Interviews by Ken Davis, 12 August 1986. WBEZ-FM Radio, Chicago, Illinois.

McDonald, Webster

Holway, John. "Historically Speaking: Webster McDonald." *Black Sports* (May 1974): 54–55.

_____. "'They Made me Survive.'" *The Sporting News,* 18 July 1981, 48–49.

Obituary. *The Sporting News,* 28 June 1982, 54.

"Webster McDonald Will Quit Baseball in 1936." *Chicago Defender,* 20 April 1935.

Welsh, John. "Mac was a Hero." *Times,* (St. Cloud, MN), March 1991, 1A, 3A.

Minoso, Minnie

"Around the Minors." *The Record,* 17 July 2003.

Holway, John. "Minoso, Oliva, Other Cuban Stars Cited." *The Sporting News,* 6 June 1983, 20.

Lindberg, Richard C. "Minoso by Any Other Name." *The National Pastime* 12 (July 1992): 55–57.

"Minnie Minoso." *Black Sports* (December 1977): 30.

"Minnie Minoso Lands Job with Ball Team in Mexico." *Jet,* (16 May 1974): 52.

Minoso, Minnie. *Extra Innings. My Life in Baseball.* Regency Books, 1983.

"Tears of Joy for Minoso." *Chicago Tribune,* 24 August 2004.

Van Dyck, Dave. "Minoso Staute Unveiled." *Chicago Tribune,* 20 September 2004.

"Whatever Happened to Minnie Minoso?" *Ebony* (July 1978): 58–60.

"Writers Pick Minoso 2d to Yankees' Star, 13–11." *Washington Post,* 16 November 1951, B15.

Moseley, Beauregard

"Attorney B. F. Moseley." *Broad Ax,* 26 April 1910.

"Att'y Beauregard F. Moseley Shoots to Kill." *Chicago Defender,* 18 February 1911, 1.

"B. F. Moseley a Presidential Elector of Ill." *Chicago Defender,* 9 November 1912.

"Call for a Conference of Persons Interested in the Formation of a National Negro Baseball League." *Broad Ax,* 17 December 1910.

"Death and Funeral of Col. Beauregard F. Moseley." *Broad Ax,* 6 December 1919, 1.

"Hon. B. F. Moseley." *Chicago Defender,* 30 April 1910, 1.

"Mayor Thompson and B. F. Mosely Laud Lincoln and Douglass." *Chicago Defender,* 12 February 1916.

Moseley, Beauregard. "A Baseball Appeal of a Worthy Undertaking." *Broad Ax,* 21 January 1911.

_____. The World Series." *Broad Ax,* 13 October 1917.

"Negro Baseball League." *The Post,* 27 December 1910.

Obituary. *Chicago Tribune,* 2 December 1919.

Redding, Richard "Dick" "Cannonball"

"Dick Redding." In *Baseball, The Biographical Encyclopedia,* edited by David Pietrusza, Matthew Silverman, and Michael Gershman. Kingston, New York: Total Sports Publishing, 2000, 920.

Evers, John. "Redding, Richard 'Dick,' 'Cannonball.'" In *Biographical Dictionary of American Sports, Baseball,* edited by David L. Porter. Westport, CT: Greenwood Press, 2000, 1258–1259.

Holway, John. *Smokey Joe and the Cannonball.* Washington, DC: Capital Press, 1983.

Holway, John B. "The Cannonball (Dick Redding)." *Baseball Research Journal* 9, (1980): 99–103.

"Lundy and Dick Redding to Lead 'Original Bacharachs.'" *Chicago Defender,* 18 March 1922.

"Redding Is Hit Hard but Wins, 11 to 8." *Chicago Defender,* 15 May 1926.

"Redding Pitches Lincoln Giants to Double Win." *Chicago Defender,* 16 September 1916.

"Redding Wins His Twentieth Straight Game." *Chicago Defender,* 24 July 1915.

"Redding Wins His Seventeenth Straight Game." *Chicago Defender,* 10 July 1915.

Shalin, Mike, and Neil Shalin. "Dick Redding, Jose Mendez, Ray Brown." In *Out* by a Step: The 100 Best Players Not in the Baseball Hall of Fame. Lanham, MD: Diamond Publications, 2002, 202–205.

"Thinks Dick Redding Class of Speed Ball Pitchers." Norfolk Journal and Guide, 21 June 1930.

Young, Fay. "Down Memory Lane." Chicago Defender, 24 June 1939, 8.

Stearnes, Norman "Turkey"

Bak, Richard. "After Words." Detroit Monthly, (May 1989), 124.

_____. "Black Diamonds." Michigan: The Magazine, 5 April 1987, 92–107.

_____. Turkey Stearnes and the Detroit Stars, The Negro Leagues in Detroit, 1919–1933. Michigan: Wayne State University Press, 1994.

"Hall of Famer Stearnes Finally Gets Headstone." USA Today, 14 August 2002; Detroit Free Press, 14 August 2002.

Harris, Barbara. "Negro Leaguer Turkey Stearnes Inducted into Baseball Hall of Fame." Jackson Advocate News, n.d.

Henning, Lynn. "Stearnes Made a Lasting Impact." The Detroit News, 16 July 2001, 1F, 5F.

_____. "Unorthodox Stearnes Finally Elected." USA Today Baseball Weekly, March 2000, 8–14.

Holway, John B. "I Never Count My Homers Unless They Win Games." Detroit News Magazine, 15 August 1971, 384.

_____. "More Negro Leaguers for the Hall." The National Pastime, SABR, 1995, 91–95.

_____. "Stats Shine on Stars of Negro Leagues." USA Today Baseball Weekly, 14 June 1991, 48.

_____. "Turkey Stearnes, "A Humdinger of a Hitter."" Black Sports Magazine (1 July 1976): 48–49, 56.

Justice, Richard. "Sparky Anderson Elected ... Negro Leagues' Stearnes In." Washington Post, 1 March 2000, D3.

Ladson, Bill. "Talking Turkey." http://www.MLB.com.

LaPointe, Joe. "Negro League Star Turkey Stearnes, 78." Detroit Free Press, 6 September 1979, 5A.

Martin, Douglas D. "Stearnes, Norman 'Turkey.'" In Biographical Dictionary of American Sports, Baseball, edited by David L. Porter. Westport, CT: Greenwood Press, 2000), 1468–1469.

"Norman 'Turkey' Stearnes." Post-Standard, 1 March 2000, E-8.

"Norman 'Turkey' Stearnes." Solidarity, (June 2000), 7.

Obituary. Detroit Free Press, 6 September 1979.

Perkins, Dave. "Negro League Stars Deserve Their Due." Toronto Star, 24 February 2000.

Posnanski, Joe. "It's A Shame Turkey Stearnes Couldn't Be At His Hall of Fame Induction." Kansas City Star, 25 July 2000.

"Satchel Saved by Homer in Ninth." Los Angeles Times, 25 November 1935, A11.

Schabath, Gene. "Negro League Star's Grave Found Unmarked." The Detroit News, 14 May 2002.

Smith, Glenn C. "Norman Thomas 'Turkey' Stearnes (1901–1979): One of the Most Profilic Long-Ball Hitters in the Negro Leagues." Los Angeles Sentinel, 22 March 2000.

Spence, James Jr. "Signing Habits and Autograph Analysis of Norman 'Turkey' Stearnes." http://www.autographuniverse.com/articles/article_view.html, 27 June 2001.

"Stearns Leads Negro All-Star Baseball Vote." Chicago Tribune, 27 August 1933, A6.

"Turkey Stearnes." In Baseball, The Biographical Encyclopedia. Edited by David Pietrusza, Matthew Silverman, and Michael Gershman. Kingston, New York: Total Sports Publishing, 2000, 1028.

Suttles, George "Mule"

"Big League Stars Bow to Giants." Los Angeles Times, 20 October 1935, 20.

Downer, Marian. "Our Girl Scribe Sees Mule's Hit." Chicago Defender, 17 August 1935.

"Eagles Trim Senators, 7–5." Washington Post, 3 July 1938, X4.

"Elite Gaints Win from Eagles by 5 to 1." Washington Post, 17 May 1936, X4.

"George Suttles." In Out by a Step: The 100 Best Players Not in the Baseball Hall of Fame. Mike Shalin and Neil Shalin. Lanham, MD: Diamond Publications, 2002, 160–162.

Harris, Ed. "At It Again." Philadelphia Tribune, 29 August 1935.

Holway, John B. "Give These Guys Some Extra Innings." Washington Post, 5 August 2001.

_____. "More Negro Leaguers for the Hall." *The National Pastime*, SABR, 1995, 91–95.

_____. "Not all the Stars Were White (Mule Suttles' All Star Homerun)." *The Sporting News*, 1983 All-Star Special.

_____. "Stats Shine on Stars of Negro Leagues." *USA Today Baseball Weekly*, 14 June 1991, 48.

Kleinknecht, Merl F. "Suttles, George 'Mule'" in *Biographical Dictionary of American Sports, Baseball*, David L. Porter, ed., (Westport, CT: Greenwood Press, 2000), 1505–1506.

"Memphis , St. Louis and Newark Here June 11." *Chicago Defender*, 10 June 1944, 9.

Monroe, Al. "Suttles' Homerun Wins It for the West." *Chicago Defender*, 17 August 1945.

"Mule Suttles." In *Baseball, The Biographical Encyclopedia*. Edited by David Pietrusza, Matthew Silverman, and Michael Gershman. Kingston, New York: Total Sports Publishing, 2000, 1104.

"'Mule' Suttles Breaks Up Ball Game with Sensational Homer." *Indianapolis Recorder*, 17 August 1935, 12.

"Newark Buffaloes Ready for Opener." *New Jersey Herald News*, 13 April 1946, 15.

"Newark Signs Mule Suttles." *Chicago Defender*, 18 April 1936.

"Pilots Win, 7–3, on Suttles' Homer." *Washington Post*, 11 August 1932, 10.

Rea, E. B. "Suttles Poles Out Homer in Sunday's Game." *Norfolk Journal and Guide*, 8 May 1937, 17.

"Royal Giants Win, 13–4." *Los Angeles Times*, 29 November 1937, A13.

Suttles, George. "The Mule." Interview by John Holway, n.d. . Interview T207, transcript. University of Missouri — Archives and Manuscript Division, St. Louis, Missouri.

"Suttles, Gibson and Leonard Go Without a Hit." *Chicago Defender*, 12 August 1939, 8.

"Suttles Hits 2 Homers as Giants Blast Craws." *Afro-American*, 1 June 1935, 20.

"Suttles Homer Gave Fans Thrill in '33 Game." *Chicago Defender*, 5 August 1939.

"Suttles' Home Run wins for West, 11–8." *Chicago Defender*, 17 August 1935, 6.

"Suttles' Homer with 2 on Won 1935 Game." *Chicago Defender*, 17 August 1940.

"Suttles New Newark Pilot." *Chicago Defender*, 17 April 1943.

"The Speedy Mule Suttles." *Our Sports*, July 1953, 72.

"Veteran Slugger to Guide Eagles in '43." *Pittsburgh Courier*, 10 April 1943.

"Western Team Wins, 11–8." *New York Times*, 12 August 1935, 18.

Young, Fay. "Gibson, Suttles and Leondard Held Hitless." *Chicago Defender*, 12 August 1939.

Sweatt, George

Holway, John B. "Historically Speaking ... George Sweatt." *Black Sports Magazine*, September 1975, 49, 55, 58.

Taylor, Jim "Candy"

"Akron Site of Training Camp." *Pittsburgh Courier*, 3 April 1943.

"'Candy Jim' And Players Invade Sunny Southland." *Chicago Defender*, 31 March 1945.

"Elites, Cubans Divide Pair of Games." *Washington Post*, 1 June 1936, X18.

"Gen. Jim Taylor's Shock Troops Fail to Stop A's." *Chicago Defender*, 8 May 1926.

"Grays Face Giants Today in Stadium" *Washington Post*, 12 August 1945, M7.

"Grays to Face Black Yankees in Opener Today." *Washington Post*, 7 May 1944, M7.

Hughey, Robert. "'Candy Jim' Taylor, New Pilot of Grays, One of Baseball's Greats." *Pittsburgh Courier*, 24 April 1924.

"Jim Taylor Brings St. Louis Stars to Chicago for Five Games with American Giants." *Chicago Defender*, 27 June 1925.

"Jim Taylor Peeved Over Bad Weather." *Chicago Defender*, 17 April 1926.

"Jim Taylor Signs as Manager of Am. Giants." *Chicago Defender*, 13 January 1945.

Litke, Jim. "Remembered at Last." *The Indianapolis Star*, 28 September 2004.

"Memorial Honors Three of Negro League's Best." *The Tribune*, 27 September 2004.

Pride, Karen. "Negro League Players Gravesites Honored." *Chicago Defender*, 27 September 2004.

"Recognition for Three Negro League Stars." *Chicago Sun-Times*, 27 September 2004, 6.

"Taylor Seeks to Strengthen American Giants." *Chicago Defender*, 12 November 1938, 8.

Wronski, Richard. "A Fan's Tribute to Legends of Negro Leagues." *Chicago Tribune*, 25 September 2004, 1, 8.

Torriente, Cristobal

"Cristobal Torriente: 'El Hombre que Derroto a Ruth.'" Cocobeisbol.com.

"Cristobal Torriente." In *Baseball, The Biographical Encyclopedia*. Edited by David Pietrusza, Matthew Silverman, and Michael Gershman. Kingston, New York: Total Sports Publishing, 2000, 1140.

"Cristobal Torriente." In *Out by a Step: The 100 Best Players Not in the Baseball Hall of Fame*. Mike Shalin and Neil Shalin. Lanham, MD: Diamond Publications, 2002, 115–117.

Figueredo, Jorge S. "November 4, 1920: The Day Torriente Outclassed Ruth." *Baseball Research Journal*, 11 (1982): 130–131.

Holway, John B. "Cristobal Torriente." *Baseball Historical Review*, (1981), 72–74.

_____. "More Negro Leaguers for the Hall." *The National Pastime*, SABR, 1995, 91–95.

_____. "The One Man Team-Cristobal Torriente."*Baseball Reseach Journal* 3(1974): 42 45.

"Homer in 9th by Torriente; Am. Giants Win." *Chicago Defender*, 22 April 1922.

Kleinknecht, Merl F. "Torriente, Cristobal." In *Biographical Dictionary of American Sports, Baseball*, edited by David L. Porter. Westport, CT: Greenwood Press, 2000, 1557–1558.

"Torriente Goes to Kansas City for Sweatt; Cliff Bell to Birmingham; Other Deals." *Chicago Defender*, 13 February 1926.

Trouppe, Quincy

"American Giants Buy Quincy Trouppe; Made Manager." *Chicago Defender*, 10 January 1948, 10.

"Bar Negro Clubs in Decatur Park." *Chicago Defender*, 11 September 1948, 10.

Bennett, Chuck. "Remembering the Negro Leagues." *Sports Collectors Digest* (21 July 1989): 154, 156.

Cisneros, Pedro Tetro. *Enciclopedia del Beisbol Mexicano*. Mexico City, Mexico, 1992.

Elliott, Jeffrey. "Quincy Trouppe, Baseball Great and Catcher to Satchel Paige, Comments." *Sepia* 26 (December 1977): 28–33.

_____. "Quincy Trouppe: Portrait of a Superstar Negro League Player." *Negro History Bulletin* (1 March 1978): 804–807.

Forman, Ross. "Quincy Trouppe: Former All-Star Catcher Just Missed Majors." *Sports Collectors Digest* 21 (June 1991): 160–61.

Kee, Lorraine. "Son Determined to Keep 'Big Train' Trouppe's Memory Alive." *St. Louis Post-Dispatch*, 10 December 1994.

Kleinknecht, Merl F. "Trouppe, Quincy." In *Biographical Dictionary of American Sports, Baseball*, edited by David L. Porter. Westport, CT: Greenwood Press, 2000, 1568–69.

"New Rockford Gets Only Five Hits in Game There Sunday." *The Bismarck Tribune*, 21 May 1934, 6.

"Quincy Trouppe: An Invisible Ball of Dreams." Program, Pasadena Public Library, Pasadena, CA. 7 October 2001.

"Quincy Trouppe and Paul Schaefer to Make Their Debut." *Bismarck Tribune*, 27 July 1938.

"Quincy Trouppe Paces Local Hitters with .390 Average." *Bismarck Tribune*, 28 August 1934, 6.

"Trouppe, Negro Leagues Star, Dies at 80." *St. Louis Post-Dispatch*, 12 August 1993.

"Trouppe Touted as Good as Campanella." *East Liverpool Review*, 28 February 1952, 19.

Trouppe, Quincy. *Twenty Years Too Soon*. Sands Enterprises, 1977.

West, Hollie I. "Quincy Troupe's American Rag." *Washington Post*, 17 February 1979, A1.

Turner, Thomas

Erardi, John. "Tom Turner, A Third-deck Homer and a Look from a Scout." *The Cincinnati Enquirer*, 4 July 1999.

Hunter, Art. "Georgetown Man Plays, Coaches Sports over 70 Year Span." *The News Democrat* (Georgetown, OH), 26 July 1998, 1,4.

Player Panel including Bill Cash, Connie Johnson, Butch McCord, Al Surratt, and Tom Turner, June 21, 1997. SABR 27 Convention. Louisville, Kentucky.

"Thomas Turner." 19 February 2002. http://www.pointsoflight.org/dpol/dpol-home.cfm.

Wells, Willie James "Devil"

Adamek, Steve. "This Eagle Lands in Hall." *The Record*, 4 August 1997.

"Appears to be Choice." *Chicago Defender*, 27 July 1935.

"Baseball Hall of Fame Inductees." *Washington Post*, 3 August 1997, D5.

Bock, Hal. "Lasorda, Niekro Inducted at Cooperstown." *Gettysburg Times,* 4 August 1997.

Buck, Ray. "Giving the Devil His Due." *Fort Worth Star-Telegram,* 6 July 2003.

_____. "Wille Wells' Hellbent Style Made the Texan a Negro Leagues Legend." *Fort Worth Star-Telegram,* 5 July 2003.

Davis, Reyn. "He Played Here, Now He's in the Hall." *Winnipeg Free Press,* 11 March 1997, C1.

Egner, Jeremy. "Batter Up! Austin's Forgotten Baseball Hero." *Austin American Statesman,* 19 June 2003, 131.

"Ex-Negro Leaguer Willie Wells Inducted into Hall of Fame." *Jet* (18 August 1997): 51.

Fikca, Peggy. "Negro Leagues Star Wells Honored." *San Antonio Express-News,* 6 October 2004, 1B, 5B.

Fitzpatrick, Frank. "Baseball Reminisces." *The Chronicle,* 4 August 1997, B1.

Fleitz, David L. "Willie Wells." In *Ghosts in the Gallery at Cooperstown.* Jefferson, NC: McFarland, 2004, 189–201.

Holway, John B. "The Black Cal Ripken, Willie Wells." *Sports Collectors Digest* 24 (18 April 1997): 134.

_____. "More Negro Leaguers for the Hall." *The National Pastime,* SABR, 1995, 91–95.

_____. "Negro League 'Devil' Showed 40–40 Ability." *Chicago Tribune,* 9 March 1997.

_____. "Willie Wells." *Baseball Research Journal* 17 (1998): 50–53.

"Infield King." *Chicago Defender,* 15 June 1935.

Kreytak, Steven. "A New Resting Place for Negro League Star." *Cox News Service,* 5 October 2004.

"Monument Honors Negro Leagues Legend Willie Wells." *Austin News,* 2 October 2004.

"Negro League Game at West Frankfort Wednesday Night." *The Daily Register* (Harrisburg, IL), 19 July 1948, 5.

"Negro Leagues Star Buried in Place of Honor." *Washington Post,* 10 October 2004, A02.

"Negro Leagues Star Honored with Place at Texas State Cemetery." *Austin American-Statesman,* 10 October 2004.

"Negro Leagues Star Wells Honored." *San Antonio Express,* 10 October 2004.

"Negro Leagues Star Wells Reburied with Honor." *Houston Chronicle,* 9 October 2004.

"Niekro, Lasorda Inducted; Fox, Wells Also Join Hall of Fame." *Washington Post,* 4 August 1997, D5.

Ruck, Rob. "Wells, Willie 'el Diablo.'" In *Biographical Dictionary of American Sports, Baseball,* edited by David L. Porter. Westport, CT: Greenwood Press, 2000, 1648–49.

Shannon, Kelley. "Black Baseball Great Willie Wells Honored." The Associated Press, 6 October 2004.

"Shortstop Willie Wells, 82, Dies; Was Called 'One of the Greatest.'" *The Post-Standard,* 25 January 1989, B-2.

Smith, Claire. "In Cooperstown Time Stops for a Moment." *New York Times,* 4 July 1997.

"Taylor Wants Wells as Chicago Shortstop." *Chicago Defender,* 7 January 1939.

Walker, Jackie. "Willie 'Devil' Wells." *Black Sports Magazine* (June 1975): 52, 54.

Ward, Pamela. "Group Goes to Bat with Campaign to Honor Baseball Legend Wells." *Austin American Statesman,* 2 January 1977, A1, A9.

"Wells Wins Cuba with His Fine Play on Ball Diamond." *Chicago Defender,* 28 December 1935, 13.

"Willie Wells, 82, Dies; Star in Negro Leagues." *New York Times,* 25 January 1989.

"Willie Wells." In *Baseball, The Biographical Encyclopedia,* edited by David Pietrusza, Matthew Silverman, and Michael Gershman. Kingston, New York: Total Sports Publishing, 2000, 1210.

Williams, Joe "Smokey Joe"

Boone, Kevin. "Smokey Joe Williams Earned His Way to Hall." *St. Louis Post-Dispatch,* 25 July 1999.

Burley, Dan. "Smoky Joe Williams All-time Great Hurler — More on Phillips High." *Chicago Defender,* 3 May 1958, 23.

Chase, Chris. "'Smokey' Joe Remembered." *The Gazette Enterprise,* 10 February 2004.

Coates, John M. "Smoky Joe Williams." *Baseball Historical Review* (1981), 46–47.

"Council Votes to Honor 'Smokey' Joe." *The Seguin Gazette-Enterprise,* 14 April 2001.

"'Cyclone' Joe to Toss Again." *New York Amsterdam News,* 2 August 1933.

"Cyclone Joe Williams in 7–3 Victory." *Chicago Defender,* 20 February 1926.

Gilbert, Thomas. "Biz, Pop, and Smokey Joe: Race, Baseball, and the Founding of the Negro Leagues." In *The Soaring Twenties.* New York: Franklin Watts, 1996, 91, 111.

Harris, Barbara. "Negro League's Star Pitcher Smokey Joe Williams Named to Baseball's Hall of Fame." *Jackson Advocate,* 11 March 1999.

Holway, John B. "The Death of Smokey Joe." http://www.baseballguru.com

_____. "The Rube and Smokey Joe." *Dawn Magazine,* 1 September 1977, 12, 14–15.

_____. "Shutting the Door on Negro League Stars." *New York Times,* 31 July 1977, S2.

_____. *Smokey Joe and the Cannonball.* Washington, DC: Capital Press, 1983.

_____. "Texas Smokey." *Dallas Morning Post,* 23 July 1999.

"Joe Williams." In *Baseball, The Biographical Encyclopedia,* edited by David Pietrusza, Matthew Silverman, and Michael Gershman. Kingston, New York: Total Sports Publishing, 2000, 1234.

"Joe Williams." *The Intelligencer Record,* 25 July 1999, B10.

Kleinknecht, Merl F. and John Holway. "Williams, Joseph 'Smokey Joe.'" In *Biographical Dictionary of American Sports, Baseball,* edited by David L. Porter. Westport, CT: Greenwood Press, 2000, 1681–1682.

Laing, Jack. "Memory Lane." *Syracuse Post-Standard,* 14 July 1971.

Lee, Jim. "Notes on Negro League Baseball." *Minneapolis Review of Baseball* (January 1985): 11–15.

Lundquist, Carl. "Veterans Weigh Candidates." *USA Today Baseball Weekly,* 25 February 1998, 33.

Maher, John. "Seguin Celebrates Its Native Negro Leagues Star." *Austin American,* 4 April 2001, C5.

McCord, Jeff. "Color Commentary." *Texas Monthly* (August 1999): 53–54, 56–57.

O'Connell, Bill. "Honoring a Legend." *The Gazette-Enterprise,* 4 April 2002.

"Smokey Joe Williams of Negro Leagues Gets Hall of Fame Spot." *Jet* 96, no. 11 (16 August 1999): 46.

Steele, David. "Negro Leaguers Seek Entry Into Hall." *USA Today Baseball Weekly,* 16 August 1991, 17.

Wiederhold, W. Alan. "Banquet Tips City's Cap to 'Smokey Joe.'" *The Gazette Enterprise,* 10 April 2002, 1, 7.

Wilson, Johnny

Kelley, Brent. "Jumpin' Johnny Wilson." *Sports Collectors Digest,* 28 May 1999, 190 191.

Wolfolk, Lewis

"Wolfolk Makes Debut as Rogers Parks Loses, 9–1." *Chicago Defender,* 28 April 1923.

"Wolfolk Pitches Fosterites to a 4 to 0 Victory." *Chicago Defender,* 16 June 1923.

About the Contributors

Bijan C. Bayne wrote the profile of Quincy Trouppe found in chapter 4. He is the author of *Sky Kings: Black Pioneers of Professional Basketball*. In July 2002, he won the Robert Peterson Research Award for his paper "The Struggle of the Latin American Ballplayer." Bayne's chapter on black baseball in North Carolina appears in the book *Baseball in the Carolinas* (McFarland, 2002).

Ryan Bucher's biographical write-ups on Lou Dials and Lloyd Pepper Bassett appear in chapter 3. Bucher received a bachelor of arts degree in history from Kent State University in 2003, graduating with University Honors. In May 2005 Ryan earned a master's of business administration. He is now working on a second master's in economics.

Michael Harkness-Roberto contributed write-ups on Bingo DeMoss, Alec Radcliffe and Cristobal Torriente in chapter 3 and Candy Jim Taylor in chapter 4. He is a graduate of the Kent State University, Stark Campus. His research interests include United States sports history, colonial and early American history, and nineteenth and twentieth century Japan. With Leslie Heaphy, he is working on another series of articles on the history of the Negro Leagues in Kansas City.

Leslie A. Heaphy, the volume editor, is associate professor of history at Kent State University, Stark Campus. She is the author of *The Negro Leagues, 1869–1960,* published by McFarland in 2003, and co-editor (with Mel Anthony May) of the *Encyclopedia of Women and Baseball* (McFarland, 2006). She has also written numerous encyclopedia articles and reviews on the Negro Leagues. She is a member of the Negro Leagues Committee for the Society for American Baseball Research (SABR) and chairs the Women in Baseball committee for SABR.

Jim Kastro's biographical write-up on Bill Foster can be found in chapter 3. He is past president of the Jack Graney Chapter of SABR and a member of the society's Negro Leagues Committee, serving on the host committee of the Jerry Malloy Conference (2004) held in Cleveland, Ohio.

Larry Lester wrote the introduction, the Rube Foster and Dave Malarcher biographies in chapter 4, and "The East-West Classic" in chapter 5. He compiled appendices A, C, and D. His first book, cowritten with Dick Clark, is titled *The Negro Leagues Book* (1994). It was billed as "the most complete collection of information on baseball's Negro Leagues ever published." His next four books were written as part of Arcadia's *Black America Series* and focus on black baseball in Detroit, Chicago, Kansas City and Pittsburgh. In 2002, the University of Nebraska Press published *Black Baseball's National Showcase: The East-West All-Star Game, 1933–1953,* which won the Sporting News–SABR Research Award and the Robert Peterson Recognition Award. His latest book, *Baseball's First Colored World Series: The 1924 Meeting of the Hillsdale Giants and Kansas City Monarchs,* will be published by McFarland in 2006. Lester serves as cochairman of SABR's Negro Leagues Committee.

David Marasco's "Jackie Robinson Goes to Wrigley" appears in chapter 5. He is a regular writer for *The Diamond Angle,* where he has contributed a wide range of articles on the Negro Leagues and the All American Girls Professional Baseball League. Marasco is a member of the SABR Negro League Committee and has delivered a number of papers on black baseball at various conferences.

Kyle McNary, whose write-up on Double Duty Radcliffe appears in chapter 4, has been researching the Negro Leagues for fifteen years. He has written two books, *Ted "Double Duty" Radcliffe — 36 Years of Pitching and Catching in Baseball's Negro Leagues* and *Black Baseball.* He was a technical advisor for a PBS documentary on Radcliffe and is coproducer for an upcoming movie about the integrated 1935 Bismarck baseball team. McNary is married, with two children, and lives in St. Louis Park, Minnesota.

Sammy Miller has a write-up on Jimmy Crutchfield in chapter 3, and "Chicago Ballparks" appears in chapter 5. He is a longtime member of the SABR Negro League committee and writer of the monthly newsletter. Miller is also the coauthor of *Black Baseball in Chicago* and *Black Baseball in Pittsburgh* (Arcadia Publishing). He created the database about ballparks used by Negro League teams, which is held at the National Baseball Hall of Fame and Library in Cooperstown, New York.

Jason Norris contributed the profile of Ted Trent in chapter 3 and the essay "Buck O'Neil Integrates the Coaching Ranks," which appears in chapter 5. A master's student of history at the University of Akron, his primary field of research is twentieth-century American history. His current research deals with how American memorials affect the memory of the Korean civil war in American history.

Shawn Selby's write-up on Frank Duncan, Sr., and Big Bill Gatewood can be found in chapter 3, and his "Bingo and Bango Break the Cubs' Color Line" is in chapter 5. He is a Ph.D. candidate in twentieth century U.S. social and intellectual history at Ohio University and has contributed articles to the *Encyclopedia of Women and Baseball* (McFarland, 2006).

Aric Smith has write-ups on Pop Lloyd and Arthur Pennington in chapter 3. He graduated from Kent State University, Stark Campus, with a bachelor's degree in history. Aric has developed an interest in the history of mascots and is currently working on an article on this topic.

Wayne Stivers contributed the sidebar on the American Giants' back-to-back no hitters; it appears in chapter 2. A member of SABR's Negro League Committee, he has worked for the past three years with the Negro League Researchers and Authors Group researching Negro League statistics for the Baseball Hall of Fame in Cooperstown, New York.

Index

Aaron, Henry "Hank" 81
Algona Brownies 44
All-Nations 18–19, 57, 69
Anderson, Curt "Andy" 41
Anson Colts 84, 180
Armour, Alfred "Buddy" 41
Auburn Park 13
Avendorph, Julius 7

Bacharach Giants 4, 21, 25, 55, 68, 75–76,
  115, 129, 138, 159, 174
Baird, Tom 186
Baker, Gene 178, 184, 185–88, 195
Ball, Walter 13, 14, 16, 36, 42–43, 50, 74, 84,
  143
Baltimore Elite Giants 20, 29, 46, 163, 186
Bankhead, Dan 21, 114
Banks, Ernie 178, 184, 185–88, 191, 194
Barbour, Jess 22, 23, 25, 43
Barnhill, Herbert 44
Barton, Sherman 44
Bassett, Lloyd "Pepper" 28, 44–47, 58, 162
Beckwith, John 47
Bell, James Thomas "Cool Papa" 41, 47–48,
  55, 61, 76, 77, 79, 130, 159, 163, 166, 171,
  181, 186, 191
Beverly, William 48
Bibbs, Junius "Rainey" 48
Binga, William 13
Birmingham Black Barons 20, 26–27, 29, 32,
  33, 45, 50, 54, 59, 60, 63, 79, 82, 85, 94, 98,
  100, 114, 117, 118, 125, 162, 167–68, 169, 177
Bissant, John 33, 34, 48–49, 51, 58, 112
Blount, Tenny 4, 135
Booker, James "Peter" 50, 144
Bostock, Lyman, Sr. 50
Bowe, Randolph 41, 50–51, 141
Brewer, Chester Arthur "Chet" 51–52, 87,
  167, 180
Brooklyn Royal Giants 11, 50, 51, 101, 104,
  115, 122, 123, 135, 138
Brown, David "Lefty" 25, 52, 53, 70

Brown, George 8–9
Brown, James 53–54, 68
Brown, Larry 54–56, 171
Brown, Ray 168
Brown, Willard 117, 180
Buckner, Harry 10, 11, 12, 22, 56, 74
Byas, Dick "Subby" 37, 56–57, 112

California Winter League 24, 66, 83, 94, 111,
  135
Campanella, Roy 46, 183
Campbell, Andrew 14
Carter, Marlin 57
Charleston, Oscar 20, 41, 55, 61, 76, 77, 79,
  84, 93, 127, 158, 166
Chicago Amateur Baseball Association 8
Chicago American Giants 3, 4, 18–31, 32, 39,
  41, 43, 44, 45, 47, 49, 50, 52, 54, 55, 57, 58–
  59, 60–62, 63–64, 66–69, 69–70, 70–71, 71–
  73, 74–77, 77–78, 81, 82, 85, 86, 87–89, 90,
  93–94, 94–95, 96, 97–98, 99–100, 101–3,
  105, 106, 108–9, 110–11, 115, 116, 117, 120–21,
  123–25, 125–26, 127–29, 129–31, 132–33,
  134, 135, 137, 139–40, 141, 148, 152, 156, 162,
  166, 167, 169, 170, 171, 174, 175, 178, 179
Chicago Blue Stockings 7, 8–9
Chicago Brown Bombers 32–34, 66, 80, 95,
  97, 111, 137, 178, 196
Chicago City League 42, 175
Chicago Excelsiors 174
Chicago Giants 4, 17, 35–36, 38, 47, 50, 69,
  76, 81, 94, 100, 104, 133, 147, 174, 175
Chicago Monarchs 37, 57
Chicago Society Baseball League 7–8
Chicago Union Giants 11, 12–14, 32, 36–37,
  38, 42, 56, 62, 74, 91, 95, 103, 104, 142–43
Chicago Unions 3, 9–11, 12, 56, 62, 74, 85,
  91, 103, 142, 175, 180
Chirban, Lou 30, 169
Cincinnati Clowns 27, 33, 58, 85, 113, 114, 196
Cincinnati Tigers 48, 167
Clarizio, Luis 30, 169

Cleveland Bears 27, 30
Cleveland Buckeyes 41, 51, 61, 105, 140, 171, 177
Cleveland Giants 68
Cole, Robert A. 5, 31, 55, 96, 115, 154–55, 171
Coleman, Clarence "Pops" 57
Cole's American Giants 48, 55, 112, 125, 133, 154–55, 171
Columbia Giants 3, 10, 12, 36–37, 56, 85, 86, 139, 142, 174
Columbus Buckeyes 26
Comiskey Park 5, 27, 29, 51, 69, 87, 89, 109, 113, 123, 151, 161, 162, 168, 173, 176–77, 180, 181, 194
Cooper, Andy 35
Cornelius, William "Willie," "Sug" 28, 58–59, 124, 125, 130
Crawford, Samuel 59, 113, 127–28
Cross, Norman 34, 35, 59, 112
Crutchfield, John W. "Jimmie" 28, 60–62, 112, 162, 163
Cuba 52, 83, 87, 89, 93, 101, 110, 125, 127, 134, 135, 138, 151, 193–95
Cuban Giants 10, 106
Cuban Stars 25, 79–80, 83, 84, 101, 127, 134, 196
Cuban X-Giants 10, 11, 12, 42, 82, 149
Currie, Rube 20, 21, 62, 159

Dandridge, Ray 61, 107
Daniels, Zack 8–9
Davenport, Lloyd 21, 27, 62–63, 85, 163, 177
Davis, John 14, 63
Davis, Lorenzo "Piper" 117, 180
Davis, Peanut 29
Davis, Roosevelt 32–33, 34–35
Davis, Saul 62–63
Davis, Walter "Steel Arm" 64, 68, 171
Day, Leon 61, 64, 181
Dayton Marcos 4, 37, 96
DeMoss, Bingo 25, 32–34, 62, 64–66, 69, 115, 134, 138
Denver Post Tournament 82
Detroit Cubs 33
Detroit Motor City Giants 33, 37, 96
Detroit Stars 4, 26, 30, 37, 55, 64, 68, 77, 79, 81, 110, 121, 135, 157, 164
Detroit Wolves 47, 125, 130, 138
Dials, Alonzo "Lou" 66–69
Dismukes, William "Dizzy" 66, 113, 115, 162
Donaldson, John 18–19, 35, 38, 57, 69–70, 135, 163
Dougherty, Charles "Pat" 3, 16, 20, 22–24, 70, 74, 83, 84, 144, 151
Douglas, Jesse Warren 70–71, 100, 109, 177
Dunbar, Ashby 22, 24

Duncan, Frank "Pete," Sr. 22, 24, 55, 58, 65, 71–73, 113
Dunlap, Herman 30, 73
Durham, Joseph Vann 73
Dyll, Frank 30

East Chicago Giants 33, 104, 168
East-West Classic 5, 19, 20, 21, 41, 45, 47, 48, 51, 54, 56, 58, 60, 62, 64, 69, 70, 73, 76, 85, 86, 87, 94, 99–100, 101, 108, 112, 114, 122, 123, 130, 140, 155, 161, 167, 171, 176–77, 180, 181–83, 193, 196
Eastern Colored League (ECL) 4, 75, 152
Eclipse 13
Ethiopian Clowns 33, 45, 50, 197

Ferrell, Willie 28, 74
Footes, Robert 11, 74
Foster, Andrew "Rube" 3, 4, 13, 15, 17, 18, 19, 20, 22, 24, 31, 42, 43, 50, 52, 55, 59, 65, 66, 68, 74–77, 82, 86, 90, 93, 94, 104, 107, 115, 126, 128, 135, 138, 139, 142–44, 147, 148–54, 157–61, 170, 174, 175, 189
Foster, James 32
Foster, Willie 20, 55, 74–77, 124, 131, 159

Gamble, L.H. 32, 34
Gardner, Floyd "Jelly" 71–72, 77–79, 140
Garrett, Al H. 11, 144
Gatewood, William "Big Bill" 16, 17, 21, 22, 23, 47, 50, 79–80, 90
Gibson, Josh 29, 45, 47, 55, 61, 76, 77, 163, 164, 166, 177
Gilkerson, Robert 11, 14, 38
Gilkerson's Union Giants 14, 38–40, 51, 52, 57, 64, 69, 70, 96, 100, 119, 120, 128, 137, 164
Gordons 7
Grand Crossing Park 174
Grant, Charlie 12
Great Lakes Naval Team 27, 53, 62, 195–97
Green, Joe 4, 16, 17, 35–36, 126
Greenlee, Gus 5, 45, 61, 159
Gulley, Napoleon "Nap" 80
Gunther, Charles 15
Gunther Park 17, 175
Gunthers 15, 16, 17, 43, 83, 84, 175
Gurley, James Earl 81

Hackley, Albert 11
Hall, Horace G. 5, 31, 51, 154, 155, 171
Hamilton, Thomas 9
Hardy, Paul 81
Harlem Globetrotters 80, 114, 122, 140, 168
Harris, Nate 81, 144
Havana Las Palomas 34
Hawkins, Lemuel "Hawk" 81

Hayes, Malvin 36
Haywood, Albert "Buster" 81–82
Hill, J. Preston "Pete" 3, 16, 17, 22, 25, 65, 82–84, 104, 107, 115, 134, 135, 144, 151
Hill, Samuel 85, 180
Hilldale Daises 62, 71, 152, 174
Holland, William 11, 85
Homestead Grays 21, 37, 45, 47, 48, 51, 68, 76, 85, 87, 94, 96, 117, 121, 130, 138, 141, 158, 162, 163, 166, 168, 177, 196, 197
Hopkins, George 11
Horne, William "Billy" 11, 14, 51, 85, 162
Hoskins, David 85–86
House of David 26, 168
Hudson, Willie 28, 141
Husband, Vincent 30
Hutchinson, Fred 22, 24, 86
Hyde, Cowan "Bubba" 86
Hyde, Harry 11, 14

Indianapolis ABCs 4, 19, 55, 61, 65, 90, 91, 104, 106, 113, 115, 125, 157, 161, 163
Indianapolis Clowns 29, 30, 34, 82, 87, 89, 105, 185
Irvin, Monte 61, 84, 99, 182

Jackson, Major Robert R. 11, 12, 15, 146
Jackson, Stanford "Jambo" 86
Jacksonville Red Caps 44, 140
Jessup, Joseph Gentry "Jeep" 21, 27, 28–29, 29–30, 41, 58, 87–89, 180
Johnson, Allen 37
Johnson, Don "Groundhog" 89–90
Johnson, George "Chappie" 90
Johnson, Grant "Homerun" 3, 12, 151
Johnson, Louis "Dicta" 22, 23, 26, 90
Johnson, Tom 27, 90–91
Johnson, W.P. 9
Johnson, William "Judy" 61
Jones, Abe 9
Jones, Bert 10–11, 91
Jones, Willis 11, 14, 91

Kansas City Monarchs 4, 20, 26, 28, 29, 30, 33, 35, 37, 39, 44, 47, 48, 51, 58, 59, 64, 65, 68, 69, 71, 74, 75–77, 81, 87, 97, 99, 100, 101, 104, 113, 117, 120, 122, 125, 126, 128, 130, 141, 152–53, 158, 162, 168, 174, 177, 182, 185, 187, 189–93
Kenyon, Harry 91, 140

Lake Front Park 173–74
Lamar, E.B. 42
League of Colored Baseball Clubs 3, 142
Leland, Frank C. 3, 9–11, 12–14, 14–17, 18, 38, 42, 81, 83, 142–44, 146, 147
Leland Giants 3, 14–17, 32, 50, 62, 70, 72, 79, 83, 85, 90, 93, 95, 97, 105, 110–11, 117, 135, 138, 140, 142–44, 145, 147, 150, 151, 161, 174, 175, 180
Leland Giants Baseball and Amusement Association 143, 146
Leonard, Buck 109, 112, 115, 181
Libeaux, Wilbert 26
Lincoln Giants 25, 52, 54, 77, 93, 98, 115, 135, 138
Lindsay, William "Bill" 3, 22–24, 94
Little, William 31, 154, 155
Lloyd, John Henry "Pop" 3, 16, 20, 25, 83, 91–94, 104, 115, 135, 151, 160
Lockett, Lester 94–95
Logan Square Park 173, 176
Logan Squares 26, 84, 151, 176
Longest, Bernell 34, 95
Longest, Jimmy 33
Louis, Joe 66, 181
Louisiana Pinchbacks 10
Louisville Buckeyes 31
Lyons, Jimmie 20, 127, 153
Lyttle, Clarence 14, 95–96

Mackey, Biz 55, 60, 159, 170
Malarcher, Dave 25, 26, 32, 65, 75, 77, 96, 113, 153, 156, 157–61
Man-Dak League 89, 95, 169
Manley, Effa 61
Manning, Clery 9
Marshall, Bobby 16
Marshall, Jack 34, 96, 112
Martin, Dr. J.B. 21, 29, 31, 107, 109, 112, 155–56
Mathis, Verdel 27, 179, 180
Matthews, Dell 14, 96–97
McClellan, Dan 22–24, 98, 149
McCoy, Walter 31, 58, 97
McCurrine, James "Jim" 29, 97–98
McDonald, Webster 20, 21, 98–99, 159
McKinnis, Gread "Lefty" 28, 29, 33, 37, 58, 99–100, 109, 169
McLaurin, Felix 100
McNair, Hurley 38, 100
McNeal, Clyde 30, 101, 141
McNichols Park 180
Memphis Red Sox 29, 37, 44, 47, 54, 57, 58, 68, 75, 86, 113, 116, 155–56, 163, 167
Mendez, Jose 76, 101, 135
Mexico 47, 58, 100, 101, 109, 130, 132, 171–72
Miarka, Stanley 30
Miles, John 98, 101–3
Miller, Joe 14, 103, 144
Milwaukee Bears 83–84
Mineola Black Spiders 57
Minoso, Orestes "Minnie" 185, 193–95
Monroe, William 11, 17, 22, 86, 104
Monroe Monarchs 62, 105, 166

Montgomery Gray Sox 47
Montgomery Red Sox 81
Moore, Harry 14, 105
Moore, Mike 11
Morney, Leroy 41, 51, 105
Morton, Sidney "Sy" 105
Moseley, Beauregard 12, 15, 16–17, 144–48
Mounds Blues 37

Nashville Elite Giants 20
National Baseball Hall of Fame 48, 91, 94, 138, 170
Negro American League (NAL) 5, 12, 27, 30, 37, 44, 58, 71, 81, 108, 112, 117, 118, 154, 156, 167
Negro National League (NNL) 4, 5, 11, 17, 19, 75, 94, 127, 130, 152, 154, 158, 159, 162, 164, 170, 171
Negro Southern League 5, 80, 159, 171
Neil, Ray 89
Nelson, Clyde 29, 41
New Orleans Crescent Stars 44
New York Black Yankees 68, 87, 100, 125, 130, 196
New York Cubans 32, 50, 51, 117, 124, 177, 193
Newark Eagles 53, 57, 61, 112, 125, 134, 177, 182
Norfolk Redstockings 12
Normal Park 83, 175
Normals 26
Norman, Billy 15

Oaklands 7
Ogden Park 174
O'Neil, Buck 18, 45, 178, 187, 188–93
Owens, Aubrey 21
Owens, Jesse 33, 64
Owens, Will "Gabie" 106

Pacific Coast Winter League 22, 69, 116, 120, 123, 187
Padrone, Juan 21, 26, 106, 134
Page Fence Giants 10, 12, 90, 103
Paige, Satchel 27, 28, 35, 44, 47, 55, 61, 69, 77, 80, 87, 89, 98, 100, 108, 109, 113, 117, 122, 131, 163, 164, 166, 167, 168, 172, 178–79, 181, 182
Palmer House All Stars 34–35, 54, 59, 64, 111, 112, 120, 137
Parker, Sonny 32
Patterson, John W. 12
Payne, Andrew "Jap" 3, 16, 106–7
Pendleton, James "Jim" 107
Pennington, Arthur David "Art" 27, 28, 100, 107–10, 177
Peters, Frank, Jr. 36
Peters, Frank, Sr. 36
Peters, William S. 9–10, 13, 38, 96, 142

Petway, Bruce 3, 14, 20, 22, 24, 25, 80, 104, 107, 110–11, 115, 144, 151
Philadelphia Giants 11, 15, 82–83, 91, 104, 111, 115, 149
Philadelphia Stars 62, 96, 105, 127, 159
Pierce, Bill 22, 23, 86
Pittsburgh Crawfords 45, 58, 60, 61, 112, 125, 159, 166, 196
Pittsburgh Keystones 82
Pollard, Fritz 12
Posey, Cumberland "Cum" 84, 158
Powell, Melvin 26, 34, 111
Powell, Willie "Piggie" 111, 159, 180
Price, Marvin 111–12

Quaker Giants 104

Radcliffe, Alexander "Alec" 28, 34, 64, 112–14, 160, 169, 171
Radcliffe, Ted "Double Duty" 21, 27, 38, 55, 57, 62, 64, 112, 116, 163–70
Ragens Colts 19
Raines, Lawrence "Lefty" 90, 114
Redd, Ulysses 114
Redding, Dick "Cannonball" 19, 36, 52, 57, 114–15, 144
Redus, Wilson 49, 115
Reed, Johnny 32
Reeves, Donald "Soup" 115–16, 141
Reynolds, Louis 11
Rhodes, Harold "Lefty" 116
Rile, Ed 21, 26, 116, 140
Ritchey, John 116
Robinson, Jackie 62, 71, 109, 168, 183, 183–84, 186, 187–88, 196
Robinson, Neil 44, 180
Robinson, Robert "Bobby" 164
Rogan, Wilber "Bullet Joe" 51, 76, 158
Rose, Haywood 14, 117

St. Louis Giants 4, 24
St. Louis Stars 20, 46, 47–48, 49, 76, 79–80, 115, 116, 125, 130, 140, 159, 162, 166, 171
St. Paul–Minneapolis Gophers 32–33, 54, 96, 161
Sampson, Tommy 46
San Marcos Giants 53
Schorling, John 30, 151, 174
Schorling Park 4, 22, 23, 25, 84, 93
Scout 52
Shields, Charles "Lefty" 117
Simmons, R.S. 156
Simms, Willie 117–18
Simpson, Herbert "Suitcase" 118
Smart Sets 22–23
Smaulding, Bazz Owen 39–40, 118–21
Smith, Eugene 89

Smith, Hilton 46, 105, 167, 172, 181
Smith, James 14
Smith, Theolic 46, 114, 121
Smith, William 11
Spearman, Alvin 37
Spearman, Clyde 45
Stearnes, Norman "Turkey" 34, 41, 115, 121–22, 124, 134, 171, 181
Strong, Theodore "Ted" 122–23, 140
Strothers, Tim 123
Summers, Lonnie 85, 123
Suttles, George "Mule" 45–46, 76, 115, 123–25, 159, 171, 178, 181, 182
Sweat, George Alexander 125–26, 128

Talbert, Dangerfield 13, 16, 126–27
Taylor, Ben 82, 84, 161
Taylor, Charles I. (C.I.) 4, 19, 65, 157, 158, 161–62
Taylor, George 14
Taylor, James "Candy Jim" 21, 22–24, 29, 32, 41, 44, 49, 50, 97, 98, 102, 108, 115, 127, 133, 141, 156, 161–63, 165
Taylor, Jelly 46
Taylor, John "Steel Arm" 22, 161
Thompson, Buddy 33
Thompson, Samuel 127
Toledo Crawfords 30, 39, 61
Torriente, Cristobal 20, 25–26, 38, 40, 59, 84, 127–29, 170
Treadwell, Harold 128
Trent, Ted 26, 58, 59, 121, 129–31
Trimble, William E. 4, 31, 154
Trouppe, Quincy 81, 112, 115, 156, 163, 167, 170–72, 180
Turner, Thomas "Highpockets" 132–33
25th Infantry Team 81
Tyson, Armand, Sr. 37

Unions 4, 142
Uniques 7, 9
United States League (USL) 32, 178

Vargas, Roberto "Lefty" 133, 180

Warren, Herman 133
Washington Pilots 51, 125, 130
Welch, Winfield 31–32, 81, 156, 163
Wells, Willie 76, 114, 115, 124, 133–34, 159, 171, 181
West, Ollie 58
West Baden Sprudels 24
White, Sol 12, 93, 139
Whitworth, Dick 25, 134–35
Wickware, Frank 3, 17, 20, 25, 36, 50, 69, 135–36, 151
Wiggins, Maurice 34–35, 137
Wiley College 49, 104
Wilkinson, J.L. 4, 69
Williams, Jesse 137
Williams, John 137
Williams, Joseph "Smokey Joe" 17, 50, 83, 93, 138
Williams, Robert "Bobby" 93, 138
Williams, Roy 30
Williams, "String Bean" 32
Williams, Tom 19, 21, 26, 138–39
Wilmington Potomacs 99
Wilson, George 139
Wilson, John "Jumpin' Johnny" 139
Wing, Charles 8–9
Wolfolk, Lewis 21, 139–40
Woods, Parnell 140
World Series 4, 18, 20, 55, 68, 71, 75, 77, 81, 94, 98, 101, 111, 125, 128, 135, 153, 158, 167, 168, 174, 181, 193
Wright, Bill 46
Wright, George 140
Wrigley Field 178–79, 183–84
Wyatt, David 11, 14, 18
Wyatt, Ralph 27, 51, 58, 140–41, 177

Young, Edward "Pep" 141
Young, Frank 26, 153, 158

Zulu Cannibal Giants 64, 107–8